ETHICAL MONOTHEISM,
PAST AND PRESENT

Program in Judaic Studies
Brown University
Box 1826
Providence, RI 02912

BROWN JUDAIC STUDIES

Series Editors 2001–
David C. Jacobson
Ross S. Kraemer
Saul M. Olyan

Series Editor 1991–2001
Shaye J. D. Cohen

Number 329

ETHICAL MONOTHEISM, PAST AND PRESENT

Essays in Honor of Wendell S. Dietrich

edited by
Theodore M. Vial and Mark A. Hadley

ETHICAL MONOTHEISM, PAST AND PRESENT
Essays in Honor of Wendell S. Dietrich

edited by
Theodore M. Vial
Mark A. Hadley

Brown Judaic Studies
Providence

ETHICAL MONOTHEISM, PAST AND PRESENT
Essays in Honor of Wendell S. Dietrich

edited by
Theodore M. Vial and Mark A. Hadley

Library of Congress Cataloging-in-Publication Data
Ethical Monotheism, past and present : essays in honor of Wendell S. Dietrich / edited by Theodore M. Vial, Mark A. Hadley.
   p. cm. — (Brown Judaic studies ; no. 329)
   Includes bibliographical references.
   ISBN 1-930675-06-2 (cloth : alk. paper)
   1. Religion and ethics. 2. Monotheism. 3. Dietrich, Wendell S.
I. Dietrich, Wendell S. II. Vial, Theodore M., 1962– III. Hadley, Mark A. , 1963– IV. Series.

BJ47 .E83 2001
291.5—dc21   2001043051

08 07 06 05 04 03 02 01   5 4 3 2 1

Printed in the United States of America
on acid-free paper

To Wendell S. Dietrich
Scholar, Teacher, Mensch

CONTENTS

PART THREE

ETHICAL MONOTHEISM AS CONTEMPORARY RESOURCE

ACKNOWLEDGMENTS

The editors would like to thank Wendell S. Dietrich, Shaye Cohen, Stanley Stowers, and Gail Tetreault for their support and wisdom. The contributors to this volume offered many moments of grace and generosity of spirit which, when combined with scholarly rigor, are the moments when the academy is at its best, and a beautiful thing. These experiences, though not public, are as much a tribute to Wendell Dietrich as the essays in the volume.

In particular, Ted Vial would like to thank Wendell Dietrich for introducing him to the intellectual life, and for his standards and passion, which continue to set inspiring goals; Mark Hadley for his unfailing good judgment and humor; and Nancy Walsh for her encouragement and insight, for making life good, and for teaching most of the important things that can be learned outside a classroom, which are most of the important things. Between the earliest stages of this project and its completion, Aubrey and Isha Grace were born, bringing great happiness, a reminder of the fragility and beauty of education and the process of transmission, and the hope that they will be as fortunate in their teachers.

Mark Hadley thanks Wendell Dietrich for sharing the joys and nuances of the intellectual quest; he thanks his co-editor Ted Vial for his generosity and perspicuity; he thanks his lovely wife, Leslie, for her graciousness and wisdom and the joy of life together; and he thanks his children, Spencer Alan and Olivia McPherson, for their wonderment and enthusiasm which has made life beyond this project rich and happy.

INTRODUCTION

Theodore M. Vial

1. *What Is Ethical Monotheism?*

Each epoch confronts a different set of problems when reading sacred texts. Augustine (354-430) argued that one must approach scripture with the "rule of charity." "What is read should be subjected to diligent scrutiny until an interpretation contributing to the reign of charity [the motion of the soul toward the enjoyment of God for His own sake, and the enjoyment of one's self and of one's neighbor for the sake of God] is produced."[1] If the literal reading of a passage led to an interpretation that violated this rule, this was a sign that the passage ought to be read figuratively. One's guide to difficult passages of scripture is the rest of scripture: "In those places where things are used openly we may learn how to interpret them when they appear in obscure places."[2] Likewise Moses Maimonides (1135-1204) writes his *Guide for the Perplexed* for those who, having studied philosophy, are perplexed by biblical anthropomorphism. In his commentary on the Mishnah he harmonizes rabbinic teachings with Aristotelian ethics. Thomas Aquinas (c. 1225-1274) undertakes an analogous project almost a century later for Christian theology. Martin Luther (1483-1546) argued that the dilemmas posed by apparently contradictory passages could be resolved if one understood that scripture was divided between "commandments" and "promises." Contemporary conservative Christian exegetes claim both inerrancy and literalism as hermeneutical principles, but will always sacrifice the latter to the former. The "this generation" of Mark 13:30 that will see the Son of Man's return, for example, must be read as referring not to the generation listening to Jesus, or Mark's original audience, but to the reader of the 21st century. For all these interpreters, scripture has one author, and is unified.

The 19th century marks a watershed in Biblical interpretation, in large part because of a cultural shift in context as great as that of

---

[1] Augustine, *On Christian Doctrine*, trans. D. W. Robertson (Indianapolis: Bobbs-Merrill, 1958), 93, 88.
[2] Augustine, 101.

Ambrose's and Augustine's reliance on neo-Platonism, or Maimonides' and Thomas Aquinas's commitment to Aristotelianism, or Luther's Renaissance humanism. The issues raised with such force, and confronted with such acumen and passion, are not the same issues that confronted Augustine, or Maimonides, or Luther. To a great extent we have inherited, and are still working through, these same issues that occupied the 19th century. The two most obvious sources of conflict created by the cultural context of the 19th century for meaningful biblical interpretation both stem from the Enlightenment: the rise of science, and the rise of a historical consciousness. Though the first is, perhaps, more dramatic, the second has posed deeper, more troubling questions, and provoked more brilliant hermeneutic efforts.

The possible effects of a Newtonian world view can best be discerned in the chapter entitled "Of Miracles" in David Hume's (1711-1776) *An Enquiry Concerning Human Understanding* (first published 1748). Hume's argument is a subtle one. He does not argue that miracles, defined as violations of laws of nature, are impossible. That sort of certainty is not available when reasoning concerning matters of fact, that is, reasoning based on cause and effect known to us through the senses and our memory.[3] Rather, Hume argues, it is wiser, based on the cumulative weight of our experience of nature and of our experience of human testimony (which is easily mistaken, exaggerated, or fraudulent), to place more confidence in the presumption of a human source for miracle accounts than in the presumption that a violation of the laws of nature has, in fact, occurred. "It is strange, a judicious reader is apt to say, upon the perusal of these wonderful historians, *that such prodigious events never happen in our days. But it is nothing strange, I hope, that men should lie in all ages.*"[4]

In placing more confidence in Newton than ancient miracle accounts, Hume also serves as an excellent example of the early stages of a truly modern historical consciousness. "Supernatural and miraculous relations . . . are observed chiefly to abound among ignorant and barbarous nations." These accounts are found in "the first histories of all nations." A human reporter tends to magnify "his country, his family, or himself." What is remarkable is not the rarity of such miraculous stories, but their abundance. They are to be expected, and are found, in every religion.[5] Who wouldn't want to be the chosen people? Hume has

---

[3] David Hume, *An Enquiry Concerning Human Understanding* (Indianapolis: Hackett, 1977), 16.
[4] Hume, 80 (italics in original).
[5] Hume, 79, 80, 86, 81.

historicized scripture. It is the product of specific humans (all too human, according to Hume) in a specific time and place, and as such is exactly comparable to the sacred writings of other religions.

In his classic *The Historian and the Believer*, Van Harvey relies heavily on Ernst Troeltsch (1865-1923) as an articulate representative of a fully developed historical consciousness and its potentially corrosive effect on faith. Troeltsch argues that "critical historical inquiry rests on three interrelated principles": 1. criticism (no historical judgment can be simply true or false, but is always a matter of degree); 2. analogy (we can only judge probability if our experience is not radically dissimilar to the one we are examining); and 3. correlation (any event is so wrapped up in the intertwining nexus of history that no event can be understood except in terms of its antecedents and consequences).[6] "Can one rest his faith on historical assertions which themselves do not seem capable of a high degree of probability," Harvey asks?[7] The problem is more than simply that history sometimes renders unfavorable verdicts, or that the kinds of verdicts believers desire lie outside its purview. The deeper problem, Harvey argues, is the historian's "awareness of the falsifying influence belief frequently exercises on critical judgment, so that he is most distrustful of just those answers he would most like to believe."[8] How is faith possible in the modern context in which a historical consciousness is part of the furniture of the mind?

One possibility for reconstructing Judaism and Christianity in the modern context is ethical monotheism: "a religious concentration and intensity that focuses singular attention on God in contrast to all creaturely reality." How does ethical monotheism serve "as the credible form of modern religion and . . . a suitable base for modern culture"?[9]

As Wendell S. Dietrich has shown, both Jewish thinkers such as Hermann Cohen (1842- 1918) and Christian Thinkers such as Ernst Troeltsch accepted the historical conclusions of Julius Wellhausen (1844-1918), the great Hebrew philologist and historian of ancient Israel who ended his career at the University of Göttingen. Wellhausen focused on the origins of biblical narrative, applying many of the same techniques Karl H. Graf had used to study and date the law codes. Assuming that forms become progressively more complex, Wellhausen,

---

[6] Van A. Harvey, *The Historian and the Believer: The Morality of Historical Knowledge and Christian Belief* (reprint: Urbana and Chicago: University of Illinois, 1996), 14-15.
[7] Harvey, 14.
[8] Harvey, 103.
[9] Wendell S. Dietrich, *Cohen and Troeltsch: Ethical Monotheistic Religion and Theory of Culture*, Brown Judaic Studies (Brown University, 1986), 1, 5.

through painstaking historical analysis of the kind scholars were also employing to understand the history of ancient Greece and Rome, reconstructed the development of ancient Israel and its religion. Well-hausen argued that, after passing through earlier stages (which show evidence of polytheism and henotheism), Israelite religion culminates in the sharp monotheism of the Hebrew prophets, with its powerful calls for social and ethical responsibility. The Priestly source, which contains most of the Mosaic Law code, is in fact a late (post-exilic) composition, which Wellhausen saw as a degeneration of the great prophetic spirit into legalism (a conclusion that Cohen did not accept). To someone troubled by evidence of historical development in the text, or hints of polytheism, or mythology, or ethically repugnant commands attributed to God (such as the slaying of the Canaanites), such a developmental approach, the result of critical history, can be redeeming. These troub-ling aspects can be seen as stages on the way to a religious conscious-ness highly developed enough to write:

> Is not this the fast that I choose:
>   to loose the bonds of injustice,
>   to undo the thongs of the yoke,
> to let the oppressed go free,
>   and to break every yoke?[10]

Such a valuation of stages of religious consciousness in the Bible also makes it clear that far more than hermeneutics is at stake. Each epoch faces not only exegetical choices, but the hard task of constructing legitimate social institutions. One's reading of the prophets will affect one's social theory and practice. Solomon Formstecher (1808-1889) found in ethical monotheism a theoretical basis for the emancipation of the Jews in Germany, and for the Reform movement. For Formstecher ethics is not a theoretical construct, but the aspiration of the historical tradition of Judaism to embody the divine and revealed moral ideal on earth. This sets Jews apart from other religions, which are either "religions of nature," or "physical monotheisms." The Jewish mission to the world, because of this difference, must be an indirect one, carried out through Christianity and Islam, which mix "pagan" and "spiritual" elements. Cohen argues that Judaic ethical monotheism more directly provides "the most appropriate religious basis for modern culture as a whole." Troeltsch will disagree, arguing that Jesus revived the prophetic tradition from a "moribund" legalism,[11] and that Christian ethical

---

[10]   Isaiah 58:6, NRSV.
[11]   Dietrich, 17, 21.

monotheism forms the basis for European culture. Part Three of this volume, in particular, will focus on the ethical questions that arise out of consideration of ethical monotheism.

The idea of development, then, allows both for rigorous historical analysis, and a basis for a conviction that scripture offers a valuable resource with authority in the modern world. It was not an idea original to Wellhausen, but has venerable precursors. We might consider Gotthold Ephraim Lessing (1729-1781), a contemporary of David Hume's, as one of the forerunners of ethical monotheism. For Hume, the human fingerprints on scripture are cause for skepticism, but Lessing makes different use of his historical awareness. In a remarkable essay entitled "The Education of the Human Race," Lessing argues that the Bible might be compared to a child's primer. It makes sense that one would not mention the doctrines of the immortality of the soul to the Israelites at a stage when they were "rough, unpracticed in thought."[12] And the Israelites could only come to see Jehovah, the national deity, as God once they had acquired from the Babylonians an aversion to "sensuous representation."[13] Lessing holds out hope that humans will continue to develop until such time as they will do what is right simply because it is right, and not because of the promise of future rewards and punishments.[14] He even contemplates a day when the historical revelations of the Bible will no longer be necessary: "And why should not we too, by means of a religion whose historical truth, if you will, looks dubious, be led in a similar way to closer and better conceptions of the divine Being, of our own nature, of our relation to God, which human reason would never have reached on its own?"[15]

Another, more direct, influence on ethical monotheism, of course, is Friedrich Daniel Ernst Schleiermacher (1768-1834). In arguing that religion is a basic aspect of human nature to modern despisers of religion to whom the Bible looks antiquated, orthodox doctrines foolish, and the church as an institution coercive, Schleiermacher opens up the theological space for comparative religion at the largely Protestant universities in Germany. His own comparative efforts come in the famous "Introduction" to *The Christian Faith*. "The various religious communions

---

[12] Gotthold Lessing, "The Education of the Human Race," in *Lessing's Theological Writings*, trans. Henry Chadwick (Stanford: Stanford University Press, 1956), 87. The same collection contains an essay entitled, "New Hypothesis Concerning the Evangelists Regarded as Merely Human Historians."
[13] Lessing, 89-90.
[14] Lessing, 96.
[15] Lessing, 95.

which have appeared in history with clearly defined limits are related to each other in two ways: as different stages of development, and as different kinds."[16] The highest form of religion is that "in which all religious affections express the dependence of everything finite upon one Supreme and Infinite Being, i.e. the monotheistic forms."[17] Of the three monotheistic religions, Schleiermacher classifies Islam as "aesthetic" because its reliance on divine will is fatalistic, while Judaism and Christianity are "teleological" ("a predominating reference to the moral task constitutes the fundamental type of the religious affections"). Judaism is more passive than Christianity, and so Christianity is the highest form of teleological monotheistic religion.[18] As a contribution to the history of religions, this introduction is somewhat embarrassing, even if Schleiermacher is not entirely to be blamed for the state of scholarship on religions in his day. Troeltsch himself calls it "a travesty in the shape of an ecclesiastical, biblical, dogmatics."[19] But it does form the basis for religious judgments that carry on "developing independently and freely harmonizing and fusing . . . with modern knowledge."[20] It is carried out on the basis of "a historical-critical, and therefore *religionsgeschichtliche* investigation of Christianity."[21] "Scarcely one stone of Schleiermacher's own teaching can remain upon another, but his programme remains the great programme of all scientific theology. It only needs working out, not replacing by new inventions."[22] One can question Schleiermacher's knowledge and assessment of other religions, but the theological groundwork for the development of ethical monotheism has been laid.

2. *Ethical Monotheism: Traditions and Prospects*

The historian Miri Rubin has described the academic division of labor that prevailed at her alma mater, Hebrew University in Jerusalem:

---

[16] Friedrich Schleiermacher, *The Christian Faith*, 2d ed., trans. and ed. H. R. MacKintosh and J. S. Stewart (Edinburgh: T. & T. Clark, 1986), 7 (31). I cite *The Christian Faith* by section, subsection if relevant, and page.

[17] Schleiermacher, 8 (34).

[18] Schleiermacher, 9, 2 (42-44).

[19] Ernst Troeltsch, "The Dogmatics of the Religionsgeschichtliche Schule," *American Journal of Theology* 17 (1913), 7.

[20] Ernst Troeltsch, "Half a Century of Theology: A Review," in *Writings on Theology and Religion*, trans. Robert Morgan and Michael Pye (Atlanta: John Knox Press, 1977), 78.

[21] Troeltsch, "The Dogmatics of the Religionsgeschichtliche Schule," 6.

[22] "Half a Century of Theology: A Review," 80.

"there was the department of Jewish History which covered all periods and places, and then the department of General History, which excluded Jews from the history of Europe and the rest of the west. It was thus possible to reach the fifth year of the study of history . . . without ever having come across the Jews."[23] While this is a dramatic example, it is not atypical. At a certain point, such a division of labor must distort the history being studied. As Dietrich has shown, for example, not only did Cohen and Troeltsch both find ethical monotheism a valuable resource for their religious traditions in the modern world, they did not do so in isolation. They read and reviewed each other's books, and corresponded. An accurate assessment of either cannot be carried out in ignorance of the other. As Dietrich writes, "we are past the time when historians of nineteenth- and twentieth-century Christian and Judaic thought can work in hermetically sealed compartments."[24] One of his great contributions to scholarship is to breach just this division. No small measure of his influence can be seen by the fact that contributors to this volume not only are roughly distributed between these two fields, but many of the essays move easily across former boundaries. In this way Dietrich can be compared to Lessing in that his scholarship is as radical as, and exemplifies the virtues of, the latter's great play *Nathan the Wise.*

In an essay on the nature and function of universities, Schleiermacher distinguishes between academies, which consist of scholars with a living sense and passion for knowledge in itself and with an awareness of the necessary interconnectedness of all knowledge, and universities, whose business is to awaken the idea of science [*Wissenschaft*] in their students. Dietrich's scholarship is certainly "academic" in this sense, but one might argue that his primary mode of influence has been as a "university" professor. And this is particularly true if one includes in the category of "student" not only those formally enrolled, undergraduate and graduate, whose life paths he has altered and who have followed him into the university, or into specific areas and modes of scholarship, but also if one includes colleagues who, in their work, on panels at professional meetings, and in informal conversations, clearly defer to and esteem him as their "professor." Both categories are well represented in this volume.

Part One consists of Peter Ochs's essay (Chapter One), a critical appraisal of the corpus of Dietrich's scholarship. Ochs, a post-modernist,

---

[23] Miri Rubin, "Whose Eucharist? Eucharistic Identity as Historical Subject," *Modern Theology* 15 (April 1999), 197.
[24] Dietrich, x.

identifies Dietrich as a modernist. Yet through a critical appraisal of the corpus of Dietrich's scholarship, Ochs identifies Dietrich's methodological principles that, when turned on Dietrich himself, make possible the retrieval of Dietrich's work as a valuable resource for post-modern scholars. In interpreting Calvin and Cohen and Troeltsch and others, Ochs argues, Dietrich reads selectively, not for reasons of abstract curiosity but to address specific "torments" of the community on whose behalf he undertakes his scholarship. These are principles in tune with ethical monotheism itself. Intentionally tendentious, Ochs's reading, he claims, results not in a "misreading" of Dietrich but a "felicitous" reading that "acknowledges the redemptive telos of such a thinker's work and thereby grants that work the power to apply itself to ever renewed contexts of healing" (39).

Part Two contains six essays that analyze different aspects of significant figures in ethical monotheism in their 19th and 20th-century contexts. Susannah Heschel (Chapter Two) demonstrates the fruits of breaking out of hermetically sealed academic compartments. She revisits Abraham Geiger, the leading figure of the *Wissenschaft des Judentums*, a 19th-century movement (with clear affinities to the *religionsgeschichtliche Schule* of Göttingen) that applied historical-critical methods to Judaism. Far from being the assimilationist traitor that most scholars, in the wake of Gershom Scholem, have assumed him to be, Heschel argues that when one reads Geiger in context with his Christian and Jewish contemporaries, it becomes clear that he is writing a kind of subversive, anti-colonialist, counter-history. The sharp responses of Christian scholars such as Renan, Harnack, and Ewald when Geiger argues that Jesus was a typical rabbi demonstrate that they were well aware of this.

Richard Crouter's essay (Chapter Three) is the first of several considerations of Schleiermacher. This is not surprising, given the looming presence of Schleiermacher to the theme of ethical monotheism. Schleiermacher's developmental schema in which all religions, though valid expressions of religious consciousness, will eventually pass over into (Protestant) Christianity (the highest form of religious expression), and his sharp words about Judaism as a "dead religion" in the fifth speech of his *On Religion: Speeches to Its Cultured Despisers*, have overshadowed interest in Schleiermacher's relation to Judaism. Historical reality is, of course, more complex, as Crouter shows in considering the exchange of letters between Schleiermacher and David Friedländer, an Enlightenment Jew and student of Moses Mendelssohn, who argued that, in the wake of emancipation the question of the Jews' civil status was best resolved by a nominal baptism that would make them full citizens but would not require confessing Christ as their savior. Schleiermacher's respectful disagreement touches on issues of religious identity and national identity, and adds nuance to the common view of his relationship to Judaism.

Peter Hodgson (Chapter Four) challenges the common assumption that George Eliot (Mary Ann Evans) "lost" religion. Hodgson argues that Eliot's religious "pilgrimage" ends in a view that he terms the religion of divine presence and sympathy. Though she lacked the language to articulate her view in conceptual terms, a close reading of two novels (*Adam Bede* and *Daniel Deronda*) shows that she is closest to Hegel, or perhaps even Whitehead, in her understanding of a God-in-process. Her efforts at social reform and her deep appreciation of Judaism (evident in the Jewish character of Deronda) make her a natural fit for a collection on ethical monotheism.

Walter Conser (Chapter Five) demonstrates the important role played by foreign missionaries on the American Frontier during the Second Great Awakening. In a way that is structurally similar to the work of Dietrich, Conser's analysis of German confessional theologians in the 19th century brings together two fields, American religious history and the history of German 19th-century theology, that should be treated together but have not been.

The last two essays of Part Two begin to address the usefulness of ethical monotheism for contemporary theology and ethical and social theory, but do so primarily through historical analysis. Walter Wyman's essay (Chapter Six) is the second of the suite of essays on Schleiermacher. Wyman tackles head on the question of the conceptual adequacy of Schleiermacher's theology in the modern world by taking, as an example, Schleiermacher's doctrines of sin and evil. If ethical monotheism is to be a contemporary resource, it must offer theological advantages. While the standard complaint about Schleiermacher is that he does not do justice to the theological norm of Christian tradition, Wyman shows that Schleiermacher, despite the technical language, does stand squarely in the tradition of Augustine. Wyman is more critical when judging Schleiermacher according to the second theological norm, that of human experience. Wyman shows just what the advantages and possible shortcomings of Schleiermacher's formulations may be.

The historical consideration of ethical monotheism comes to a close with the juxtaposition of three seminal thinkers, Ernst Troeltsch, Max Weber, and William James. By setting these three in conversation,

Mark Hadley (Chapter Seven) brings into sharp focus challenges to the usefulness of ethical monotheism as a theoretical basis for society in the contemporary world. By the end of his life Troeltsch has modified his ethical monotheism to the point where it is almost a kind of ethical henotheism. While he despairs of showing that Christianity is the absolute religion, he also recognizes that such as task is needless. It is enough if Christianity can be reformulated in such a way that it continues to form the basis of European culture. Weber is more critical of the "iron cage" of modern European capitalism, and does not see how the religious values of ethical monotheism can play a role in the modern, desacralized world outside of the private sphere. James is perhaps less pessimistic than Weber about the state of Western culture, but would argue that Troeltsch's ethical monotheism is too exclusivistic and anti-democratic for the modern context. While Troeltsch is a kind of pluralist, he fails to consider what the relation of Christianity and culture should be for minority religions dwelling within Western culture. In the wake of these astute criticisms of the leading Christian proponent of ethical monotheism, has it anything to offer the contemporary context?

Part Three addresses just this question. The first two chapters consider the possibility and adequacy of our knowledge of God, first from a Jewish, and then from a Christian theological framework. David Blumenthal (Chapter Eight) analyzes the adequacy of God-talk in the Zohar, a 13th -century mystical text. The ten *sephirot* offer, he argues, a way of talking about God that allows for divine dynamism, acknowledges the influence of human action on God, and gives resources for theodicy. All these advantages compare favorably with the possibilities offered by Christian Trinitarian monotheism.

Katherine Sonderegger (Chapter Nine) is the third consideration of Schleiermacher. She argues that critics who argue that Schleiermacher's theology of consciousness is subjective and offers no objective knowledge of God have misread him. She finds a "robust realism" in Schleiermacher, but in a fascinating systematic move argues that the epistemology that allows for such knowledge of God belongs not to the introduction to the doctrine of God in a dogmatics, as it is found in Schleiermacher, but in the doctrine of human nature.

The final six chapters form a collection that analyzes ethical monotheism as a contemporary resource for ethics. Peter Haas (Chapter Ten) shows the links between reigning theories in physics, from Aristotle (ideal forms, universe is a hierarchy) to Newton (unified causality, universe is a machine) to quantum mechanics (universe is unpredictable, there is an inherent relationship between observer and object) and moral beliefs. Haas argues that ethical monotheism is well suited to a Newtonian world view in its optimism and reliance on objective knowledge of the nature of God. He hints that in the present context ethical monotheism may not offer the resources required for ethical theory.

Robert Gibbs (Chapter Eleven), by comparing the theology of Franz Rosenzweig and the ethics of Emmanuel Levinas, argues that a kind of reformulated ethical monotheism is in fact necessary to contemporary ethical thought. Inter-human relationships require, as a third term, a God, but one who is "always . . . already passed by." There is, perhaps, less to be said about this God than would please Cohen or Troeltsch, but the disappearing God of ethical monotheism is, nonetheless, critical for contemporary ethics.

David Novak (Chapter Twelve) also places Levinas in a trajectory of ethical monotheists, but argues in the end that ethical monotheism is a wrong turn for Jewish thinkers in modernity. The attempt to do ethics from a philosophical perspective, in the tradition of Kant, leads to ambivalent attitudes to Jewish law. Novak argues that the proper starting point for Jewish ethics is to reaffirm the whole Jewish tradition, including the Talmudic distinction between transgressions against God and transgressions against other humans (which, finally, are also transgression against God).

Louis Newman (Chapter Thirteen) argues that Novak's argument that natural law has a place in Jewish tradition has limits. While agreeing that Novak's theories might find confirmation if they give practical assistance in the tasks of defining the relationship of Jews to the secular world in which they find themselves, the need to condemn the Holocaust on universal grounds, and the effort to create a Jewish democratic state, Newman indicates that one can find natural law in scripture only through forced exegesis that expects to find it there. Where Novak sees Jewish and natural law as complementary, Newman argues that this comes at the expense of revelation, and hints that Jewish law may, in fact, be subsequent to and displace natural law.

Francis Schüssler Fiorenza asks whether ethical monotheism can be ethical in a pluralistic world (Chapter Fourteen). He takes James's criticisms of Troeltsch a step further, asking whether pluralism is truly pluralistic, or if it is an American export that fails truly to hear other voices. While acknowledging the benefits of pluralism, Fiorenza argues that if the exclusive truth claims of religions are overlooked, one has failed to take them on their own terms, and has reduced them to commodities among which one may pick and choose as a consumer.

With Jeffrey Stout's final chapter (Chapter Fifteen) we circle back to many of the same issues with which Peter Ochs started us off. What is the proper method for interpreting and making use of texts? Can biblical texts provide norms for ethics, and what is the relationship of the prophet who criticizes society from a divine perspective, and human social critics? Is criticism possible in a pluralistic context? While largely agreeing with Michael Walzer's social democratic commitments to radical yet gradual change, Stout argues that it is difficult to derive warrants for this stance from the Exodus story, as Walzer claims to. Wandering in the desert is not a bad metaphor for this brand of social change, but it is difficult to see the exodus as a liberating vision of the overcoming of oppression. It is, rather, a flight; there is a danger when social critics claim to speak for God, as do prophets; and the story is less liberating when seen from the Canaanite perspective. Stout distinguishes several kinds of "critical distance," and argues that a social critic cannot choose his or her distance a priori, but only on a case by case basis.

The 19th century continues to be a focus of scholarly attention because of its profound cultural and social changes, and its stunning intellectual efforts to rethink religion and society. But as the essays in Part Three demonstrate, it is also an object of fascination because the issues confronted in the 19th century are still our issues. Our context may be more complex, and post- modernism, feminism, and the tremendous violence of the 20th century may have called into question some of the 19th century's assumptions. But far from replacing the tasks of theological, ethical, and social thought in the context of a historical consciousness, these developments have sharpened our awareness, deepened the issues to be confronted, and taught us the utter seriousness of the project. Ethical monotheism remains a useful, if contentious resource. We have inherited, not solved, the puzzles facing the 19th century.

B. A. Gerrish has written that one of the motives for studying historical theology is so that one can "make one's theological decisions in the best of company."[25] Wendell Dietrich has helped to make the figures to whom he has devoted his scholarly career lively company indeed. For the contributors to this volume, and many others in the academy, he himself has been and continues to be the best of company, for which this volume is a small token of gratitude.

---

[25] B. A. Gerrish, "Theology and the Historical Consciousness," *McCormick Quarterly* 21 (1968), 206.

PART ONE

CHAPTER ONE

ETHICAL MONOTHEISM WHEN THE WORD IS WOUNDED: WENDELL DIETRICH REREAD

Peter Ochs

Introduction

Wendell Dietrich's presence in Jewish academia represents one of those rare expressions of balm and care that the Jews receive in years after their terrible destructions. I don't say this merely as a token of gratitude for his personal presence and contributions, but also as a way of acknowledging the *type* of presence he embodies in Jewish life. What type of philosophic academic can embody balm for the Jews after *this* Destruction? There is a transcendental condition to be met! It must be a Christian, in order for it to embody the reversal of oppression — undoing the main features of European civilization under which the Jews were oppressed. Among these features were Christian universalism (/imperialism) and its secularized substitute: what many of us lazily perhaps but also somewhat helpfully label "modernism," thinking of such features as "foundationalism," "secular humanism," and the various academic imperialisms that have accompanied these.

Wendell Dietrich — from here on, I will write WD — is not a post-modernist. That is to say, his way of responding to the oppressive features of modern Europe has not been to negate modernity in general, but to search out and selectively promote modernity's deeper capacities for inner reform: imperialist Europe's working toward that form of Christian philosophy that would overcome Europe's imperialism. Hence the balm mentioned earlier: a balm for European thought and, therefore, a balm as well for Jews in the West after the horrible culmination, this century, of Europe's oppressive tendencies. But WD's response to oppression is more than a balm *for* the Jews touched by European civilization. It is also a balm *of* the Jews, because WD's response is to locate commandments for Europe within the Jewish heritage of Europe's own Christian heritage.

This is a Jewish heritage that, without negating its own inner concerns, turns also outside itself to speak to Europe — or to the Christian-

and-secular West — to remind it of its own roots in Biblical Judaism, to caution it against its imperialist, totalizing proclivities, and to draw it forward to a renewal of its primordially prophetic faith. This renewal is what may be termed "ethical monotheism": WD's reading of Hermann Cohen's vision of biblical faith as ethical rule for the modern West, a rejudaized Christian West. Ethical monotheism does not negate the modern West but extends its arms, instead, to envelope it in the stern and directive love that emerges from out of the biblical word to define Europe's present purpose.

But what do we do when the word itself is wounded? Wounded, because we do not, after the Shoa, know so clearly how the biblical Word commands, what it promises, or what it threatens. And wounded, as well, because we also do not know so clearly how our own reason is to be trusted as a vehicle for deciphering the command, the promise, and the threat. This is the question, in different terms, of how WD's version of ethical monotheism can respond to the challenges of postmodernity. In response to this question, I offer four stages of re-reading WD's ethical monotheism. In stage 1, I offer an introductory typology of the central theses of WD's ethical monotheism, interpreted as an intentionally selective and pragmatic re-reading of John Calvin, of Ernst Troeltsch, and, in particular, of Hermann Cohen. I suggest that WD displays the religious purpose of his ethical monotheism in his reading of Calvin, and its ethical purpose in his readings of Cohen and also Franz Rosenzweig (with passing references to Emmanuel Levinas). In stage 2, I offer my own selective and pragmatic re-reading of WD's ethical monotheism as it might now respond to the challenges of postmodernity. This complex re-reading is divided, in turn, into four sub-stages. Stage 2a addresses the early modern sources of WD's ethical monotheism. I suggest that, to serve the needs of our own age, WD may be interpreted as having reread Calvin as a selective, pragmatic reader of his own community's scriptural tradition. Stage 2b addresses the modern context of WD's use of Calvin. I reconstruct the ethical monotheism WD attributed to Calvin as WD's way of re-addressing Calvin's monotheism to the needs of a modern age. Stage 2c addresses the postmodern context of our own uses of WD's work. I identify two "torments of postmodernity"; 2d I suggest how these torments may challenge WD's ethical monotheism; and then 3 I offer a way to re-read this ethical monotheism so that it responds appropriately to the torments. In conclusion, 4 I suggest how WD's work may be brought into dialogue with some contemporary movements of postmodern philosophical theology.

1. *Wendell Dietrich's Ethical Monotheism: A Brief Typology*

WD is one of those cheerier scholars who write about thinkers they like and write about them felicitously. His felicity is not mere generosity, however; it also reflects a method of selectively re-reading previous thinkers in ways that will enhance their capacity to serve the deep needs of a contemporary society of readers. This method provides the means, moreover, of reading WD as he reads these others: reading him felicitously and then re-reading him in ways that extend his service to our community of readers. WD introduces the method through the way he describes Troeltsch. WD writes,

> When Troeltsch moves from . . . reflection on the work of the historian to the work of a systematic thinker, he acknowledges that systematic thought requires selection among varieties of Christian belief. Such selection requires responsible risk-taking. . . . Troeltsch's selection of resources from the tradition is . . . shaped by his estimate of the modern sensibility. Modern man is not occupied with death and other-worldly immortality as is the man of the Ancient Church. . . . A proper modern reinterpretation of Christianity will show that Christianity provides significance to man as moral personality by relating him to the one God.[1]

So too, WD begins his analyses as a historian of religious and ethical thought, but then rereads his authors' words selectively, taking risks to argue how these authors speak from out of their own historical contexts to address matters of urgent concern in the context WD shares with his readers. In the language of his other central author, Hermann Cohen, this is WD's own process of "idealization."

Cohen is the central source for the terms of WD's work. As WD notes, Cohen offers a systematic scheme for understanding Judaism, what WD calls his "ethical monotheism." This is, however, no essentialistic reduction of Judaism, but "a postulatory scheme in which the idea of God functions in certain ways."[2] The scheme "is filled out in a specific way when data is brought into the scheme from religious life and from the sources of Judaism."[3] Is that not, nonetheless, simply to adopt an abstract postulate and then "fill in the details" to suit the given case of Judaism? WD does not think so. First of all, he believes Cohen has drawn the terms of his scheme from readings of the classic Biblical and rabbinic sources that are warranted by the historical scholarship of his

---

[1] Wendell Dietrich, *Cohen and Troeltsch, Ethical Monotheistic Religion and Theory of Culture* (Atlanta: Scholar's Press for Brown University, 1986), 19.
[2] Ibid., 10.
[3] Ibid.

day: "modern biblical criticism helps to set the agenda for Cohen's own systematization and 'idealization' of Judaism as a religion of reason."[4] Second, this scholarship portrays the Biblical and rabbinic texts themselves as the products of multiple layers of redaction, each layer of which is guided by its own postulatory scheme for selectively rereading previous layers. The third and key issue is how these schemes arise. Did Cohen believe that the schemes arise out of each generation's conviction that its teachers have glimpsed "the one truth" more clearly than any other? If so, then we might suspect Cohen of seeking to do the same: to promote what we would now call his own "foundational" vision of the essence of Judaism. What if, however, he believed that each generation of teachers must select from its text traditions those specific lines of reasoning that will redeem the generation from its present woes? If so, then Cohen would be guilty of ignoring his generation's specific needs if he read the text traditions of Judaism as mere historian or academic. His obligation would be, in addition to historical scholarship, to take the risk to *judge* what his community needed and how some aspects of the text tradition could speak to those needs.

I believe WD reads Cohen in this second sense and that this represents WD's own purpose as well: to pursue what we might call a "redemptive — or pragmatic — scholarship" that places the last stage of scholarly interpretation in the service of an explicit, ethical and religious end. WD reveals significant aspects of his religious purpose in his reading of Calvin and his ethical purpose in his reading of Cohen-Rosenzweig.

Calvin and Scriptural Monotheism

In his essay, "Calvin's Scriptural Ethical Monotheism," WD draws out of Calvin's entire corpus, the *Institutes* in particular, a single, coherent system of religious thought.[5] Following Troeltsch, he argues that Calvin constructs this system by asking, selectively, what social and religious directives scriptural Christianity can offer the Western civilization of his day. In the next stage of reading, I will examine WD's method of reading Calvin's method of reading. In this stage, my goal is only to identify the results of WD's reading: a system of religious rules,

---

4   Ibid., 11.
5   Wendell Dietrich, "Calvin's Scriptural Ethical Monotheism: Interpretation, Moral Conscience, and Religious System," in *Faith and History: Essays in Honor of Paul W. Mayer*, ed. John Carroll, C. Cosgrove, and E. Johnson (Atlanta: Scholars Press, 1990), 360-377.

including the following rules for fulfilling the religious ends of scholarship.

- God communicates to humanity by way of scripture.
- This communication is made by way of the scriptural readings that are offered *by* particular communities of readers *with respect to* the particular social/historical conditions of life that stimulate their reading.
- By itself, the scriptural text therefore communicates God's word vaguely or multivalently; univalent meanings are disclosed only with respect to the specific social/historical context of the community of readers.
- While we cannot say a priori what the content of any such reading will be, we can say what a priori conditions it should fill: God's word will, in some context-specific way, command the community of readers to act in a certain way, on behalf of the God of all creatures, on behalf of all humanity, and as a means of redeeming the community itself from its sin and suffering.
- The culminating, Gospel narrative of Christ's life was conditioned, finally, by

  the tormented consciences of fallen human beings who are so alienated from God that they persistently turn in upon themselves and must constantly be converted in order that they might refer all life and its benefits to God and not to themselves.[6]

  As WD reads Calvin, God enters humanity as Christ only in response to humanity's sin and the torment of its unredeemed fall. Christ is thus the mirror of the special election of the individual believer, who is relieved of his or her torments through Christ and comes, through him, to the moral and social obligations of God's word.

- For his own Christian society, Calvin read the scriptural record as a summons to form a plurality of communities covenanted with God as was Israel: "construing the universal church as an association of churches in different nations."[7] Each community was obligated to the "two tables of the law": the first table of the Ten Commanments that obliges Israel and the Church to be devoted to God and the second table that obliges all humanity to moral relations with its neighbors[8]. God commands freely and commands all humanity.

---

6 Ibid., 362.
7 Ibid., 367.
8 Ibid., 373-4.

- As a religious response to the needs of the modern era in general, Calvin's religious doctrine can be reread as a "scriptural ethical monotheism." In the same way that the "tormented conscience" of fallen humanity conditions Christ's redeeming presence, so do each of the major "torments" of the modern era warrant Calvin's redeeming doctrine.

In sum, scholarship should serve the life of Christ, responding redemptively to the specific symptoms of humanity's fall that one encounters in contemporary society. These are, in general, symptoms of humanity's "tormented conscience." Therefore, the goal of scholarship is to read scripture as vehicle of God's redeeming word; to read it through the history of successive, community-specific readings that links us, today, to the primordial reception of scripture; and to reread scripture now, in light of that history, as vehicle of God's redeeming word *for us here, specifically, in our particular condition of torment.* From this perspective, both Calvin's and WD's selective readings are selective *as* vehicles of this redeeming word. Since that selectivity is specific to present day needs — and self-consciously so — it should not be condemned as symptom of some foundationalist reduction of the scriptural tradition to the terms of some a priori scheme. It serves, instead, a "postulatory scheme," whose value is ultimately instrumental: true, in a pragmatic sense, if it redeems; false to the degree that it does not.

Cohen/Rosenzweig/Levinas and Ethical Monotheism

The redemptive goal of WD's Christian scholarship is, at the same time, an ethical goal, since humanity's "torment" is not only sin, but also suffering. This connection between suffering and moral conscience is made clearest in WD's reading of Cohen, which extends, in its major theses, to his readings of Rosenzweig and Levinas.

A succinct statement of Cohen's ethical monotheism comes in WD's "The Character and Status of the Concept of History in Three Twentieth Century Systems of Judaic Thought: Cohen, Rosenzweig, Levinas."[9] According to WD, Cohen derives three postulates from his reading of Jewish sources: "[i] the one, unique God, in his transcendent ethical

---

[9] Wendell Dietrich, "The Character and Status of the Concept of History in Three Twentieth Century Systems of Judaic Thought: Cohen, Rosenzweig, Levinas," in *From Ancient Israel to Modern Judaism: Intellect in Quest of Understanding*, eds. Jacob Neusner, E. Frerichs, and N. Sarna (Atlanta: Scholar's Press for Brown University, 1989), 197-211.

ideality; [ii] unitary human history; and [iii] the ideal goal, never to be fully attained, of a unified Messianic humanity."[10] The "universally valid criterion" by which changes in humanity's unitary history are to be judged is "*justice*," which primarily concerns the redistribution of "social power in modern industrial society," and which also serves the end "of fostering human emancipation."[11] This is emancipation from "status oriented, hierarchically structured pre-modern societies" to the messianic society Cohen envisions. Or, in what WD considers Troeltsch's complementary terms, humanity's utopian goal and "highest purpose, attainable only through religion, is to achieve that authentic human freedom that entails a transition from finite-egoistic creatureliness to a self surrendered to the divine will."[12] The people Israel's purpose is to serve as instrument of humanity's achieving this goal, which means that, for WD, following Cohen, Jewish ethical monotheism should be a regulative principle for all western society.

WD's commitment to this conclusion is evident in the aspects of Rosenzweig's monotheism that he does *not* accept. Rosenzweig — and Levinas after him — notes that the Jewish people's attachment to the one, transcendent God constitutes its resistance to the violence of history and, thus, its capacity to guide humanity to the end of history. For WD, this is good, ethical monotheism. But, Rosenzweig — perhaps unlike Levinas — also appears to value this people as more than mere instrument, focusing "on the Jewish ethnos as a concrete realization of transcendent goods without regard for ethical monotheism's instrumental conception of the Jewish people . . . as bearer of the universal criterion of justice as an *unaccomplished* eternal task."[13] For WD, this is not good; it is a "serious defect" in Rosenzweig's reasoning, that shows him to be "basically a conservative . . . at odds with a social democratic version of Judaic ethical monotheism."[14] Rosenzweig's position notwithstanding, WD has shown us the force of his own ethics. It is not good for Christians or Jews to live in an end-time. Human fallenness remains a condition for ethical as well as religious life, because it means that all our institutions — the profession of scholarship included — remain potentially suspect

10 Ibid., 199.
11 Ibid.
12 Wendell Dietrich, *Cohen and Troeltsch*, 22.
13 Wendell Dietrich, "Is Rosenzweig an Ethical Monotheist? A Debate with the New Francophone Literature," in *Der Philosoph Franz Rosenzweig (1886-1929) Internationaler Kongress Kassel 1986*, ed. Wolfdietrich Schmied-Kowarzik (Freiburg: Karl-Alber Verlag, 1988), 898 (italics mine).
14 Ibid.

until the one end of time: potentially unjust, potential sources of oppression. Our capacity for autonomy is thus emancipatory in the present world only when it is a power to free us from our violent history and the institutions that embody it. And we acquire this power only when, with the grace of God, we participate in all of our institutions as instruments of justice and of rectifying injustice. For us as scholars, this means refusing to participate in the profession of academia as if it were an end in itself, rather than an instrument of ethical service.

In sum, WD's ethical reading of Cohen overlaps with his religious reading of Calvin. In both cases, the end of reading is to contribute to healing humanity's torments. The reader encounters the torment of human sin by way of its manifestations in specific cases of human injustice and suffering, and, in responding to injustice and suffering, the reader responds to the conditions of human sin. From this perspective, WD's writings on scriptural-ethical monotheism may themselves be re-read as expressing the following Calvinist/Cohenian doctrine of religious-ethical scholarship:

- Humanity suffers. This is the consequence of the universal condition of human sin, as manifested in community-specific instances of suffering.
- By way of scripture, God communicates a redeeming word to this suffering humanity.
- This word is directed to humanity universally, but vaguely. The word is received, clearly, only as it, in context-specific ways, commands a specific community of readers to act in a certain way, on behalf of all humanity, but in response to community-specific instances of sin and suffering.
- Any specific reading — or project of reading — should have a specific context in the life of the community of readers: it should respond to their defining "torment of conscience," as WD puts it in terms gleaned from Calvin. In religious terms, this represents the specific aspect of human sin and fallenness that warrants both God's redeeming grace *and* the scholar's work: for this work succeeds only through divine grace. In moral terms, this represents the specific conditions of injustice and suffering to which the reading must respond.
- Scriptural readings of this kind are guided by community representatives specifically educated for this purpose.
- Scriptural-philosophers of the scriptural traditions — like the subjects of WD's inquiry, Cohen, Troeltsch, Rosenzweig, and Levinas

— have the qualifications to be numbered among these representatives, provided they accept the responsibility. And they should accept it.

- As community representatives (and representative readers), these scriptural philosophers carry the heavy responsibility of proposing how God's scriptural word offers its commanding and redeeming voice *to* the specific conditions of need or "torment" that mark a given community of readers and that warrant scriptural scholarship. Scriptural scholarship is not for its own sake, but for the sake of delivering a redeeming word to its communal context. The scholarship should include three activities:

  1. Reading: careful familiarity with the text-reading traditions that link the present community of readers to the scriptural sources. This means study of scriptural sources, rabbinic (or patristic) commentaries, and medieval and modern text-and-philosophic interpretations.

  2. Observation: attentiveness to the empirical conditions of social and communal life that warrant scriptural study today.

  3. Responsive (or redemptive) Interpretation: selective re-reading of the text traditions in order to suggest how the scriptural word may command specific responses to contemporary conditions of suffering and injustice.

- Philosophic reflection is integrated with practices of text reading throughout all three of these activities. In Cohen's terms, the scholar's obligations to act are rooted, ultimately, in the scriptural revelations and their interpretations; the scholar's capacity to clarify the meanings of the revelatory tradition draws, ultimately, on the rules of philosophic logic recommended by Greek philosophic traditions and their interpreters. While the scriptural traditions should, indeed, retain their moral privilege, the details of ethical monotheism reflect many levels of interaction between text and philosophic practices. Furthermore, while it requires philosophic discipline to clarify the rules of scriptural scholarship, this discipline itself reflects a history of interaction between philosophers and text scholars.

- The second and third activities of scriptural philosophy require concrete engagement with the specific community of readers out of which the scholar works. For example, there must be some actual case of injustice and suffering in some actual society, as observed by some actual scriptural readers. The selectivity of scriptural reading is based, ultimately, on the specificity of this concrete engagement, which is the basis, as well, of the scriptural logic of the absolute. For a scriptural philosophy, the kind of universality one associates with pure generality must be nominal, alone. This is the generality of mere convention or artifice, as when one says "let us define the term 'hard' to refer to *any* object (in general) that scratches but cannot be scratched," and so on. Real generality — or that which may be predicated of whatever actually exists — is attributable only to attributes of what we may call the "absolute." This is that one reality to which everything in the universe refers, relating to it as creature to creator, but of which nothing is known in general. Attributes of the absolute are displayed only in relation to historically and experientially concrete events or engagements: for example, "divine grace," as displayed in the capacity of a particular group of scriptural philosophers to rediscover the relationship between scriptural reading and the modern scholar's obligation to respond, as scholar, to conditions of communal suffering.

2. *But What If the Word Is Wounded? Challenges to WD's Ethical Monotheism*

Readers of this book will be sufficiently familiar with postmodern criticism to expect that, if stated baldly, ethical monotheism would seem to be a candidate for just that kind of criticism. As a species of "universalism," this monotheism might be expected to attract criticisms of its foundationalism, or its efforts to construct a total, conceptual scheme on the basis of which all claims to human knowledge and all norms for human conduct could be judged. As a form of theism and of scripturalism, ethical monotheism might be expected to attract criticisms of its potential contribution to cultural oppression: imposing the master narrative of some confessional group on those who may not share the confession. Students of academic methodology might be expected to criticize what appears to be its unwarranted reduction of Jewish and Christian ethics to a single set of concepts. And so on. My purpose in this section is to ask to what degree ethical monotheism can or cannot speak to a postmodern age. Nonetheless, there are two reasons why I will not attempt to get an answer by applying these more well-known kinds of postmodern criticism. One reason is that I am afraid that, within the limited space of this essay, I would have to reduce subtle lines of argument to mere slogans. A second and more important reason is that, unless it is to be employed in an imperialistic way, postmodern criticism must be offered first with respect to a philosophic, religious, or cultural program's own internal rules of inquiry. To ask about the pertinence of WD's ethical monotheism is, therefore, first to ask how this monotheism would evaluate itself today.

While modern- or liberal-sounding in its ethical universalism, and while clarified through the tools of transcendental philosophy, WD's ethical monotheism remains rooted in a reading of God's commanding and redeeming word, as read through scripture, both Old and New Testament, and through the history of scripture's reception right up to the present day and its torments. This ethical monotheism therefore rests on faith in the commanding and redeeming presence and power of God's word, but not on mere faith. As detailed in the previous section, it offers a rational method for receiving, clarifying, and falsifying its claims. These claims are "postulatory schemes," rather than foundational dogma. They represent a self-consciously selective reading of the scriptural traditions, rather than a mere reduction of these traditions to the terms of an a priori scheme. This selection, furthermore, is made on behalf of pragmatic criteria drawn from out of the traditions themselves. Abstracted from out of the practice of ethical monotheism, these criteria could be re-framed, for the present occasion, as rules for testing the strength of this practice. Here, then, is an illustrative list of three of these internal rules for testing the claims of ethical monotheism:

1. The *legitimacy* of these claims is tested against one's communal tradition of scriptural reading: this is scripture as witness to the presence of God's word and one's communal tradition as witness to the witness. It may be simplest to say that a given community *urges* a set of readings of scripture and that the claims are tested against these readings.

2. The *power* of these scriptural readings is tested, in turn, in their success in commanding behavior that relieves the kinds of suffering, injustice, or torment that characterize a given community in a given age. To be pragmatically testable, in other words, one's scriptural reading must be selective and the selection must be directly influenced by the conditions of torment that the reading should help relieve.

3. *Reason* is the *vehicle* for articulating any of these claims from out of a tradition of scriptural reading and for applying to them the tests of communal reading and of pragmatic efficacy. This is not simply "reason in general," but the specific form reasoning takes when scriptural reading is adopted as the basis for generating ethical norms and when those norms are to be tested pragmatically, as noted in Rule 2. There is no single, a priori rule for determining

the form that reasoning will take in this monotheism. The form it takes — or the set of rules for determining that form — is simply urged on what we may call the sub-community of ethical monotheists through their direct encounter with God (or what they consider to be such an encounter). *That* they encounter God in this way is not itself a testable or falsifiable claim but is one of the a priori conditions for engaging in ethical monotheism, as is the claim *that* a form of reasoning is urged on them and that this reasoning makes irresistible and indubitable commands. What remain testable and falsifiable are their claims about *what* specific forms this reasoning takes and *what* it specifically commands. For example, the "universality" of ethics is *not* an a priori category for reasoning in this way. "Universality" is, instead, an attribute of the ethical monotheist's *claim* about the ethical meaning of scripture and is therefore a testable and falsifiable aspect of ethical monotheism.

To test the pertinence of ethical monotheism to a postmodern age, perhaps the most important aspect of the preceding rules is the *selectivity* of monotheistic claims: the requirement that each claim is made *with respect to* historically specific conditions of suffering and injustice or "torment." This aspect, alone, protects ethical monotheism from the baldly stated range of postmodern criticisms mentioned earlier. WD's claims must be evaluated with respect to their contribution to *the modern European conditions of torment to which they are addressed. To re-evaluate their contribution to our own context, WD's claims must first be re-applied to the postmodern conditions of our communities of scriptural reading.* Since WD's modernism is itself articulated against the backdrop of *early modern* scriptural monotheism, I find it helpful to add his reading of early modernism as yet another context for this evaluation.

2a. *The Early Modern Context of Scriptural Ethical Monotheism: Calvin as Reread by WD*

Earlier, I listed rules of scholarship that are suggested by WD's reading of Calvin: his selective way of re-reading Calvin's scriptural, ethical monotheism in light of his own community's needs (above, 19). To test or justify WD's rereading, we should try to reconstruct what WD takes to be the early modern communal context to which Calvin addressed his ethical monotheism. This way, we can imagine a perennial *albeit vague* ethical monotheism that can appear in one way for Calvin's community and another for WD's. We would be practicing a version of Cohen's "idealization," but the *vagueness* of our ideal should protect the exercise against charges of reductionism or foundationalism. The ideal would function like a personal being that appeared in this or that way at different times, reliably there as a representation of our readings, but never reducible to a single set of appearances. So, here is a reconstruction of Calvin's context as WD reads it:

- Calvin offered his reading of scripture for an early modern community that, among other crises, was disappointed by the failings of natural science; was therefore confused theologically by the lingering religious naturalism it inherited, still, from Thomism; was confused morally and socially by Luther's two kingdoms doctrine and its accompanying dichotomization of law and grace; and lacked, as yet, a theo-political doctrine that would enable it to participate, as a Christian community, within the emergent plurality of European nation states.
- Calvin recognized the context-specific character of both Old and New Testament receptions of God's word.
- Calvin re-read scripture in terms of its own three major contexts. The Old Testament narratives of creation were conditioned by the general election of humanity to life with God and by the fall of humanity.[15] The elemental conditions for this fall were humanity's sins: infidelity to God and rebellion against God's commandments; sloth; and following the idols of its own false imagining and thus suppressing the truth.[16] The Old Testament narratives of Israel's history were conditioned by the general election of the people Israel, along with its subsequent exile and restoration, all of which are also types for the later election, exile or loss and restoration of subsequent Christian nations. The culminating, Gospel narrative of Christ's life was conditioned, finally, by "the tormented consciences of fallen human beings."[17]

2b. *The Modern Context of WD's Own Scriptural Ethical Monotheism*

We may next reconstruct the way WD re-reads the monotheism that addresses Calvin's community but *now* as it addresses WD's own *modern* community. For the sake of comparison, I will offer this reconstruction

---

15 Wendell Dietrich, "Calvin's Scriptural Ethical Monotheism," 364.
16 Ibid., 366.
17 Ibid., 362. See above, 19-20.

in terms of WD's reading of Calvin, but it could also be offered in terms of his readings of Cohen, Troeltsch, et al.

- In the same way that the "tormented conscience" of fallen humanity conditions Christ's redeeming presence, so do each of the major "torments" of the modern era warrant a reapplication of Calvin's redeeming doctrine.

  1. *Calvin's universalism responds to the "torments" of modern atomism, in which each nation, people, and denomination is potentially at war with every other.* Consistent in this respect with the rationality and universalism of Kant's categorical imperative, Calvin recognizes a single humanity, universally obliged to overcome self-interest out of devotion to God and to God's moral law.

  2. *Calvin's scriptural monotheism responds to the "torments" of modern secularism, in which the enlightened philosopher seeks a universalism, but without God.* Without God, "universal humanity" represents a mere concept — well intentioned, perhaps, but nonetheless an idol of human imagination and desire, which cannot represent humanity universally, because it cannot be fully detached from the historical conditions of representation. As portrayed in the scriptural narrative, however, "universal humanity," or *adam*, is no mere concept, but, rather, an *index of* that creative act of God's through which all human beings find their commonality.[18] Scriptural references to *adam* function as a set of *rules for seeking out* the universally human, rather than as any sort of reductive *description* of some general being or essence. The *scriptural* portrayal works this way, because it defers, implicitly, to the one, infinite God as its author and, thus, reserves for the Infinite, alone, the capacity and privilege to complete any reader's effort to determine the *particular one* to which the portrait refers. Secular philosophic concepts of humanity *cannot* work this way, because they defer, by definition, to merely human authors, who lack the capacity and privilege to delimit their readers' efforts to determine meaning. In sum, without a scripture whose author is infinite, humanity can be characterized in only non-universal ways.

  3. *Calvin's ethical monotheism responds to the "torments" of modern, religious irrationalism and docetism.* Here, religious critics seek a false

---

[18] WD does not articulate a semiotic notion like this — distinguishing the universality of the *indexical symbol*, as opposed to a mere concept, or icon. Nevertheless, I believe this notion supports his reading of Calvin and extends it into a vocabulary appropriate to contemporary discussions.

alternative to modern atomism and secularism by condemning reason, altogether, as if it were not an instrument of God's word, and by condemning the worldly realm, altogether, as if it were not also part of God's creation, and as if the secular philosophers who inhabited it were not also neighbors, made in the image of God's beloved. Calvin's ethics — the "second table of the Law" — is dictated to all humanity by the one "sovereign and free commander who shows himself as the one who has the right to command."[19] It is dictated by way of the scriptural word, mediated by Christ as God's truth, and addressing humanity's "troubled and guilty moral conscience."[20]

WD notes that there are other elements in Calvin's writings that do not seem to fit this ethical monotheism: for example, Calvin's writings on Christ as priest who cleanses humanity of its pollution[21] and on the transmission of "hereditary sin." *However*, he believes that, to read Calvin's words religiously, as witnesses to God's word, and not as a mere collection of completed ideas, is to read them the same way Calvin read the scriptures: as texts that communicate God's redeeming word *to* some tormented community of believers in its social-historical context and religious need.

In sum, as it addresses modernity, WD's ethical monotheism retains Enlightenment-like optimism, but it is not optimism about modern reason per se. It is optimism about the divine Word's capacity to repair modernity's wounds. What do we do, however, if the Word itself is wounded?

2c. *A Postmodern Context for Re-reading and Evaluating WD's Scriptural Ethical Monotheism*

WD addresses his ethical monotheism to a modern, rather than a postmodern context. To reread him in the felicitous way he rereads previous monotheists, it is therefore best to identify specifically postmodern conditions of "torment" and *then* ask if and how ethical monotheism can be reapplied to these conditions. In this concluding section, I perform this exercise by, first, isolating two dominant torments of postmodernity; then, summarizing *modern* ethical monotheism's incapacities to relieve these torments; and, finally, suggesting some of the features of a more

---

[19] Dietrich, "Calvin's Scriptural Ethical Monotheism," 372.
[20] Ibid., 361.
[21] Ibid., 369.

adequate, postmodern ethical monotheism. The reader may now note that, from the beginning of this essay, I have already been reading WD from the perspective of this postmodern version of his monotheism. This is not mis-reading, but the kind of selective rereading that his own scholarly method requires.

1. *Two torments of postmodernity*

According to what we may call the witness of scripture's postmodern interpreters, the Word is wounded today in two ways. First, by the testimony of postmodern ethicists, the Word is wounded because reason is wounded, and human reason serves as the scriptural word's messenger, delivering it to the places of suffering and torment that receive it as healer and redeemer. Eugene Borowitz summarizes the general Jewish version of this complaint, as directed, in this case, against the *modern* formulation of Cohen's ethical universalism: modernity betrayed our faith.

> For most of two centuries almost all Jews who could modernize did so. They knew that modernity was good for them, that the great gains that equality and opportunity brought made the problems connected with modernization acceptable. But as the twentieth century waned, doubts about modernity's beneficence arose throughout Western civilization. People were profoundly disturbed by the deterioration of the quality of life. A great deal of their unhappiness was disappointment. The Enlightenment, the intellectual credo of modernity, had promised that replacing tradition with rational skepticism, hierarchy with democracy, and custom with freedom would bring messianic benefit — and certainly it hasn't. . . . On a much deeper level, this loss of confidence in Enlightenment values has come from the collapse of its philosophical foundations. All the certainties about mind and self and human nature that once powered the bold move into greater freedom now seem dubious.[22]

Where they once served, in disproportionate numbers "as the prophets of [modern] humanism and taught the secular salvation of politics, intellect, and high culture,"[23] Jewish thinkers now turn, again in disproportionate numbers, to the deconstructive arts of postmodernism, undermining what they take to be the false idols of modern rationalism. From their perspective,

> Cohen's rationalist monotheism remains too close to this kind of idolatry. Cohen's paradigm [of a 'religion of reason'] has been problematic to many

---

22 Eugene Borowitz, *Choices in Modern Jewish Thought: A Partisan Guide*, 2d ed. (West Orange, NJ: Behrman House, 1995), 283.
23 Eugene Borowitz, *Renewing the Covenant: A Theology for the Postmodern Jew* (Philadelphia: The Jewish Publication Society, 1991), 283.

Jews [in postmodernity] because, to begin with, asserting the dominance of human reason makes Judaism a hostage to whatever version of rationalism the thinker finds convincing. . . . The other great complaint against this model is the inability of a stringent universalism to legitimate a substantial Jewish particularity. In neo-Kantian and similar systems, only ethics is directly required by the God-idea, which, itself being fully universal, has no special relation to any particular people or land.[24]

And, one of the lessons of modernity for the Jews is that theories of universal ethics offer no protection for the dignity and safety of human communities, in their "mere" particularity.

From a second perspective — testimony from the people Israel's survivors in this century — the Word itself is wounded, and not merely its messenger. In our age, the Word that commands does not command clearly or unambiguously, and the Word that redeems seems to delay its own coming. Most readers will be familiar with the question that haunts Eli Wiesel's *Night*: "where is God? . . ." For the Talmudist David Halivni — a fellow survivor from Wiesel's town of Sighet — the challenge is not to locate God, but, rather, to face the current reality of God's speaking a word that is "maculate" — not immaculate. "As religious Jews," Halivni writes,

we have to know that without God there is no humanity. . . . 'Walk humbly with the Lord thy God' (Micah 6:8) — like a child holding hands. You must hold hands, and walk. But this does not mean that you always have to say, particularly in remembrance of the Holocaust, 'What you did was right.' It was terribly wrong.[25]

A sensitive survivor — and particularly one who has the opportunity or the leisure to pursue intellectual activity — must work . . . under the influence of mutually contradictory forces. . . . The Shoah signifies that whatever one considered the pattern of life one should choose — the ideal standard — collapsed. . . . Something must be changed. . . . On the other hand, the person who has survived, and has been wounded so deeply, needs that support, that holding-on-to, which only tradition can provide. 'Though he slay me, yet I will trust in Him' (Job 13:15). . . . That mankind could sink so low and inflict this kind of violence upon children: one must react to this spiritually. And at the same time, one must seek spiritual solace. . . .
    On the one hand, . . . not criticizing the past is being like those who justify. . . . On the other hand, if you acknowledge the wrong [in God and tradition that is!] then you run the risk of cutting off the branch on which you rest. . . . Therefore the struggle this person has is the struggle to do both: to find a way of criticizing tradition, but of holding steadfastly to it. Criticizing affirms that something went wrong — badly wrong, deeply wrong. Yet there

---

24 Ibid., 64-65.
25 David Weiss Halivni, *The Book and the Sword, a Life of Learning in the Shadow of Destruction* (New York: Farrar, Straus and Giroux, 1996), 164.

must be something to come home to. . . . Personally, I found this balance in
the critical study of Jewish texts, in a combination of criticism and belief in
the divine origin of the text.[26]

Halivni bases his doctrine of text criticism on a Talmudic tradition
according to which *the words of the Hebrew Bible are holy, yet they by
themselves are not fully reliable vehicles to knowing God's will.* Because of the
"sins of Israel" during the period of the monarchy, the words transmitted to us are maculate. Through divine inspiration, Ezra worked to
restore these words. In many cases, he left the explicit meaning of the
written words unclear, but he then transmitted the "oral Torah" through
which these meanings can be clarified by the sages of each generation
in response to the context specific needs of each generation. In Halivni's
terms, the unclear texts are "maculate," and this maculation is also an
index of the maculation — or what I am calling the "wounds" — of our
world as well of the words of the One who created this world. Maculate
texts are clarified only in the process of responding to the specific
maculations of our lives in this world: to clarify a text of Torah is, thus,
no act of merely technical scholarship, but an act of *tikkum olam,* "repair
or restoration of the world" — as well as of the word.[27]

Halivni's reading illustrates a tendency of Jewish thinkers after the
Shoa neither to abandon the scriptural word as sign of divine will *nor* to
trust that that word can be known clearly, nor that that will can be
followed without jeopardy. How would such thinkers receive the
postulates of ethical monotheism? What shall we of this generation do,
more generally if, for the ethical humanist's community of readers
today, reason does not appear to offer its commands unambiguously? If
the word it delivers does not appear to heal or redeem? And if the
community, in fact, offers ambiguous witness to the presence of God's
word?

2d. *Challenges to modern ethical monotheism*

For the following reasons, these two torments of postmodernity would
appear to pose some unanswerable challenges to the *modern* variety of
ethical monotheism.

1. Calvin-Cohen's universalism is significant as a response to
   modern atomism, but it overstates the response, as if there were no

---

[26] Ibid., 160-62.
[27] This thesis on maculation is presented in David Weiss Halivni, *Revelation
Restored: Divine Writ and Critical Responses* (Boulder, CO: Westview Press, 1997).

other means of avoiding atomism, outside of a strict universalism. Modern ethical monotheism appears to be posed within the terms of a strictly binary opposition between strict universalism and strict particularism. According to the postmodern critique of reason, there is no reason to presume the adequacy of such an opposition, as if there were no third term.

2. The notion of a single humanity may function, asymptotically, as a regulative and messianic ideal, but, in practice, fixation on this ideal has tempted ethical monotheists to denigrate the individual's this-worldly obligations to family, community, and people, as if these particularities were not also instruments of ethical messianism. It is not possible, in clear terms, to define what the notion of a "single humanity" means.

3. To identify universal humanity with *adam*, the single creature of God, is an appropriate way to avoid reducing ethical universalism to a merely abstract concept. However, there is no reason to presume that we understand clearly the relation of single creature to infinite creator, nor the relation of universal humanity to the individual human being.

4. To avoid spiritualizing ethics, it is appropriate to locate its source in the "Ten Commandments" as commands directed to all humanity. Like all of scripture, however, the Commandments do not speak without context-specific rereading. Without such rereading, there is no way to distinguish this "universal commandment" from what, as we have noted, remains a strictly regulative and messianic ideal. Once the Commandments are subject to rereading, however, their meanings are disclosed only to the context of some particular community of readers, weakening, or at least complicating, claims about the universality of these commandments. WD's own discomforts with Rosenzweig's ethnic particularism may also represent discomforts with context-specific readings of this kind.

5. While granting the historical specificity of each generation's reading, the modern variety of ethical monotheism appears to be inattentive to potential differences of readings within any community, let alone within the text itself.

6. Modern ethical monotheism may idealize the capacity of even a pragmatic reasoning to discern unambiguously just what torments a particular community, just what it suffers and thus just how its reading of scripture will prove redemptive.

3. Rereading WD's Ethical Monotheism for a Postmodern Setting

Almut Bruckstein has recently argued that postmodern critics fail to appreciate the hermeneutical moves implicit in Cohen's scriptural monotheism. Her reading of Cohen suggests, in fact, ways of rereading WD's ethical monotheism for a postmodern community of readers. To take one example, consider her reading of Cohen on "the creativity of the concept":

> Cohen maintains that the very acts of interpretation and of criticism — both of which are acts of 'calling into question' — create the infinity of content that characterizes Jewish oral tradition, whereas any religious truth-claim produced by history, dogma, or emotional conviction turns out to be a mere derivative, a limited reading of the biblical tradition, presented in the garb of absolute religious truth. Such a dogmatic reading . . . harbors the dangers of violence and totalitarianism. . . . Cohen condemns such dogmatic limitation of the biblical text, calling it 'idol worship.' . . . 'Idol worship' in this context is characterized by a loss of 'originality,' resulting in a closure of the text, betraying the Jewish tradition of innovative interpretation and of creative textual reasoning. The term *originality*, or *origin*, is defined in Cohen's logic as the infinite creativity of human resourcefulness and critical reasoning. . . . The concept of origin refers to the 'limit of knowledge' by what has not yet been explored. . . . The primacy of this principle . . . implies a way of interpreting religious traditions in which the past is predicated upon the future. To this way of thinking, nothing is 'given' but the originality of the interpretation that links the facts into a coherent objective structure. . . . The logical primacy of innovative interpretation is predicated on . . . 'monotheism' and 'messianism."[28]

On Bruckstein's reading, Cohen shares with postmodernist philosophers a vision of the infinite process of interpretation through which texts *and* facts are rendered meaningful and through which the reading of both texts and facts is freed from premature closure. Textual words and facts are *given as* subjects of interpretation, but *what they are* is never given, only disclosed through interpretation. On this reading, Cohen's ethical monotheism might be protected from challenges #3-6 (above, 33). To meet these challenges, we would have to assume that "universal humanity" (in #3) and "universal commandment" (in #4) represent only regulative ideals in the ongoing interpretation of what "*adam*" means. And we would have to assume that the ethical monotheist offers only provisional and context-specific readings of the "torments" of any age and of the meaning of any text. Unless claims about "transcendental

---

[28] Almut Bruckstein, "Joining the Narrators: A Philosophy of Talmudic Hermeneutics," in *Reasoning After Revelation: Dialogues in Postmodern Jewish Philosophy*, Steven Kepnes, P. Ochs, and R. Gibbs (Boulder, CO: Westview Press, 1998; 105-121), 112-13.

conditions" are somehow protected from such disclaimers, then we would have to assume that the ethical monotheist also offers only provisional and context-specific formulations of classical Jewish and Christian doctrines.

Robert Gibbs's complementary reading of Cohen's principle of correlation may help protect Cohen's ethical monotheism from challenges #1-2. "[For Cohen,] logic requires the possibility of recognizing the correlation of two independent realities. . . . Cohen claims that any concept is not merely an answer, but is itself a question."[29]

In the terms of Bruckstein's argument, the creativity of the concept involves what Cohen calls the "reciprocal determination" of question and answer. In the pragmatic terms I have used in this essay, every reading of the text idealizes the text — generating some concept from it — but only as answer to some question put, for example, by the problematic facts of our social condition. Our reading now contributes to the 'givens' of our social condition and thus to the questions posed to us for subsequent reading, and so on.

"In the *Ethics*, moreover, Cohen presents the 'I' and 'you' as correlation . . . [T]he 'I' is correlate with the other. . . . To become aware of myself as I, I must first become aware of the other."[30] Once again, every formulation of the "I" is thus correlative to some set of relations: not only of I to you or to this community to which I belong, but also of the I of "us" as a human community to another community, and of our concept of the "I" of humanity to our concept of the "you" of God.

> Correlation, in Cohen's *Religion*, is a methodological reciprocity between our concepts of the human and the divine. We can neither understand what a human being is without understanding the same of God, nor vice versa. The basis of this correlation is the creation of the human being in reason. . . . God creates the human being in order to be known and loved.[31]

In terms of Gibbs's reading, Challenge #1 (32) may be met by introducing some "correlation" as a third term between the poles of strict universalism and strict particularism. The ethical monotheist may explain that the concept of any universal is correlative to the concept of some particular. In these terms, the modern monotheist's concept of strict universalism would appear, correlatively, only as an effort to ameliorate the modern concept of atomism, and the concept of atomism

---

[29] Robert Gibbs, *Correlations in Rosenzweig and Levinas* (Princeton: Princeton University Press, 1992), 85-86.
[30] Ibid., 86.
[31] Ibid.

would itself appear only as an effort to ameliorate some other, antecedent concept, and so on. To respond to Challenge #2, in turn, the ethical monotheist may explain that the messianic ideal of a single humanity is correlative to the life of some particular community of human beings in this world — *and vice versa.*

In sum, it is possible to reread WD's ethical monotheism, out of a postmodern context, in ways that parallel Bruckstein's and Gibbs's rereadings of Cohen. The "postmodern" ethical monotheist may argue that postmodernity retains many of the torments of modernity, for which the concepts of ethical monotheism still provide a healing response. Among these are:

1. The torments of the contemporary West's persistent atomism, in which each nation, ethnic group, and religion remains, still, potentially at war with every other. The "postmodern condition" has not reduced the dangers of this atomism, nor, therefore, the appeal of this Kantian aspect of Calvin's and Cohen's universalism: the messianic goal of seeking a single humanity, universally obliged to overcome self-interest out of devotion to God's moral law.

2. The torments of the Enlightenment West's tendency to define ethical universalism as if it were incompatible with the individual's devotion, as well, to particular relations and to local or finite communal life. This suspicion of community and relationship accompanies the Enlightenment West's tendency to promote atomistic individualism and, with it, the unintended consequences of self-isolation and self-absorption. Calvin's Christian communalism remains appealing, in this regard, as a foil to the extremes of modern individualism, although his communalism is always tempered by his doctrine of the special election of the Christian individual.

3. The torments of the contemporary West's secularism, since, as noted above, mere humanism cannot underwrite ethical universalism. Calvin's and Cohen's scriptural monotheism remains appealing in the way it guarantees a universal telos (all humans are creatures of the one God) and a universal source of ethical obligation (this God obliges all humans to one another).

4. The torments of anti-modern irrationalism in the contemporary world. Calvin's and Cohen's scripturalism remains appealing in the way that, unlike recent religious anti-modernisms, it combats secular individualism by appealing to a scripturally warranted rationality. Here, reason is an instrument for interpreting God's

ethical commands as they appear when applied to the unpredictable contexts of actual social and political life. Calvin-Cohen therefore illustrate how, within a given historical context, it is possible to avoid both conceptual dogmatism (theology considered apart from its bearing on actual social and political life) and irrationalism.

5. Finally, the persistent perils of totalitarianism in the contemporary world. Calvin's and Cohen's critiques of idolatry have lasting pertinence, as a warning against the human tendency to suppress truth, in favor of self-justifying and non-falsifiable projects of world-repair and redemption. Whether religious or secular in self-description, these projects share, in the end, the logic and perils of totalitarianism. A contemporary, scriptural ethical monotheism must be pluralistic.

There, then, is a condensed rendition of WD's ethical monotheism, as its draws on Calvin's and Cohen's scriptural, ethical monotheism and as reinterpreted for a postmodern community of readers. As a response to various "torments" of contemporary life, it offers a non-atomistic, non-egocentric, non-secular, non-dogmatic, non-totalitarian, this-worldly but God-centered, universalist but pluralist, rational but scripturally-based doctrine of ethical life. But is it also polyanna-ish, or can this collection of seemingly incompatible principles respond successfully to the torments of postmodernity?

4. Conclusion
Scriptural Ethical Monotheism in Dialogue with Scriptural and Textual Reasoning

This essay has been guided by two maxims: i) read the work of a scriptural philosopher selectively, with respect to the conditions of social and religious concern that stimulate your scholarship; ii) evaluate the work of a scriptural philosopher with respect to these conditions and, correlatively, with respect to what you believe are the philosopher's rules of inquiry, as displayed in his or her writings.

Following Maxim #1, I have read WD's writings on ethical monotheism, specifically, to see if and how they might help a community of postmodern theologians respond to a contemporary "torment." The community, loosely defined, includes members of the Societies for Textual Reasoning (STR) and for Scriptural Reasoning (SSR). Formed in 1991, STR gathers philosophers and text scholars of Judaism who share what, as we heard earlier, Borowitz calls the postmodern "disappointment" in the promises of modern inquiry (above, 30). While not abandoning the university, these thinkers believe that indigenous forms of Jewish inquiry, such as Talmudic methods of text interpretation, provide resources, as well, for university studies of both Judaism and of other subject matters in the arts and sciences. Formed in 1996, SSR extends the interests and concerns of STR to scholars of the three biblical or Abrahamite faiths. The Society studies the patterns of reasoning that emerge out of philosophically disciplined readings of sacred scriptures by Jews, Muslims, and Christians who seek alternatives both to the foundational or reductive discourses of secular academia and to the anti-modern or anti-rational religious fundamentalisms that sometimes replace them.

Both Societies are beginning now to share the first fruits of their inner dialogues with the rest of the academic world. And, in doing this, both encounter one shared problem above all: to articulate how it may be possible for members of three different communities of scriptural readers to argue together about issues of truth. The goal, of course, is to argue together without reverting *either* to what modernists call the self-enclosed discourses of the pre-modern religions *or* to what postmodern-ists call the imperialistic and rationalistic formulations of modern inquiry. Without conceptual constructions, however, how do they now "stretch" their reading of God's word — to paraphrase Hans Frei, of blessed memory — so that it provides shelter for dialogues outside the precincts of their finite communities of reading? In a discussion among members of the STR, Elliot Wolfson put the problem this way:

> The postmodern turning back to Jewish textuality is a corrective to the mod-ernist turning away from Judaism, the abandonment of 'Jewish particularity for the sake of the abstract universal.' . . . [But,] if the fallacy of modernism lay in its universalizing approach to revelation and in its consequent tenden-cy to ignore the contextual nature of specific traditions, the risk of post-modernism is a potential emphasis on the particularity of a tradition to the exclusion of others. . . .
>
> To emphasize a Jewish particularity isolated from the larger cultural ma-trix in which it takes shape may result in the reification of the ethnocentric elements of traditional texts. . . . The postmodern study of Jewish texts must be predicated on a critical assessment of the tradition in all its multivocality. . . .
>
> The challenge for postmodern Jewish philosophy is to facilitate the growth of a culture based on the textual specificity of the past without losing sight of the place that Judaism must occupy in the human community at large.[32]

---

[32] Elliot Wolfson, "Listening to Speak: A Response to Dialogues in Postmodern Jewish Philosophy," in *Reasoning After Revelation*, 101-104.

Following Maxim #2, I have examined WD's ethical monotheism only from the perspective of its potential contribution to this postmodern inquiry. If my reading was selective, it was selective, however, from out of some version of what I could defend as — to borrow the rabbinic term — a "plain-sense reading." This was an effort to identify certain rules of reading — and rules of scholarship — that are implicit in WD's writings and, then, to apply a selection of those rules to reading his own studies of ethical monotheism. The result was a reading of WD's ethical monotheism reread selectively according to his own rules of reading and selectively, again, as it might contribute to the postmodern dialogue. One result of this end-driven way of reading is that, right from the start of this essay, each of my readings of WD already anticipates the post-modern questions I will be asking of him in the end. Rather than a *misreading*, I believe this is a route to a more felicitous reading of WD, or any scriptural philosopher, because it acknowledges the redemptive telos of such a thinker's work and thereby grants that work the power to apply itself to ever renewed contexts of healing.

Following this process, this is what I have learned in response to my initial question: what do we do — with scriptural, ethical monotheism — when the word itself is wounded?

1. Scholars must continue to follow the deeper scholarly rules practiced by the scriptural ethical monotheist. These rules remain the same in any situation we can imagine. In the modern period, ethical mono-theists in the Kantian mode would say that these rules represent "transcendental conditions" for the conduct of this inquiry. In a premodern period, these rules might be called, for example, attributes of the divine mind or basic commandments. In this postmodern period, we might, following WD's Calvinist side, call them "redempt-ive rules of inquiry"; or we might call them "pragmatic rules of inquiry."[33] As drawn, for example, out of WD's studies of Calvin,

---

[33] To help envision how pragmatic rules work, the philosopher Charles Peirce proposes a thought experiment: "You may recognize . . . two kinds of reasoning which we may call A-reasonings and B-reasonings. You may think that of the A-reasonings very few are seriously in error, but that none of them much advance your knowledge of the truth. Of your B-reasonings, you may think that so many of them as are good are extremely valuable in teaching a great deal. Yet of these B-reasonings you may think that a large majority are worthless, their error being known by their being subsequently found to come into conflict with A-reasonings" (*Collected Papers of Charles S. Peirce Vol 2*, ed. Charles Harteshorne and Paul Weiss [Cambridge: Harvard University Press, 1931,1933] Par. #189.) It is helpful to think of a socio-cultural complex, like "modernity" or "medieval scholasticism," as a vast

Cohen, Troeltsch, and Rosenzweig, these include the scholar's obligation to study the scriptural tradition for the sake of confronting injustice and healing suffering (including the tormented moral consciousness) in the community of readers and its wider society. This community belongs, at once, to a tradition of scriptural reading, to the university tradition and society, to some socio-political realm, and to the human community most broadly; the scholar serves all these.

2. In the postmodern period, all of these societies are tormented by disappointments with the modern university's dominant rules of inquiry, with the dominant religion's capacities to train the human heart and to account for evil and for what evils God may allow, and with the dominant socio-political systems of promoting human safety and well-being. At this time, scholars need to acknowledge the powers of modern inquiry to contribute to healing specifically modern torments, such as fears of communal and political atomism or of the lack of any shared human values across a world of competing ethnic, religious, political, and economic groups and interests. But, recognizing the context-specificity and finitude of each redemptive inquiry, scholars need to acknowledge as well that modern inquiry will necessarily fail to heal other sorts of torment, including those to which it may contribute. Facing some of the continuing burdens of modern society, postmodern inquiry will continue some of the rules of modern inquiry. But facing new burdens, as well, this inquiry must also reform and replace some of the modern rules.

3. Among the most needed reforms are these:

- To correct modern inquiry's tendency simply to overstate and overstretch its conclusions: to assume, for example, that an entire system or religion or philosophy is "wrong," when only some of its claims are falsified; or to assume that reforms for such a system require "true universality," where "something simply more-than-particular" would do.

---

collection of visible B-reasonings that offer explicit rules about how to act in the world and normally invisible A-reasonings. Brought to consciousness by the failings of our B-reasonings, these A-reasonings do not offer any information about the world, but they offer rules for correcting B-reasonings. The A-reasonings correspond to what we are calling "pragmatic rules of inquiry." According to the scriptural pragmatist, scripture is a place where these normally invisble rules are made visible. [See Peter Ochs, *Peirce, Pragmatism, and the Logic of Scripture* (Cambridge: Cambridge University Press, 1998), 177f.]

- To correct modern inquiry's complementary tendency to frame criticisms and corrections in terms of a strict law of excluded middle, as if for every claim X that is falsified, there is a claim -X that is true (where the set of contraries [X + -X] constitute the universe of possible claims, rather than the set of contradictories [X, Y, Z, Q . . .].

- Therefore, and by way of illustration, to replace the binary pair "universal or particular" with some correlation uCp, so that any universal claim (u) is made correlative to (C) some particular context of inquiry (p) for which the universal claim serves some corrective or regulative function. According to this rule, "universality" and "particularity" conflict only in the absence of the mediating third that correlates one with the other.

- To legitimize philosophic claims about "absolutes," where an "absolute" is predicated of claims that are neither universal nor particular but vague. These claims illustrate some correlation that is predicated of all humans universally but that is definable and observable only in specific contexts. Examples of names of absolutes are "God's love," "Israel as God's beloved," "justice," and so on. A specific narrative about justice will illustrate only a kind of justice as achieved or sought in some situation. This rule suggests that a modern thinker's typical binary pairs (individual vs. community, freedom vs. law, universality vs. particularity) can be mediated only by absolutes.

- To note that scriptural scholars are those who identify sacred Scripture as source of the absolutes with respect to which they make claims that correlate universals and particulars. These scholars therefore conduct three kinds of inquiry: i) *reading*: studies of the plain sense of scripture, which disclose to them, within their communities of reading, the names of absolutes and their relations one to the other within the corpus of scripture. This includes studies of the rereadings of scripture throughout the history of their traditions of reading; ii) *observation*: studies of the conditions of suffering, injustice, or torment in their societies that warrant scripturally grounded, redemptive responses. This includes critical studies of scriptural or other academic inquiry that fails to fulfill (or incompletely fulfills) its obligations to respond to such conditions; iii) *interpretation*: judgments about how, as both guided by and illustrating certain absolutes, specific conditions of suffering may be remedied by certain lines of action or rules of conduct. It is in formulating these rules that the scholar correlates particular descriptions of suffering with specific sets of concepts. This list itself may be taken as an example, since it belongs to an effort to remedy certain problems in postmodernity. Some absolutes that inform this list are "God's love and compassion," "the imitation of God," "the obligation to reason as a means of responding to suffering." These absolutes guide my correlating a set of concepts like "over-stretching" and "excluded middle" with a particular description of what I take to be a torment in modern inquiry. The result is a claim about the scriptural philosopher's obligation to correct modern inquiry's tendency to over-stretch its use of the law of excluded middle.

Strengths of This Response to Postmodern Torments

This way of rereading WD's ethical monotheism appears to respond successfully to several postmodern concerns. It offers a non-exaggerated way of appreciating the continuing contributions of the modern model, while making needed reforms as well. It strengthens the pragmatic dimension of WD's reading of Cohen-Calvin. By rereading each monotheistic inquiry as a response to context-specific conditions of suffering, this model corrects foundationalist tendencies in the modern model. It assures the postmodern scriptural scholar that, even when an inherited tradition seems to fail (including a modern tradition), it still offers access to deeper, pragmatic rules for correcting the tradition. By identifying these rules with scriptural absolutes, this model provides the community of readers a continued source of faith, hope, and knowledge amidst the disappointments and confusions of postmodernity. By characterizing the absolutes as "vague," and thus irreducible to conceptualized dogmas, the model seems to protect the interests of both localized community and the "other" to any such community. Local community is protected, because it alone provides a context for clarifying the actual meaning of these absolutes for concrete action. Those outside the community (or "others" to the community) are protected, for one, because the absolutes belong to them as well as to the community: the community "owns" only its context-specific clarifications of the absolute, nothing more general than that. Others — and otherness — are protected, for two, because the absolute is clarified by correlating certain particular descriptions (of need or suffering) with certain sets of concepts. Each of these concepts is a universal, in the sense that it (unlike the absolutes) may have a general definition and is potentially usable by any community on any occasion: the way a brick may become part of my house, alone, but could also become part of yours. Outsiders to the community may therefore not appreciate precisely why a community has defined its absolutes on some occasion in some specific way, but they can still understand each conceptual element of the definition. With that understanding, they can enter into dialogue with community members — keeping "tabs" on the community as it, as well, keeps tabs on them.

Weaknesses of This Response to Postmodern Torments

To identify various weaknesses of the postmodern model, it is necessary to examine it from various perspectives. This means that there is not simply one "counter-model," but rather a potential dialogue — or debate among several. Here is an illustrative sampling.

- Bruckstein, as we saw, argues that Cohen rejects both dogmatic rationalism and dogmatic textualism, holding that "the very acts of interpretation and of criticism — both of which are acts of 'calling into question' — create the infinity of content that characterizes Jewish oral tradition" (above, 34). This reading of Cohen would appear to lend support to our notion of the vagueness of scriptural absolutes, but to undermine our implicit assumption that these absolutes bring the infinite with them, so to speak, rather than having infinity lent to them by the interpreter. In other words, Bruckstein might argue that our postmodern model attributes relatively too much givenness or authority to the text and too little freedom to the reader. In this sense, our model would appear to move too far away from modern models of personal autonomy.

- According to Gibbs's reading of Cohen (above, 35), our model may treat the two poles of each correlation as too dependent on one another, rather than as "two independent realities" that stand in correlation. Wolfson and WD himself might be expected to share in this concern: that our absolutes are too strong and that the relation of the absolutes to local conditions of knowledge may therefore overdetermine our pragmatic responses to conditions of suffering. This would be to argue, again, that our model has moved too far from modern universalism and expresses too much confidence in the redemptive power of scripture's absolutes. WD would undoubtedly extend to our model the criticism he offers of Rosenzweig's particularism. The vagueness of our absolutes implies that it may, in practice, be too difficult to transcend the communal borders of our relations to the absolute.

- From Borowitz's perspective, on the other hand (however much he might share Bruckstein's concerns about autonomy), our model may appear to have retained too much of Cohen's rationalism. Pragmatism can also be a kind of rationalism, if we are too confident in the capacity of scriptural readers to perceive just what is wrong in society and just how a scripturally based reasoning may correct what is wrong.

- Finally, more radical Holocaust theologians might, along with more radical postmodernists, argue that our model does not take seriously enough our own theme of "the brokenness of the word." Edith Wyschogrod has argued, for example, that the kind of scriptural reasoning displayed in this postmodern model of ethical monotheism may still have *too* much to say about the word, even if it is to talk about its brokenness. Such talking is an explicit effort to repair, it seems, and thus to move beyond the fact of brokenness and its source: "It is the historical traumas of the twentieth century that call the values of modernity into question. . . . Although attributable largely to deep-seated anti-Semitism, the building of the camps can be seen, at least in part, as an outcome of modern social organization and new technologies rooted in modernist conceptual foundations. The Shoah is generally acknowledged to open a new era, one in which the modes of rationality invoked to explain the event fail to account for it while at the same time they are seen as implicated in causing it. . . . [It brings forward] the problem of unsayability [itself]. When the unsayable is spoken in the straight-forward language of journalism, its horror is flattened out; when it is mythologized, archetypical meanings are foisted upon it."[34] And, she suggests, is a return to theological discourse after the Shoa — a return that is exemplified in our postmodern model — not an effort to say now, and so soon, what cannot be said? Should we not, instead, share "in the words of the Master of the Universe in the text of Menachot *29b* . . . : 'Silence. Thus it came to mind?'"[35]

All of these potential criticisms of our model are strong ones, and I do not believe that there is any systematic way to repair the model so that it responds to all of them. According to its own rules, a postmodern model of ethical monotheism should not be universally useful, but should

---

[34] Edith Wyschogrod, "Trends in Postmodern Jewish Philosophy: Contexts of a Conversation," in *Reasoning After Revelation*, 133-4.
[35] Ibid, 135.

represent a context-specific way of resolving a given problem. The limits of the model should correspond to the finite character of the problem, and contradictory models should represent opportunities for bringing the perspectives of a variety of problem-specific inquiries into conversation. This does not mean that every model represents a point of fruitful dialogue with every other. Some models belong to a community of models; some do not. The postmodern monotheist might argue that a set of contradictory models belongs to a community when all the models are actively informed by a family resemblance class (or overlapping sets) of absolutes (or rules of correlation). On one level, all scriptural philosophies should belong to a community, since they all draw on scripture's absolutes. This is one reason why postmodern scriptural reasoners *ought* to enter into a community of dialogue with modern ethical monotheists: they have bases for dialogue. On a second level, scriptural philosophies that are stimulated by similar problems or torments should belong to a more intimate community. Textual Reasoners and Scriptural Reasoners form close communities because they are drawn to similar concerns about modernity and postmodernity. When they are identified and self-identified as strict modernists, ethical monotheists keep or are kept outside such communities. As reread in this essay, however, WD's ethical monotheism may also be identified differently. Modernist or not, ethical monotheism can be read as a mode of reasoning, within a community of readers, from conditions of social torment to the need for scripture's word and of reasoning from that word to some program for redemptive or responsive action. This sounds very much like the work of Scriptural and Textual Reasoning. Such reasoners are bound to differ among themselves; informed by different specific torments and differently selective inquiries, so they should. These differences are conditions of fruitful dialogue and of the kind of relationality that must substitute, in postmodernity, for what the moderns called "universality."

PART TWO

CHAPTER TWO

HOW THE JEWS INVENTED JESUS AND MUHAMMED: CHRISTIANITY AND ISLAM IN THE WORK OF ABRAHAM GEIGER

SUSANNAH HESCHEL

Wendell Dietrich has influenced two generations of scholars by reorienting our consideration of modern Jewish thought. Calling our attention, over and over again, to the remarkable intellectual similarities between Jewish and Christian thinkers in Germany, he has made us aware that our contextualization of Jewish ideas must be ever broader. He has pointed out to us, for example, that Leo Baeck's highly popular *Wesen des Judentums* must be seen in light of Adolf Harnack's *Wesen des Christentums*. The parallels he noted were not merely the accidental confluence of a similar era, but rooted more directly in Baeck's critical review of Harnack's work, and more generally in the widespread Jewish interest in contemporary Christian theology. Just as Uriel Tal made us aware of the serious interest in Judaism taken by Christian thinkers of the Second Reich, Wendell Dietrich has made us realize that the reverse was also true, and that Jewish thought in Germany was deeply concerned with questions of Christianity. Thanks to him, a reorientation of scholarship on modern Jewish thought is now underway, with rich and fruitful results.

One example of Wendell Dietrich's insistence that German-Jewish thought be contextualized within the larger framework of Christian thought is the reconsideration of the Wissenschaft des Judentums (WJ). Some non-Jewish influences and parallels of thought have been occasionally noted, such as Ismar Schorsch's comparison of Saviny with Graetz, but the impact of much broader currents of historiography on the WJ have too long been neglected. Yet the WJ itself was deeply involved in the historiography of its day, as evidenced by explicit references and implicit arguments. When seen in the larger context, the pioneers of the WJ turn out to have been serious and often audacious challengers of conventional assumptions regarding Western history. Indeed, failing to place their work into a broader context results in erroneous conclusions, such as that of Gershom Scholem, who, in a 1944 article, accused the WJ of being "demonic figures," nothing more than Judaism's "grave-diggers and embalmers, even eulogizers."

When the WJ is seen within the context of the contemporaneous non-Jewish historiography, Scholem's attacks become strangely erroneous. Far from having "tendencies toward historical suicide, of destruction and dismantling," as Scholem claimed, the WJ seems rather to have had a political thrust, seeking a reorientation of Western history in order to place Jews and Judaism at its center. Far from being a desiccated fossil whose generative powers ceased with the end of classical prophecy, Judaism, the WJ argued, stood as the font of Western civilization, giving birth to the monotheistic religions of Christianity and Islam.

The political nature of the WJ argument received its classic formulation in the work of Abraham Geiger, one of the founders of the WJ, and was then carried forward by subsequent generations of German-Jewish historians. Geiger's own work was focused primarily on a reinterpretation of the origins of Islam and of Christianity within the context of Judaism. Given both his interest in Christianity and his leadership within Reform Judaism, Geiger has long been considered a paradigmatic figure of modern Jewish assimilationism. Although not the most radical of the reformers, he nonetheless advocated curtailing the synagogue service, praying and sermonizing in German rather than Hebrew, eliminating many home-centered religious rites, playing the organ in synagogue services, and other changes that transformed the synagogue after the model of Protestant worship. Moreover, Christian theology was one of Geiger's lifelong interests and a central theme of his scholarship.

Was Geiger, in fact, seeking to remodel Judaism after the image of Christianity? Only a broad analysis of his work, including his scholarship, within the context of German religious thought in his day, can indicate the meaning of his arguments in their own time. The reception of Geiger's work among Christians, which was overwhelmingly hostile, is one important clue to the underlying thrust of his interest in Christianity. That hostility makes it clear that he was not writing to ingratiate himself, or Jewish theology, in Christian eyes. The polemical edge of his writings on Christianity can only be brought to the surface by placing Geiger's intellectual efforts in historical context and examining the reception of his work among Christians as well as Jews. Just as the Jews of Germany engaged in a long struggle over civic emancipation, Geiger was engaged in a struggle over Judaism's theological emancipation. What his writings reveal is not an effort at assimilation of Judaism to Christian behavioral and intellectual norms, but a radical effort to subvert the basis of Christian hegemony in Western civilization and liberate Judaism from Christian colonial domination.[1]

Throughout the centuries, Judaism had functioned within Christian theology as a colonized religion. From its inception, Christianity appropriated Jewish concepts, practices, and sacred scriptures, reinterpreting them to fit its own purposes while simultaneously delegitimizing Judaism's own independent understanding of its sources. Not only on the level of ideas, but also on the level of the physical, Jews were colonized under Christian political and economic control; at times, the Jewish body became the metaphoric or even actual embodiment of the satanic within the Christian religious system. Economically and spiritually, the Jewish experience of Western civilization was of domination and regulation at Christian hands.

The Jewish revolt against Christian colonialism was an intrinsic component of modern German-Jewish thought. Expressed with increasing vigor by leaders of the nineteenth-century WJ, beginning with Leopold Zunz, the revolt reached its zenith in mid-century with the work of Geiger. Geiger's scholarship itself set the agenda for subsequent generations of German-Jewish thinkers who barely deviated from the pattern he established regarding the relationship between early Christianity, the Qur'an, and rabbinic Judaism[2]. The process itself has been thoroughly misunderstood, most significantly by Gershom Scholem, whose vituperative attack on the fathers of the WJ, his own discipline, is striking for its lack of differentiation and contextualization. His attack has been widely accepted, with the result that figures such as Geiger have acquired images as traitors to the Jews. Writing in Palestine in 1944, Scholem declared that while Geiger "was without any doubt the most talented among the scholars of destruction, insofar as anyone can measure his talents," in Geiger's "words one can smell priestly

---

[1] Many of the themes in this article are developed more fully in my recently-published book, *Abraham Geiger and the Jewish Jesus* (Chicago: University of Chicago Press, 1998).

[2] Geiger's argument that Jesus was a Pharisee and that Paul was responsible for the establishment of Christianity, his claims regarding the Pharisees as the liberalizers of Jewish law, and his demonstration of rabbinic influence on the Qur'an, became the standard Jewish explanation, found in the writings of his contemporaries, including Joseph Derenbourg and Kaufmann Kohler, and in later generations, including Joseph Eschelbacher, Leo Baeck, Abraham Katsch, and Samuel Sandmel, among others.

hypocrisy, clerical pride, and the ambition of an archbishop. . . . [He] rapes the facts for the sake of his construction."[3]

For Scholem, the WJ was marked by a driving effort to enter German bourgeois culture and sap Judaism of any authenticity. Jewish thieves were omitted from historical accounts of the Jews, as were phenomena such as the mystical and apocalyptic, all of which were held to be "degenerate." Judaism became spiritualized, disembodied of peoplehood, and the historians themselves, according to Scholem, were manifestations of the *Sitra Ahra*, the satanic cosmos. In the end, Judaism was "liquidated as a living organism."[4]

Scholem's statements are based on a thorough misunderstanding of the nature of the WJ project, the result of his failure to investigate the intellectual circumstances in which figures such as Geiger wrote, and his ignorance of the impact of Geiger's work on both Jewish and Christian historians. Geiger, Graetz, and numerous others of their generation and the ones that followed often called themselves theologians, rather than historians, and rooted their historical arguments in the ongoing debates among Protestant theologians concerned to determine the historical origins and development of both Christianity and Judaism. By describing the prior generations of German-Jewish historiography as degenerate forces, Scholem then claimed that Zionist historiography would "liquidate the liquidation" (*hisul ha-hisul*) by freeing Jewish history from being a handmaiden to political apologetics or theological dogmatism. The redeemer, of course, was to be Scholem himself, who used kabbalistic imagery to describe his own messianic role in the redemption of Jewish historiography: "Yet there is life hidden in this Judaism. It awaits the breaking of the spell and the release which is often missing in the great works of the WJ." That "release," according to Scholem, would come with a renewal of what the WJ had lost, namely, a living relationship to Jewish literature.

Not only is Scholem's evaluation of the WJ rooted in his ignorance of the larger context of German theological scholarship in which the WJ was formulating its arguments, but he was also unable to recognize the

---

3 Gershom Scholem, "Reflections on Modern Jewish Studies" (Hebrew), chap. in *Luah Ha-Aretz* (1944), 94-112; trans. Jonathan Chipman in *On the Possibility of Jewish Mysticism in Our Time and Other Essays*, ed. Avraham Shapira (Philadelphia: Jewish Publication Society, 1997), 51-71.

4 Gershom Scholem, "The Science of Judaism — Then and Now" (German), *Bulletin, Leo Baeck Institute* III (Tel Aviv, 1960), 10-20; trans. Michael A. Meyer in *The Messianic Idea in Judaism and Other Essays on Jewish Spirituality* (New York: Schocken Books, 1971), 304-13.

subversive quality of the WJ. That subversive edge was directed at undermining the configurations that mark the history of the Christian West — the values that govern it, the powers that shape it, the judgment of its significance. It was through the WJ's attention to the history of Christian origins that Judaism, the subaltern voice of Europe, began to speak back, resisting and disrupting the hegemony of Christianity. Judaism's voice began its resistance and disruption by not only presenting its own history through the WJ, but by reconfiguring the history and significance of Christianity by undermining its central claims.

The agenda of the WJ coincided with significant shifts in German Protestant theology during the nineteenth century. The so-called quest for the historical Jesus, which began with Hermann Samuel Reimarus, during the late eighteenth century, was an outgrowth of an earlier Lutheran effort to reconstruct the historical and linguistic context of the New Testament. That context, in turn, was required to achieve a proper understanding of the biblical word, upon which Christian faith was to be based — in contrast to the institutional authority of Roman Catholicism. Since the New Testament was composed within the milieu of first-century Judaism, a new attentiveness arose to the reconstruction of early Jewish history. The historical investigation, however, raised a new set of theological dilemmas. The problem for Christians was that if the divinity of Christ was embodied in the historical Jesus, and the historical Jesus was a first-century Palestinian Jew, the heart of Christian faith was now located within Judaism. What was Christian about Jesus' teachings, and how far did Jewish influences over him extend? Christian scholars portrayed Jesus as the antithesis of Judaism, but since they barely knew Jewish sources from the era, their claims were weak and based on a small set of rabbinic citations that were passed down from one generation of scholars to the next.[5] For his part, Geiger was the first to identify Jesus as a Pharisee, and he claimed that Jesus' message was neither original nor unique, but taken over from Judaism. Because Jesus was thoroughly immersed in the faith of Judaism, Geiger declared that Christianity was merely a religion constructed about him, bearing little resemblance to Jesus' own faith. Geiger sought in this way to sever the connection between Christianity and Jesus, just as Christian theologians of his day were attempting to sever the link between Jesus and Judaism.

Far from liquidating Judaism, Geiger launched the WJ as one of the earliest efforts at colonialist revolt within Europe. Nineteenth-century

---

[5] E. P. Sanders, *Paul and Palestinian Judaism* (Minneapolis: Fortress Press, 1977), 1-59.

German-Jewish historians were the first to call into question accepted "truths" about the history of the West and the respective roles played in it by Christianity and Judaism. Geiger, Heinrich Graetz, Zunz, and others recognized the institutional power of the church to transform falsehoods into accepted truths, creating power through its theologically-based ideological regime. They realized that the dominant ideology was a Christian one, attempting to disguise itself as modern, secular moral and cultural values, and equating Christianity with the highest expression of religion, rather than as one particular religion whose claims required justification before the bar of reason and historical investigation. Postcolonial theory's recognition that minority literature is characterized by counterdiscursive practices helps to illumine the WJ, inasmuch as the logic of its historical arguments represented an inversion of accepted European self-understanding. The arguments of the WJ were not assimilationist, their scholarship was not an effort to Christianize Judaism, and it is not surprising that Christian reactions were marked by outrage.

The nature of Geiger's historiographical argumentation is best understood as a form of counterhistory, a genre which has been operative since antiquity, but which has not been identified as such until the recent studies by Amos Funkenstein and David Biale.[6] Counterhistory is a form of polemic in which the sources of the adversary are exploited and turned "gegen den Strich," in Walter Benjamin's phrase.[7] Counterhistory is the genre that characterizes the Jewish re-telling of the Jesus story in the *Toldot Yeshu*, or Gottfried Arnold's history of Christian heresy, or Karl Marx's history of the modern state, or Gershom Scholem's history of Jewish mysticism.[8] It is also the genre that characterizes Christian histories of the Jews, particularly of the biblical and post-biblical eras, inasmuch as they take Jewish sources and revise them as anticipations (theological promises) of the coming of Jesus, and as explanations for the rise of Christianity (the degenerate state of post-exilic Judaism). As counterhistory, these Christian revisions of Judaism, whether or not they intend it, "deprive the adversary of his positive identity, of his self-image, and substitute it with a pejorative counter-image."[9]

---

[6] Amos Funkenstein, *Perceptions of Jewish History* (Berkeley: University of California Press, 1993), 36-37.

[7] Walter Benjamin, *Illuminations*, trans. Hannah Arendt (New York: Schocken Books, 1969), 257; cited by Funkenstein, *Perceptions of Jewish History*, 36.

[8] Funkenstein, *Perceptions of Jewish History*, 39-44; on Scholem, see David Biale, *Kabbalah and Counter-History* (Cambridge: Harvard University Press, 1979).

[9] Funkenstein, *Perceptions of Jewish History*, 48.

Geiger sought to defend Judaism by writing a counterhistory of Christian counterhistory. That is, he did not simply offer a straightforward rendition of the history of Jews and Judaism, but presented Jewish history in the context of his own, original counterhistory of Christianity, with the focus on Jesus and Christian origins. His efforts had a variety of motives, to be sure, including providing a historical justification for the reform of Judaism, but prime among them was ending Christian anti-Judaism with the challenge of a counterhistory of Jesus. While he did not succeed, of course, in ending the theological animosity of German Christian theologians toward Judaism, Geiger did succeed in demonstrating the false bases of their accounts of Judaism.

I see Geiger not as attempting an assimilation of Judaism into Christianity, but as a precursor of contemporary multicultural theory. In his studies of Christianity, Geiger destabilized the dominant metanarrative of his day by rearranging the elements of that metanarrative on terms made possible by an understanding of the suppressed history of the Jews, a group devalued by the hegemonic majority, the Christians. This use of subaltern subjectivity is precisely what characterizes the multiculturalist movement of the past two decades. Going further, Geiger also destabilizes the unified construction of the concept of the Jew. Rather than an inherited identity, Jewishness is shown to be reliant on its own view of Christianity. If the significance of Judaism lies, at least in part, on its generation of Christianity and Islam, its pride of place relies on their success. "The forger of a counteridentity of the other renders his own identity to depend on it."[10] The implied dependence of Judaism on Christianity that emerged with the WJ reached its full flowering only in the twentieth century, with the sycophant tenor of Martin Buber's writings on Christianity, and in the Christian imagery found in some Jewish post-Holocaust writings.[11]

To write a counterhistory of one's adversary in the absence of any responsible historical defense by that adversary is one kind of success. To continue to do so after the adversary has mounted a serious response carries different implications. Geiger's arguments presented his Christian colleagues with a new challenge to their counterhistory of Judaism: awareness of their ignorance of a vast quantity of primary source materials — rabbinic literature — and hence of the limitations of their historical reconstructions. Their persistence thus could no longer be a

---

10 Funkenstein, *Perceptions of Jewish History*, 48.
11 Martin Buber, *Two Types of Faith*, trans. Norman P. Goldhawk (New York: Collier Books, 1951), 12-13.

mark of involuntary ignorance, but a deliberate effort to present a false record as the truth. The effort occurs most significantly when the histories of the two adversaries are intimately connected, as in the case of Christian and Jewish origins.

Even in his own day the claims of Geiger and other Jewish thinkers to an objective scholarship and to a benign interest in mutual Jewish-Christian understanding were betrayed by the triumphalism implied by the Jewish version of Jesus. The seventeenth- and eighteenth-century Christian critics of Christianity had severed the link between the New Testament and the Old Testament, as Richard Popkin has shown,[12] while D. F. Strauss separated Christ from Jesus.[13] In a similarly radical manner, Geiger attempted to sever the link between Christianity and Jesus. Jesus' religion was Judaism; the religion of Christianity was utterly different from it. The implied threat was, if Jesus was preaching nothing more than classical Pharisaic religion, what was left as the basis for Christianity? And if Jesus was a Jewish religious teacher, what was the basis for Christianity as an independent religion?

The intimacy shared by knowledge and power in nineteenth-century Europe has been most influentially illustrated by Edward Said's 1978 study, *Orientalism*, which describes the modern European academy's construction of "Orientalism" as a field of study put to use by European colonizers.[14] While the book abounds in problematic assertions and has been subjected to widespread attack for misunderstanding the field of Islam, the course of modern European history, and for overlooking "the potential contradiction between [Foucauldian] discourse theory and Gramscian hegemony,"[15] it has nonetheless become a banner for multicultural studies concerned with the politics of scholarship. What Said neglects to mention is that during the modern European construction of "Orientalism" no Arabs or Muslims were present to participate or protest, but as "Judaism" was constructed by modern European Christian scholars, Jews were present and did talk back. The

---

[12] Richard H. Popkin, "Jewish Anti-Christian Arguments as a Source of Irreligion from the Seventeenth to the Early Nineteenth Century," *Atheism from the Reformation to the Enlightenment*, ed. Michael Hunter and David Wootton (Oxford: Clarendon Press, 1992), 158-181.

[13] Hans Frei, "David Friedrich Strauss," chap. in *Nineteenth Century Religious Thought in the West*, ed. Ninian Smart, John Clayton, Steven Katz and Patrick Sherry, 2 vols. (Cambridge: Cambridge University Press, 1985), vol. 1, 215-260.

[14] Edward Said, *Orientalism* (London: Routledge & Kegan Paul, 1978).

[15] Dennis Porter, "Orientalism and Its Problems," chap. in *Colonial Discourse and Post-Colonial Theory: A Reader*, ed. Patrick Williams and Laura Chrisman (NY: Columbia University Press, 1994), 150-161; 160.

Jewish scholars who shaped the first generation of the WJ condemned the exclusive control of Jewish knowledge by Christians. Judaism was being portrayed in a "hateful light" by Christian theologians, asserted Immanuel Wolf, who published the first manifesto of the WJ in 1823.[16] Zunz complained of the tendentious view of Jews in academic writings. Jews, according to Zunz, are depicted either as witnesses or opponents of a victorious Christianity, but always as representatives of disputed principles, never as subjects of their own, self-defined historical narratives.[17] Whatever the case, Zunz suggested that Christian scholars took on a "demonic nature" when studying Judaism.[18]

In an omission that begs for interpretation, Said neglects to note that modern scholarship on Islam came into being with the publications of German-Jewish scholars. The earliest was Geiger's first book, *Was hat Mohammed aus dem Judenthume aufgenommen?*, published in 1833, which argues for the derivation of some of Islam's central teachings from rabbinic literature.[19] Passages in the Qur'an which altered Old Testament stories, for example, were neither sheer inventions nor derived from Christian heretical teachings, as scholars had believed, but stemmed from Midrashic retellings of those stories. Geiger's insight was considered astounding and the book was showered with praise by all the major European scholars of his day.[20] Jews received the book with pride: Geiger had proven that Judaism had given the world Islam. Ever since Peter the Venerable (c. 1092-1156) had deemed Judaism responsible for the distorted presentation of Old and New Testament teachings in the Qur'an, a new motif in Christian anti-Judaism had arisen, blaming the Jews for producing Islam and thereby hindering the conversion of the Arabs to Christianity.[21] Geiger's reinterpretation is an example of his use of counterhistory: Rather than blaming the Jews for the folly of Islam, he gave Judaism pride of credit for producing

---

[16] Immanuel Wolf, "Über den Begriff einer Wissenschaft des Judenthums," *Zeitschrift für die Wissenschaft des Judenthums*, vol. 1 (1823): 1-24.

[17] Leopold Zunz, *Zur Geschichte und Literatur* (2. Auflage. Berlin: Louis Lamm, 1919).

[18] Cited by Altmann, "Jewish Studies," 84.

[19] Abraham Geiger, *Was hat Mohammed aus dem Judenthume aufgenommen? Eine von der Königl. Preussischen Rheinuniversität gekrönte Preisschrift* (Bonn, 1833; 2nd ed., Leipzig: M. W. Kaufmann, 1902). Translated as *Judaism and Islam* by F.M. Young. (Madras, 1898; 2nd ed., New York: Ktav, 1970).

[20] See the reviews of Geiger's book by Antoine de Sacy, *Journal des Savantes* (1835): 162-74; Friedrich Karl Umbreit, *Theologische Studien und Kritiken* 1, no. 1, (1841): 212-266; Heinrich Ewald, *Gottlingische gelehrte Anzeigen* 1 (1834): 438-440.

[21] See Norman Daniel, *Islam and the West: The Making of an Image* (Edinburgh: The University Press, 1960), 188-194 and passim.

Islam by demonstrating the influence of rabbinic literature on the Qur'an. Islam remains, as with Peter the Venerable, a religion of human, rather than divine, creation. But in the new nineteenth-century context in which historiography has replaced sectarian polemics, what matters is not to disprove Islam's claims to divine revelation, but instead, to prove its status as unoriginal in terms of the human religious imagination. Judaism, then, becomes the source for Islam, not in Peter's terms, but in a fully new context. Geiger wrote:

> Islam is the youngest great form of religion, not — a new religion. There is only one religion of revelation, Judaism. Christianity was carried in the womb of this religion, Islam more indirectly suckled and nurtured by it. . . . Over against the fantasies of paganism and the limits of speculation through intellectual contemplation — and this is revelation — [Judaism] has grasped the eternal religious truths, filled and spread them with the whole embers of conviction, and these truths remain in their steadfastness despite all trials and doubts. Christianity and Islam possess the manifestation of Judaism . . . without establishing a new religion.[22]

What marks Geiger's work on the Qur'an as a breakthrough in Islamic scholarship is not only his demonstration of Jewish influences on the text, but his development of a scholarly vocabulary that accords both Muhammad and the Muslim religion respect and respectability within the world of theological scholarship. In his 1833 book, Geiger lifted Muhammad from the categories of deliberate deceiver and seducer, the two adjectives that predominated in the literature of the Enlightenment and of nineteenth-century Oriental Studies, and de-scribed him as an authentic religious personality who was genuinely convinced of the divine origin of his mission.[23] Muhammad drew from Judaism as an effort to encourage Jews to join his movement, but more important, according to Geiger, was Muhammad's genuine conviction that Jewish monotheism and halakhic practices were religiously meaningful. Preserving some degree of Muhammad's integrity and intelligence was necessary to Geiger's construct, since Muhammad would otherwise be unable to comprehend the value of the Jewish religious teachings he was transmitting — or, it would be implied, those teachings did not require much intelligence to be understood. In Geiger's presentation, Muhammad is genuine in his belief that he had a

---

[22] Geiger, review of *Das Leben und die Lehre des Mohammad*, by Aloys Sprenger, in *Jüdische Zeitschrift für Wissenschaft und Leben* (*JZWL*) vol. 2 (1863): 185-191; 186.

[23] Geiger modified his positive presentation of Muhammad's personality and character in his writings of the 1860s; see *Das Judentum und seine Geschichte*, vol. 2, lecture 4.

divine mission. Still, as a human, he was ambitious and loved power, so that he created a suitable version of his divine mission to meet his own goals. Nevertheless, Geiger was equally unwilling to present Muhammad either as a prophet or as an original religious teacher. Had Geiger presented Muhammad as a true prophet, he would have had to accept the Qur'anic parallels with Judaism as divine in origin, rather than as historical borrowings.

Geiger opens his book by arguing that the major theological and moral ideas of Islam, as expressed in the Qur'an, were deliberately taken over by Muhammad from Judaism. Convinced of his own divine mission,[24] Muhammad did not want to found a new religion,[25] but to align his teachings with those of the prophets. Muhammad himself felt ambivalent toward Jews and Judaism, according to Geiger; at first he wanted to please the Jews and win them over with promises of equality and efforts to accommodate their customs, but later he became hostile when their response was not positive.[26] In that way, Qur'anic passages favorable and unfavorable toward the Jews could be explained by Geiger as expressions of different periods in Muhammad's relationship with the Jewish community. Ultimately, Muhammad wanted to persuade the Jews that "his views were on the whole the same as theirs with some few differences,"[27] yet at the same time to "borrow from Judaism . . . so long as the Jewish views were not in direct opposition to his own."[28]

Finally, Geiger's approach to Muhammad, and later to Paul, serves as a model for his own stance as a Jewish theologian. Just as Muhammad and Paul were strong and creative misreaders of Jewish texts and beliefs, so, too, Geiger was a strong misreader of the literature they themselves produced. Muhammad and Paul misread Judaism in order to use its theological insights for the purpose of establishing their own religious traditions, just as Geiger misread Islam and Christianity to gain support for the religious tradition he was creating.

Geiger's approach was far from assimilationist, as Scholem would have it. Rather than trying to reconstitute Judaism after the model of the dominant religion, Christianity, he presented a radical revision of both Islam and Christianity. Rather than simply trying to create room for the study of Judaism within the scholarship of his day, he introduced

---

24 Abraham Geiger, *Was hat Mohammed aus dem Judenthume aufgenommen?*, 25.
25 *Judaism and Islam*, 21.
26 *Judaism and Islam*, 12-16.
27 *Judaism and Islam*, 14.
28 *Judaism and Islam*, 17.

Jewish sources to revise radically the history and teachings of Christianity and Islam. Neither was what it appeared to be; both were derived from the very religion they held in contempt.

While his book on Islam was hailed by scholars throughout Europe as an important, breakthrough work of scholarship, Geiger's application of the same methods to an analysis of Christianity's derivation from Judaism elicited a completely different response. Geiger began by redefining the texture of Judaism from the Second Temple to the Mishnaic period in his magnum opus, *Urschrift und Übersetzungen der Bibel*, published in 1857, as well as in shorter articles and lectures.[29] The crucial element of his argument defined the period as an ongoing conflict between Pharisees and Sadducees, which he found described in apocryphal, rabbinic, and New Testament texts and implied in subtle textual emendations and mistranslations of the biblical text that he identified in the Targumim (Aramaic translations of the Bible) as well as in the Greek and Syriac biblical translations. The most controversial element of the *Urschrift* was Geiger's definition of the two tendencies, Pharisaic and Sadducean, as a liberal and a conservative proclivity, respectively. The Pharisees, far from being the figures of hypocrisy depicted in the New Testament, attempted to liberalize and democratize halakha, Jewish religious law, to make its practice easier. The Sadducees, by contrast, represented the narrow interests of the priestly aristocratic elite seeking to preserve its privileges by a conservative reading of Jewish law. Each group set forth its own halakha, with the Pharisaic reading becoming the governing law of rabbinic Judaism and the Sadducean, repressed by the victorious Pharisees, re-emerging later in Jewish history as Karaism. Geiger claimed to have found traces of Sadducean halakha within the Mishnah, Targumim, and apocryphal literature, a claim that was widely disputed by both Jewish and Christian scholars, who clung to Josephus' insistence that the Sadducees had no oral law.

Most controversial, however, was Geiger's claim that the Pharisees were the liberalizers of Jewish law. Christians found the assertion unacceptable because the Pharisees had acquired an unsavory, if not evil, reputation through the centuries. Christian polemicists had argued since

---

[29] *Urschrift und Übersetzungen der Bibel in ihrer Abhängigkeit von der innern Entwickelung des Judenthums* (Breslau: Julius Heinauer, 1857); the second edition was published with an introduction by Paul Kahle, a postscript by Nachum Czortkowski, and a Hebrew essay by Geiger, reprinted from *Ozar Nechmad* 3 (1860): 1-15, 115-121, 125-128 (Frankfurt am Main: Verlag Madda, 1928); in Hebrew translation, *Ha-Mikra v'Targumav* (Jerusalem: Bialik Foundation, 1949; reprinted 1972).

the Middle Ages that Jews during the rabbinic period had introduced deliberate falsifications into the talmudic texts and Targumim in order to avoid what would otherwise be proofs for the truth of Christianity. A contradictory charge was of Jewish *Buchstabendienst*, literal-mindedness at the expense of deeper meaning, a charge against Judaism made as early as the Church Fathers. Implied was that the Jews were so absorbed in the letter of the biblical text that they were unable to appreciate its spirit, let alone the fulfillment of its promises in the figure of Jesus, a charge that came to flourish within Lutheran theology. For Geiger, however, proof of the freedom of the Jewish spirit was precisely the literal-minded attentiveness of the ancients that motivated their emendations of the text and alterations of its meaning through translations. This showed that the canon was not hard and fixed, but underwent adjustments in every generation in response to changes in the religious and political circumstances.

The *Urschrift* set forth a new background for the Jewish environment within which Jesus lived and taught, and Geiger spent most of the rest of his life writing about the implications of the *Urschrift* for Christian origins. In *Das Judentum und Seine Geschichte*, published in 1863, Geiger became the first scholar to present Jesus as a Pharisee, an identification that infuriated Christian scholars.[30] He went further, arguing that Jesus taught nothing unique or original, but simply repeated the common wisdom of the rabbis of his day, which is why his message made no great impact on his Jewish listeners. Christianity's success came when Paul took the pure monotheism of Judaism to the pagans and polluted it with polytheistic teachings, creating a religion that would be more palatable to the heathens, namely, Christianity.

Geiger's arguments touched a raw Christian nerve. The liberal Protestants of his day, having rejected the supernatural elements of the New Testament, claimed they were seeking the faith *of* Jesus, rather than the religion *about* Jesus, but their efforts to discover the historical Jesus led to the frightening realization that Jesus was a Jew whose faith was Judaism. The scandal over this discovery was not only spurred by associating Jesus with a despised religion, but by the theological problem of defining the originality and uniqueness of his faith and what relation it bore, if any, to the religion called Christianity. Ultimately, Jesus' Jewishness could not be denied, and the parallels Geiger had demonstrated between his teachings and those of the rabbis could not be disputed or

---

[30] Geiger, *Das Judentum und seine Geschichte*, 3 vols. (Breslau, 1865-71); English translation, *Judaism and Its History*, trans. Charles Newburgh (New York, 1911).

overlooked. The paths Christian theologians chose out of the discomfiting claim included painting first-century Judaism in repugnant colors and shifting the significance of Jesus as a historical figure from his teachings to his racial identity. The problem of Jesus' Jewishness became tied to significant political developments. Jewish claims to Jesus' Jewishness were rejected as a Jewish defamation of the integrity of Christianity.[31] With the rise of German nationalism, suggestions began to be heard among Protestant theologians that Jesus was a Jew by religion, but an Aryan by race. Racial arguments were useful in shifting the significance of Jesus' Jewishness away from the linkages made by Geiger between Jesus' teachings and those of the rabbis, and preserved Jesus' originality in racial, if not intellectual terms. The theological appropriation of racial theory, found primarily among German liberal Protestants, came into vogue well before 1933, although the advent of National Socialism provided an additional incentive.[32]

For Christians and Jews in Germany, the Jewishness of Jesus served as a central trope for defining the historical-theological consciousness of each group. The greater or lesser degree of Jesus' ties to Judaism measured the bond between the two religions and also the acceptability of Jews within modern German society. The more Jewish Jesus could be shown to have been, the more Christians would respect Judaism — or so many of the German Jews hoped. Christians had a different agenda. For them, the more Jewish Jesus was shown to be, the less original and unique he was. Geiger's writings were nothing less than an assault on the basis of Christianity. If Jesus had simply preached the ordinary Judaism of his day, the foundation of Christianity as a distinctive and unparalleled religion was shattered.

Toward the end of his life Geiger expressed increasing hostility toward Christianity, which he blamed for exercising a nefarious influence on the course of Western civilization and for freezing the development of Jewish theology in the rabbinic and medieval periods. In a posthumously published essay, Geiger writes that German Jews, as well as the church, err in calling Christianity the mother of modern culture. Rather, "human culture and literature have no greater enemy than

---

[31] See Treitschke's attack on Graetz: Heinrich von Treitschke, "Ein Wort über unsere Juden," *Preussische Jahrbücher* (1879); reprinted in Walter Böhlich, ed., *Der Berliner Antisemitismusstreit* (Frankfurt am Main: Insel Verlag, 1965).

[32] For additional elaboration of these developments, see my article, "Nazifying Christian Theology: Walter Grundmann and the Institute for the Study and Eradication of Jewish Influence on German Church Life," *Church History* 63, no. 4 (December, 1994): 587-605.

Christianity. . . . Christianity destroyed ancient civilization, it spread barbarism."[33] On the other hand, the victory of Christianity over paganism was not due to the greatness of Jesus or any truths specific to Christianity, but to "eternal truths borrowed from Judaism." Today, however, Christianity is in the same situation "to which the philosophical paganism in the days of Celsus was sunk."[34] "The Christian religion, the Church as her body, has always fought against Wissenschaft, it has declared every light that wants to be illumined next to her to be false, that it must be extinguished."[35]

Geiger's conflicts with Christian theologians are embodied in his exchange with Ernst Renan, whose best-selling *Vie de Jesus* was published in 1863. The two men had met in Paris in 1855 and Renan had read the *Urschrift* and other of Geiger's publications. In his introduction to the *Vie de Jesus*, Renan praised Geiger and urged consideration of rabbinic sources in reconstructing Jesus' life:

> In the history of the origin of Christianity, the Talmud has hitherto been too much neglected. I think with M. Geiger, that the true notion of the circumstances which surrounded the development of Jesus must be sought in this strange compilation, in which so much precious information is mixed with the most insignificant scholasticism.[36]

Yet Renan's book repeated the old stereotypes about the Pharisees and maintained the sharp contrast between them and Jesus:

> Now, the Pharisees were the true Jews; the nerve and sinew of Judaism. . . . They were, in general, men of a narrow mind, caring much for externals; their devoutness was haughty, formal, and self-satisfied. Their manners were ridiculous, and excited the smiles of even those who respected them.[37]

Jesus, for Renan, was no Pharisee: "Jesus recognized only the religion of the heart, whilst that of the Pharisees consisted almost exclusively in observances."[38] Nor was Jesus a reformer of Pharisaism: "Far from Jesus having continued Judaism, he represents the rupture with the Jewish spirit. . . . The general march of Christianity has been to remove itself more and more from Judaism. It will become perfect in returning to Jesus, but certainly not in returning to Judaism. The great originality of

---

[33] Geiger, "Scartazzini über den Einfluss des Christenthums auf die gesammte Culturentwickelung," *JZWL* 11 (1875): 190-195.
[34] Geiger, "Celsus," *JZWL* 11 (1875): 182-5.
[35] *Das Judentum*, 143, 144-5.
[36] Renan, *Life of Jesus*, introduction.
[37] Renan, *Life of Jesus*, 299.
[38] Renan, *Life of Jesus*, 300.

the founder remains then undiminished; his glory admits no legitimate sharer."[39]

Geiger countered forcefully, but he was limited to his own publications; as a Jew, he could not receive an academic appointment at a German university and he was barred from publishing in the major Protestant theological periodicals of the day. In a personal letter to his friend, the scholar Joseph Derenbourg who lived in Paris, Geiger wrote,

> That . . . Christian scholarship should be so unusually sensitive is truly incomprehensible to me and can only be explained by an immeasurable arrogance with which it wants to oppress with club-beating any rebellion that hurts its self-esteem. While Christian literature year after year insults Judaism and its followers with diverse expressions to the point of loathsomeness, while it prides itself on introducing prejudice into the souls of unsuspecting human beings by way of a most disgusting missionary institution, spends millions to annihilate Judaism, it [Christian literature], the strong one, [nevertheless] is so irritated when the weaker one [Judaism] dares utter a word of retort, and weighs and measures it [the word] as to whether it is decent enough not to injure its ear. . . . And when so-called Christian scholars, who cannot read an unvocalized Hebrew word, who only know how to serve the fragile crutches of earlier malicious or superficially knowledgeable scribes, bring their silly judgments to the market with sovereign self-assurance, then it is obligatory to put a stop to their game.[40]

Yet even while conducting his assault against Christianity, Geiger was unintentionally making Judaism increasingly dependent upon it for its own significance. There is no Christian faith without Judaism, he argued, but in the end, Judaism's significance to Western civilization is tied to the success of its "daughter" religions, Christianity and Islam.

Internal Jewish reasons also motivated Geiger's arguments concerning Christianity. His revisionist view of the Pharisees was motivated not only to counter Christian scholarship, but also to defend against claims that reform of Judaism was nothing more than an acceptance of Jesus' critique of Jewish law. Although the *Urschrift* said nothing explicit about contemporary reforms of Jewish religious practice, the implication of his presentation of the Pharisees, precursors of the Talmudic rabbis, as liberalizers of Jewish law was sufficiently provocative for opponents of reform. Even as he suggested that reforming Judaism would be a return to the original impulse of rabbinic Judaism, Geiger came under attack by the Orthodox for betraying rabbinic law. In one of the major attacks on him by Orthodox opponents, in 1849, the prominent Galician rabbinics scholar Zvi Hirsch Chajes, wrote, in *Darkhei Moshe*, that

---

[39] Renan, *Life of Jesus*, 391.
[40] *JZWL* 10 (1872): 310.

Geiger's reforms placed him in the same category as the sectarians of antiquity, the Sadducees, Essenes, early Christians, and Karaites.[41] In response, Geiger claimed that his reforms were not breaking Jewish law; the *Urschrift* sought to demonstrate that rabbinic literature was not unitary, but had developed as a challenge of the liberalizing, newer halakha of the Pharisees to the conservative, older halakha of the Sadducees.

The very presence of a Sadducean counter-force within the heart of the Talmud contributed to Geiger's attack on rabbinic rigidity and hegemony. On the one hand, the *Urschrift*, Geiger suggested, would show that the Babylonian Talmud must be removed from its pedestal as the authentic expression of Jewish antiquity, because it is a relatively late compilation of rabbinic writings, demonstrating conflicting interpretive methods between the Mishnah and the Gemara. On the other hand, if change and development within the Talmud can be demonstrated, as the *Urschrift* also tries to do, Reform Judaism can be seen as a restorative heir to the Talmud.

As Christianity spread and came to dominate Judaism, its theological inferiority ultimately led to the disastrous mentality of religious and intellectual oppression that has prevailed in the West since antiquity. Geiger wrote to Derenbourg in 1865:

> I may be mistaken about many things, but I am not mistaken when I view Christianity as the adversary of great cultural endeavor. Christianity takes great pains to reveal the full extent of its intolerance; the papal encyclicals and the spoutings of the High Consistories, the synods and Church Days truly contribute their share in this effort. And think of the cowardice with which all of this is accepted.[42]

The Jewish scholarship on the New Testament that was inaugurated by Geiger and its impact on the world of Christian theology is part of the story of how historical investigation of Christian origins was transformed from supporting to undermining the basis of liberal Protestantism. The Christian debate which crystallized around Geiger's work, particularly around his contentions regarding the historical Jesus, played an important role in a tradition of Christian anti-Judaism since the Protestant Reformation in Germany that sought to place the New

---

[41] Zvi Hirsch Chajes, *Minhat Kenaot* (1849), reprinted as vol. 2 of *Kol Sifrei Maharatz Chajes* (Jerusalem: Divrei Hakhamim, 1958); Geiger, *Ansprache an meine Gemeinde* (Breslau, 1842).

[42] Letter to his friend M. A. Stern, January 5, 1865; *Abraham Geigers Nachgelassene Schriften*, ed. Ludwig Geiger, 5 vols. (Berlin: Louis Geschel Verlagsbuchhandlung, 1878; reprinted New York: Arno Press, 1980), 5:291.

Testament within its historical context, while at the same time presenting Jesus in sharp contrast to Judaism. By painting as negative a picture
as possible of first-century Judaism, and by rejecting rabbinic sources as
a-historical, these liberal theologians tried to elevate Jesus as a unique
religious figure who stood in sharp opposition to his Jewish surroundings. At the heart of their arguments, however, stood Geiger's claim:
that Jesus was a Jew whose teachings were the typical liberal Pharisaic
teachings of his day. Geiger's claims were not accepted, but they were
also difficult to refute. Sometimes, the response to Jesus' Jewishness
became a descent into vulgar antisemitism. The *Giessen Mishnah*, a
project of translation and commentary led by Protestant New Testament
scholars during the first decades of the twentieth century, often became
an opportunity for reproducing crude antisemitic stereotypes. At its best,
the project presented the Mishnah as the Jewish "contrast" to the New
Testament; at its worst was Georg Beer's suggestion, in his edition of the
Mishnah's tractate *Pesachim*, that Passover gave evidence for Jewish
efforts at world domination and was the occasion for Jewish ritual
execution.[43] A less flagrant example is Adolf von Harnack's classic
statement of liberal Protestantism, *Das Wesen des Christentums*, written in
1900, which attempts a response to Geiger. For Harnack, the issue was
not whether Jesus had taught anything new; he conceded that he had
not. What was important was that Jesus' teachings were pristine:

> "What do you want with your Christ," we are asked, principally by Jewish
> scholars; "he introduced nothing new." I answer with Wellhausen: It is
> quite true that what Jesus proclaimed, what John the Baptist expressed before
> him in his exhortations to repentance, was also to be found in the prophets,
> and even in the Jewish tradition of their time. The Pharisees themselves
> were in possession of it; but unfortunately they were in possession of much
> else besides. With them it was weighted, darkened, distorted, rendered
> ineffective and deprived of its force, by a thousand things which they also
> held to be religious and every whit as important as mercy and judgment.
> They reduced everything to one dead level, wove everything into one fabric;
> the good and holy was only one woof in a broad earthly warp. You ask again,
> then: "What was there that was new?" The question is out of place in
> monotheistic religion. Ask rather: "Had what was here proclaimed any
> strength and any vigor?" I answer: Take the people of Israel and search the
> whole history of their religion; take history generally, and where will you
> find any message about God and the good that was ever so pure and so full of

---

[43] Georg Beer, *Pesachim (Ostern): Text, Übersetzung und Erklärung. Die Mischna, II.
Seder: Moed, 3. Traktat* (Giessen, 1912), 94-5, 102, 150f. Cf. Christian Wiese, *Wissen-
schaft des Judentums und protestantischen Theologie im wilhelminischen Deutschland*
(Tübingen: Mohr Siebeck, 1999), 322-27.

strength — for purity and strength go together — as we hear and read of in the Gospels?[44]

There is something strikingly pathetic about Harnack's text. It contains a concession that Jesus was, indeed, as Geiger had suggested: utterly unoriginal. Somehow, though, Harnack must rescue Jesus' message, and he concludes that while its content may have parallels in Jewish writings, its vigor and purity must have set it apart from the rabbis and made possible Christianity's triumph over Judaism.

In his retelling of the Christian myth, Geiger directly challenged the processes of constructing and problematizing Protestant theology. Negative representations of "Judaism" in the imagination of Christians were analyzed by Geiger as expressions of an internal Christian theological problem. In his view, those representations highlighted the contradictions within Christian claims to originality and uniqueness, and, above all, to Jesus as the founder of a new, Christian religion.

Such claims are frequently understood as examples of German-Jewish assimilation into Christian culture, of a Jewish love for Germany that led to a desire for Christianizing Judaism and even to expressions of Jewish self-hatred. Yet the Jewish tradition of claiming Jesus for Judaism, which began in full force with Geiger's writings, must also be evaluated with reference to the Christian reception of such claims, if the subtleties of its argument are to be understood. Far from assimilation or love of Christianity, the argument represents a serious and potentially devastating critique of Christian claims, an effort to undermine the identification of Western civilization with Christianity, and to substitute Judaism as the source from which Christianity (and Islam) developed, in weak and distorted versions of the authentic mother religion, Judaism.

Ultimately, Scholem is correct on one point: the WJ had a political agenda. The claims of Geiger and other Jewish thinkers to an objective scholarship and to a benign interest in mutual Jewish-Christian understanding were betrayed by the triumphalism implied by the Jewish version of Jesus.

The theological challenge to liberal Protestantism implied by Geiger's work remained relatively inchoate until Harnack, but the vituperative reaction to Geiger suggests that he touched a raw Christian nerve. His arguments met little serious criticism or refutation; no

---

[44] Adolf Harnack, *What Is Christianity?* trans. Thomas Bailey Saunders (New York: Harper & Brothers, 1957), 47-8.

Protestant scholars were capable of debating his readings of rabbinic literature, so he was attacked with *ad hominem* hostility. Heinrich Ewald, Germany's grand old man of biblical studies, both praised and condemned the *Urschrift*, but did so based on prejudices; Ewald lauded the absence in Geiger of the animosity toward Christianity which "is common among many Jewish scholars" and has "no basis" in Protestant theology; Geiger's problem is that "It is futile to try to understand the history of the people of Israel correctly, if one disregards Christianity."[45] A few years later he wrote, "The views of today's Jews [heutigen Juden], Geiger and Graetz (and also Jost) on the origin and value of the Pharisees and Sadducees are wholly unhistorical and baseless, because they are themselves nothing but Pharisees and do not intend to be anything else."[46]

Franz Delitzsch, long active in missionizing Jews, attacked Geiger in an 1866 pamphlet, *Jesus und Hillel*. According to Delitzsch, Geiger had elevated Hillel "in order to rank Jesus below him. . . . Hillel, however, left everything as he found it. . . . All history, on the other hand, proclaims what Jesus has become."[47] Among the younger generation of critical biblical scholars, the attacks by Heinrich Julius Holtzmann and Julius Wellhausen were the most devastating. Holtzmann, who had already achieved prominence by the 1860s for his work on Marcan priority, attacked Geiger's presentation of Christianity as "the old resentment against the victorious daughter religion that lies deep in the hearts" of Jews.[48] Geiger's efforts to find Jewish ideas within Christianity were manipulations similar to those of conservative theologians such as Ernst Wilhelm Hengstenberg, who claimed to find Jesus' messianic prophecies within the psalms and prophetic writings.[49] Ultimately, Geiger was attempting to "chisel away" the name of the founder of Christianity out of the tablets of history.[50]

Perhaps the most important and lasting critique of Geiger's work came from Wellhausen, who devoted a series of lectures he delivered as

---

[45] Heinrich Ewald, "Übersicht der 1857-1858 erschienenen Schriften zur Biblischen Wissenschaft," *Jahrbücher der biblischen Wissenschaft* 9 (1858): 94-275; 103.

[46] Ewald, *Geschichte des Volkes Israel* (Göttingen: Dieterischen Buchhandlung, 1864), 5: 477, note 1.

[47] Franz Delitzsch, *Jesus und Hillel: Mit Rücksicht auf Renan und Geiger* (Erlangen: Verlag von Andreas Deichert, 1866).

[48] H. J. Holtzmann, "Jüdische Apologetik und Polemik," review of *Das Judentum*, vol. 1, in *Protestantische Kirchenzeitung* 10 (March 11, 1865): 225-237; 228.

[49] Holtzmann, "Jüdische Apologetik und Polemik," 236.

[50] Holtzmann, "Jüdische Apologetik und Polemik," 231.

Professor of Old Testament at the University of Greifswald to a refutation
of Geiger's *Urschrift*.[51] The lectures formed the basis of his book, *Pharisäer
und Sadducäer: Eine Untersuchung zu inneren jüdischen Geschichte*, which was
originally published in 1874 and was reprinted in 1924 and 1967,
remaining a well-read volume among theologians until very recently.[52]
The significance of Wellhausen's critique of Geiger's work stems from
the detail with which he examined Geiger's arguments and from Wellhausen's reputation as a scholar, which lent prominence to his claims.
The harsh tone Wellhausen adopted toward Geiger's work is not in
itself significant, since it can be found in all of his criticisms of fellow
scholars; Wellhausen seems to have been bombastic even when the
difference in question was minor, as in his argument of the 1890s with
Eduard Meyer.[53] That he would devote an entire volume to a detailed
refutation of Geiger's work is far more revealing of Geiger's significance, indicating the extent to which Geiger's publications, and the
influence they exerted, were taken seriously. Some of Wellhausen's
criticisms centered on Geiger's readings of Mishnaic sources. To Wellhausen, the third-century redaction of the Mishnah indicates that it
cannot be reliably used as a historical source for first-century controversies between Pharisees and Sadducees, a seemingly valid criticism.
On the other hand, Wellhausen did not hesitate to accept the historical
authenticity of gospel accounts that reported Jesus' notorious accusations
against the Pharisees as evidence for what he accepted as the actual
nature of Pharisaism. The Pharisees represent the nature of Judaism and
were characterized, according to Wellhausen, by a "religious materialism" that "killed nature through the commandments. 613 written
commandments and 1000 other laws and they leave no room for
conscience. One forgot God and the way to him in the Torah."[54]

---

[51]   There is a discrepancy about the date of the lectures. Wellhausen himself writes
in the preface to *Die Pharisäer und die Sadducäer* that the lectures were held during
the winter semester, 1871-72, but records at the University of Greifswald indicate
that the lectures were held on Saturdays from 12 to 1 during the summer semester,
1873; University of Greifswald Archives, Hgb. 39 Bd. 29. Wellhausen's lectures were
entitled, "Über die jüdischen Parteien zur Zeit Christi." See also Alfred Jepsen,
"Wellhausen in Greifswald: Ein Beitrag zur Biographie Julius Wellhausens,"
Festschrift zur 500-Jahrfeier der Universität Greifswald, 2: 47-56; 49.

[52]   Wellhausen, *Die Pharisäer und die Sadducäer: Eine Untersuchung zu inneren jüdischen
Geschichte* (Greifswald: Bamberg, 1874; second edition, Hannover: Orient- Buchhandlung H. Lafaire, 1924; third edition, Göttingen: Vandenhoeck & Ruprecht,
1967).

[53]   See Christhard Hoffmann, *Juden und Judentum im Werk deutscher Althistoriker des
19. und 20. Jahrhunderts* (Leiden: E.J. Brill, 1988), 159-165.

[54]   Wellhausen, *Die Pharisäer und die Sadducäer*, 19.

Wellhausen and Holtzmann deserve the greatest credit for undermining Geiger's reputation as a scholar among Christian theologians,
but it was changes in the noetic structure of Protestant theology at the
turn of the century that obviated any substantive role for Judaism in the
analysis of Christian origins. Whereas conservatives abjured historical
investigation of Jesus in favor of classical affirmations of dogmatic
christology, liberal Protestants attempted to bring historical method into
the dogmatic system of christology, without abandoning the major
contours of the latter. The outcome was similar to the German political
phenomenon called "reactionary modernism," which attempted to
speak simultaneously of modernity and traditional culture, combining
technology with romantic and antirational visions.[55] Liberal Protestantism was characterized by a comparable reactionary modernism,
attempting to combine the latest techniques of critical, presuppositionless
historical investigation with an old-fashioned theological vision informed by romantic and antirational elements. Even with the sophisticated debates over dating the gospel sources, and the skepticism in
judging the sayings as authentic, Jesus' inner spiritual life was retained
as a legitimate category and made the basis of claims for his uniqueness. The threat perceived by liberal Protestantism was not only from
conservatives, who claimed that historical method would undermine
Christianity, but from a figure such as Geiger, who demanded that
historical method be thoroughly applied, without the hindrances of
theological commitment. Liberal Protestants were not willing to take
that step. Nor, from their perspective, was it even necessary. For them,
the rhetoric of anti-Judaism served the crucial function of bridging the
limited application of historical method and the retention of the
theological category of Jesus' uniqueness. In painting a negative picture
of the religion of the Pharisees, Jesus could stand out in sharp contrast,
his extraordinary nature preserved intact.

Given the fruitless polemics that resulted from the struggle to claim
Jesus, it is well worth asking why the WJ expressed such a strong
fascination with the origins of Christianity. After all, the Jesus story has
been responsible for inordinate Christian violence and Jewish suffering.
Why not dismiss or refute or ignore Jesus and the gospels? Here, gender
theory may be helpful in clarifying some of the hidden motivations.
The position of Jews entering the world of Christian theology is not

---

[55] Jeffrey Herf, *Reactionary Modernism: Technology, Culture, and Politics in Weimar and
The Third Reich* (Cambridge; Cambridge University Press, 1984), 2.

unlike the position of women novelists entering the nineteenth-century literary world. In their landmark study of women novelists in Britain, Sandra Gilbert and Susan Gubar argued that women were required to "kill the angel in the house," the aesthetic ideal of the female promoted in male literature, before they could generate their own literature.[56] Similarly, Jewish theologians initiated an effort to destroy the image of Judaism within Christian theology as part of their project of self-definition. Nina Auerbach has observed in connection with women writers in Victorian England who appropriated male-authored misogynous myths, that the power of mythologies lies both in their ability to oppress and in their ability to endow strength.[57] To deny a myth or try to side-step it will neither destroy its power nor subvert its meaning. The nineteenth century witnessed the rise of women's efforts to cope with the misogynist myths of literature by retelling the conventional narrative but subverting its plot. In a similar pattern, modern Jewish thought has been formed not simply by creating a Jewish historical narrative, but by attempting a rebirth of the Christian mythic potential under Jewish auspices. What is particularly interesting in Geiger's work is not so much his denial of individual Christian anti-Jewish myths, but the second look he takes at those myths and the power he reclaims from them. Like women characters in the English novel, the Jewish victim of Christian persecutions — slain, dismembered, powerless — is revived, made whole, and empowered through a Jewish retelling of the Christian story. In this theological construction, Jews are thereby enabled to become the self-restoring hero who tries, in Auerbach's words, to merge "imperceptibly with the lives of those who believe in [the myth] and thereby into the history they make."[58] Increasingly after the middle of the nineteenth century, Jewish theologians, beginning with Geiger, developed the strategy of writing a counterhistory of Christianity, claiming Jesus in his entirety for Judaism. Jesus' extraordinary religious consciousness was not unique, Geiger argued, but simply a typical example of the religious genius of the Jewish people. Seen in this light, the modern Jewish re-telling of Christian origins is not merely a matter of Jews wishing to "set the record straight." Rather, it demonstrates a Jewish desire to enter the Christian myth, become its hero, and claim

---

[56] Sandra M. Gilbert and Susan Gubar, *The Madwoman in the Attic* (New Haven and London: Yale University Press, 1979).
[57] Nina Auerbach, *Woman and the Demon: The Life of a Victorian Myth* (Cambridge, Mass.: Harvard University Press, 1982), 12.
[58] Auerbach, *Woman and the Demon*, 15.

the power inherent in it. Reform Jews in particular concentrated so much attention on early Christianity in part to uncover a model for their own acts of revisioning Judaism, since they saw Christianity itself as beginning in a strong misreading of Judaism.

From the Christian perspective, the widespread research on the Jewish background to the New Testament became so prevalent during the nineteenth century not simply to gain information about Jewish history. Rather, it was a necessary element in constructing the hegemony of Christian scholarship. Studies of first-century Judaism provided information about the historical background of the New Testament, but, more important, they established the preferred Christian interpretation under the pretense of an objective, scholarly gaze. The creation of a devalued Judaism as "Other" to Christianity made the Christian theological gaze seem to be a transcendent, rational subject able to undertake analysis without affective subjectivity.[59]

Christian scholarly investigation of Jewish history established a radical dichotomy between Christianity and Judaism, which was required to maintain Christian theological order. Presenting the historical relationships between the two religions was simultaneously a construction of contemporary social relations and of relations of power within the realm of scholarship. The Christian made himself the transcendent subject of theological Wissenschaft, necessitating a radical dichotomy with an "Other" in order to maintain order. The gaze of historical theology was Christian; the ordering of history, the questions raised, the evidence examined, all revolved around the central issue, explaining the rise of Christianity. Other religions, other peoples' histories, other texts, were viewed from the Christian perspective, weighed and evaluated with reference to the Christian standard of measurement. Edward Said has noted the function of the Orient in the imagination of Christian Europe: "European culture gained in strength and identity by setting itself off against the Orient as a sort of surrogate and even underground self."[60] The role of the constructed "Jewish" in the European Christian imagination is very similar, even in the parallel metaphors that establish both the Jewish and the Oriental as feminine.

---

[59] The effort was similar to the establishment of the transcendental rational subject outside of time and space as a necessary part of the nineteenth-century colonialist enterprise. See Nancy Hartsock, "Foucault on Power," chap. in *Feminism/Postmodernism*, ed. Linda J. Nicholson (NY: Routledge, 1990), 160.

[60] Said, *Orientalism*, 3-8.

To return to Scholem: There still remain several questions to be raised concerning the motivation of his 1944 critique of the WJ and the positive reception it received then and in subsequent years. What function does it serve to contemporary Israeli, American, and European Jewish historiography to hold the WJ as seeking the liquidation of Judaism, rather than the conquest of European self-understanding? Perhaps Scholem felt the need to slaughter the angel in the house through a misreading of his predecessors, out of his own anxiety of influence. Finally, it is not the WJ that requires a eulogy, but Scholem's ignominious characterization of it that must be laid to rest.

CHAPTER THREE

SCHLEIERMACHER'S *LETTERS ON THE OCCASION* AND THE CRISIS OF BERLIN JEWRY

RICHARD CROUTER

Just how and why Jewish emancipation into civil society came to be addressed in a set of six fictive letters by Friedrich Schleiermacher forms a complex but compelling story. How did a rising young Christian theologian within the Berlin romantic circle come to use his gifts of satire, irony, and substantial insight into religion to address a socio-political situation with immense implications for Christians as well as Jews? If comparable moments exist in the history of Christian theology where a major theologian so directly (and constructively) engages the religious teaching and socio-political striving of contemporary Jews, they must be few in number.[1] Of course, Schleiermacher's life (1768-1834) coincides with the era of democratic aspirations. The quest for universal rights of late eighteenth-century Europe epitomized by the neighboring French revolution had a great impact on Prussia, with a Jewish population many times that of France. Although French Jews (mostly living in Alsace) were emancipated in 1790 and 1791, it would take Prussia another eighty years to grant full civil and political rights to its Jews.[2]

---

[1] One thinks of Reinhold Niebuhr in twentieth-century America as a possible analogy. See, e.g., "The Relations of Christians and Jews in Western Civilization [1958]," in *The Essential Reinhold Niebuhr: Selected Essays and Addresses*, ed. Robert McAfee Brown (New Haven: Yale University Press, 1986), 182-201.

[2] The "Law of the Equality of Religions as Regards Common and State Civic Rights in the North German Confederation" was passed in July 1869 in the movement towards German unification; see Michael Brenner, "Between Revolution and Legal Equality," in *German-Jewish History in Modern Times*, ed. Michael A. Meyer, III (New York: Columbia University Press, 1997), 297. See also Werner E. Mosse, "From 'Schutzjuden' to 'Deutsche Staatsbürger Jüdischen Glaubens': The Long and Bumpy Road of Jewish Emancipation in Germany," in *Paths of Emancipation: Jews, States, and Citizenship*, ed. Pierre Birnbaum and Ira Katznelson (Princeton: Princeton University Press, 1995). The move in this direction arose in the eighteenth-century Enlightenment with its discovery of universal human political rights, was embodied in the French Revolution, and as a result of the Napoleonic Wars, their immediate

Eventually known as the premier theologian of modern Protestant liberalism, translator of Plato into German, Schleiermacher served with distinction as teacher at the University of Berlin from 1810 until 1834. His youthful 64-page pamphlet, *Letters on the Occasion of the Political-theological Task and the Open Letter of Jewish Householders* (July, 1799) has received modest attention in the scholarly literature.[3] His involvement in German-Jewish and Jewish-Christian relations in Berlin is all the more striking since there is little doubt that Schleiermacher — like most Christian theologians — maintained the supersessionist view that Christianity's truth has supplanted that of Judaism.[4] Christian anti-Judaism

---

aftermath and settlement, became an urgent matter in Prussia. Especially after 1797, with the coming to power of Frederick William III (1797-1840), the way seemed open to get an authentic hearing on these matters. Although the call for emancipation dates from Christian Wilhelm von Dohm's *Concerning the Amelioration of the Civil Status of the Jews*, 1781 [excerpts of which are found in Paul Mendes-Flohr and Jehuda Reinharz, eds., *The Jew in the modern world: A documentary history*, 2d ed. (New York: Oxford University Press, 1995), 28-36], and was fostered through the Enlightenment thought of Moses Mendelssohn (1729-1786), it reached great ferment in the 1790s and early 1800s prior to the 1812 Prussian Edict of Emancipation. By hindsight, however, all this constituted a phase of "proto-emancipation." The actual emancipatory thrust dates from well after the Congress of Vienna (1815). During and after 1848 a firmer footing for emancipation was produced, but restrictions on civil and political rights of Jews were only overcome in law in 1869. In addition to other essays in *German-Jewish History*, I-IV, ed. Michael A. Meyer, see Meyer, *The origins of the modern Jew: Jewish identity and European culture in Germany, 1769-1824* (Detroit: Wayne State University Press, 1967); Reinhard Rurup, *Emanzipation und Antisemitismus: Studien zur Judenfrage der bürgerlichen Gesellschaft* (Göttingen: Vandenhoeck und Ruprecht, 1975); David Sorkin, *The Transformation of German Jewry, 1780-1840* (New York: Oxford University Press, 1987).

[3] H.-J. Birkner, *Schleiermacher-Studien* (Berlin/New York: Walter de Gruyter, 1996), 137-156 on "Der politische Schleiermacher," does not mention this controversy; Joseph W. Pickle, "Schleiermacher on Judaism," in *Journal of Religion* 60 (1980/2) 115-137; Kurt Nowak, ed., *Friedrich Schleiermacher, Briefe bei Gelegenheit der politischen theologischen Aufgabe und des Sendschreibens jüdischer Hausväter* (Berlin: Evangelische Verlagsanstalt, 1984), 67-86; Gunter Scholtz, "Friedrich Schleiermacher über das Sendschreiben jüdischer Hausväter," in *Judentum im Zeitalter der Aufklärung, herausgegeben vom Vorstand der Lessing-Akademie* (Bremen, Wolfenbüttel: Jacobi Verlag, 1977), 297-351; Bernd Oberdorfer, "Sind Nur Christen Gute Bürger? Ein Streit um die Einbürgerung der Juden am Ende des 18. Jahrhunderts: Verheißungsvoller Ansatz für ein friedliches Zusammenleben oder erster Schritt zu den Nürnberger Gesetzen?" *Kerygma und Dogma* 44 (Oct-Dec 1998), 290-310; Micha Brumlik, "Die Duldung des Vernichtenden: Schleiermacher zu Toleranz, Religion und Geselligkeit — Eine Fallstudie zur Dialektik der Anerkennung" in *Kritik Und Geschichte Der Intoleranz*, eds. Rolf Kloepfer and Burckhard Dücker (Heidelberg: Synchron, 2000), 41-56.

[4] This position is reflected in his notorious remark in the fifth speech of Schleiermacher's *On Religion*; see note 12, and accompanying text.

(prejudice based on religious commitments) and its relationship to anti-Semitism (racial hatred) is well established by a myriad of recent studies.[5] In addressing religious and political aspirations of his acculturated Jewish contemporaries in Berlin Schleiermacher was walking on perilous ground, which is further haunted by our knowledge of the subsequent fate of German Jewry. It is the contention of this paper that we still have much to learn from this, and similar, moments of authentic interreligious dialogue.

1. *Setting of the* Letters on the Occasion

The direct spark for Schleiermacher's *Letters on the Occasion* was an exchange of views between David Friedländer (1750-1834), silk merchant, intellectual and spiritual heir of Moses Mendelssohn in the Berlin Jewish community and Wilhelm Abraham Teller (1734-1804), Provost of the Berlin Protestant Church. Friedländer and Teller were both deeply under the spell of Enlightenment ideas about universal reason, human dignity and morality, and both wished for a progressive political-religious life where, as Jew or Christian, these values could be fostered. To bring these voices to life through the eyes of Schleiermacher is to revisit the religious conflict and political-social pain faced by Berlin's Jewish community in the era of the French and American democratic revolutions.[6]

Wilhelm Abraham Teller had served since 1767 as Provost or head of the Protestant Church in Berlin. In the 1790s he was recognized as a leading Enlightenment theologian of that city. His influential publications sought to square Protestant Christianity's age-old dogmas with

---

[5] Paul L. Rose, *Revolutionary Antisemitism in Germany: From Kant to Wagner* (Princeton: Princeton University Press, 1990), like the older work by Nathan Rotenstreich, *Jews and German philosophy: the polemics of emancipation* (New York: Schocken Books, 1984) does not include Schleiermacher in its treatment of the German intellectual tradition's attitudes towards Jews.

[6] The works in question are [Anonymous:] "Politisch-theologische Aufgabe über die Behandlung der jüdischen Täuflinge," in *Berlinisches Archiv der Zeit und ihres Geschmacks* 5 (Berlin 1799), Teilbd. 1, 228-239 and [David Friedländer:] *Sendschreiben an Seine Hochwürden, Herrn Oberconsistorialrath und Probst Teller zu Berlin, von einigen Hausvätern jüdischer Religion*, Berlin 1799, reprinted in Friedrich Schleiermacher, *Kritische Gesamtausgabe* I.2: 373-413, and [Friedrich Schleiermacher:] *Briefe bei Gelegenheit der politisch theologischen Aufgabe und des Sendschreibens jüdischer Hausväter* in *KGA* I.2: 325-369. I am currently collaborating on an English translation and edition of these three works, plus the response of Wilhelm Abraham Teller.

Enlightenment moral-religious teaching. Indeed, *The Religion of the Perfect* (1793, 2d ed.) as well as his earlier *Dictionary of the New Testament for Explaining Christian Doctrine* (1785, 4th ed.) attempted to separate the "Jewish-Oriental," i.e., sacrificial, elements of Christian teaching on reconciliation from what he took to be universally acceptable as Christian, while putting forth the thesis that it would suffice for a Jewish convert to confess Jesus as the founder of "a better moral religion."[7] Without advocating Jewish emancipation but by putting a Christian missionary agenda on the table, Teller set the stage for Friedländer's political-religious overture.

Teller's liberal Enlightenment views might be described as a form of eighteenth-century deism with a Christian flair. These views, plus his considerable influence, made him a natural recipient for Friedländer's *Open Letter to His Most Worthy, Supreme Consistorial Counselor and Provost Teller at Berlin, from some Householders of the Jewish Religion* (April, 1799). More a treatise than a letter, Friedländer's 86-page document provides its readers with a thoughtful reflection of Haskalah (Enlightenment) Judaism in Berlin. Friedländer's proposal has been pilloried by Jews and Christians alike for urging conversion to Protestant Christianity as the vehicle for Jewish emancipation into Prussian civil society. Even with its main qualification (refusing to confess Jesus Christ as Son of God) few persons, then or now, can see merit in quasi-baptism as a vehicle for attaining civil rights.

Yet a close reading of Friedländer's treatise reveals a remarkable mind in great turmoil. Here was a human plea for understanding and dignity in face of the marginality of German Jewish existence under the growing commercial and political conditions of modernity. However little merit we may see in linking political rights to church membership, Friedländer's dignified tone and rhetoric tell a nuanced story that reveals this self-styled Moses Mendelssohn disciple's keen intelligence and pride in his Jewishness (even amid his severe quarrels with Orthodoxy and its rabbis). Published anonymously, the document set off a firestorm of some twenty-three pamphlets (including Schleiermacher's), plus ten newspaper or journal articles.[8] Despite the work's anonymity, readers quickly associated it with Friedländer and his circle,[9] along

---

[7] *Religion in Geschichte und Gegenwart*, 3d ed., VI, 678.
[8] Ellen Littmann, "David Friedländers Sendschreiben an Probst Teller und sein Echo," *Zeitschrift für die Geschichte der Juden in Deutschland* 6 (1935): 92-112.
[9] At first denying any involvement Friedländer acknowledged writing the Sendschreiben in 1819 and subsequently re-affirmed this; see Littmann, 93.

with the March, 1799, 11-page essay, "Political-theological Task Concerning the Treatment of Baptized Jews."[10]

In April 1799 Schleiermacher had just completed his celebrated early book, *On Religion: Speeches to its Cultured Despisers*. Here he argues that religion arises from a distinctive "intuition of the universe" and "whether we have a God as a part of our intuition depends on the direction of our imagination."[11] Indeed, one infers from the apparent liberalism of such passages that their author was well beyond thinking that one religion can be truer or better than another. Given what looks like a perspectival view of truth, one is invariably startled by reading in that work's fifth speech: "Judaism is long since a dead religion, and those who at present still bear its colors are actually sitting and mourning beside the undecaying mummy and weeping over its demise and its sad legacy."[12] The description of Judaism seems so prejudicial and dismissive (not to mention its being patently false) as to raise many questions about how and why its author would publish an anonymous pamphlet that same summer that engaged the living aspirations of a faith he considered dead.

Since February 1799 Schleiermacher had been in Potsdam in an interim post as preacher to the court, though his regular position was a hospital chaplain at the Berlin Charité. His romanticist friends, the Schlegel brothers, Henriette Herz, and his earlier friend Alexander von Dohna had all been instrumental in urging him to write *On Religion*, which he did during February-April 1799, while remaining in close

---

[10] See n. 6.

[11] *On Religion*, 53. Years ago Rudolf Otto credited Schleiermacher's *On Religion* with rediscovery of the numinous and coined this term from the Latin *numen* (a place where deity dwelt). For Schleiermacher, lived religion arises from intuitions of the universe and is more closely aligned with poetry and feeling than with metaphysics and morals. He thus defends positive in contrast with the natural religion of the eighteenth-century Enlightenment. By contrast Friedländer's deist principles (God, immortality, virtue and dignity of humankind) rested on the older rationalism of Moses Mendelssohn and were antithetical to Schleiermacher's way of starting and ending all argument about religion with the particulars of one's own experience.

[12] The passage continues, "Moreover, I speak of it, not because it was somehow the forerunner of Christianity; I hate that type of historical reference in religion. Its necessity is a far higher and eternal one, and every beginning in it is original. But Judaism has such a beautiful, childlike character, and this is so completely buried, and the whole constitutes such a remarkable example of the corruption and total disappearance of religion from a great body in which it was formerly found." *On Religion: Speeches to its Cultured Despisers*, ed. and tr. Richard Crouter (Cambridge: Cambridge University Press, 1996), 113-114.

touch with these friends. Although surely too neat and schematic, the three spheres of literary expression (Friedrich Schlegel), Jewish life (Herz) and government service (Dohna) all have an impact on the fictive letters. The son of a noble family in Schlobitten, East Prussia, where Schleiermacher earlier served as a tutor, by the late 1790s Alexander von Dohna held a position in the Prussian government and had ushered Schleiermacher into Berlin's social circles, including the Jewish salon of Henriette Herz frequented by the von Humboldts and other persons among the cultural elite.

His correspondence shows Schleiermacher discussing the *Political-theological Task* with Henriette Herz (16 March 1799) and pledging to respond to it in the Berlin journal where it appeared. In addition, a letter to Herz (9 April 1799) speaks of receiving and exchanging materials pertaining to Jewish emancipation from Alexander von Dohna.[13] Having already begun the task of translating Plato's dialogues, Schleiermacher was well aware of the power of indirect communication and the dialog form as means of discourse for topics that resist simple definition or resolution. Indeed, Schleiermacher's skill in fashioning conversational discourse worked to his advantage in addressing thorny issues surrounding Jewish emancipation. Indirect communication enhanced a sense of dispassion and distance, enabling him to relate the political and religious issues to matters he had just presented at length in *On Religion*. The very next year he would again use the literary form of an exchange of pseudonymous letters to defend another unpopular work: Friedrich Schlegel's *Lucinde*, a notorious self-revelation of Schlegel's love life with the daughter of Moses Mendelssohn, Dorothea (Veit) Schlegel.[14]

The *Letters on the Occasion* are artfully conceived as letters from a concerned preacher to an editor and political leader in Berlin. The letters read as if Alexander von Dohna had collected and published letters from Schleiermacher; their artistry is seen in the way that the politician's views are only inferred from the preacher's responses, while the fact that a politician collected and presents the letters gives their ideas

---

[13] *KGA* I.2, LXXXII-LXXXIII. That Schleiermacher's first fictive letter is dated 17 April, two days after he finished *On Religion*, further links the two projects.

[14] Here, as in the *Letters on the Occasion*, Schleiermacher was able to defend Schlegel, while presenting a nuanced and objective review of the work. The strategy of indirect communication of this work, re-issued in the 1840s, made such an impact on the young Søren Kierkegaard that the Danish philosopher appears to have based his own refined use of this method of pseudonymity on Schleiermacher's example. See Richard Crouter, "Kierkegaard's Not so Hidden Debt to Schleiermacher," *Zeitschrift für Neuere Theologiegeschichte/Journal for the History of Modern Theology* 1 (1994/2): 205-225.

presumed status in the eyes of the state. A sharp call for political responsibility on behalf of Prussia's Jews had just been made by the anonymous, satirical *Political-theological Task*, which appeared in a Berlin journal of art and culture. In turn these fictive letters frame and analyze theological, moral, and historical arguments in light of this denial of full political rights to Prussia's Jews. No stranger to the use of a sharp tongue, wit, and satire, Schleiermacher's *On Religion* delights in turning contempt towards religion back in the face of religion's cultured despisers, and his *Letters* take delight in needling the state for failing to confront directly its widespread and malicious contempt toward Jews. A lovely ruse is exhibited in the politician-recipient's cover letter (with its "prefatory reminder" of how they came into being) as well as in the dating of the letters, which purport to have been written from the 17th of April to the 30th of May while the war of pamphlets was in process. Such detail enhances verisimilitude and underscores the realistic voice assumed by Schleiermacher. In what follows these literary inventions by Plato's young German translator are frequently cited simply as "the preacher" and "the politician."

2. *The Argument of* Letters on the Occasion

In the First Letter Schleiermacher chides his politician friend's arrogance for doubting that writers, who only work with words, could have anything useful to say about a matter of practical politics. He contrasts the purely rhetorical appeal of *Political-theological Task* with the *Open Letter*, a more somber work that puts an actual proposal on the table (334).[15] The preacher acknowledges that the *Open Letter* is beautifully written and notes its acknowledgment of mysticism as the seed of piety and religion — a view that permeates Schleiermacher's recently completed *On Religion* — yet chides the author for not integrating this aspect of religion into his work as a whole (333).

It is a moot question whether at the time of writing Schleiermacher knew Friedländer was the author of the *Open Letter*. Most interpreters think he must have known.[16] If Schleiermacher did know, his pitting of the "splendid Friedländer" (335) against the anonymous author of *Open*

---

[15] Parenthetical page references to the *Political-theological Task* and *Open Letter* are from *KGA* I.2.
[16] Ellen Littmann, "David Friedländers Sendschreiben an Probst Teller und sein Echo," 92-112; Michael A. Meyer, *The origins of the modern Jew: Jewish identity and European culture in Germany, 1769-1824* (Detroit: Wayne State University Press, 1967); See Kurt Nowak, Gunter Scholtz, n. 3.

Letter was an especially brilliant rhetorical ploy. Yet caution is urged in view of Schleiermacher's random jottings on Jewish emancipation in his *Gedanken* (youthful notebooks).[17] Private entries on the *Political-theological Task* and on Friedländer's earlier *Akten-Stücke* on emancipation do not directly link Friedländer with the *Open Letter* where we might have expected him to do so. What is not in doubt, however, is that Schleiermacher connects Friedländer's earlier publications with the 1799 emancipation debate. It seems reasonable to think that Schleiermacher must have surmised that Friedländer was somehow behind the *Open Letter*. But since the Teller letter's dual proposals regarding (i) quasi-conversion and (ii) dropping ceremonial law both went against Friedländer's (not to mention Mendelssohn's) earlier published views, it would have been difficult to name him as their author[18].

Schleiermacher identifies the *Open Letter's* call for "quasi-conversion" (334) to Protestantism as the plot of the drama, which requires direct action by the head of Berlin's Protestant community, Provost Teller, and by the Prussian state. By contrasting the current document with Friedländer's previous efforts in the *Akten-Stücke* the preacher's political realism is seen (335). The *Open Letter* writer is chided (i) for acting alone in 1799 unlike the earlier situation, which had broader backing, and (ii) for breaking with Mendelssohn, who wished to retain the ceremonial law.[19]

The core of Schleiermacher's position on Jewish emancipation, which echoes the separation of church and state arguments of *On Religion*,[20] is set forth early on:

> Reason demands that all should be citizens, but it does not require that all must be Christians, and thus it must be possible in many ways to be a citizen and a non-Christian — which surely any number of them already have become — and to discover among them those who are suited to our situation and the case at hand; that is the task that no one can escape who wishes to speak openly about this matter, and which thus far has not been treated so that one might leave it alone as settled (335).

---

[17] None of the three entries that touch on the *Sendschreiben* mention Friedländer's name; one entry ironically speculates that the *Sendschreiben's* author might be a Christian because of its tendency to split hairs in an argument in a crypto-Jesuitical manner; *KGA* I.2, 45-48.

[18] In addition, the *Open Letter* further veiled its origin by purporting to have been written by a group of "Jewish householders."

[19] That Schleiermacher had read and known Mendelssohn's argument from *Jerusalem* is apparent not only from the First Letter but also from Schleiermacher's earlier unfinished work (1796-97) on the nature of contracts, *KGA* I.2, 62-64.

[20] *On Religion*, Speech IV, 90, "Away, therefore, with every such union of church and state!"

Being Christian and converting to Christianity are by no means necessary conditions for full and effective citizenship. Here Schleiermacher speaks directly to the polemical satire of *Political-theological Task*. In agreement with that document's satire he playfully assaults the "lazy reason" of statecraft, which avoids thinking of new solutions and falls back on old, settled understandings as a (false) means of solving problems. "How should it not be a case of irresponsible cowardice to give up on that very thing that is known to be not only desirable but necessary:" (336)

> Whoever does not wish to contribute to the final and satisfactory solution of this task directly by making new proposals, or seeking to resolve difficulties that one could not overcome until now, must — if one just doesn't say to him that he should better have been silent — at least make an indirect contribution. He must tackle things in their present situation, bring forth the incoherence and inconsistencies in the present conduct of so-called Christian states and place things in some kind of new light; he must apply some kind of stimulus to tease them out of their laziness, so that from their side they finally begin to make proposals and — which they alone are capable of — proceed at the same time with the work at hand (336).

In light of this statement the *Letters* attempt to tease the state out of its laziness while stimulating some useful proposals, perhaps along lines of the recently enacted "East Prussian Regulation of the Jews" (1797). The state cannot be reluctant solely on the economic grounds that it receives "protection money" (*Schutzgeld*) from Jews, a view of an unenlightened government that Schleiermacher rejects (336). Rather the preacher strongly associates himself with the view of the *Task* and *Open Letter* that critiques the dogma that "the inner corruption of the Jews" makes it "dangerous to accept them into civil society." This view he finds "very widespread among men of your estate, and God knows how in the matters they have thought and written about in their official duties, about which little is ever reported to the public, this belief may have been shaped into a full-blown theory" (337). Schleiermacher critiques the *Open Letter* for failing to present a more historical account of the dogma of a corrupt Jewish character, and the *Task* for not questioning the state's assumption of this dogma more severely.

In his Second Letter Schleiermacher chides his politician friend for taking issue with the rage and indignation of the taskgiver's tract while knowing that the state's policies regarding conversion and citizenship are utterly inconsistent. His friend's objection to the *Task's* argument against proselytism on grounds that it disrupts families is technically correct, but limited and not realistic because it minimizes the power of the natural bonds of social sentiments. It is wrong to dislike the sarcastic and angry tone of the "honest satire" when the cold reasoning of the state has been so inadequate. On the preacher's view, this sarcastic tone could even be sharper, "for I am concerned that many persons will think the author has adopted the political option [mass conversion of the whole Jewish nation] in earnest." But the preacher agrees with his friend's emphasis on the *Open Letter's* seriousness and dignity, even if there are annoying features in the letter: (i) The presumption of an opposition between mysticism and enlightened reason is viewed as a typically Jewish position, as if it could not arise among Christians, (ii) suggesting that the "authentic meaning" of ceremonies pertains solely to priests, and (iii) showing a "restrained bitterness" when the work engages directly in discussions of how the state relates to Christianity (340). On the whole, for an anonymous document where no prior knowledge of an author can shape a favorable opinion, it is all the more remarkable that the *Open Letter* has received such praise.

Yet the sense of bitterness toward Christianity and the state is in conflict with the work's "obtrusive, unwarranted expectation" of a demand for conversion to Christianity. Here Schleiermacher identifies the contradictory impulse that runs between the *Open Letter's* apparent aversion to Christianity and its willingness to embrace the larger tradition (albeit for political ends). The preacher sees how steeped the letter is in Judaism's "basic truths," how it even seeks precedents in Moses and the rabbis for abolishing law, while aligning its position with the teachings of the psalms and the prophets; how Christianity's "basic truths" are depicted only as faith claims, while Judaic truths are viewed as rational convictions (341). By contrast certain phrases praise Christianity's openness to the hilt. How is one to weigh these apparent contradictions? In the preacher's words:

> All of this taken together brings me to the thought that the author cannot be serious even in half the way he proposes for converting to Christianity; but that his intention is only to proceed in such a way as to make the idea compelling that such a half-way transition is the highest that could be demanded of a reasonable and educated man, quite apart from the fact that one should not require anything of the kind. This secret meaning will satisfy the nation, which is so clever in matters of interpretation, while it literally has the appearance for Christians of being about peace and dignity; the former to embarrass them, the latter to keep them in a good mood (342).

On this view the *Open Letter* engages in a secret meaning, perceptible to its Jewish readers, which undercuts Christian claims to truth, while purporting *in some fashion* to wish to join the Protestant Church. Here lies the sharp edge of disagreement between the preacher and open letter writer; the latter insists on the sheer incompatibility of modern reason with the Christological dogma, whereas the former took pains to come up with an arguably reasonable, yet normative understanding of Christ in *On Religion*.[21] The Second Letter doesn't consider the actual reasoning provided in the *Open Letter* for avoiding the phrase "Son of God" in making a confession that will end up with Christian approbation and with citizenship.

In his Third Letter the preacher's grounds and motivation for involvement surface. His politician friend has apparently wondered how a Christian could object to Jewish conversions, as if that were the supreme goal of all right-thinking Christian theology. Yet the preacher explains that his fears lie in just this sphere, coupled with the view that if the *Open Letter* has no effect and fails to get the desired notice, the disruptive practice of conversion will continue. As a convinced Christian the preacher takes the conversion of Jews "to be the worst thing that can happen" (344). Twenty or thirty years earlier such a gulf separated Jews and Christians that — apart from occasional marital ties — the problem didn't arise. Yet even if not harmful to the state, the mixed motives and political end of Jewish conversions will surely do great harm to the Christian church. "By far most of the people whom we can expect among us will be the sort of persons who are wholly indifferent towards anything having to do with religion" (345). They are ruled by worldly sentiments or are convinced Kantians who equate their own morality with religion.

Here we see Schleiermacher's roots in Moravian pietism with its teaching about an experiential faith, views endorsed in *On Religion* with the sensibility of romantic poetry. There's too much external adherence to religion as it is, and this has been aided and abetted by political compacts like the Peace of Westphalia (1648), which re-enforced the territorial religious settlement of the Peace of Augsburg (1555). The argument here contains a strong critique of the *Open Letter's* "truths of reason," which the preacher relegates to a form of Kantian moralism that equates morality with religion. Schleiermacher appears to conflate the *Open Letter's* endorsement of quasi-baptism with the satirical and ironic call for a time of education (*Bildungszeit*) to follow mass baptism as a means of overcoming the faults of Jewish character. Even if the latter extends twenty years, the preacher asserts, it would still remain inadequate. The idea of proposing a "time of education" seems wrong-headed to Schleiermacher, since misunderstood irony might encourage the view that such a time is actually needed.

---

[21] *On Religion*, Speech V, 115-121.

But the underlying religious insulation of Jewish and Christian communities appears most generally to rest on Schleiermacher's romanticist view of positive religions as virtually organic entities:

> It is impossible for anyone who really has a religion to accept another one; and if all Jews were most excellent citizens, not a single one of them would be a good Christian; but they would bring along a great many peculiarly Jewish elements in their religious principles and convictions which, just for this reason, are anti-Christian (347).

Since this teaching would appear to allow no growth or transference between religions, one might wonder how any new religion could ever arise. The point reflects Schleiermacher's considered teaching that each religious awakening is unique and, once awakened, becomes so all-consuming and deeply set in the fabric of existence that it cannot be replaced. Most abhorrent to him is the idea that one might traffic in religions just as one trades on the commodities market! His political objection to conversion is then supported by a more specific stance that argues against law-based religion as a form of works righteousness: "Indeed, a judaizing Christianity would be the true disease against which we should still inoculate ourselves!" (347). For Schleiermacher this theological issue was resolved in Paul's letters in Christian antiquity (e.g., Galatians 2-3), which defend the freedom of the Christian life against positions that would place law at the center of religion.[22] There is no point in just trying to put a good face on a process as onerous as wanting to convert Jews and make them into Christians.

In the Third Letter the preacher continues to pose other explicitly Christian objections to the conversion of Jews. In coming to a decision on these matters his politician friend should take to heart objections coming from within the believing traditions. Far from welcoming Jews into its midst, the Church should resist this process, for "if it endures this now all the more decadent governmental courtesy even longer, it will pay with its complete ruin much too dearly indeed for this politeness" (347). This is the case, even though Jews increasingly take part in the process of German education in ways that approximate those of Christians. If the *Open Letter* has a plea for Teller, the preacher's plea is that Teller will realize that the Church "should decisively declare itself to this effect: that it request the state to put an end to such an oppressive

---

[22] See *On Religion's* frequent appeal to the contrast between letter and spirit; and Schleiermacher's sermon "Evangelical Faith and the Law," in *Servant of the Word: Selected Sermons of Friedrich Schleiermacher*, ed. and trans. Dawn DeVries (Philadelphia: Fortress Press, 1987), 136-51.

course of action" [i.e. conversion]. Rather than encourage baptisms of Jews, the church, although it cannot prescribe to the state, can "declare before the whole world that it has nothing at all against" allowing Jews "into the unlimited pleasure of civil liberty" (348). On the related matter of matrimony between Jews and Christians the preacher argues that, though it may not be advisable — for various practical reasons — nothing within religion speaks against it; the practices of the early church obviously sanctioned it, and nothing in sacred scripture speaks against it. Although Schleiermacher conceives of religions virtually as self-contained, if not exclusive enclaves of meaning, the allowance of interfaith marriages tempers that insight with realism.

In opening the Fourth Letter the preacher complains that his politician friend has mistaken his desire not to have Jews in the church for enmity toward Jews, or perhaps a secret belief in their "moral degradation." In a sharp retort the letter writer reminds his friend that he also wishes that "the greatest portion of Christians," including good friends and the politician himself, were not in the church. But he chooses not to defend himself further, urging this non-resistance on grounds of his being a Christian (351). When the politician appears to have pressed him for more practical solutions and suggestions, the preacher responds that his discussion partner simply hasn't paid attention to the previous letters. This remark, however, in no way prevents the preacher from becoming more specific in his recommendations and ideas. In passing, a reader soon realizes that Schleiermacher's preacher has already carefully studied the earlier Jewish reform efforts led by David Friedländer.[23]

The Fourth Letter specifically maintains that (i) ceremonial law is a political hindrance and that (ii) the current method of naturalizing Jews as citizens requires a cumbersome, tedious, and unfair investigatory process. In not requiring that Jews should "completely reject ceremonial law but only subordinate it to the laws of the state" (352), the preacher's demand is less stringent than that of the *Open Letter*. In agreement with the *Open Letter* the preacher also requires Jews to renounce the hope for a messiah, while wryly noting that Friedländer's *Akten-Stücke* complains about Jews being treated as foreigners, but refers to the Jewish people as a nation and re-enforces the idea that their allegiance may belong to some entity other than the German state. Even if belief in a messiah has "few true followers". . . "as long as it remains a public confession the

---

[23] The fact that Friedländer's documents from that period (the *Akten-Stücke*) are cited several times (352) points to Schleiermacher's involvement with the issue of emancipation prior to the summer of 1799.

state cannot treat them other than by assuming that they believe in it." Acknowledging the need for a smooth working relationship with society, the preacher notes that a level of moral corruption that inhibits assimilation can even occur among his own people: "Who would wish to deny that our own common people are well-inclined to deceive foreigners?" He observes the social cohesion that German society feels in the Jewish community and defends it by saying: "Only for this reason do they separate themselves from other fellow citizens, so that when the time of departure comes, they may be as little entangled as possible, while being bound together as much as possible" (353).

Schleiermacher's final requirement in response to the politician's challenge to become more concrete is that Jews "constitute a special ecclesiastical society" (353). This would establish an "altered Judaism" in the form of a state-recognized (reform or Enlightenment) Judaism that embodies the two prior conditions of (i) subordinating ceremonial law to German civil law and (ii) giving up the hope in a messiah. In both instances, citizenship requires accepting the full legitimacy of the state and its lawfulness as well as sharing in its maintenance and well-being. Recognizing that even the *Open Letter* stops short of proposing full organic union with the church and (against initial appearances!) seeks a way to preserve one's Jewishness, the preacher paraphrases St. Paul to write that "if one in accord with law has to destroy the law for the sake of the eternal, one still remains under the law, i.e., in Judaism" (354-55).[24] In effect, the passage wishes to suggest that the choice of sub-ordinating (outmoded religious) law to (living) German law creatively ensures the survival of one's (truly religious) Jewishness through the use of law.

Although the Fourth Letter rejects the idea of Jews attaining civil liberty via the church, it argues strongly for a non-Christian alternative that would parallel the *Open Letter's* proposal to Provost Teller. Far from polemicizing against the *Open Letter*, Schleiermacher believes he has "shown that it is full of the spirit of Judaism and of love for the same and that the conversion to Christianity is a false deed that does not belong in it" (354). Against reader expectation, and against the expectation of his fictionalized interlocutor, the preacher thinks he has captured not just the spirit of the *Open Letter* but even improved on that document by denying any need to ensure Jewish civil liberties through church

---

[24] Adapted from Galatians 2:19: "For I through the law I died to the law, that I might live to God" (RSV).

membership. Only an "evil demon" could have driven its author to want to unite with the church in order to have an assured place in the society; if this aim can be granted short of conversion, that is an improvement for both Jew and Christian.

> Once one has wholly excluded its false elements, the *Open Letter* contains everything that the state can demand from the Jews and is the true codex of a new Judaism, capable and worthy of political existence in every respect. You see how little I am against the *Open Letter* when I allot it this place! I see the "Task" and the *Open Letter* as necessary and complementary pieces and believe that, taken together, both contain everything that the Jews have to do for their benefit: the former indirectly by provoking the state to depart from its accustomed way; the latter directly by opening a new way to it (355).

This statement unambiguously endorses both of the Judaic documents to which Schleiermacher responds through his preacher. Thus Schleiermacher as Christian theologian, who might well have taken a strongly anti-Judaic line on religious grounds, uses his *Letters on the Occasion* to support the proposals that derive from Friedländer's circle of Haskalah Jews. He ends the fourth letter by challenging his imaginary political interlocutor, and thus his readers, to come up with valid objections to what he proposes.

It remains only to characterize the Fifth and Sixth Letters in light of the preceding arguments. The Fifth Letter constitutes an effort to make the proposal for a new Jewish sect more plausible in view of the natural skepticism of political realism. The preacher first seeks to disarm potential objections to new recognition of a Jewish sect based on the 1648 Peace of Westphalia's strictures against the creation of new religions (356). This older imperial law (of the Holy Roman Empire) is less important than the immediate matters at hand and needs of Prussia. (Indeed, the old empire did come to an official end in 1806.) In addition, he maintains that having a new sect of elite, educated, and enlightenment Jews will have practical benefits; among these, the natural bonding within the Jewish community will not cease to help poorer classes of Jews who remain in Orthodoxy, and will serve as a leadership group to counterbalance the interests of Orthodoxy, among whom there are also persons of wealth. If the Orthodox continue to grow and fan the flames among the poorer class of Jews, this will "support hatred of Christians and the fatherland far more strongly than is the case up to now" (357). If there had been such "a select group of the Jewish nation" (here Schleiermacher also uses the term "Jewish nation") at the time of the earlier reform efforts, something salutary would have happened, at least for these people. Granted, one might simply institute a new Jewish regulation on the model recently enacted in East Prussia.[25] But then "even less would be achieved towards that which our German Jews want and what I as a Christian have wished for them" (358).

Letter Six stands apart from the debate pursued thus far and responds to other reactions to the *Open Letter* that the politician has sent the preacher. Indeed, we mentioned at the outset that Friedländer's letter to Teller set off a firestorm of reactions and protests in the Christian world. It was largely to counter these reactions that Schleiermacher produced his own pamphlet of fictive letters. Letter Six, dated the 30th of May, 1799, is especially concerned to mock a particularly obnoxious reaction to the *Open Letter* signed "by a preacher in Berlin."[26] His own work "by a preacher outside of Berlin" constitutes a direct rejoinder to this document. Schleiermacher goes to great lengths to attack this document, while sarcastically wondering why more sensible Protestant clergy in Berlin have not become involved. His personal motivation is clear when he writes: "I am ashamed when I think it is possible that worthy Jews, who know so few clergy, and hardly have a proper idea of this class of persons, might draw inferences from this to other instances" (360). The Sixth Letter's final paragraph ends the exchange by noting that Herr Teller's response (which had been written in the meantime) is instructive and gracious, states his private opinion and uses "his insight to clarify the matter about which he's been asked" (361). In fact Teller denied the baptism proposal but remained open to full Jewish civil rights. In the perspective of Friedrich Schleiermacher the cycle of debate had now run its course.

3. *Conclusion*

What then is one able to conclude with regard to this exchange of views? Basically, two quite fundamental and interrelated points emerge from careful study of the *Letters on the Occasion*. These consist of (i) the fact that Schleiermacher's views as a Christian theologian who is antithetical to Judaism on religious-theological grounds remain fully in place. (These were subsequently re-enforced by his dogmatic theology

---

[25] *Das General-Juden-Reglement für Süd- und Neu-Ost-Preußen* from 17 April 1797 is printed in Ludwig von Rönne and Heinrich Simon, *Die früheren und gegenwärtigen Verhältnisse der Juden in den sämmtlichen Landestheilen des Preußischen Staates [Die Verfassung und Verwaltung des Preußischen Staates*, Vol. 8/3] (Breslau: G. P. Aderholz, 1843), 292-302.

[26] [Anonymous:] *An einige Hausväter jüdischer Religion, über die vorgeschlagene Verbindung mit den protestantischen Christen. Von einem Prediger in Berlin* (Berlin, 1799).

[*The Christian Faith*], by various of his sermons, and by his writings on the history of the Christian church.) Abundant evidence points to the reality that Schleiermacher, whose New Testament faith emerged from German pietism, had a lifelong aversion to Hebraic religion, i.e., what he takes to be legalistic religion of the Old Testament; and (ii) a distinction must be made between intra-confessional theological agreement (which is never achieved) and the fact that theological agreement is not a prior condition for (a) civil discourse about theology or (b) granting practitioners of diverse religions civil rights under a common polity. On separation of church and state Schleiermacher comes closest to his Enlightenment peers. His fictive letters recognize the likely devastating consequences if the call for Jewish emancipation is either completely blocked or allowed to drift, and he combines this rational appeal with an appeal to the powers of human empathy. On balance, one must conclude that the justifiable restrained bitterness of both Judaic documents found as deep a resonance in him as it did among his Jewish friends in the circle around Henriette Herz.[27] With these associations in mind the demand for emancipation (with minimal conditions) looked not just reasonable but long overdue. Here, as elsewhere, Schleiermacher's realism and progressive political temperament[28] was profoundly shaped by his generation's experience with the French Revolution and the distantly admired American case of church and state separation.

Far from Friedländer directly selling out his tradition to Christianity an argument can be made that in a situation where he saw the temptations of conversion on a daily basis and the social as well as political benefits that flowed from being assimilated, he desperately sought a solution for an intolerable situation that was, as it turned out, too messy for immediate social resolution. At a time when conversions seemed inevitable and began to happen more frequently among educated Jews, Friedländer sought an accommodation whereby, once within what he genuinely took to be a largely deist Protestant community, at least his Jewish existence and that of like-minded Jews (and their progeny) could be preserved without having to confess Christ as savior! If this

---

27   For the impact of the Jewish salons on Schleiermacher's Berlin see the recent work by Deborah Hertz, *Jewish High Society in Old Regime Berlin* (New Haven: Yale University Press, 1988; Steven M. Lowenstein, *The Berlin Jewish community: enlightenment, family, and crisis 1770-1830* (New York: Oxford University Press, 1994); Peter Siebert, *Der literarische Salon. Literatur und Geselligkeit zwischen Aufklaerung und Vormaerz* (Stuttgart: Metzler, 1994).

28   See Richard Crouter, "Schleiermacher and the Theology of Bourgeois Society: A Critique of the Critics," in *Journal of Religion* 66 (1986/3): 302-323.

reading of the document (which goes beyond Schleiermacher's reading) seems extreme, that is only because it requires us to leap even further into Friedländer's own world. It is just this Jewish horror not just of giving up one's own people with its shattering of family and other ties, but of confessing Christ as savior that is poignantly expressed in the *Open Letter* and its precursor, the *Political-theological Task*. Although not uncritical of their details, Schleiermacher entered deeply into these Judaic works and ended by defending both of them as necessary, useful, and complementary.

On this reading Schleiermacher's *Letters on Occasion* constitute more than an extended footnote to the negative comments on Judaism of the Fifth Speech of *On Religion*. They reflect the beliefs and aspirations of Schleiermacher's circle of Jewish friends, who were deeply alienated from their roots in Talmudic tradition, in a situation where, as Friedländer puts it, knowledge of Hebrew was "diminishing daily." The proximity of *On Religion* and the *Letters* in 1799, plus evidence that their author was pondering work on the latter while writing the former, tie the two works together in the life of their author.[29] Indeed, if *On Religion* was written especially against the background of the Enlightenment with his artistic and literary friends in mind, the *Letters* are written against this same background but with his Jewish friends, especially the circle around Henriette Herz in mind. In effect, of course, life in the salons constituted the Judaic side of the early Romantic movement, but always mixed with healthy respect for Enlightenment rationality. To modern minds, like those of Friedländer as well as Schleiermacher, the claims and practices of Orthodox Judaism were indeed perceived as "long since dead." However biased and short-sighted that belief may have been — whether in its own day or ours — it is to Schleiermacher's credit that he could live with the incompatible imperatives of rival religions, while arguing that citizenship requires no religious test. Two-hundred years later the human community continues to struggle towards a just civil and political order in the face of irreconcilable religious rivalries and their immense social tensions.

---

[29] See Günter Meckenstock, *KGA* I.2, LXXXII-LXXXIV; Jacob Katz's classic account of the movement of Jews into civil society, *Out of the Ghetto: The Social Background of Jewish Emancipation 1770-1870* (New York: Schocken Books,1973), 120, has the order of publication reversed: "Speeches on Religion, published shortly after he had taken a stand on the Jewish issue, did a great deal to rescue religion from its subordination to rationalism."

CHAPTER FOUR

GEORGE ELIOT'S RELIGIOUS PILGRIMAGE[1]

Peter C. Hodgson

1. *A Religious Pilgrimage*

The conventional wisdom about George Eliot — Mary Ann (Marian) Evans, 1819-1880 — is that, after her exposure to higher criticism and German theology, she abandoned the fervent evangelical faith of her youth and became a disciple of the "religion of humanity." Thereafter, it is thought, she lost interest in religion and turned to the exploration of other subjects in her novels.

On a simple factual level the latter statement, at least, is demonstrably false. Religion is a topic of central interest in her first and last novels (*Scenes of Clerical Life, Adam Bede,* and *Daniel Deronda*), and it plays a significant role in the others as well (*The Mill on the Floss, Romola, Felix Holt,* and *Middlemarch*). Moreover, religious figures, roles, beliefs, and practices are treated with both an understanding and a sympathy rare in modern literature. Yet the recent critical studies of George Eliot virtually ignore her engagement with religious issues or find various deconstructive devices to explain it away. The critics simply assume that she was a non-believer who used religion to achieve certain aesthetic, psychological, political, or moral effects.[2]

---

[1] I am pleased to contribute this essay in honor of Wendell Dietrich. He was an "elder classmate" of mine at Yale for whose erudition and scholarship I have had the greatest respect. George Eliot's religious pilgrimage took her in the direction of an ethical monotheism and a deep appreciation of Judaism, both of which are concerns in the distinguished career of Professor Dietrich. This essay is adopted from *Theology in the Fiction of George Eliot: The Mystery Beneath the Real,* published by SCM Press in May 2001, and by Fortress Press in July 2001.

[2] See, for example, E. S. Shaffer, *Kubla Khan and The Fall of Jerusalem: The Mythological School in Biblical Criticism and Secular Literature, 1770-1880* (Cambridge: Cambridge University Press, 1975), chap. 6; Thomas Vargish, *The Providential Aesthetic in Victorian Fiction* (Charlottesville: University Press of Virginia, 1985), chap. 4; and Mary Wilson Carpenter, *George Eliot and the Landscape of Time: Narrative Form and Protestant Apocalyptic History* (Chapel Hill: University of North Carolina Press, 1986). Carpenter traces in great detail the biblical imagery and number symbolisms employed in George Eliot's novels, but her approach to the texts is not theological;

Basil Willey, noting Lord David Cecil's remark that George Eliot was "not religious," responds as follows:

> 'Religious' seems to me to be just what she was . . . ; the whole predicament she represents was that of the religious temperament cut off by the *Zeitgeist* from the traditional objects of veneration, and the traditional intellectual formulations. She was not, of course, a 'practising Christian,' but in her estrangement from the 'religion *about* Jesus' she was none the further from the 'religion *of* Jesus.' She knew the hunger and thirst after righteousness, and the need for renunciation — the need to lose one's life in order to gain it. And, though her religious consciousness was pre-eminently moral, it was not exclusively so; she also had the faculty of reverence, the capacity to acknowledge the reality of the unseen.[3]

I believe that Willey is correct, and I want to expand his interpretation by proposing that George Eliot's life and literary career form a kind of religious pilgrimage. She herself, four years before her death, in response to a query about her religious views, said that her writing "is simply a set of experiments in life" in order to determine "what gains from past revelations and discipline we must strive to keep hold of as something more sure than shifting theory." The "supreme subject" with which she found herself engaged is "how far the religion of the future must be one that enables us to do without consolation."[4] Similarly, she wrote to Harriet Beecher Stowe that "a religion more perfect than any yet prevalent, must express less care for personal consolation, and a more deeply-awing sense of responsibility to man."[5] To a close friend she insisted that "I have too profound a conviction of the efficacy that

---

in fact, it is anti-theological. By contrast, Valerie A. Dodd, in *George Eliot: An Intellectual Life* (New York: St. Martin's Press, 1990), notes George Eliot's wide exposure to theology and her continuing interest in religion, but finally offers an aesthetic rather than a theological interpretation. The most recent biographies — Frederick R. Karl, *George Eliot: Voice of a Century* (New York: W. W. Norton & Co., 1995); Rosemary Ashton, *George Eliot: A Life* (London: Hamish Hamilton, 1996; Penguin Books, 1997); Kathryn Hughes, *George Eliot: The Last Victorian* (New York: Farrar, Straus and Giroux, 1999) — offer very little on the subject of religion. William S. Peterson notes this deficit in his review of Ashton in *The New York Times* (27 July 1997). He refers to "Eliot's life-long search for some larger meaning in the cosmos," and suggests that it would be helpful if the next biographer would tell us not only about "Eliot the beleaguered woman" but also about "Eliot the beleaguered religious skeptic." Unfortunately, the next biographer, Hughes, does not; she assumes that George Eliot's religion reduces to a Feuerbachian humanism and at best serves a psychological function, a substitute perhaps for the lack of maternal love.

[3] Basil Willey, *Nineteenth Century Studies* (London: Chatto & Windus, 1955), 238.

[4] *The George Eliot Letters*, ed. Gordon S. Haight, 9 vols. (New Haven: Yale University Press, 1954-56, 1978), 6:216 (to Dr. Joseph Frank Payne, 25 January 1876).

[5] *Letters*, 5:31 (8 May 1869).

lies in all sincere faith, and the spiritual blight that comes with No-faith, to have any negative propagandism in me. . . . I care only to know, if possible, the lasting meaning that lies in all religious doctrine from the beginning till now."[6] It seems evident George Eliot never arrived at any final or secure knowledge of this lasting meaning. Like the characters in her last novel, *Daniel Deronda*, she was on a journey, seeking an appropriate "pathway" through life, perhaps in the hope that her pathway and those of others might, in the words of Mordecai, be "bound together in that Omnipresence which is the place and habitation of the world."[7] There are many pathways, many pilgrimages, and she was convinced of the importance of a diversity of religious views and traditions to avoid cultural imperialism and to preserve what she was to call "separateness with communication."[8]

George Eliot's own religious pilgrimage took her through at least three phases or way stations: evangelical Christianity, the religion of humanity, and a religion of divine presence and sympathy. The first two stations were not simply left behind but incorporated into a growing and more complex vision.

I. *Evangelical Christianity*

The story of Mary Ann Evans's intense involvement with evangelicalism at an early age is well- known. Through the influence of a boarding school governess, she experienced the need for conversion, repentance, and acceptance of Christ at about age fifteen. She studied the Bible and read religious books intensively. A few years later she had frequent conversations with her Aunt Elizabeth Evans, who as a young woman had been a Methodist lay preacher, and who told her the story around which *Adam Bede* was constructed.[9] All this collapsed rather suddenly at age twenty-two when she became acquainted with the liberal Unitarianism of the Bray and Hennell families after she and her father moved to the vicinity of Coventry in 1841. In a forthright letter to her father, she

---

[6] *Letters*, 4:95 (to Barbara Bodichon, 26 November 1862).

[7] *Daniel Deronda* (1876), edited with an introduction by Barbara Hardy (London: Penguin Classics, 1986), chap. 63, 818. Because the novels are published in different editions, I cite chapter numbers (the same in all editions) followed by page numbers (for the particular edition indicated) — e.g., 63:818.

[8] Ibid., 60:792. See the introduction by Jane Irwin to her edition of *George Eliot's Daniel Deronda Notebooks* (Cambridge, Cambridge University Press, 1996), xxxvi-xxxviii. See also Dodd, *George Eliot*, 194-97, 286-87.

[9] See Gordon S. Haight, *George Eliot: A Biography* (London: Penguin Books, 1986), 18-29.

explained why she stopped attending church,[10] but she retained a life-long association with the Unitarians[11] and never renounced the Church of England. Her deep knowledge of Scripture, her devotion to the gospel proclaimed by Jesus, her understanding of the power of the central Christian symbols, and her appreciation for all genuine religious piety are lasting heritages of her evangelical involvement.

It was the lack of such piety that chiefly bothered her in evangelical teachers like Dr. John Cumming. In a brilliant review of his writings, she found in him "no indication of religious raptures, of delight in God, of spiritual communion with the Father. He is most at home in the forensic view of justification, and dwells on salvation as a scheme rather than as an experience. He insists on good works as the sign of justifying faith, . . . but he rarely represents them as the spontaneous, necessary outflow of a soul filled with Divine love."[12] She identified three striking characteristics of his theology: unscrupulosity of statement (free play of prejudices, no regard for truth), absence of genuine charity (hatred of everyone not in the clan), and perverted moral judgment (egoistic passions, dogmatic beliefs, everything reduced to serving the "glory of God").[13] In evangelical Christianity as a whole she found well-repre-sented what Paul Ricoeur has described as "the rotten points" present in every religion — accusation and consolation, taboo and shelter, the fear of punishment and the desire for protection. "In destroying the shelter offered by religion and liberating men from the taboos imposed by

---

[10] *Letters*, 1:128 (to Robert Evans, 28 February 1842). "While I admire and cherish much of what I believe to have been the moral teaching of Jesus himself, I consider the system of doctrines built up from the facts of his life and drawn as to its materials from Jewish notions to be most dishonourable to God and most pernicious in its influence on individual and social happiness."

[11] The Unitarian chapel in Hampstead was within walking distance of where George Eliot and George Henry Lewes lived from 1863 to 1878. A letter from Catharine T. Herford to *The Guardian*, 2 July 1980, written in response to letters questioning the propriety of placing a memorial to George Eliot in Westminster Abbey on the hundredth anniversary of her death, states the following: "George Eliot was no atheist, even if her parish church was closed to her. My mother — living in Hampstead until her marriage in 1886 and brought up as a member of the Rosslyn Hill (Unitarian) Chapel — used to tell us that she remembered the author attending the chapel more Sundays than not, and finding there a spiritual home denied in other recognised communities." I am indebted to David Pailin for confirming the details of this letter, to which reference is made in Dodd, *George Eliot*, 86.

[12] "Evangelical Teaching: Dr. Cumming" (*Westminster Review*, Oct. 1855), in *Selected Essays, Poems and Other Writings*, ed. A. S. Byatt and Nicholas Watten (London: Penguin Classics, 1990), 41.

[13] Ibid., 43-65.

religion, atheism clears the ground for a faith beyond accusation and consolation."[14]

II. *The Religion of Humanity*

George Eliot was searching for a religion beyond accusation and consolation. And indeed in her case it was the implicit atheism of the German and French critics of mythical and dogmatic Christianity that cleared the ground for such a faith. But it would be misleading to suggest that she became a disciple of David Friedrich Strauss and Ludwig Feuerbach, whose works she translated, or of Auguste Comte, whose "religion of humanity" was in vogue among the intellectuals with whom she associated in the early 1850s.

She was put off by the "coldbloodedness" and single-mindedness of Strauss's *Life of Jesus,* telling Caroline Bray that she was "Strauss-sick — it made her ill dissecting the beautiful story of the crucifixion, and only the sight of her Christ-image and picture made her endure it."[15] While endorsing the historical-critical method with its rejection of supernaturalism, and accepting Strauss's analysis of the role of myth in the Bible as well as his critique of the orthodox doctrine of the God-man, George Eliot was not attracted to the portrayal of the historical figure of Jesus that emerged from Strauss's study. Strauss's Jesus was an apocalyptic enthusiast who confused his own identity with that of the messianic Son of Man coming on the clouds of heaven, whereas George Eliot's Jesus was the Man of Sorrows who proclaimed the friendship of God and exemplified a life of service and self-renunciation.

Feuerbach, too, disappointed her. She disliked Feuerbach's "crudity of expressions," warning Sara Sophia Hennell that the translation drafts of *The Essence of Christianity* that she had shared with her were quite literal, "so you have the *raw* Feuerbach — not any of my cooking. . . . With the ideas of Feuerbach I everywhere agree, but of course I should, of myself, alter the phraseology considerably."[16] The reference to "cooking" and the tongue-in-cheek nature of the remark about "everywhere agreeing" — for it is quite clear that there was no single thinker with whom George Eliot could everywhere agree — should warn us that the

---

[14] Paul Ricoeur, "Religion, Atheism, and Faith," in Alasdair MacIntyre and Paul Ricoeur, *The Religious Significance of Atheism* (New York: Columbia University Press, 1969), 60.
[15] *Letters,* 1:206 (Caroline Bray to Sara Sophia Hennell, 14 Feb. 1846); 217-18 (George Eliot to Sara Sophia Hennell, 20 May 1846); Haight, *George Eliot,* 50-51, 261.
[16] *Letters,* 2:153 (29 April 1854).

"cooked" version of Feuerbach that appears in George Eliot's fiction will differ in significant respects from the "raw" version.[17] Nor is "altering the phraseology" as innocent as it sounds, for *how* things are said shapes the substance of what is said.

George Eliot found support in Feuerbach for her own conviction about the primacy of feeling and emotion in human experience, and she responded affirmatively to his emphasis on the essentially communal nature of human beings as expressed in love and the I-Thou relationship, which has of necessity for embodied beings a sensual and sexual aspect. The category of "sympathy" that proved so important for her interpretation of religion derived in part from Feuerbach's *Mitgefühl* ("fellow-feeling"). She agreed with his (essentially Kantian) insight that religious images and theological concepts are constructions of the human imagination. But the question is what calls forth and justifies such constructions. I find no evidence in her writings that George Eliot ever embraced the central (and tediously reiterated) dogma of *The Essence of Christianity*, namely that human beings simply project onto a screen of transcendence all their own essential attributes and qualities, thereby objectifying and idealizing them in a supreme being. The source of the idea of God, Feuerbach believed, is human consciousness coming to know itself; it is a purely fanciful idea, having no reference in reality other than to the idea of humanity, the so-called species-essence (*Gattungswesen*), to which the divine attributes properly apply. By contrast for George Eliot the idea of God or divinity, as I shall attempt to show, is not an illusion arising out of psychological needs but a response to something awesome, mysterious, and overwhelming that presents itself in experience and demands reverence. Expressed in Hegelian terms, which are not incompatible with her own deep conviction, the idea of God is not the self-projection of finite consciousness into the infinite, but the self-manifestation of the infinite in finite consciousness's

---

[17] See Kathryn Bond Stockton's discussion of "Cooking Feuerbach" in *God Between Their Lips: Desire Between Women in Irigaray, Brontë, and Eliot* (Stanford: Stanford University Press, 1994), 186-92. Stockton argues that George Eliot read a "spiritual materialism" out of (or into) Feuerbach's work. God on this reading is neither a purely spiritual being nor the material essence of the cosmos but that which stands between and unifies the material and the spiritual — an Hegelian idea that appears also in Derrida and Irigaray. Whereas Feuerbach moved away from this dialectical insight to a strict philosophical materialism, George Eliot held on to it in her vision of a mystery *beneath* (not above or detached from) the real. While my interpretation differs from Stockton, I find her insight helpful. My view is that what emerges in George Eliot's fiction has more the character of a material spirituality than of a spiritual materialism.

awareness of the infinite, an awareness that is characteristically accompanied for religious people by self-denial rather than self-seeking, a centering on God (or ultimate reality) rather than on self. The difference here is between a naturalistic and a critically realistic account of religious experience. Thus it is not surprising that Feuerbach's rationalism, as well as his materialism and naturalism, which became more evident in later writings, were of little interest to George Eliot, and after 1854 she did not discuss his ideas.[18]

As for Comte, while attracted to some of his utopian ideals, including the principles of altruism and sympathy, she found his system of positivism rigid and ideological, and she never gave unqualified approval to the "religion of humanity."[19] Comte thought it necessary to invent such a religion, in which the so-called "Great Being" is identified with the ideal of humanity, in order to have a compelling basis for developing sympathetic instincts and moral values as a counterbalance to the exercise of material power in the realm of politics. But in fact his system remained utilitarian and deterministic. Pointing out that Comte did not believe that objective reality conforms to humanity's subjective values, T. R. Wright observes that "the Religion of Humanity . . . offers a comforting fiction in the face of a hostile and meaningless universe."[20] George Eliot was not interested in such comforting fictions, and she could not accept a disconnection between reality on the one hand and morality and religion on the other, which reduces the latter to the utilitarian function of promoting happiness and harmony. Moreover, Comte's compartmentalization of gender roles (according to which women are assigned to the realm of emotion as opposed to intellect, and to family as opposed to public life) must have given her pause.

---

[18] See Dodd, *George Eliot,* 181-90. On the distinction between naturalistic and critically realistic interpretations, as well as on the transition from self-centeredness to reality-centeredness, see John Hick, *An Interpretation of Religion: Human Responses to the Transcendent* (New Haven: Yale University Press, 1989).

[19] Dodd, *George Eliot,* 115-20; Haight, *George Eliot,* 301, 506. Dodd writes: "Fascinated though she was by systems, she ultimately, however, felt the repugnance of a sceptic for them. She steadfastly refused to be identified with the English Positivists. . . . It was characteristic of her eclecticism that, during the period when she was reading Comte, she also turned to the works of Hegel, who, like Comte, explored the link between a new logic and the historical process, but from a very different viewpoint" (120). According to Haight George Eliot insisted that she could not submit her intellect or soul to the guidance of Comte and that she was never a Comtist, although because they were a "poor unfortunate sect" she would not renounce them (301-2).

[20] T. R. Wright, *The Religion of Humanity: The Impact of Comtean Positivism on Victorian Britain* (Cambridge: Cambridge University Press, 1986), 21.

While affirming that religion ought above all to promote human flourishing, her sense of human evil and historical tragedy was too deep to allow her to embrace a religion that might actually worship or idolize human beings either as individuals or as a species — those very humans whose tendency, out of ambition or fear, is to draw everything into themselves. Her insight into the human condition was more profound and also more tragic than that of Feuerbach and Comte. Hers was a religion of humanity directed, not to veneration, but to service and sympathy. But what calls forth, motivates, and empowers such service and sympathy? Her intent was to reorient human beings from self-centeredness to reality-centeredness. But what is (ultimate) reality?

George Eliot read widely, deeply, and continuously, and was subject to no controlling influence. Referring to Rousseau and George Sand, she commented: "The writers who have most profoundly influenced me . . . are not in the least oracles to me. It is just possible that I may not embrace one of their opinions, that I may wish my life to be shaped quite differently from theirs."[21] This statement should warn us against over-emphasizing the influence of Feuerbach and Comte on her thinking. Her mind was engaged by deeper thinkers and greater poets than they — not only Rousseau but also Spinoza, Kant, Hegel, Shakespeare, Goethe, Coleridge, Carlyle, and Wordsworth.[22] She first read Spinoza in 1843 and began translating the *Tractatus Theologico-Politicus*, but neither it nor her mid-1850s translation of his *Ethics* was ever published. Spinozistic motifs are evident in her essays and novels. Her life-partner, George Henry Lewes, commented that "Spinoza's Pantheism is in truth the grandest and most religious of all philosophies, and as such it is recognized by Goethe and the German philosophers who all embrace his creed."[23] Later George Eliot claimed to have freed herself of the influence of pantheism, writing to Harriet Beecher Stowe: "I do not find my temple in Pantheism, which, whatever might be its value speculatively, could not yield a practical religion, since it is an attempt to look at the universe from the outside of our relations to it (that universe) as human beings."[24] It is clear that she was attracted to speculative systems and

---

[21] *Letters*, 1:277 (to Sara Sophia Hennell, 9 February 1847).

[22] Dodd, *George Eliot*, 87-96, 121-24, 250-53.

[23] Ibid., 249-53; Haight, *George Eliot*, 69, 172-73, 199-200. See Dorothy Atkins, *George Eliot and Spinoza* (Salzburg: Salzburg Studies in English Literature, Romantic Reassessment, no. 78, 1978). Atkins focuses on the interaction of freedom and determinism in George Eliot's novels. While this is a very helpful study, I think she overstates the case by giving a tightly Spinozistic reading of *Adam Bede*.

[24] *Letters*, 5:31 (8 May 1869).

holistic visions, but her skeptical eclecticism prevented her from falling under the sway of any of them. Her philosophical-theological sensibility was closer, perhaps, to that of Hegel than of any other major thinker, but she was not a Hegelian and was probably acquainted only with his philosophy of history and his aesthetics, not his philosophy of religion or his phenomenology of spirit, logic, and ethics.[25] Above all she was impressed by life's complexity and the ultimate mystery of things. She resisted simplistic solutions, whether on the side of supernaturalistic theism, materialistic atheism, scientific reductionism, or political utopianism. I believe she actually embraced a form of panentheism, but she

---

[25] Her familiarity with the *Lectures on the Philosophy of World History* would have come through her friendship with John Sibree, who translated this work into English in the late 1840s. She does allude to Hegel's *Aesthetics* in a letter to Sibree, 8 March 1848 (*Letters*, 1:247-48). Darrel Mansell argues that George Eliot incorporated two aspects of Hegel's theory of tragedy into her novels: that tragic conflict is between two relative forces of good (the individual protagonist and the general life of society) rather than between good and evil principles; and that the resolution of tragic conflict entails a reestablishment of the common social fabric, thus enabling life to go on after the heroic struggle to transcend or change it. Tragedy is moral in George Eliot's view if evil does not prevail, but a relative good. See "A Note on Hegel and George Eliot," *The Victorian Newsletter*, 7 (Spring 1965): 12-15. Of course George Eliot became indirectly acquainted with Hegel's thought through her translations of Strauss's *Life of Jesus* and Feuerbach's *The Essence of Christianity;* but Strauss and Feuerbach were both left-wing Hegelians who gave a slanted version of his philosophy. George Henry Lewes was directly familiar with Hegel, had considerable appreciation for his thought, and wrote several articles and book chapters about him. His earliest piece, a lengthy review of Hegel's *Vorlesungen über die Aesthetik* (Berlin, 1835), in *The British and Foreign Review*, 13 (1842): 1-49, provides a survey of Hegel's life and thought, summarizes Hegel's view of the connection between art and religion (a view adopted by Lewes himself), and excerpts a passage in which Hegel expresses appreciation for the realism of Dutch painting. George Eliot was surely acquainted with this review by the time she began living with Lewes. On various Hegel references in her and Lewes's writings, see Anthony McCobb, *George Eliot's Knowledge of German Life and Letters* (Salzburg: Salzburg Studies in English Literature, Romantic Reassessment, No. 102:2, 1982), 15-16, 114-16.

I believe that George Eliot was ultimately closer to Hegel than to Spinoza in philosophical sensibility (even though she was much more directly acquainted with the thought of Spinoza) because she did not subscribe uncritically to the Spinozistic doctrine of substance; reality had for her as well the qualities of subjectivity, historicality, relationality, and difference, which are the central Hegelian categories. Hegel's claim that substance is subject, and subject substance, seems to be implicit in her thinking: thus her view that divinity has the aspect of both moral order and infinite loving presence. Moreover, she was closer to both Spinoza and Hegel than to Feuerbach since from her point of view it is fundamentally wrong to confuse one's finite mode of existence or even the human species as a whole with the totality that is God as absolute substance/subject. Humans share in the divine reality but certainly do not exhaust it.

would have rejected that label as too abstractly philosophical, preferring instead to emphasize the way redemptive transformation is concretely experienced in people's lives.

III. A Religion of Divine Presence and Sympathy

My argument is that George Eliot was seeking to identify and advance a future religion, a religion without accusation and consolation, oriented to human flourishing, grounded in a faith in divine presence, sympathy, suffering, friendship, empowerment. She lacked the categories to articulate the theological aspects of this religion very clearly. What she needed was an understanding of a God-in-process, a God who does not control the course of world events but interacts with them, becoming God through a process of self-divestment and self-reunion, a fellow-sufferer who empowers humans through a kind of sympathetic presence, a God who preserves and transforms all things within the divine life. She did not know Hegel well enough to acquire such a vision from him, and she preceded Whitehead by some fifty years. But this is the idea of God implicit in her novels. I shall outline four themes in George Eliot's religion of divine presence and sympathy: a stress on feeling and deed rather than doctrine, the necessity of doing without opium and consolation, a reverence for the mystery beneath the real, and the idea of a sympathetic, suffering, present God. The first two themes are also compatible with the religion of humanity, while the third and fourth represent a transition to a more distinctive cosmotheandric perspective.[26]

1. A stress on feeling and deed rather than doctrine. In Adam Bede the narrator observes: "Faith, hope, and charity have not always been found in a direct ratio with sensibility to the three concords; and it is possible, thank Heaven! to have very erroneous theories and very sublime feelings."[27] And Adam Bede himself says that "it isn't notions sets people doing the right thing — its feelings." "Doctrines," he adds, simply are "finding names for your feelings." Rather than arguing about doctrines, "I found it better for my soul to be humble before the mysteries o'

---

[26] The term "cosmotheandric" is borrowed from Raimon Panikkar and refers to the interaction of world, God, and humanity. See The Cosmotheandric Experience (Maryknoll, N.Y.: Orbis Books, 1993).

[27] Adam Bede (1859), edited with an introduction by Stephen Gill (London: Penguin Classics, 1985), chap. 3, 82. The "three concords" may be a reference to the Lutheran Formula of Concord, or to the three ancient creeds acknowledged by all Anglicans: Apostles', Nicene, and Athanasian (see 595, n. 7).

God's dealings."[28] By these statements George Eliot is telling us to trust our emotions, our feelings, to regard them as putting us in touch with what is real and true, and to view doctrines as interpretations of feelings rather than vice versa. While she seemed to have no objection to doctrines in principle, she saw them being used principally to impose a set of inhumane, rationally indefensible beliefs and practices. And she regarded the role of the artist to be the evocation of feelings in relation to concrete figures and experiences rather than the advancement of the writer's religious, philosophical, or moral theories.[29] There is, to be sure, a powerful didactic element in George Eliot's novels, but it is a teaching that proceeds inductively from experienced realities rather than deductively from abstract principles. It arises out of her genius for acute observation and penetrating description. Religious feelings have both a mystical and a practical dimension. Mystically, they entail the fruits of the Spirit, the peace of God, the "bathing of the soul in emotions which overpass the outlines of thought";[30] practically they lead to a life of service and sympathy, a sharing in the suffering love of Christ.[31]

2. *The necessity of doing without opium and consolation.* Responding to Barbara Bodichon's query as to whether it was acceptable to turn to the "forms and ceremonies" of religion for comfort, George Eliot wrote: "I have faith in the working-out of higher possibilities than the Catholic or any other church has presented, and those who have strength to wait and endure, are bound to accept no formula which their whole souls — their intellects as well as their emotions — do not embrace with entire reverence. The highest 'calling and election' is to *do without opium* and live through all our pain with conscious, clear-eyed endurance."[32] No statement is closer to George Eliot's own religious struggle. She was deeply aware of the human need to make sense of life, to find meaning and direction in history, to face the future with courage in the absence of certainty about one's own destiny. She knew how tempting it is to dull the pain of life through such escapes as gambling and alcohol,[33] or

---

28 Ibid., 17:226-28.
29 Hence her critique of the "oracular" species of novels in "Silly Novels by Lady Novelists" (*Westminster Review*, October 1856), *Selected Essays*, 148-56. To Joseph Frank Payne she wrote: "I become more and more timid — with less daring to adopt any formula which does not get itself clothed for me in some human figure and individual experience, and perhaps that is a sign that if I help others to see at all it must be through the medium of art" (*Letters*, 6:217 [25 January 1876]).
30 *Letters*, 6:89 (to Harriet Beecher Stowe, 11 November 1874).
31 *Selected Essays*, 41.
32 *Letters*, 3:366 (26 December 1860).
33 See the description of Thias Bede's gradual descent into alcoholism in *Adam*

to provide consolation through superficial assurances of divine rescue and salvation.[34] She did not believe that God intervenes episodically in history to save people from disasters, to reward piety, to punish wrongdoing, or to bring about desired outcomes. Rather the natural and moral worlds are governed by laws that assure an invariability of sequence and the inexorability of consequences. To suggest that God contravenes these laws is immoral and irrational; rather the laws constitute God's system of government. In such a world human beings are free and responsible agents, and they must accept the consequences of their actions. Thus the effects of sin cannot be expunged, but the course of wrong-doing need not be continued. Repentance can change the future but not obliterate the past.[35] By living through our pain with conscious, clear-eyed endurance, new and higher possibilities may open up — but *we* must make them happen.[36] In all of this, truthfulness, honesty, clarity, and avoidance of illusion are absolutely essential. "Falsehood is so easy, truth so difficult."[37]

Is it possible for religion "to do without opium"? Perhaps George Eliot was thinking of Karl Marx's famous comment that religion is "the opium of the people," offering illusory happiness in place of real happiness. But that is a sweeping dogma, true in some instances but not in others. Certainly the religion of Dinah Morris in *Adam Bede* was no opium of the people; she never tried to make things seem better or different than they were, and she avoided illusions. She provided comfort without consolation; by her sympathetic deeds and truthful speech she manifested God's presence in the world.

3. *A reverence for the mystery beneath the real.* Commenting on Darwin's *Origin of Species,* George Eliot made another revealing observation to

---

Bede, chap. 4, and the critique of gambling as a form of amusement in *Daniel Deronda,* chap. 1.

[34] "Life, though a good to men on the whole, is a doubtful good to many, and to some not a good at all. To my thought, it is a source of constant mental distortion to make the denial of this a part of religion, to go on pretending things are better than they are." *Letters,* 4:183 (to Caroline Bray, 18 March 1865).

[35] See George Eliot's reviews in 1851 of works by R. W. Mackay and W. R. Greg (*Selected Essays,* 271, 293-94). Here the influence of Spinoza is especially felt (Dodd, *George Eliot,* 94-95, 250-53).

[36] This is a central theme of all the novels, especially *Adam Bede, Middlemarch,* and *Daniel Deronda.* To a despairing friend she wrote, "The progress of the world — which you say can only come at the right time — can certainly never come at all save by the modified actions of the individual beings who compose the world." *Letters,* 6:98-100 (to Mary Elizabeth Ponsonby, 10 December 1874).

[37] *Adam Bede,* 17:222.

Barbara Bodichon: "To me the Development theory and other explanations of processes by which things came to be, produce a feeble impression compared with the mystery that lies under the processes."[38] This
letter was written shortly after the publication of *Adam Bede,* in which
she was concerned with both the divine mystery and realism in art.
The mystery that lies under the processes is "the mystery beneath the
real"[39] — a phrase that can serve as a motto for her work as a whole. The
narrator of *Adam Bede* associates the mystery with the kind of deep love,
religious feeling, and musical harmony[40] that "bring with them the
consciousness that they are mere waves and ripples in an unfathomable
ocean of love and beauty: our emotion in its keenest moment passes
from expression into silence; our love at its highest flood rushes beyond
its object, and loses itself in the sense of divine mystery."[41] This
mystery is to be found not above and beyond the real but beneath and
within it. What is required to find the mystery is not a denial of the real
and commonplace but an imaginative penetration and intensification of
it, a discovery of the good, true, and beautiful in the midst of the
common, ugly, and everyday — a discovery that is possible only for
those who have eyes to see. This is the "rare, precious quality of truthfulness" in many Dutch paintings, which find beauty not simply in the
"secret of proportion, but in the secret of deep human sympathy." We
may paint angels and madonnas if we like, but "do not . . . banish from
the region of Art those old women scraping carrots with their work-
worn hands, those heavy clowns taking holiday in a dingy pot-house,

---

[38] *Letters,* 3:227 (5 December 1859).
[39] Jennifer Uglow, in *George Eliot* (London & New York: Virago/Pantheon Pioneers, 1987), uses this phrase in the title of her chapter on *Adam Bede,* but she does
not analyze it.
[40] Peter Mudford, in his editorial introduction to *Silas Marner, The Lifted Veil,
Brother Jacob* (London: Everyman Library, 1996), says that George Eliot's sense of
mystery was closely associated with her love of music, and that she associated
musical harmony with human sympathy (xx). A journal entry describes how she
was caught up in the singing of the mass in the Nürnberg Frauenkirche: "How the
music that stirs all one's devout emotions blends everything into harmony —
makes one feel part of one whole, [in] which one loves all alike, losing the sense
of a separate self" (Haight, *George Eliot,* 256). To John Sibree she wrote: "No mind
that has any *real* life is a mere echo of another. If the perfect unison comes occasionally, as in music, it enhances the harmonies. It is like a diffusion or expansion of
one's own life to be assured that its vibrations are repeated in another, and words
are the media of those vibrations. How can you say that music must end in silence?
Is not the universe itself a perpetual utterance of the One Being?" (*Letters,* 1:255 [8
March 1848]).
[41] *Adam Bede,* 3:81.

those rounded backs and stupid weather-beaten faces that have bent over the spade and done the rough work of the world."[42] In these common human faces may be seen the face of God; in ordinary human sympathy, the divine sympathy.

4. *The idea of a sympathetic, suffering, present God.* George Eliot's artistic vision clearly refers the reader to a mysterious reality that transcends the self and nature, reverberates in the rhythms of nature and the events of history, draws the self out of itself into an unnameable whole, molests and drives human beings until they collapse and are reborn.[43] Sometimes it comes under the guise of the "hard unaccommodating Actual, which has never consulted our taste and is entirely unselect."[44] Other times it appears as "a pitying, loving, infinite Presence, sweet as summer to the houseless needy."[45] But what is it in and for itself? Is it simply the fatality and necessity of history, the cosmic and moral law that exacts consequences for every action?[46] Is it an impersonal trans-individual essence, having perhaps the quality of "maternity," a

---

[42] Ibid., 17:222-23.

[43] For this interpretation I am partly indebted to John P. McGowan, *Representation and Revelation: Victorian Realism from Carlyle to Yeats* (Columbia: University of Missouri Press, 1968), chap. 6 ("The Development of George Eliot's Realism"). Gordon Haight and Valerie Dodd point to the influence of John Ruskin's aesthetic theory on George Eliot's visionary realism: see Haight, *George Eliot*, 239-40; and Dodd, *George Eliot*, 295-98. If she knew anything of Hegel's philosophy of art, she would have found resources there as well. See above, n. 25; and Stephen Houlgate, "Hegel and the 'End' of Art," *The Owl of Minerva*, 29 (fall 1997): 1-21.

[44] *Daniel Deronda*, 33:430.

[45] *Adam Bede*, 3:81-82.

[46] F. W. H. Myers reported a conversation with George Eliot in 1873 in which she pronounced the words "God, Immortality, Duty," and remarked "how inconceivable was the *first,* how unbelievable the *second,* and yet how peremptory and absolute the *third.* Never, perhaps, have sterner accents affirmed the sovereignty of impersonal and unrecompensing Law. . . . I [Myers] seemed to be gazing . . . on vacant seats and empty halls — on a sanctuary with no Presence to hallow it, and heaven left lonely of a God" (*Century Magazine,* 23 [November 1881]: 62-73). Quoted in Haight, *George Eliot,* 464. This account was written from recollection eight years after it occurred, and it is difficult to know how much credence to give it. Rosemary Ashton doubts its veracity, believing that it is couched in overwrought language George Eliot would not have used and that it turns her into the evangelist of a gloomy rationalism (*George Eliot: A Life,* 333-34). God, while in the strict sense "inconceivable" (as the apophatic tradition has always insisted), may nonetheless be necessary for the idea of duty. In *Middlemarch,* the epigraph to chapter 80 quotes Wordsworth's *Ode to Duty,* where God and duty are linked rather than divided. In *Daniel Deronda,* which George Eliot began to write shortly after this conversation, she seems to be preoccupied, in the Jewish parts, with precisely the question of a hallowing presence.

nurturing, sacrificial love?[47] Or is it a God who, while not personal in any finite sense, nonetheless is experienced as subject, present and active in nature and history? On this question I think George Eliot did not arrive at a clear and definitive answer; she remained agnostic. She seems to have oscillated between a more personal view of a compassionately engaged, suffering God, as in *Adam Bede,* and a more impersonal, Spinozistic view of a divine omnipresence at work in things, as in *Daniel Deronda.* In some ultimately inconceivable sense God is, as Hegel argued, both subject and substance.

To her former landlord in Geneva George Eliot wrote:

> Ten years of experience have wrought great changes in [my] inward self: I have no longer any antagonism towards any faith in which human sorrow and human longing for purity have expressed themselves; on the contrary, I have a sympathy with it that predominates over all argumentative tendencies. I have not returned to dogmatic Christianity — to the acceptance of any set of doctrines as a creed, and a superhuman revelation of the Unseen — but I see in it the highest expression of the religious sentiment that has yet found its place in the history of mankind, and I have the profoundest interest in the inward life of sincere Christians in all ages.[48]

Note the qualifiers in this statement: she has not returned to *dogmatic* Christianity, to the acceptance of doctrines *as a creed,* or to a *superhuman* revelation. This leaves open the possibility of reconstructing a non-dogmatic, non-creedal form of Christianity (the highest expression thus far, she claims, of human religion), and of affirming an innerhuman revelation of the Unseen.

In her critique of Dr. Cumming's evangelical teaching, George Eliot sketched an intriguing alternative to his vengeful, compensatory God.

> The idea of God is really moral in its influence . . . only when God is contemplated as sympathizing with the pure elements of human feeling, as possessing infinitely all those attributes which we recognize to be moral in humanity. In this life, the idea of God and the sense of His presence intensify all noble feeling, and encourage all noble effort, on the same principle that human sympathy is found a source of strength: the brave man feels braver when he knows that another stout heart is beating time with his; the devoted woman who is wearing out her years in patient effort to alleviate suffering or save vice from the last stages of degradation, finds aid in the pressure of a friendly hand which tells her that there is one who understands her deeds, and in her place would do the like. The idea of a God who not only sympathizes with all we feel and endure for our fellow-men, but who will pour new life into our too languid love, and give firmness to our vacillating purpose, is an extension and multiplication of the effects produced by human

---

[47] See Uglow, *George Eliot,* 112-13.
[48] *Letters,* 3:231 (to François d'Albert-Durade, 6 December 1859).

sympathy; and it has been intensified for the better spirits who have been under the influence of orthodox Christianity, by the contemplation of Jesus as 'God manifest in the flesh.'[49]

There are, to be sure, Feuerbachian elements in this statement, but there are also important differences from Feuerbach. Some "cooking" has occurred: the role of the human imagination is affirmed, but also the reality of what is imagined. The idea of God may be a fiction, but a true and necessary fiction. After all, theology as a whole is a kind of fiction that creates imaginative variations on what history offers as "real." The theologian and the artist alike are engaged in a creative act, a *poiēsis*, an envisionment of a possible world in which human beings might dwell humanly. In this case, George Eliot is telling us that we need the sympathetic presence of a friend in order to have the courage and strength to act under difficult circumstances. Human friends alone will not do given the fragility and transience of the human condition: we need a God who will "pour new life" into our languid love and empower our vacillating resolve. Such a God does not act directly, miraculously, superhumanly, but through the mediation of human friends: just this is the meaning of God becoming manifest in the flesh of Jesus. For believers this "fiction," this theological idea, is a palpable reality, not an empty illusion. For George Eliot the idea of God does not satisfy a psychological need or serve a social function, as claimed by Feuerbach and Comte; rather it refers to the fundamental condition of being human and existing morally in a tragically conflicted world. God comes forth as real in redemptive transformations wrought by the power of sympathy and love.

George Eliot's fiction can be read as a series of theological experiments in which she explored the character of religious life and the idea of God as they manifested themselves in a variety of traditions, theologies, practices, and life-styles. In the strict sense we cannot claim to know George Eliot's innermost thoughts and deepest convictions from her fiction. What is available to us is a series of texts that reverberate with religious images, motifs, and characters. We can offer a *theological reading* of these texts, attempting to identify not only compelling ideas but perhaps even an encompassing vision whose relevance for present-day theology is noteworthy. The extent to which these ideas and vision coincide with George Eliot's own point of view is ultimately unanswerable. More important is what is written in the texts themselves. Surely a

---

[49] *Selected Essays*, 66-67.

theological reading of George Eliot's fiction is as plausible as a feminist reading, a humanist reading, or a psychological reading. Ideas and insights may be presented in her work that prove illuminating to theological reflection in ways not intended or foreseen by the author. In the final analysis, the reader provides the hermeneutical lenses that bring the texts into focus in particular ways. An adequate presentation of my reading would require a study of all the major novels. In the remainder of this article I am able to consider briefly only two of them, *Adam Bede* (1859) and *Daniel Deronda* (1876). By choosing an early and a late writing, I am trying to show that George Eliot's engagement with religious questions continued to the end of her literary career.

2. *Feeling the Divine Presence: Adam Bede*

Most of the recent critical literature has focused on the relationship between Adam Bede and Hetty Sorrel, and has not known what to make of the "preacher-woman" Dinah Morris. George Eliot herself saw it differently. She originally conceived of this story as another "scene of clerical life," with Dinah as the central figure.[50] The irony with which the novel was named *Adam Bede* reflects the irony with which Marian Evans named herself "George Eliot." In letters and her journal she described how her Aunt Elizabeth Evans suggested the figure of Dinah but was entirely different. "How curious it seems to me that people should think Dinah's sermons, prayers, and speeches were *copied* — when they were written with hot tears, as they surged up in my own mind!"[51] To Barbara Bodichon, who recognized her to be the author merely from excerpts in reviews, she wrote that this book "has come from my heart of hearts."[52]

The story in brief: Adam Bede, a fine carpenter of manly virtues but limited vision, has become infatuated with Hetty Sorrel, a beautiful girl with remarkable capacities for self-deception and vanity. Unbeknownst to Adam, Hetty has her eyes on Arthur Donnithorne, the landed gentleman who will inherit the estate on which the common people of Hayslope labor, and who, like Hetty, is egocentric and self-deceiving, but also affectionate and generous. Arthur knows that the laws of social class will not permit a marriage between himself and Hetty, but he does

---

[50] Haight, *George Eliot,* 249. See also her journal entry for 30 November 1858, printed as an appendix to the novel (585-88).
[51] *Letters,* 3:174-76 (to Sara Sophia Hennell, 7 October 1859).
[52] Ibid., 3:63 (5 May 1859). Bodichon was in Algiers at the time.

seduce her on a fine summer's night of 1799. When Hetty discovers she is pregnant, she cannot bear to tell her uncle and aunt, the Poysers, with whom she lives. Instead she runs away and begins a fruitless search for Arthur, who has left Hayslope for a period of military service. After much aimless wandering, Hetty gives birth to a child in a stranger's house. The next day she abandons the child in the woods, and it dies of exposure. She is found out, is placed on trial for child murder, and condemned to death, although she denies everything.

Dinah Morris is a lovely young Methodist lay preacher. We meet her in the second chapter when she preaches on the village green of Hayslope. She works among the poor of a mining village, Snowfield, but frequently visits her Aunt Rachel Poyser, the wife of Hetty's uncle, in Hayslope. As the story progresses, Dinah becomes the central figure. She is the antitype to Hetty, utterly self-giving, gifted with the power of divining the mystery beneath the real. Whereas Hetty is preoccupied with mirrors in which to see her reflected face, Dinah delights in her bedroom window from which she can look out upon the fields (15:194-202).[53] For Hetty water is an image of death by drowning (35:410-11), while for Dinah it is an image of life: she experiences the inspiration of the divine Spirit as a rushing stream and a deep flood (8:134-35). When Hetty is imprisoned and condemned, Dinah goes to her in the prison cell to stay with her to the last. There she brings about Hetty's confession and repentance, and Hetty is saved from the hangman's rope by a last-minute reprieve from the magistrate. But she is "transported" to Australia, the colony for exiled criminals, and is never seen again. Adam, too, is transformed by this baptism through suffering. Two years later he and Dinah are married; she, proscribed from further preaching by an edict of the Methodist Conference in 1803, becomes a wife and mother, but carries on her ministry of human caring.

George Eliot's portrayal of Dinah Morris is quite extraordinary and of considerable theological interest. While perhaps not exactly a Christ figure, Dinah is the mediatrix of a divine redemptive presence. She is in fact a Madonna figure (17:224, 26:326), inspired by Raphael's painting of the Sistine Madonna in Dresden, where George Eliot wrote part of the novel.[54] God is not seen or known directly in this world but is reflected, made manifest, in the speech and actions of persons like Dinah. Dinah's speech has a clarity, simplicity, and insight that are luminous

---

[53] The page references following chapter numbers (hereafter cited in text) are to the Penguin Classics edition of *Adam Bede* (see above, n. 27).

[54] Haight, *George Eliot*, 264.

and transformative. The preaching on the Hayslope green (chapter 2) is the most remarkable instance of this. George Eliot created an eighteenth-century Methodist evangelical sermon, using as a historical model the preaching of Mary Bosanquet Fletcher. But the sermon and other speeches were her own artistic creation, composed, as she said, "with hot tears, as they surged up in my own mind." Dinah's actions are as effective as her speech. She soothes, touches, calms, feeds, and heals by her physical presence (10:153-58). She does not deny suffering when it is real, does not offer false assurances, does not engage in abstract exhortations. She knows intuitively when quiet sympathy is best, and when it is appropriate to speak. As she comforts Adam's mother Lisbeth after the death of her husband, we are told that "there was faith, love, and hope pouring itself forth that evening in the little kitchen" (10:159).

Who is Dinah's God? The central theme is annunciated in her sermon: God is one who is present and available to those who have need of God, especially the poor, the broken-hearted, those who are lost and who suffer. God is not remote and lofty but has come near and is our friend — above all in the words and deeds of Jesus, who was not just a good man:

> He was the Son of God — 'in the image of the Father,' the Bible says; that means, just like God, who is the beginning and end of all things. . . . So then, all the love that Jesus showed to the poor is the same love that God has for us (2:68-71).

Dinah seems to address and answer George Eliot's central religious question: "Will God take care of us when we die? and has he any comfort for us when we are lame and sick and helpless? Perhaps, too, he is angry with us; else why does the blight come, and the bad harvests, and the fever, and all sorts of pain and trouble? For our life is full of trouble, and if God sends us good, he seems to send bad too. How is it? how is it?" The answer is that God does not directly cause these things, is not angry with us, does not reward or punish us. Rather God simply "lasts when everything else is gone." God is our everlasting, ever-present friend, who sustains us when we are sad and rejoices with us when we are glad. "What shall we do if he is not our friend?" (2:70).

The theme that runs through Dinah's discourses is that of the presence of a suffering, infinite love, which is God's very being. Those to whom she has spoken have had their souls "suffused . . . with the sense of a pitying, loving, infinite Presence, sweet as summer to the houseless needy" (3:81-82). The divine presence is "the presence of a

Love and Sympathy deeper and more tender than was breathed from the earth and sky" (15:202). The infinite love is a suffering love:

> I feel it, I feel it — Infinite Love is suffering too — yea, in the fulness of knowledge it suffers, it yearns, it mourns; and that is a blind self-seeking which wants to be freed from the sorrow wherewith the whole creation groaneth and travaileth. Surely it is not true blessedness to be free from sorrow, while there is sorrow and sin in the world: sorrow is then a part of love, and love does not seek to throw it off. . . . Is there not pleading in heaven? Is not the Man of Sorrow there in that crucified body wherewith he ascended? And is He not one with the Infinite Love itself — as our love is one with our sorrow?" (30:374).[55]

In reflecting upon Hetty's hidden dread and forthcoming agony, the narrator comments: "Such things are sometimes hidden among the sunny fields and behind the blossoming orchards; and the sound of the gurgling brook, if you come close to one spot behind a small bush, would be mingled for your ear with a despairing human sob. No wonder man's religion has much sorrow in it; no wonder he needs a Suffering God" (35:410). We need a suffering God. The theology and church doctrine that George Eliot knew did not give such a God. She lacked the philosophical categories of a Hegel or Whitehead to express the idea of a God of self-divestment, world-embodiment, process and becoming. But this is the kind of God she envisioned through her own religious sensibility and artistic imagination.

Dinah "felt the Divine Presence more and more" as she sat in the prison cell with Hetty. She felt "as if she herself were a part of it, and it was the Divine pity that was beating in her heart." God, she thought, "manifest[s] himself by our silent feeling, and make[s] his love felt through ours" (45:494). A bit later we are told that "the pitying love that shone out from Dinah's face looked like a visible pledge of the Invisible Mercy" (46:505). Dinah, in other words, is a mediatrix of the redemptive divine presence; she is an instrument by which this presence can become a transformative reality in people's lives. Without such human mediation there would be no divine presence. How do we know that it is really the *divine* presence that is mediated, as opposed, let us say, to merely the innate human capacity for love and sympathy? There is no way that we can know this with logical certainty, no way to disprove

---

[55] Edward Farley quotes this passage in the epigraph to chap. 19 of *Divine Empathy: A Theology of God* (Minneapolis, Fortress Press, 1996). I find intriguing similarities between Farley's theology of divine empathy and George Eliot's religion of divine sympathy. In this essay I cannot show how Farley's categories might provide a vehicle for unpacking some of the theological implications of George Eliot's fiction.

definitively the Feuerbachian inversion of theology into anthropology. But we can listen to the testimony of those like Dinah who are filled in a special way with the divine presence. What they testify to is a sense of being *channeled, called, laid upon,* and *led on* by a gratuitous power not at their disposal. Those who so testify include women. As Dinah and Mr. Irwine discuss "women's preaching," she remarks wryly: "It isn't for men to make channels for God's Spirit, as they make channels for the water-courses and say, 'Flow here, but flow not there.'" And she continues:

> Sometimes it seemed as if speech came to me without any will of my own, and words were given to me that came out as the tears come. . . . Sir, we are led on, like the little children, by a way that we know not. I was called to preach quite suddenly, and since then I have never been left in doubt about the work that was laid upon me (8:134-135).

In another context, the narrator observes: "As Dinah expressed it, 'She was never left to herself; but it was always given her when to keep silence and when to speak.' And do we not all agree to call rapid thought and noble impulse by the name of inspiration? After our subtlest analysis of the mental process, we must still say, as Dinah did, that our highest thoughts and our best deeds are all given to us" (10:158-159). Is this the gospel according to Feuerbach or another, truer Gospel — the Gospel not of achievement but of gift?

Dinah, then, is a holy, inspired figure, and we are told that the crowds gazed at her with awe (47:507). But at the same time George Eliot is careful to depict her as a real, flesh-and-blood, warm and sensuous human being. She weeps at the thought of her repressed affection for Adam (49:523, 50:530). She, whose calling is to minister to others and not to have joys and sorrows of her own (3:79), allows herself nonetheless to be drawn into the human community and to be ministered unto. She benefits from the sacrifice of another woman, Hetty Sorrel, and has to live with the knowledge of that fact. She consents to marriage, recognizing that her love of Adam may compete with her love of God (52:554, 54:576). And after her marriage she acquiesces in the prohibition against women preaching — even though she is not completely silenced, for, as Adam observes, Dinah goes on "talking to the people a bit in their houses" and is "not held from other sorts o' teaching" (epilogue: 583) — a hint that in a subversive way her ministry continues. But for the most part she has to give up one aspect of the Madonna role, proclamation and spiritual guidance, to assume another aspect, that of motherhood and domesticity. It is after all only fragile human beings, caught in life's ambiguities, who mediate God's presence.

In *Adam Bede,* redemption prevails over loss, but not unambiguously. Hetty repents and is saved from execution, but she dies before she can return from exile. Arthur obtains her reprieve, is genuinely remorseful, and after several years is welcomed back into the community, but he agrees with Adam that "there's a sort of wrong that can never be made up for" (epilogue: 584). The novel teaches the hard truth that deeds cannot be revoked, and that agents of deeds must live with the consequences of their actions. Yet life goes on. Tragedy is clearly present, but it does not prevail; the vision is comic, or better tragicomic. In George Eliot's later fiction, the tragic elements of the vision deepen. She never again created a hero or heroine as thoroughly good as Dinah Morris. Daniel Deronda is the closest approximation, and we shall have occasion to compare these two figures. In the later novels, George Eliot continued to explore religious traditions and practices, and the central themes of sin and guilt, suffering and loss, grace and redemption are present in all of them.

Even in the greatest and most secular of her novels, *Middlemarch,* George Eliot did not abandon the possibility of redemptive acts in a broken and unredeemed world.[56] The central female figure, Dorothea Brooke, is compared with Saint Theresa of Avila, whose "passionate, ideal nature demanded an epic life," and who "found her epos in the reform of a religious order."[57] Dorothea was one of those many Theresas who found for themselves no epic life, whose social ideals and passionate nature led to no great reforming achievement. "Her full nature, like that river of which Cyrus broke the strength, spent itself in channels which had no great name on the earth. But," continues the narrator,

> the effect of her being on those around her was incalculably diffusive: for the growing good of the world is partly dependent on unhistoric acts; and that things are not so ill with you and me as they might have been, is half owing to the number who lived faithfully a hidden life, and rest in unvisited tombs.[58]

This, I believe, is a profoundly religious insight, which tells us more about God's real presence in the world than all the sermons of glory and

---

[56] To her publisher, John Blackwood, she wrote that there is "no unredeemed tragedy in the solution of the story" (*Letters,* 5:296 [4 August 1872]).

[57] *Middlemarch,* edited by Rosemary Ashton (London: Penguin Classics, 1994), 3-4 (prelude).

[58] Ibid., 838 (finale). George Eliot wrote Blackwood that her design for *Middlemarch* "is to show the gradual action of ordinary causes rather than exceptional, and to show this in some directions which have not been from time immemorial the beaten path" (*Letters,* 5:168 [24 July 1871]).

triumph, all the naive belief in divine purpose and protection. It also hints at a form of subjective immortality to which George Eliot was attracted.

3. *Finding the Pathways: Daniel Deronda*

Daniel Deronda is a much longer and more complex novel than *Adam Bede*, approximating *Middlemarch* in breadth and depth of vision, and picking up several of its unfinished themes. Again, the story in brief: Daniel Deronda observes a beautiful young English woman gambling away her money at a German spa. When she is called home unexpectedly because of a family financial crisis, she pawns her necklace for return fare; upon an impulse, Deronda purchases it and returns it to her anonymously. The young woman, Gwendolen Harleth, is one of George Eliot's most brilliant creations. Witty, smart, vivacious, egocentric, and driven, she consents to marry Henleigh Mallinger Grandcourt for money rather than love, even though she knows that he has a son by a former mistress to whom he is morally obligated. Gwendolen thinks that she can master Grandcourt but discovers the opposite to be true: soon she is reduced to a passive shadow of her former self.

Deronda lives nearby with his guardian, Sir Hugo Mallinger, Grandcourt's uncle. He becomes a kind of spiritual confessor to Gwendolen, helping her to bear up under her misery and to reorient herself to larger human purposes. It is clear that they are passionately attracted to each other, but at the same time Deronda has become involved with another young woman whom he rescued from suicide by drowning. She is Mirah Lapidoth, a Jewess, a talented musician, a woman of pure soul and devout faith who is fleeing from a tyrannical father and has despaired of finding her long-lost brother, Mordecai. It happens that Deronda discovers Mordecai in a London pawnbroker's shop and reunites brother and sister. Mordecai is a Jewish sage and mystic, modeled on Judah Halevi, a medieval Spanish poet and philosopher. He initiates Deronda into the history, theology, and spirituality of Judaism, adopting the young man as his disciple and successor.

Deronda eventually discovers his own Jewish identity and resolves to marry Mirah rather than Gwendolen, whose husband drowned in a boating accident off the coast of Genoa, a drowning for which Gwendolen holds herself partly responsible. In the final anguished scenes between Daniel and Gwendolen, she undergoes a kind of death and resurrection, resolves to live and to become a better person. "Do not think of me sorrowfully on your wedding-day," she writes him. "I have remembered your words — that I may live to be one of the best of women, who make others glad that they were born. . . . I only thought of myself, and I made you grieve. It hurts me now to think of your grief. You must not grieve any more for me. It is better — it shall be better with me because I have known you" (70:882).[59] Shortly thereafter, Mordecai dies and Daniel and Mirah set out for the East on the vague mission of finding a homeland for the Jews.

The recent publication of George Eliot's *Daniel Deronda Notebooks* makes clear the extraordinary lengths to which she went to immerse herself in the history, life, and thought of Judaism. She visited synagogues, learned Hebrew, and read broadly in ancient, medieval, and modern Jewish literature, with a special interest in the Kabbalah, thereby supplementing her knowledge of and love for the Hebrew Bible acquired in youth.[60] In a letter to Harriet Beecher Stowe, she explained quite explicitly her purposes:

> Precisely because I felt that the usual attitude of Christians towards Jews is — I hardly know whether to say more impious or more stupid when viewed in light of their professed principles; I therefore felt urged to treat Jews with such sympathy and understanding as my nature and knowledge could attain to. Moreover, not only towards the Jews, but towards all oriental peoples with whom we English come in contact, a spirit of arrogance and contemptuous dictatorialness is observable which has become a national disgrace to us. . . . Towards the Hebrews we western people who have been reared in Christianity, have a peculiar debt and, whether we acknowledge it or not, a peculiar thoroughness of fellowship in religious and moral sentiment.[61]

The "spirit of arrogance and contemptuous dictatorialness" of the English upper classes is brilliantly depicted in this novel,[62] and the cause of a Jewish national home, which George Eliot learned from her friendship with Emanuel Deutsch, is embraced by it.[63] But the last

---

[59] The page references following chapter numbers (cited hereafter in text) are to the Penguin Classics edition of *Daniel Deronda* (see n. 7).

[60] See Jane Irwin's introduction to her edition of the *Daniel Deronda Notebooks* (above, n. 8). George Eliot also had to battle against her own youthful prejudice against Judaism (see *Letters*, 1:246-47 [to John Sibree, 11 February 1848]).

[61] *Letters*, 6:301-302 (29 October 1876).

[62] In this article I have done scant justice to George Eliot's social criticism, which is present throughout her work but is especially powerful in her last novels. She had a deep sense of oppressive ethnic, creedal, gender, and class structures, and it is more in the realm of individual relationships that redemptive acts seem possible. The social is above all the realm of the tragic. Yet she does not permit her characters (or her readers) to abandon efforts at social reform when some good can be accomplished.

[63] Haight, *George Eliot*, 469-70.

sentence of the letter may provide a clue as to why she seemed so driven to acquire an understanding of Judaism: she found in it a fellowship of religious and moral sentiment. Daniel Deronda is partly George Eliot finding her own spiritual identity.

Certainly Daniel has some of Dinah Morris's qualities. He is not motivated and driven by worldly success (16:219-20). He combines affectionateness with independence of judgment, has deep sympathy for those who are in difficulty and suffering, and seems attracted to persons whom he can rescue (28:367-70). He is more than a moral counselor, a provider of practical wisdom: he is a priest, a confessor, a redeemer (36:505-10). Mirah's visionary impression that Daniel was a divinely-sent messenger (37:522) may be compared with Lisbeth's that Dinah was the angel at the grave of Jesus (*Adam Bede*, 51:542-43). Daniel assumes from the dying Mordecai the mission to unify his race and ultimately humanity as a whole (63:819-20). He is a messianic figure of obscure background and uncertain parentage, but he falls in love and marries a woman.

What does Daniel (and his artistic creator) discover in Judaism? Put in briefest terms, he finds in it a genuine moral and religious community that thrives on inner diversity and debate, that has a distinctive mission to humanity as a whole, and that believes in a God who is mysteriously present in every human face and natural entity, who gives to human beings a diversity of pathways through life, and is the ultimate, incomprehensible, unnameable ground of the unity of all things.

The narrator comments that when the great moments of the world enter like an earthquake into our own lives,

> it is as if the Invisible Power . . . became visible, according to the imagery of the Hebrew poet [e.g., Psalm 104], making the flames his chariot and riding on the wings of the wind, till the mountains smoke and the plains shudder under the rolling, fiery visitation. Often the good cause seems to lie prostrate under the thunder of unrelenting forces. . . . Then it is that the submission of the soul to the Highest is tested, and even in the eyes of frivolity life looks out from the scene of human struggles with the awful face of duty, and a religion shows itself which is something else than a private consolation (69:875-76).

Judaism at its best is such a religion, though it too has its failings (as Deronda's mother Leonora testifies [51:689-90]). Deronda teaches a similar truth to Gwendolen when he tells her that "the refuge you are needing from personal trouble is the higher, the religious life, which holds an enthusiasm for something more than our own appetites and vanities" (36:507-8).

The apocalyptic images found in chapter 69 raise the question of the meaning and goal of history — a question that fairly haunts this novel. Conventional views of divine providence are juxtaposed with expressions of despair and hopelessness. In the epigraph to chapter 41 (567), Aristotle is quoted: "It is a part of probability that many improbable things will happen." The improbable things that happen in this story — the chance meetings, the coincidences of time and place — are attributed by its author to probability rather than to divine plan. God's providence manifests itself differently — by empowering individuals to make something good of the opportunities that present themselves in life, and by creating a moral universe in which deeds yield inexorable consequences. Deronda tells Gwendolen that "no evil dooms us hopelessly except the evil we love" (57:765). She *can* make efforts to start over, yet her deeds have left her a life without love. The Hebrew liturgy that Daniel heard recited in Frankfurt seeks for nothing special, asks for no divine favors, but rather is "a yearning to escape from the limitations of our own weakness and an invocation of all Good to enter and abide with us." It is "a self-oblivious lifting up of gladness, a *Gloria in excelsis* that such Good exists; both the yearning and the exultation gathering their utmost force from the sense of communion in a form which has expressed them both, for long generations of struggling fellow-men" (32:416). Such a religion is without private consolation and without special divine intervention. It rather simply rejoices that the Good exists and abides with us, sustains us by its steadfast presence in a communion of human beings that spans the generations.

Gambling is a false response to the probabilities and improbabilities of history — a veneration of the goddess of luck in the desire to escape historical necessity or to gain something for oneself at another's expense, a way of finding passion in life, of fighting boredom through amusement (1:36-42, 2:45, 15:193-94, 56:757). "What we call the dulness of things is a disease in ourselves," Daniel tells Gwendolen, who learns from bitter experience that by her marriage to Grandcourt she gambled and lost everything (31:402, 35:464).

The alternative to the roulette table as an image of history in this novel is the image of the pathway. Mordecai tells Daniel that human beings must find their pathways: at first they were visible foot-tracks, now they are swift and invisible, the thoughts and feelings that lead to actions and suffering (40:560, cf. 16:202). Have we found all the pathways yet? Who shall say where they lie? (43:602). The pathway is a recurring image in Hebrew poetry, and the use of it in *Daniel Deronda* is indebted to the *Sefer Yetzirah,* "The Book of Creation," which is the oldest of all Kabbalistic texts. It develops the idea of thirty-two mystical paths of wisdom, which are manifest as the ten numbers and twenty-two letters of the Hebrew alphabet. These are paths that must be found and blazed by each individual. Barbara Hardy suggests that "Mordecai uses the image to express the hidden but secure workings of Providence."[64] In a climactic conversation, Mordecai reminds Daniel that,

> from the first, I have said to you, we know not all the pathways. Has there not been a meeting among them, as of the operations in one soul, where an idea being born and breathing draws the elements towards it, and is fed and grows? For all things are bound together in that Omnipresence which is the place and habitation of the world [Psalm 91:9], and events are as a glass where-through our eyes see some of the pathways (63:818-19).

Daniel himself, he continues, has found a chief pathway by his loving will, which led him to rescue Mirah and to become a brother to Mordecai. Had he not taken this path he would not have discovered his Jewish identity and his life's vocation.

There are, in other words, a great diversity of pathways, all of which are ultimately bound together in the divine Omnipresence, and some of which are reflected in the events of history. It is up to each individual to find the pathway that is appropriate for him- or herself, and this requires a life-long pilgrimage with many false turns and lost ways. God, presumably, does not choose the right pathway for us, but provides a multitude of opportunities and possibilities. Those that are actualized contribute to the nourishment and growth of the divine life.

Do the pathways of history actually converge upon an Omnipresence that is the dwelling place of the whole world? Such at least, claims Mordecai, is the *Shemah* of the people of Israel, the confession of the divine Unity: "Hear, O Israel: The LORD our God is one LORD" (Deuteronomy 6:4).

> This made our religion the fundamental religion for the whole world; for the divine Unity embraced as its consequence the ultimate unity of mankind. . . . Now, in complete unity a part possesses the whole as the whole possesses every part: and in this way human life is tending toward the image of the Supreme Unity (61:802).

Parts that do not possess the whole would be merely fragmented, scattered, continuously in conflict with each other. Something is

---

[64] *Daniel Deronda,* chap. 39, n. 6 (897). On the *Sefer Yetzirah,* see Aryeh Kaplan, *Sefer Yetzirah: The Book of Creation* (York Beach, Maine: Samuel Weiser Inc., 1990), introduction, chap. 1, and appendix 2; and Leonard R. Glotzer, *The Fundamentals of Jewish Mysticism: The Book of Creation and Its Commentaries* (Northvale, New Jersey: Jason Aronson Inc., 1992), introduction and chap. 1.

needed to draw and drive them into communion with each other, but without reducing them to the same — the idea of "separateness with communication" enunciated by Deronda's grandfather (60:792). Thus the premise for a genuine ethical universalism, for the great goal of human unity-in-diversity, seems to be a religious vision of the divine Whole that possesses and preserves every part *as a part* (the nonhuman as well as the human parts).

What can actually be known of the divine unity, that Omnipresence wherein all things dwell? In her notebooks on the Kabbalah, George Eliot emphasized the connection of its doctrines with the negative theology of the Neoplatonists, especially Proclus.[65] The Kabbalah, she said, called God the *En Soph,* the Incomprehensible One, to whom no name can be given and no attributes applied. This is a God beyond all being, thinking, knowing, in the strict sense non-existent, *das Nichts.* This God is *arrētos* and *agnōstos,* the inexpressible and the unknown. George Eliot's own agnosticism is to be understood in this sense: to be agnostic is not to deny God's "existence" — a term that in any event represents a category mistake as applied to divinity — but rather to honor the divine mystery in accord with the great tradition of apophatic theology. Yet this mystery comes forth, becomes kataphatic, manifests itself in the creation of the world by the Sephiroth, the emanations that disperse the divine light into the intellectual, sensuous, and material realms of reality. Each part is a microcosm of the whole and contributes to the whole by reflecting refracted light back upon it. The eye of the novelist is focused upon the parts, tracking their patterns, connections, movements, seeking therein traces of the whole, the mystery beneath the real. This was the central religious insight to which George Eliot was drawn, through her engagement with Judaism, at the end of her fictional career.

---

[65] See George Eliot's *Daniel Deronda Notebooks,* 173-74, 454. Her knowledge of the Kabbalah derived principally from the work of Christian David Ginsburg and Heinrich Hirsch Graetz.

CHAPTER FIVE

MORAL ORDER ON THE AMERICAN FRONTIER: LUTHERAN MISSIONS IN THE 1840s

WALTER H. CONSER, JR.[1]

In 1834 Lyman Beecher published *A Plea for the West*, one of the classic expressions of nineteenth-century American Protestantism's missionary consciousness. Here in his call to meet the religious challenges presented in the trans-Mississippi West, Beecher epitomized that earnestness so typical of the Second Great Awakening. The West was being rapidly populated, Beecher informed his Atlantic seaboard brethren, yet it had a dearth of those spiritual and moral institutions which provided a real foundation for society. The task was to supply clergy and teachers, churches and schools and thereby establish the groundwork for the extension of those other important voluntary associations, the tract and reform societies, which had been so successful in the East. Just as the challenge was great, Beecher rhapsodized, so too was the potential for success. Yet Beecher also reminded his listeners that this opportunity to form a model society in the West faced competition from Roman Catholicism. In his depiction of the struggle between Catholics and Protestants for souls in the West, Beecher not only invoked a familiar missionary argument, but also contributed to the rising nativist sentiment in the early republic.[2]

In his summons to an interdenominational Protestant assault on the forces of spiritual ignorance, one augmented by the agencies of moral reform and the exertions of prayerful Easterners, Beecher represented the mainstream of the missionary efforts of the Second Great Awaken-

---

[1] My first consideration of conservative confessionalism occurred in my dissertation at Brown University for which Wendell Dietrich served as a reader. It is a pleasure to return to the theme again in this volume honoring him.
[2] Lyman Beecher, *A Plea For the West*, 2nd ed. (Cincinnati: Truman & Smith, 1835). On the very night that Beecher delivered this address in Boston, the Roman Catholic convent in Charlestown was sacked. Beecher always maintained that it was a coincidence. See *The Autobiography of Lyman Beecher*, ed. Barbara M. Cross, 2 vols. (Cambridge: Harvard University Press, 1961), 1: 251.

ing. Yet exclusive attention by scholars to the activities of figures such as Beecher neglects important collateral efforts and skews the picture of missionary work in America. Specifically, it overlooks that the West, and America as a whole, was seen as a missionary field by European Protestants, particularly among those traditions, such as the Lutherans, which still maintained strong ties between America and Europe. Beyond that, the very success of the interdenominational organizations and activities, which Beecher so ably typified, raised additional questions for those groups which believed in placing all missionary work within a strict confessional framework.[3]

This Continental missionary concern for America conceived within a confessional standpoint is aptly exemplified in the efforts of the German Lutherans, Wilhelm Löhe and Ludwig Petri. Attention to their views on the proper nature of missions gives us insight into an influential set of debates in nineteenth-century Christianity and illustrates significant similarities in the ecclesiastical situations in Germany and America during the first half of the nineteenth century. Beyond that, in their models for moral order on the American frontier these Germans represented those principles of patriarchalism and conservatism which Ernst Troeltsch identified as classically Lutheran in their orientation and meaning.[4]

Just as the United States between roughly 1790 and 1840 experienced a cultural and religious revival in the form of the Second Great awakening, so too did Germany have its own early nineteenth-century *Erweckungsbewegung*. Detailed discussion is beyond our present purposes, but the core of the German movement's message was clear. As its participant-historian, Gottfried Thomasius, put it, the *Erweckungsbewegung* focused on "the need of mankind for salvation from sin and death, the belief in the free grace of God through Christ and the justification from sin by grace through faith." Upon this basis general regional tendencies developed in which the southwestern and northwestern areas of Germany favored a nonconfessional approach to religion, while the northeastern and Bavarian portions adopted a more strictly confessional orientation.[5]

---

[3] See the studies by Charles C. Cole, Jr., *The Social Ideas of the Northern Evangelists, 1826-1860* (New York: Columbia University Press, 1954); Clifford Griffin, *Their Brothers' Keepers: Moral Stewardship in the United States, 1800-1865* (New Brunswick: Rutgers University Press, 1960); Robert H. Abzug, *American Reform and the Religious Imagination* (New York: Oxford University Press, 1994).

[4] Ernst Troeltsch, *The Social Teachings of the Christian Church*, 2 vols. (New York: Harper & Row, 1960), 1: 573.

[5] Gottfried Thomasius, *Die Wiedererwachen des evangelischen Lebens in der lutherische*

The legacy of this split and of the *Erweckungsbewegung* in general for mission work was significant. For during roughly the first third of the nineteenth century the spirit of a nonconfessional orientation to missions reigned supreme in Germany, only to be superseded during the second half of the century by a starkly confessional perspective. The impulse for the development of missionary organizations during the early nineteenth century in Germany came from two major sources. The first originated with evangelicals in England, such as the London Missionary Society. Not surprisingly, this English influence was strongest on the North Sea coastal area, with results such as the establishment of the "Mustard Seed Society" in East Friesland in 1798. The second source issued from the *Erweckungsbewegung* itself, and could be prominently seen, for example, in the founding of the German Christian Society by Johann Urlsperger in 1780. A general consensus pervaded both of these societies, one which regarded confessional differences as nonessential and thus welcomed as members Lutheran, Reformed, and Unionist believers. Within this nonconfessional perspective contact with specific church traditions was maintained, but its importance was downplayed and the societies themselves attempted to remain independent of control by ecclesiastical administrations. Instead, missionary activity was presented as the concern of regenerated individuals, and its context and point of contact always remained individual to individual. Finally then, missionary agents were qualified through the strength of their personal faith and their sense of inner calling to such work, not through ecclesiastical ordination or rites of any sort. The message of this nonconfessional perspective was salvation from sin through faith in Jesus, never a distinctly confessional interpretation and never an appeal to join a particular tradition. It was on this basis, then, that a network of mission societies was developed with those at Basel (1815), Berlin (1824) and Barmen (1828) the most prominent.[6]

It was in the spirit of this nonconfessional perspective that the Northern German Mission Society was founded in April 1836. Although it was located in a predominantly Lutheran section of Germany, this missionary society took an ecumenical and comprehensive view of its task. "Mission as a work of belief and love," stated Friedrich Mallet, one

---

Kirche Bayerns (Erlangen: Deichert, 1867), 1; Friedrich Kantzenbach, *Die Erweckungsbewegung* (Neuendettelsau: Freimund Verlag, 1957), 146.

[6] See Henry Holze, *Kirche und Mission bei Ludwig Adolf Petri* (Göttingen: Vandenhoeck & Ruprecht, 1966), 14-21; Johannes Aagaard, *Mission, Konfession, Kirche: Die Problematik ihrer Integration im 19. Jahrhundert in Deutschland*, 2 vols. (Lund: C. W. K. Gleerup, 1967), 1: 237-244, 264-279.

of the leaders of the Northern German Society, "takes its standpoint neither in Wittenberg, nor in Geneva, nor in Rome, but rather in Jerusalem . . . with the disciples of the Lord on the Mount of Olives." And with Mallet's words as their motto, the Northern German Missionary Society became a leader in the growing network of nonconfessional missionary associations. Yet this ecumenical perspective provoked opposition, especially among those German Lutherans who, in the wake of the battles over the Prussian Union, the Tercentenary of the Augsburg Confession, and the separation of the "Old-Lutherans," felt that a distinctly confessional standpoint was necessary for proper missionary work. Consequently, in August 1836 the Dresden Missionary Society was formed as an explicitly Lutheran missionary association and in conscious opposition to the Northern German Mission Society.[7]

It is in this context of conflicting interpretations over the correct basis for missionary work symbolized by the opposition of the Northern German and Dresden missionary societies that Ludwig Petri should be located. For in 1841, amidst continuing debate in ecclesiastical and secular periodicals, Petri weighed in on the side of the Dresden society with his book, *Mission and Church*. Ironically, however, Petri arrived at his confessionalist perspective only after an initial attraction to theological rationalism. Petri was born on 16 November 1803 in Lüthhorst, the thirteenth child of a family in which both the father and father-in-law were ministers. Petri followed his father's calling and in 1824 began his study of theology at the University of Göttingen, which at this time was one of the chief centers of rationalism in Germany.[8]

While Petri's early exposure to and interest in rationalism is important, his slow transformation between 1829-1836 into a confessional Lutheran is more significant in the present context. This changeover reflected his involvement with pietist circles in Hannover, and with colleagues such as Claus Harms and August von Arnswaldt, as well as renewed biblical studies which he undertook in performance of his pastoral duties. One of the earliest signs of Petri's break with theological rationalism came in 1832 with the publication of his pamphlet, *The*

---

[7] On the North German Mission Society, see Aagaard, *Mission, Konfession, Kirche* 1: 250-257, quotation of Mallet, 253. For the Dresden Society, see Aagaard, *Mission, Konfession, Kirche* 1: 357-72; Holze, *Kirche und Mission*, 67-71.

[8] After his studies at Göttingen were completed, Petri was called to a church in Hannover. For biographical details on Petri's life, see Holze, *Kirche und Mission*; E. Petri, *D. Ludwig Adolf Petri*, 2 vols. (Hannover: Hahnschen Hofbuchhandlung, 1888-1896); Thomas Jan Kück, *Ludwig Adolf Petri: Kirchenpolitiker und Theologe* (Göttingen: Vandenhoeck & Ruprecht, 1997).

Needs and Wants of the Protestant Church in the Fatherland. Central here was Petri's discussion of the nature of the church and his insistence that the church was not a humanly created, even less a state organization, but rather "a necessary and divinely established holy institution." The implications of Petri's disenchantment with rationalism for his view of missionary work soon became evident. In 1834 he penned a short essay on the nature of missions which still regarded mission work as the province of the individual as that person felt called by God. Two years later in the *Annual Report of the Hannover Mission Association,* however, Petri completely dropped his earlier conception for one which located missionary efforts distinctly within the church. By 1836 Petri had gone a long ways towards establishing a confessional position regarding both mission work and the church.[9]

The culmination of Petri's metamorphosis into confessionalism was signaled in 1841 by his small book, *Mission and Church.* Once again Petri sought to clarify the relationship of mission work to the church by providing a discussion of the nature of the church. Petri proposed four points as the basis of his discussion. First, he argued that Christianity must be mediated through the church, through the spiritual community with Christ and not in a subjective and arbitrary isolation of the individual believer. Second, Petri insisted that the church was organic in nature, growing over time and incorporating the individual into a body which in its totality was greater than the sum of its parts. Third, he reiterated that the church was a divinely established institution and neither the creation of rational ecclesiastics nor well-meaning states-men. Finally, Petri asserted that emphasis upon the invisible church over the visible was erroneous, for the invisible was the kernel of the visible and inseparable from it.[10]

Petri's four premises reflected his indebtedness to wider intellectual currents in Germany during the first half of the nineteenth century and clearly identified him with the developing Neo-Lutheran move-ment. Beyond that, they provided him with a basis upon which to sharpen his attack on the nonconfessional perspective on missions. "Mission work, I now conclude, must have this churchly affiliation and character," Petri wrote, "it must proceed from the church and contain

---

[9] Petri, *Die Bedürfnisse und Wünsche der protestantischen Kirche im Vaterlande* (Hanno-ver: Hahnsche Hofbuchhandlung, 1832), 13; Petri, *Zur Verständigung über des Mission-wesens* (Hanover: Hahnsche Hofbuchhandlung, 1834); Petri, *Zweiter Jahresbericht des Hannoverschen Missionsvereins* (Hannover: Hahnsche Hofbuchhandlung, 1836).

[10] Petri, *Die Mission und die Kirche* (Hannover: Hahnsche Hofbuchhandlung, 1841), 16-22.

itself within the church. It must be nothing other than the church itself in its mission activity." Such a view amounted to a flat repudiation of missionary societies conceived of as voluntary associations outside of and separate from a confessional tradition. For Petri argued that it was the responsibility of the tradition to superintend and control all missionary activities and that no missionaries should adapt liturgies or offices to fit circumstances. The church needed a missionary component just as missionary work needed an ecclesiastical foundation. Here then, in his call for "eine missionirende Kirche," Petri provided a theological grounding for the confessionalist position on missions.[11]

Petri closed out his essay with a parting shot at the Northern German Mission Society. Noting that this group claimed to be free of any specific confessional orientation, Petri countered that their ordination procedures and sacramental beliefs were simply a conflation of available interpretations. "This is clearly not Wittenberg, Geneva, or Rome," he stated, "but likewise it certainly is not Jerusalem and the Mount of Olives. It is, to speak truthfully, absolutely nothing." Just as missionary work must adopt a self-conscious ecclesiological perspective, Petri argued, so too was it best to avoid any mixed efforts by Reformed and Lutheran believers but rather to allow each to carry out their own independent work. As Petri phrased it, the differences between the Reformed and Lutheran faiths were not simply "formal" but rather "real" ones. Again, unionism in ecclesiastical or missionary affairs was inappropriate and potentially quite harmful.[12]

In *Mission and Church*, Petri had provided a thorough rationale for confessionally-based missionary work. It would not be long before he would have the opportunity to apply his views in the missionary field of North America. This possibility appeared in the person of Friedrich Wyneken. Born in 1810 and educated at the University of Halle under August Tholuck, Wyneken pledged himself to missionary work and left for America in 1838. In October 1841, after ministering to German immigrants in Indiana and Ohio, Wyneken returned to Germany in the hopes of obtaining financial and moral support for the American missionary cause. Previously, Wyneken had written several appeals to German missionary societies, such as the Evangelical Association for

---

[11] Petri, ibid., 27-28. For a discussion of the Neo-Lutheran movement, see Holstein Fagerberg, *Bekenntnis, Kirche, und Amt in der deutschen konfessionellen Theologie des 19. Jahrhunderts* (Uppsala: Almquist, 1952) and Walter H. Conser, Jr., *Church and Confession: Conservative Theologians in Germany, England, and America, 1815-1866* (Macon: Mercer University Press, 1984), 55-96

[12] Petri, *Mission und Kirche*, 40, 45.

German Protestants in North America in Bremen, calling on them for aid, but these had met with little success. Ironically, when Wyneken left for America, he sympathized with the nonconfessional perspective on missions. His experience in America, particularly as a witness to the camp meetings, had transformed him into an advocate of strict confessionalism, and upon his return to Germany he sought out the leaders of the confessional movement.[13]

In May 1842 Wyneken wrote a long letter to Petri and requested his assistance. The message of Wyneken's letter was that thousands of German immigrants were arriving in America each year and moving westward. There, in the "expansive wilderness of the American West," they existed in spiritual isolation, cut off from their European roots and lacking proper Lutheran schools, churches, teachers, and preachers. This religious void was not going unnoticed in America, for Methodist circuit-riders as well as Roman Catholic missionaries were increasing their efforts and winning impressive numbers of converts. Citing the extravagance of the camp meetings, the growth of "fanaticism," and the "anti-Christian spirit of individualism," Wyneken painted a grim picture of the situation in America. He repeated the message from earlier appeals, that only help from Lutherans in Germany could save their American counterparts from certain spiritual collapse and the disappearance of the church as these confessionalists understood it.[14]

Petri was impressed by Wyneken's appeal. He distributed it to other church leaders in Germany, and two of these, Edward Huschke and Adolf von Harless, wrote back with pledges of assistance. Harless also sent a copy to his Bavarian colleague, Wilhelm Löhe. Löhe replied to Harless commending the project and underscoring the need for correct confessional Lutheranism among missionaries sent to America. Beyond that, Löhe felt that gifts of books to seminaries would be appropriate. Where Huschke suggested sending university-trained individuals under the jurisdiction of a central organization, Löhe favored the creation of a decentralized organization which could send men with less formal education. The benefit to be gained, in Löhe's view, was one of flexibility and speed in meeting the distressful situation in America.[15]

Recent historical scholarship confirms the size of German migration to America during the nineteenth century. While perhaps as many as

---

[13] For biographical information on Wyneken, see the article on him in *Allgemeine Deutsche Biographie*, 56 vols. (Leipzig: Dunckes & Humblot, 1876-1912), 44: 400-403.
[14] A partial text of the letter is given in Petri, *Ludwig Petri*, 1: 273-279.
[15] See the discussion in Petri, ibid., 1: 283-291.

100,000 persons left from Germany for North America from the seventeenth century through 1815 and the Congress of Vienna, some 5.5 million individuals made the same trip during the next hundred years. Deteriorating economic conditions and political unrest in Germany together with positive reports from America all attracted would-be immigrants. Likewise, improved transportation systems and easier arrangements for actually financing such trips made it easier by the decades of the 1830s and 1840s to emigrate than it had been earlier.[16]

The appeal by Wyneken in 1841-1842 had found an audience, and the relationship between Petri and Löhe continued to develop through the 1840s from these indirect beginnings. The backgrounds of Löhe and Petri, however, were different. Wilhelm Löhe was born in 1808 at Fürth near Nürnberg. After his studies at Erlangen, Löhe held several temporary posts until 1837, when he accepted a pastorate in the village of Neuendettelsau. Although he remained there until his death in 1872, Löhe supported a score of missionary and charitable activities both within and outside Germany during his lifetime.[17]

During the 1840s, however, his consuming passion was the plight of Germans in North America. Löhe was aware of both Wyneken and Petri prior to his contact with them in 1842. In 1840 the missionary association at Stade had reprinted a portion of one of Wyneken's pleas for help in a pamphlet entitled, *The Need of German Lutherans in North America.* Löhe read this in December 1840 and produced two short pieces of his own. The first, entitled "The Lutheran Emigrants in North America," was published in January 1841. Here Löhe sounded Wyneken's challenge in his depiction of diasporic Germans wandering in the "wilderness of North America," and falling prey to the "servants of the Pope and admirers of sects." In the second article, published in August 1841, Löhe drew attention to the recent publication of Petri's *Mission and the Church* and recommended it highly. In so doing, Löhe underscored his agreement with Petri's perspective, first by insisting himself on the importance of mission activity and, second, by placing all missionary activity directly in the center of the church rather than under the supervision of a voluntary religious association. Just as Petri had done,

---

[16] See Mack Walker, *Germany and the Emigration, 1816-1885* (Cambridge: Harvard University Press, 1964); Günter Moltmann, "The Pattern of German Emigration to the United States in the Nineteenth Century," in Frank Trommler and Joseph McVeigh, eds., *America and the Germans: An Assessment of a Three-Hundred Year History,* 2 vols. (Philadelphia: University of Pennsylvania Press, 1985), 1: 14, 16, 21.

[17] For biographical information on Wilhelm Löhe, see J. Deinzer, *Wilhelm Löhes Leben,* 3 vols. (Gütersloh: C. Bertelsmann, 1880-1901).

Löhe charged all members of the church with responsibility for and participation in missionary work. In this way, Löhe highlighted several common themes which he shared with Petri and marked the beginning of what was to become a fruitful collaborative effort between them during the rest of the decade.[18]

The ties between Hannover and Neuendettelsau continued to grow when in July 1842 two men, Adam Ernst and Georg Burger, responded to Löhe's call for missionary candidates and became the first of several men sent by Löhe to America as "emergency helpers" (*Nothelferen*). The background of these two men was humble; Ernst was a cobbler and Burger a weaver, and their preparation was simple. Under Löhe's direction they studied English grammar, the Bible, and the major Lutheran confessions, along with a smattering of world geography and church history. In addition they received instruction in pastoral counseling and homiletical duties. Although Lutheran clerics traditionally received extensive schooling and were thoroughly grounded in theological, linguistic, and historical studies, Löhe argued, as he had earlier in his response to Harless and Wyneken, that abbreviated training was justified by the circumstances of the present crisis in America. Consequently, after their preparatory work was completed, the men received Löhe's formal blessing and were sent to Petri for specific information on emigration. They left Bremen in August and landed in New York City on 26 September.[19]

As the basis of this German missionary endeavor to America became more solidly established, three developments took place. First, a concentrated effort was made by Löhe to obtain further information about the situation in America and to publicize it in Germany. As he wrote to Adam Ernst,

> America is becoming much closer and better known to us. In part through your efforts and in part through other means — a large assortment of American journals (both in German and English) . . . as well as American calendars, ministerial pronouncements, synodical protocols, writings, by [Samuel] Schmucker, etc.

With all these materials at his disposal, Löhe began publication of the journal, *Kirchliche Mittheilungen aus und über Nordamerika*, in March 1843. Through this vehicle, Löhe hoped to disseminate the factual reports and circular letters which he received regarding American missions, as

---

[18] Löhe, "Die lutherische Auswanderer in Nordamerika," in Wilhelm Löhe, *Gesammelte Werke*, ed. Klaus Ganzert, 7 vols. (Neuendettelsau: Freimund Verlag, 1951-) 4: 16-19, quotation on p. 18; Löhe, "Die Mission und die Kirche," *Werke*, 3: 4-11.
[19] See Deinzer, *Löhes Leben*, 3: 4-11.

well as to continue to appeal for men, money, and materials which could be sent to America.[20]

The second development which occurred was a clearer division of labor between Löhe and Petri. It had been Petri who in 1841 had first issued the programmatic manifesto for confessionally-based missionary work with his pamphlet, *Mission and Church*. By 1843, with this work underway, Petri was willing to pull back from the limelight and allow Löhe to take over the daily administration and supervision of the missionary efforts. In July 1843 Petri congratulated the Bavarians on the commencement of the *Kirchliche Mittheilungen* and observed that it had fallen to them to lead the work in American missions. Yet if Petri adopted a less prominent role in missionary activities, he still retained an active interest in them. Raising money for the American missionary cause, donating theological books for the fledgling Lutheran seminaries in America, or producing candidates and providing a regular stopover for missionaries leaving for or returning from America — in all these ways Petri collaborated with Löhe and supported the development of confessionally-oriented mission work within the Lutheran church. But it was Wilhelm Löhe, as Petri declared in 1849, who became the "center for all those who desired a firm and pure Lutheran standpoint for America." And it is true that through his close ties with other confessionalists throughout Germany and his gradual assumption of administrative duties, Löhe made his parish at Neuendettelsau an important headquarters for the missionary movement.[21]

The third development to occur between 1842 and 1844 built on these first two and amounted to an expansion by Löhe of the scope of his missionary activities in America. Soon after Adam Ernst and Georg Burger arrived in New York in 1842, they journeyed to Ohio to begin their missionary work there among fellow Germans. As reports of their work and that of others of Löhe's *Nothelferen* reached Bavaria, Wilhelm Löhe began to reconsider the missionary needs of America. The conceptual basis upon which he and Petri had begun their work remained the same — mission work was an integral part of the church's ethical responsibility in the world; the church was a divine institution, an

[20] Löhe to Adam Ernst, 28 October 1843, Wilhelm Löhe Papers (Löhe Archiv, Neuendettelsau, Bavaria, Federal Republic of Germany). For Löhe's hopes regarding American missions, see Deinzer, *Löhes Leben*, 3: 15; Löhe to J. F. Wucherer, 13 March 1843, Löhe Papers.
[21] Petri to J. F. Wucherer, 19 July 1843, quoted by Deinzer, *Löhes Leben*, 3: 17. For an assessment of Petri's continuing interest and work, see Petri, *Ludwig Petri*, 1: 299-300.

Anstalt, and all missionary work should be centered in it rather than in a voluntary association; and, finally, that the missionaries should hold fast to orthodox Lutheranism and avoid any alliances with Reformed, sectarian, or Roman Catholic Christians. Löhe's reformulation was to enlarge missionary work in America from exclusive concern with fellow Germans to include non-Germans as well. "Domestic (*innere*) mission work leads us to foreign (*aussere*) mission activity," Löhe noted, and such an observation had two important ramifications for confessional missionaries. First, where American missionary boards defined foreign and domestic missions in geographical terms, (i. e., domestic missions as within North America, foreign missions outside it), the German use of *aussere* and *innere* tended to represent an ethnic definition. Consequently, Löhe's initial concern with German immigrants in America fell easily within the traditional understanding of *innere Mission*, while his new interest signified a change of focus.[22]

The second implication concerned the nature of the training which missionary candidates received. Where Löhe's earlier justification for shortened instruction reflected the immediacy of the need and the availability of men who could be pressed into service, Löhe now began to explore the possibility of establishing a seminary in America where additional education could be provided for the candidates. This interest grew in importance during the rest of the decade, for Löhe and his missionaries always tried to cooperate with existing Lutheran synods in America when it was possible without a compromise, in their view, of confessional principles. In this connection the establishment of a seminary remained an attractive and important consideration, though one fraught with conflict.[23]

By 1844, then, Löhe had developed a missionary agenda for America. While initially oriented towards settling German immigrants in the United States, it also eventually included a mission to American Indians, and thereby exemplified Löhe's understanding of the reciprocity between *innere* and *aussere* mission, still conceived within a confessional framework. Beyond this programmatic level, Löhe's plans, even more importantly, epitomized his understanding of the moral challenges presented in the physical, social, and religious circumstances of the American frontier, and his vision of the appropriate remedies to meet those challenges. For Löhe conceived of these immigrant settlements in ways reminiscent of John Winthrop's ideal for the New England

---

[22] See the discussion by Löhe, *Werke*, 4: 625.
[23] See the statement, quoted by Petri, *Ludwig Petri*, 1: 296.

Puritans. These nineteenth-century voyagers, Löhe proclaimed, were to be knit together by the bonds of allegiance to the Lutheran confessional tradition and to German language and culture and reinforced by the success of their missionary enterprises.

In 1845 German settlers, sent by Löhe and under the direction of August Craemer, established the missionary outpost of Frankenmuth. The settlement was near Saginaw City, Michigan, which was a trading center for fur trappers, farmers, and local Indians as well. From the outset, Löhe envisioned Frankenmuth as "a holy gathering place for Christians and heathens." For it was to be both a model German Lutheran community and a base for missionary activity among the local Native Americans. August Craemer was an interesting choice to lead the group. Born in 1812 in Bavaria, he studied theology and philology. For a time he served as a tutor in England and later was professor of German language and literature at Oxford University. At Oxford he had come across the appeal by Friedrich Wyneken concerning North America, and it had convinced him to dedicate his energies to working with Löhe in establishing mission colonies in North America.[24]

The intentionality and purposefulness of the Frankenmuth group was evident in their subscription to a *Kirchenordnung* devised by Löhe. In addition to organizing church affairs in the community under the direction of the pastor, it stipulated that all settlers in the community had to accept the Lutheran confessions and, furthermore, that only the German language could be used in community affairs. No marriages between Lutherans and non-Lutherans were allowed, all children were to be educated in and for the Lutheran church, and adultery was the only permissible grounds for divorce. Anyone who dissented from these regulations or who could no longer subscribe to the confessions of the Lutheran church should withdraw from the community.[25]

Interest in a possible mission field among "the North American heathen" appears in Löhe's correspondence in 1843. However, it was not until 1844 that the project finally got underway. Georg Hattstädt was sent to America as a *Nothelfer* in June 1844, and upon his arrival was assigned to a congregation in Michigan. On the basis of Hattstädt's reports and additional information from Friedrich Schmidt, president of

---

[24] See the discussion in Homer R. Greenholt, "A Study of Wilhelm Loehe, his colonies, and the Lutheran Indian missions in the Saginaw valley of Michigan," (Ph. D. diss., University of Chicago, 1937), 68, 117, 257; and James L. Schaaf, "Wilhelm Löhe's Relation to the American Church" (Heidelberg: published by the author, 1961), 67-69.

[25] See Greenholt, "A Study of Wilhelm Loehe," 216-218.

the Michigan Synod, Löhe began organizing an Indian mission. By November 1844, as Löhe informed Petri, a sizable number of candidates for the Indian program were ready to embark for America.[26]

In the following year in any essay entitled, "The Mission to the Heathen in North America," Löhe summarized the accomplishments of these new missionaries and put forward his rationale for Indian missions in America. Löhe's argumentation was a blend of classic appeals to save "the lost son of the wilderness" combined with a cost-benefit analysis, which contended that the expenses were only a third as much to send and maintain a missionary in North America as they were for one in East Asia. Within this framework Löhe alluded to what he considered the depravity of Indian habits, but argued that this was offset by the many evidences of their deeply felt religiosity. He was convinced that the American Indian had innate religious sentiments, and like scores of previous missionary apologists, Löhe saw the task as one of directing this religiosity into the proper channels. Finally, while certain obstacles such as language problems, competition with other Christian missionaries, and the migratory habits of Indians were real, Löhe suggested that the Indians' proximity to existing Christian settlements, such as Frankenmuth, as well as the ongoing work of the Michigan Synod, promised excellent results for any one courageous enough to take up the challenge.[27]

Löhe's hopes were put into practice at Frankenmuth by Pastor Craemer as he struggled to learn the local Chippewa Indian language and to establish schools for the Chippewa children and the children of the German immigrants. The immigrants' school taught all its lessons in German, while that for the Chippewas conducted lessons in spelling, reading, and writing in German and religious instruction in English with the aid of a translator. As all religious materials were in German, they needed to be translated first into English and then into the local native language. The use of English, especially for instruction in religion, deeply disappointed Löhe. However, Craemer insisted that the exigencies of the situation prevailed over the commitment to the use of German. Once the Indian students became proficient in their use of the German language, then substitution of German religious materials could take place.[28]

---

[26] Löhe to A. G. Rudelbach, 1 September 1843; Löhe to Ludwig Petri, 5 November 1844; Löhe to Ludwig Petri, 23 January 1845, Löhe Papers.

[27] Löhe, "Die Heidenmission in Nordamerika," *Werke*, 4: 102-112.

[28] See Löhe to Ludwig Petri, 5 November 1844; Löhe to Ludwig Petri, 23 January 1845, Löhe Papers; Greenholt, "A Study of Wilhelm Loehe," 176, 168.

If its German origins made it somewhat unusual as a mission to American Indians, Frankenmuth's subsequent history demonstrated its accommodation to the American scene. In 1849, with the knowledge of Löhe, administration of the Indian mission at Frankenmuth was transferred from the Michigan Synod to the Missouri Synod. While this decision was defended as a reaffirmation of confessional standards, it effectively removed power from Löhe's missionaries at the mission station and gave it to church officials in St. Louis. Thus by 1850 when he left to take a seminary position, August Craemer could take pride in having baptized some thirty Indians and in the establishment of a school for Indian children. However, the school was not as successful as Craemer had wished, and he admitted that resentment over Teutonic discipline by the Indians, interference by white traders, competition from a nearby Methodist school for Indian children, and, finally, the removal of the Chippewas by the Federal government to land twenty-five miles away in order that the Indians could take up their lands in severalty all prevented the accomplishment of his and Löhe's educational plans.[29]

Three further settlements for German Lutherans were established under Löhe's direction in areas near Frankenmuth. None of these three initiated missionary programs for Indians. However, all were bound together by their dedication to Lutheran confessionalism and the hope that the examples of their lives and the moral order of their community would serve missionary purposes on the American frontier. In 1847 the colony of Frankentrost was established with Johann Heinrich Gräbner as its leader. Modeled on a German village with compact houses in neat rows, rather than spread across the countryside, Frankentrost had thirty families living there. All of these families had subscribed to a *Kirchenordnung* similar to that of Frankenmuth and were equally dedicated to upholding the confessional standards so dear to Löhe.[30]

The next missionary colony, Frankenlust, began in 1848 under the leadership of the Hannoverian clergyman Georg Ferdinand Sievers. While this settlement, which grew from seventeen individuals to thirty families by 1850, reflected the same attachment to Lutheran principles, Löhe tried to finance it by using a revolving credit plan. With initial capitalization from local German banks, Löhe hoped to purchase large sections of land which in turn would be sold to emigrating Lutheran settlers. The money from these sales would be reinvested in the fund and then later drawn on to purchase another section of land. The plan

---

[29] See Greenholt, "A Study of Wilhelm Loehe," 257; Deinzer, *Löhes Leben*, 3: 55-56.
[30] See Greenholt, "A Study of Wilhelm Löhe," 124-125, 130.

was used in the establishment of Frankenlust. However, the political turbulence in Germany in 1848 made such a distant venture appear increasingly risky to the fund's underwriters and they withdrew their support.[31]

In the third settlement, Frankenhilf, Löhe responded to the revolutionary events of 1848 in Germany with a plan for settling indigent Germans in the New World. As early as 1843, Löhe had envisioned "a small colony of workers, (masons, carpenters, etc.), gathered together under the leadership of a minister and teacher." In this idyllic setting, Löhe conceived of the settlement purchasing a piece of land and building a church, earning its bread, and living a life of Christian cooperative harmony. This was essentially the ideal which informed the Frankenmuth model. However, by 1848, amidst news of the revolutionary developments in Paris, Berlin, and Vienna, Löhe felt that these political events had added even greater urgency. "In these times," Löhe wrote, "America appears as an asylum, as a peaceful brook of Siloam. I cannot get rid of the idea that an emigration of poor persons at government expense would be an inexpensive remedy against proletarianization and pauperism."[32]

The proposal that the government bear the cost of such emigration did not meet with approval. Neither were many poor Germans nor politicized '48ers attracted to Löhe's brand of Lutheran confessionalism. Finally, while Löhe, like many others, saw in the availability of land in America an answer to the social questions of their mid-nineteenth century society, his fundamentally conservative outlook and the religious and cooperative program of his colonies contrasted sharply with the often individualistic assumptions and practices which characterized much of the settlement process in frontier America.

In addition to settling immigrants, another development in the mid-1840s which bore the mark of Löhe's influence was the establishment of a seminary. As the decade had progressed, Löhe's hopes for better prepared missionaries had increased and then crystallized in plans for the establishment of a Lutheran seminary in America which could maintain confessional standards and represent what he considered a proper German influence. At one level, the establishment of such a seminary

---

[31] See Löhe, "Etwas über die deutsche-lutherische Niederlassungen in der Graffschaft Saginaw, Staat Michigan," *Werke*, 4: 165-170; Greenholt, "A Study of Wilhelm Loehe," 131, 140.

[32] Löhe to K. von Raumer, 21 February 1843; Löhe to U. von Maltzan, 22 March 1848, Löhe Papers.

was a simple matter, for as the numbers of individuals going as missionaries to America grew, the need became clear for a formal institution which could receive these persons, orient them to the specifics of the American situation, and provide any additional remedial instruction which might be necessary. Yet Löhe knew that the ecclesiastical situation in America was a complex one and that there would be disagreements over the proper directions for the seminary to take. "In North America, there are several parties which lay claim to the name of the Lutheran Church," Löhe wrote to Adam Ernst. Here Löhe specified the two groups of recent northern German immigrants led by C. F. W. Walther and J. Grabau. These men were committed to maintaining confessional standards and were headquartered in St. Louis and Buffalo. The other major party, located at Gettysburg under the direction of Samuel Schmucker, was willing to accommodate to the American religious scene, even to the point of revising creeds and supporting "new measures" revivalism.[33]

In a pastoral letter which he wrote to Lutherans in America in 1845 and sent by way of his missionaries, Löhe focused directly on the need for adherence to high confessional standards. He warned against the adoption of new measures revivalism and recommended traditional methods of instruction. He also reiterated that only the German language be used in churches. This issue became more acute in 1845 when the Ohio Synod, reversing a previous decision, adopted English as the official language of all its synodical business. When he heard of the decision, Löhe abandoned plans for locating a seminary under the Ohio synodical auspices, and reaffirmed the importance of the German language. Writing to Johann Höfling in the spring of 1846, Löhe pointedly asserted,

> One can learn the Lutheran faith only from German institutions. German seminaries are thoroughly necessary unless through a progressive Anglicization, Germans are to receive the Lutheran church in the English tongue. There never has been an English translation of the Symbolical Books — it is the calling of the German seminaries to preserve the Lutheran church in spite of the Yankees.[34]

---

[33] See Löhe to Adam Ernst, 3 February 1845, Löhe Papers and Löhe's retrospective discussion of the need for a seminary in "Rechenschaftbericht," Werke, 4: 132-137.

[34] Löhe, "Zuruf aus der Heimat an die deutsche-lutherische Kirche Nordamerikas," Werke, 4: 68-85; Löhe to Johann Höfling, 18 March 1846, Löhe Papers. On the broader question of the connection of ethnic and linguistic identity, see Marion Huffines, "Language Maintenance Efforts Among German Immigrants and their Descendants in the United States," in Trommler and McVeigh, eds., America and the Germans, 1: 241-250.

Though Löhe's concern for ethnic and linguistic identity would be more ambiguously resolved, his theological issues were answered in 1846 with the establishment of a seminary at Fort Wayne, Indiana. This institution, directed by Wilhelm Sihler, one of Löhe's most promising and best-trained missionaries, became a center for German-educated students to conclude their studies for a ministry in America. The seminary soon became affiliated with the Missouri Synod, to which Löhe had also given active support in its initial stages, and thus together with the seminary at St. Louis, the Fort Wayne institution became a standard bearer for confessionalism within American Lutheranism.[35]

By the late 1840s, confessional Lutheranism's missionary enterprises were entering a new phase of consolidation and increasing independence from German control. Emblematic of this new stage was the formation in Neuendettelsau of the Society for Domestic Lutheran Missions in 1849. With the establishment of this group Löhe was freed from supervision of American missionary projects. Relieved of this responsibility, Löhe turned his personal attention increasingly to charitable and mission activities in Bavaria. Similarly, on the other side of the Atlantic, several events indicated a growing sense of autonomy. Sievers, for example, sold some of the land belonging to the Frankenlust colony in 1849 without Löhe's knowledge. Not long after that, the issue of synodical affiliation came to a head. Although they had affiliated with the Missouri Synod in 1846, within five years Löhe's men had withdrawn to inaugurate the Iowa Synod. Interestingly, this doctrinal strife with the Missouri Synod over a number of issues, but principally that of congregational autonomy, figured significantly in Löhe's contribution to the Neo-Lutheran movement in Germany during the 1850s. In these circumstances, then, the confessional battles in America exerted their own small degree of influence on the German religious scene.[36]

By the early 1850s Löhe's model societies of Lutheran confessionalism and moral order had begun a discernible process of transformation. Loss of élan over time is a perennial challenge in such intentional communities. Similarly, the problem of maintaining harmony and peace emerged as some settlers who had not subscribed to Löhe's *Kirchenordnung* and other settlers who did not share the same cultural assumptions of Löhe's groups moved into the area. Finally, changes in

---

[35] On Wilhelm Sihler and the establishment of the seminary at Fort Wayne, see Lewis W. Spitz, *Life in Two Worlds: A Biography of William Sihler* (St. Louis: Concordia Publishing House, 1968).

[36] See Löhe to L. Focke, 12 October 1849, Löhe Papers; Deinzer, *Löhes Leben*, 3: 31; Schaaf, "Löhe's Relation to the American Church," 76.

personnel, as in the transfer of August Craemer, signaled opportunities for those who wished to promote such revisions as English language usage or greater flexibility in confessional interpretation. Changes were underway, and though some settlements continued through the 1850s, their style and spirit were markedly different from their beginnings a decade earlier.[37]

Ernst Troeltsch once wrote that purity of worship, proper congregational organization, and the application of Christian ideals to daily life were characteristic of the missionary literature of the early Christian church. In their own ways, the missionary enterprises of Wilhelm Löhe shared these same concerns as they sought to impose moral order on the sprawling social and physical geography of the American frontier. For in this endeavor, though in ways more reflective of a social concern than Troeltsch found in the early Christian missionary impulses, the settlers bound themselves under the vision of Löhe's *Kirchenordnung*. Emphasizing religious discipline, hierarchical authority, and collective purpose, Löhe's settlements sought cohesion and continuity within a reaffirmation of tradition. In the end, despite their inability to fulfill completely Löhe's commission and dreams for them, Frankenmuth and the other colonies would be remembered for their confessional stance, their German-language mission to the Chippewas, but above all, for their experiment in building a model of German Zion in the wilderness of the American frontier.[38]

---

[37] See Greenholt, "A Study of Wilhelm Loehe," 219.
[38] Troeltsch, *Social Teachings*, 1: 39-40; Löhe to Ludwig Petri, 7 May 1851, Löhe Papers.

CHAPTER SIX

TESTING LIBERALISM'S CONCEPTUALITY: THE RELATION OF SIN AND EVIL IN SCHLEIERMACHER'S THEOLOGY

WALTER E. WYMAN, JR.

In his brief characterization of "the splendid failure that was liberal theology," Schubert Ogden asserts:

> In seeking a formulation of the Christian faith which would respect all that was valid in modern man's understanding of himself and his world, [the liberals] too often proceeded uncritically and thus failed also to respect the distinctive claims of the faith itself. In many instances, to be sure, the trouble lay in their perforce having to make use of conceptualities that obscured their real intentions. Recall, for example, Schleiermacher's definition of religion in terms of "feeling" (*Gefühl*). . . .[1]

Whether liberal theology was a failure, splendid or otherwise, is too large a question to be decided here. But Ogden's judgment does suggest a somewhat more modest preliminary question: did Schleiermacher, as the "father of liberal theology," employ an inadequate conceptuality in his revisionist formulation of the Christian faith?

Ogden's reference to "feeling" draws our attention to the "feeling of absolute dependence," the central concept in terms of which Schleiermacher's dogmatic theology is articulated. I do not propose, however, to investigate the question of the adequacy of Schleiermacher's conceptuality by remaining in the forecourt of the gentiles and exploring yet one more time the "propositions borrowed from ethics" in the Introduction to *The Christian Faith*. To be sure, some aspects of those propositions will have to be touched on. But the focal point of my discussion will be Schleiermacher's doctrine of sin. To focus on sin is to enter into the substance of Schleiermacher's dogmatics, for he analyzes the Christian consciousness (in Part Two of *The Christian Faith*) into the consciousness of sin and that of grace. A close examination of Schleiermacher's

---

[1] Schubert M. Ogden, *The Reality of God and Other Essays* (New York: Harper and Row, 1966), 4.

concept of sin displays Schleiermacher's conceptuality as it does actual dogmatic work, and thus should expose both its theological possibilities and limits. (It goes without saying that Schleiermacher's exposition of the consciousness of grace, or some aspect of it, could equally well have been chosen to test his conceptuality.) Schleiermacher understands sin in terms of an inhibition (*Hemmung*) of the God-consciousness (that is, of the feeling of absolute dependence). Does that conceptuality fall under Ogden's strictures as an inadequate conceptuality that obscures his own intentions and fails "to respect the distinctive claims of the faith itself"?

As the title of my essay indicates, I will further focus the investigation by examining not only Schleiermacher's concept of sin, but the relation of sin and evil in his thought. The "doctrine of evil" appears in Schleiermacher's *Glaubenslehre* under the doctrine of sin, in the section on "the constitution of the world in relation to sin," and thus is relevant to questions about the adequacy of the conceptuality used to unfold the Christian consciousness of sin. Writing of natural evil (*Übel*), Schleiermacher states: "Man, were he without sin, would not feel what are merely hindrances of sensuous functions as evils (*Übel*); the very fact that he does so feel them is due to sin."[2] One's initial reaction may well be to find something unsatisfactory about this statement. To see evil as a "mere hindrance of the sensuous functions" may appear to be dry and devoid of empathy for the excruciating experience of evil. Moreover, it may imply a dualism of the physical and spiritual which has become problematic in our day. Finally, this assertion appears to be a subjectivistic reduction of the reality of evil: evil seems here to be merely the consciousness of evil; if only one is sufficiently pious, one would not experience evil. One might well be tempted to react: this doesn't seem right; surely something has gone wrong with the conceptual framework. But has it? A just assessment requires an answer to a prior question: has Schleiermacher's meaning been correctly grasped?

1

Schleiermacher uses a number of different concepts, some more technical (deriving from his philosophical analysis of self-consciousness)

---

[2] Friedrich Schleiermacher, *The Christian Faith*, translation edited by H. R. Mackintosh and J. S. Stewart (Edinburgh: T. & T. Clark, 1928); *Der christliche Glaube*, 7th edition, ed. by Martin Redeker (Berlin: Walter de Gruyter, 1960), §76.2. Unless noted otherwise, I have followed the Mackintosh and Stewart translation. Further references to this text will be given in the body of the text, and (in cases of ambiguity) will be designated Chr. Gl.

and some more biblical (deriving from Paul's letters), in order to expound the consciousness of sin. Already in the Introduction to *The Christian Faith*, in his definition of the essence of Christianity, Schleiermacher presents a technical definition of sin (without actually using the word). In order to define Christianity as a religion of redemption, he needs to show that it is redemption from an "evil condition" (*schlechten Zustand*). That condition is "an obstruction or arrest of the vitality of the higher self-consciousness, so that there comes to be little or no union of it with the various determinations of the sensible self-consciousness. . ." (§11.2). In non-technical language, this is the state of "God-forgetfulness"; it is "an absence of facility for introducing the God-consciousness into the course of our actual lives and retaining it there" (§11.2).

Schleiermacher's technical language derives from the analysis of human consciousness developed in the "propositions borrowed from ethics." Human sensible (*sinnlich*) life consists of, on the one hand, the perceptions (*Wahrnehmungen*) or intuitions (*Anschauungen*) that constitute objective consciousness, and, on the other hand, of "all determinations of self-consciousness which develop from our relations to nature and man" (including "social" and "moral" feelings) that constitute the sensible self-consciousness (§5.1). The higher self-consciousness or God-consciousness is, by contrast, an immediate, pre-reflective consciousness prior to all thinking or doing: "the consciousness that the whole of our spontaneous activity comes from a source outside us" (§4.3). The higher self-consciousness is in itself an abstraction from a moment of consciousness; it can only appear in conjunction with the sensible self-consciousness (see §5, §§32-33). In Schleiermacher's distinctive technical terminology, the condition of the possibility of sin is the constitution of the human self as consisting of sensible self-consciousness and higher self-consciousness or God-consciousness: the two enter into a relation in order to constitute a moment of consciousness, but the sensible self-consciousness is capable of outweighing or obstructing the God-consciousness. Piety or blessedness (*Seligkeit*) is the relative strength of the God-consciousness with respect to the sensible self-consciousness; the consciousness of sin is the reverse — the sensible self- consciousness is the more powerful, and thus dominates the moment of consciousness.

This technical conceptuality is presupposed in the initial description of sin in Part Two of the *Glaubenslehre*: "We have the consciousness of sin whenever the God-consciousness which forms part of an inner state, or is in some way added to it, determines our self-consciousness as pain; and therefore we conceive of sin as a positive antagonism of the flesh against the spirit" (§66). Given the method of the *Glaubenslehre* as a theology of consciousness (*Bewußtseinstheologie*), the theologian's task is to describe the consciousness of sin. But the consciousness of sin is itself an abstraction from the Christian consciousness, which is always already a consciousness of redemption. This situation explains the wording of §66: the consciousness of sin is the Christian's consciousness of the inadequacy of his or her God-consciousness in any given moment, which is experienced as a "painful" self-consciousness.

It is important to note the ease with which Schleiermacher shifts in §66 from his characteristic technical philosophical conceptuality to biblical language: the "antagonism of the flesh against the spirit." He regards the two forms of expression as equivalent. The sensible self-consciousness is the equivalent of "flesh," and the higher self-consciousness or God-consciousness is the equivalent of "spirit." Interestingly, *Die christliche Sitte* is dominated by the non-technical language of flesh/spirit rather than the technical terminology of the *Glaubenslehre*. For example, two of the three forms of Christian activity are deduced from the opposition of flesh and spirit. "In the consciousness of the Christian there is always something opposed, a remainder of the independence of the lower life-potency, the lusts (*Gelüst*) of the flesh against the spirit, and the inhibition (*Hemmung*) which proceeds from this is felt as pain."[3] The experience of pain gives rise to purifying or restorative action (*reinigendes, wiederherstellendes Handeln*) which aims at restoring the spirit's dominion over flesh "as its organism."[4] On the other hand, pleasure "is posited when a lower life power comes under the claim of the higher and does not resist it . . . so that its subordination to the higher power becomes possible."[5] This pleasure gives the impulse to broadening or disseminating activity.[6]

The distinction of flesh and spirit, of sensible and higher-self-consciousness, is crucial to Schleiermacher's developmental account of the origin of sinfulness in the human species. According to this account, both in the evolution of the species and in the maturation of the individual, the sensible self-consciousness appears first and gains the

---

[3] Friedrich Schleiermacher, *Die christliche Sitte*, edited by L. Jonas, *Friedrich Schleiermachers Sämmtliche Werke* Part I, Volume 12, 2nd edition (Berlin, G. Reimer, 1884), *Nachscrift* , 44. Cited hereafter as CS. In my references I will distinguish between the *Beilage* (which consist of Schleiermacher's manuscripts) and the *Nachschrift* (which derive from student notes of Schleiermacher's lectures).

[4] CS *Beilage* A, 18-19; *Nachschrift*, 44-45.

[5] CS *Nachschrift*, 45.

[6] CS *Nachschrift*, 45. John Shelley uses "disseminating" to translate *verbreitend* in Friedrich Schleiermacher, *Introduction to Christian Ethics*, trans. by John C. Shelley (Nashville: Abingdon, 1989); see 27.

upper hand, as it were (§67). Flesh, the sensible self-consciousness, "has habit on its side as the real law of its members" and obstructs the spirit or higher self-consciousness (§68.2; Schleiermacher's footnote cites Romans 7:23).

On first reading it appears that this conceptuality of the higher and lower self-consciousness is a departure from traditional understandings of the nature of sin. An inhibition of the God-consciousness seems to be something quite different from pride, rebellion against God, or concupiscence. A number of years ago I concluded:

> For Schleiermacher, the root of the problem lies neither in the will nor in the direction of one's love, but at a prior level (prior to willing or sensible feelings), in the inability to integrate one's consciousness of the divine with the rest of one's conscious life. This shift in location suggests that a shift away from the Augustinian notion of concupiscence has taken place.[7]

Still, the echoes in §68 of Romans 7 and the Pauline dualism of flesh and spirit are unmistakable. While that evidence does not settle the question, it does seem exaggerated to claim, with Ogden, that Schleiermacher has "proceeded uncritically and thus failed to respect the distinctive claims of the faith itself." Rather, B. A. Gerrish's judgment may be closer to the mark: "Schleiermacher's theology . . . was a reworking of inherited materials in a new age" out of the conviction that "the dogmatic language inherited from Augustine was rich and deep enough to be serviceable still, if handled with good sense."[8] But a just assessment requires answers to some hard questions. Did Schleiermacher handle his materials with good sense? Is an "inhibition of the God-consciousness" an adequate way of conceptualizing the Christian consciousness of sin? Is it appropriate to read the dualism of flesh and spirit as the "independence of the lower life-potency" against the higher or God-consciousness? And does Schleiermacher's revisionist terminology really signify a departure from the notion of concupiscence?

Remaining close to Schleiermacher's own texts and inquiring into how the dualism of flesh and spirit, or lower and higher self-consciousness, actually works in the discussion of sin will put us in a position to make some assessment of the possibilities and limits of the conceptuality.

---

[7] Walter E. Wyman, Jr., "Rethinking the Christian Doctrine of Sin: Friedrich Schleiermacher and Hick's 'Irenaean Type'," *Journal of Religion* 74 no. 2 (April 1994), 206.

[8] B. A. Gerrish, *Continuing the Reformation: Essays on Modern Religious Thought* (Chicago: University of Chicago, 1993), 7.

Schleiermacher characterizes actual sin in this statement:

> Throughout the entire range of sinful humanity there is not a single perfectly good action, i.e., one that purely expresses the power of the God-consciousness; nor is there one perfectly pure moment, i.e. one in which something does not exist in secret antagonism to the God-consciousness (§73.1).

Actual sins are those actions which proceed from the flesh or sensible self-consciousness — that is, the sensible self-consciousness rather than the higher consciousness has given the impetus to act. Not even the regenerate are entirely free from sin, that is, from the relative weakness of the God-consciousness, and thus sanctification is a process, not a finished state of blessedness (§110.1, §111). Nor are actual sins limited to deeds; thoughts, too, can be actual sins:

> Actual sin in the precise sense is present even where the sinful element shows itself only internally, and enters into a moment of consciousness merely as a thought or a desire (*Begierde*). Just as love, as an inward affection, is the fulfilling of the law, since it infallibly manifests itself in outward act on every given opportunity, so for the same reason, evil desire (*Begierde*) though only working within, is already actual sin (§73.2).

The term translated here as "evil desire" (*Begierde*) can also be translated as "lust" or "concupiscence."[9] Clearly Schleiermacher intends the term in a broad sense, inclusive of yet not restricted to sexual desire. Nevertheless, the possibility of reading "desire" as "concupiscence" in crucial passages suggests that Schleiermacher's conceptuality is a reworking of (rather than a departure from) an Augustinian notion of concupiscence. This possibility can be tested by turning to several passages discussing sexual ethics (there aren't very many) in *Die christliche Sitte.*

Consider this example from a discussion of dancing.[10] The context is a discussion of the principle that the same action can be innocent for one person but sinful for another. What distinguishes the two is whether the spirit or the flesh has given the impulse to the activity.

> No sensuous activity (*sinnliche Tätigkeit*) is in itself sinful or the opposite. For example, if one sees dancing as the patterned communal movement of the body which expresses a joyful mood, then it is nothing sinful. But if in the coming together of the sexes lust (*Wollust*) enters in, then dancing is

---

[9] Schleiermacher explicitly equates *Begierde* and *concupiscentia* in Chr. Gl. §61.5.

[10] This passage was drawn to my attention by James M. Brandt's dissertation, "Die Christliche Sittenlehre: A Reassessment of Schleiermacher's Theological-Ethical Vision" (Ph. D. diss., The University of Chicago, 1991), chap. 4.

immoral. Whether it is sinful or not is not externally apparent, unless the dance is voluptuous in its entire construction.[11]

This passage makes clear that it is the presence of lust or concupiscence, that is, the predominance of the sensible (or "lower") dimension of life that constitutes actual sin. Is Schleiermacher, then, suspicious of the body — does he equate "flesh" with bodily life, thereby reproducing an Augustinian dualism? It is important not to oversimplify Schleiermacher's flesh/spirit dualism; I do not think that it cashes out as a body-soul dualism. At the same time, there are grounds for suspecting a kind of dualism in Schleiermacher's conceptuality. A second illustration from his discussion of the virtue of chastity or purity (*Keuschheit*) helps to clarify his meaning.

Chastity is a virtue in those in whom the spirit has dominion over the flesh; for them, sense impressions and sensual pleasures do not give rise to desire (*Begierde*) or *epithymia*.[12]

> So when Christ says, you should not look at a woman to lust after her, otherwise you have already committed adultery, that means that with the arousing of desire [*Begierde*] immorality has already been posited. But he does not mean by any means the woman next to you ought not to please you [*soll dir gar nicht wohlgefallen*], for that would be a natural *apatheia*. He is far from reducing chastity to that. Rather, the sense impression should arise, and Christ presupposes it in his discussion; but the pleasure should be held pure, so that desire [*Begierde*] does not arise. . . . Sensual pleasure [*sinnliche Wohlgefallen*] should not be lacking, but it should never give the impulse, for in the spirit no motive lies to make it the impulse; in and for itself it should be nothing but receptivity, and may first become spontaneity when it is permeated with spirit. That is chastity in sensual pleasures of this sort.[13]

Schleiermacher is walking a very fine line in his employment of the dualism between flesh and spirit, sensible and higher self-consciousness. He is clear that actual sin arises from the dominion of flesh over spirit, of the lower over the higher self-consciousness. At the same time he is not dismissive of the pleasures of sense; he is not fully in agreement with Augustine, who scolds himself for taking too much pleasure in food, singing, and even the spectacle of a hound chasing a rabbit, not to mention sex.[14] The line Schleiermacher draws is between

---

[11] CS *Nachschrift*, 637.

[12] CS *Nachschrift*, 608-609.

[13] CS *Nachschrift*, 609, 611.

[14] Saint Augustine, *Confessions*, trans. by R.S. Pine-Coffin (Baltimore: Penguin Books, 1961), Book X, chaps. 29-37. See Chr. Gl. §61.5, where Schleiermacher criticizes Augustine for equating the "proper life-process" of the "lower functions" with desire or concupiscence.

pleasure (*Wohlgefallen, Lust*) and desire or concupiscence (*Begierde*). The pleasures of sense are not in themselves morally problematic, as they apparently were for Augustine; but the spirit must always remain in control.

This brief foray into Schleiermacher's Christian ethics suggests some of the possibilities of his revisionist conceptuality. Schleiermacher's novel conceptuality is a way of making sense, in a different idiom, of Paul's dualism between flesh and spirit. It enables him to retrieve an Augustinian notion of concupiscence, without the other-worldly excesses of Augustine's own position. The conceiving of sin as an "inhibition" of the God-consciousness allows him to give a reading of the problem of flesh in Christian experience that centers on misplaced priorities.

Whether this reading is fully adequate to Paul's understanding of the divided self under the law is another question.[15] It does seem that a shift akin to Augustine's understanding of Paul's dualism of flesh and spirit has taken place. "Flesh" in Paul can refer to an orientation of the whole self; "it designates man's being and attitude *as opposed to and in contradiction to God and God's spirit.*"[16] "Flesh" in Schleiermacher is interpreted as the sensible dimension of human experience, the "determinations of self-consciousness which develop from our relations to nature and man" (Chr. Gl. §5.1). In this reading, Schleiermacher is closer to Augustine than to Paul, for "flesh" refers not to an orientation of the *whole* self, but to impulses originating in the life of the senses.[17] Without drawing a final conclusion as it its adequacy, I mean only to suggest that Schleiermacher's reinterpretation of sin in terms of the categories provided by his analysis of consciousness is able to make considerable contact with a significant strand of Christian thinking about sin; to that extent it cannot be said to "fail to respect the distinctive claims of the

---

[15] Schleiermacher devotes a sermon to the problem: "Christus der Befreier von der Sünde und dem Gesetz" in Friedrich Schleiermacher, *Predigten,* Fünfte Sammlung, in *Friedrich Schleiermachers Sämmtliche Werke,* Part II, Vol. 2, 21-35. Future references to the sermons in the *Sämmtliche Werke* will be designated SW. An English translation of this sermon can be found in Friedrich Schleiermacher, *Servant of the Word: Selected Sermons of Friedrich Schleiermacher,* trans. by Dawn De Vries (Philadelphia: Fortress, 1987), 43-57. This sermon was preached in 1820: see Wichmann von Meding, *Biblographie der Schriften Schleiermachers,* Schleiermacher Archiv, vol. 9 (Berlin and NY: Walter de Gruyter, 1992), 258.

[16] Günther Bornkamm, *Paul,* trans. by D. M. G. Stalker (New York: Harper & Row, Publishers, 1971), 133; italics in the original.

[17] See Augustine's reading of "flesh" in *Confessions* VIII:5 and X:29 and 30; consider Augustine's suspicion of sensuality in the entire section, X:29-35.

faith itself."[18] The question remains, however, of whether it is possible to pit spirit against flesh in this way without introducing the suspicion of other-worldliness, at least in the form of want of consideration for the significance of life in the world, including its physical necessities. A consideration of the adequacy of Schleiermacher's conceptuality to formulate a doctrine of evil throws further light on this question.

2

The correct grasp of Schleiermacher's understanding of evil is complicated by the fact that he uses two different words that can be rendered into English as "evil," *das Übel* and *das Böse*. In the passage on natural evil cited previously, Schleiermacher uses the word *Übel*: "Man, were he without sin, would not feel what are merely hindrances of sensuous functions as evils (*Übel*); the very fact that he does so feel them is due to sin" (Chr. Gl. §76.2). In his discussion of actual sin, Schleiermacher asserts: "every observant person discovers in himself so many anticipations and, so to say, germs of all evil (*Bösen*) that . . . any kind of evil (*Böse*), if not habitually, yet in particular cases, might emerge as actual sin" (§73.2). Thus a philological detour is necessary.

As the preceding citations indicate, the distinction between *das Übel* and *das Böse* is often obscured in the English translation of *The Christian Faith*. While *das Übel* is consistently rendered as "evil," a variety of terms is used for *das Böse*: "moral evil" (§48.1), "evil" (§73.2), "the bad as such" (§75.2), "wickedness" (§84.1), "badness" (§84.3), "what is bad" (§84.4). Do the two words point to a systematic conceptual distinction? How can we make sense of Schleiermacher's usage?

"Evil" (*das Übel*) is defined by Schleiermacher as "persistent cause of hindrances to life [*Lebenshemmungen*], a "hindrance [*Hemmung*] of bodily and temporal existence" (§75.1, my translation). Such hindrances can be natural, that is, obstructions which are "independent of human action"; Schleiermacher's examples are death, disease, and suffering. They can also be social, that is, due to human activity. Schleiermacher says of social evils that they either "diminish the wealth of stimuli which further men's development" (such as scarcity and want), or they "make the world less tractable to human effort" (such as oppression and antagonism) (§75.2). Perhaps what he means by "evil" in this sense

---

[18] At stake is one of Schubert Ogden's two criteria of theological adequacy: the criterion of *appropriateness* (as distinct from the criterion of credibility). See Schubert M. Ogden, *On Theology* (San Francisco: Harper and Row, 1986), 3-6.

could be better conveyed by one of the other allowable translations of *das Übel*: misfortune. That he intends to distinguish evil in the sense of misfortune from the morally evil is implied by two statements. He objects to calling social evil "moral evil" (*moralisches Übel*), "for if we say 'moral' we suggest that the bad also as such (*das Böse*) is subsumed under the concept of evil (*das Übel*)" (§75.2). Later, in arguing that evil understood as divine punishment should not be seen as retributive, he states: "Fundamentally, badness [*Böses*] (or wrong [*Unrecht*]) and evil (*Übel*) are incommensurable" (§84.3); that is, morally wicked deeds cannot be retributed by misfortunes such as physical pain. Schleiermacher's discussion presupposes the following distinction: evil (*das Übel*) is a morally neutral term; the term *das Böse*, wickedness or badness, conveys a moral judgment. This usage is identical to Kant's: in *Religion within the Limits of Reason Alone*, *das Böse* means moral evil and *das Übel* (translated by Greene and Hudson as "ills") refers to suffering, hardship, and so on.[19]

In short, the distinction between *das Böse* and *das Übel* is a systematic distinction: the former is a moral concept (wickedness, evil-doing, etc.) and the latter is a morally neutral concept referring to the ills or misfortunes of life, both natural and human caused. The "doctrine of evil" in the third section of the explication of the consciousness of sin deals only with the latter, with what is commonly referred to as the "problem of evil:" why does God permit earthquakes, death, and suffering? In effect, this section constitutes a theodicy. It is not dealing with moral evil (what is the relationship of sin to human wickedness?). There is no discussion in this part of the *Glaubenslehre* of the relation of sin to the moral conception of evil (*das Böse*).

So our question becomes: what is the relation of sin to evil in the sense of the ills or misfortunes of life? Schleiermacher's basic position is summarized in his statement: "Evil arises only with sin, but given sin, it arises inevitably" (§75.1). What does he mean? Sin, recall, is an inhibition of the God-consciousness, the failure of the God-consciousness to be dominant over the sensible self-consciousness in a moment of consciousness. Without sin, that is, given the ideal possibility of a perfect God-consciousness, "hindrances to bodily and temporal existence" such

---

[19] Immanuel Kant, *Religion Within the Limits of Reason Alone*, translated by Theodore Greene and Hoyt H. Hudson (NY: Harper and Row, 1960); *Kants Werke, Akademie-Textausgabe*, vol. VI, *Die Religion innerhalb der Grenzen der bloßen Vernunft* (Berlin: Walter de Gruyter, 1968). See Book I for the discussion of moral evil and the consistent translation of *das Böse* as "evil"; see Greene and Hudson, 67-68 and *Kants Werke* VI:73-74, footnote, for the use of *Übel* and its translation as "ills."

as death, suffering, or poverty would not be experienced as evils. Since "all the sensuous and bodily aspects of life" have been "brought into [an] exclusive relation" to the God-consciousness, "opposition" cannot be construed as an "obstruction of life" (§75.1). To the pious, the imperfections of life are not experienced as evils, but rather as "incentives" (§84.4). "If, however, the predominant factor is not the God-consciousness but the flesh, every impression made by the world upon us and involving an obstruction of our bodily and temporal life must be reckoned as an evil" (§75.1). Just as there is no sin apart from the consciousness of sin (§66.1), so there is no evil apart from the consciousness of evil. Hence, to claim that where there is sin there is evil is to say that where a lively awareness of the redeeming and sustaining presence of the divine love is dim or lacking, the unavoidable consequences of finitude — death, suffering, want — are experienced as evils.

This understanding of evil, along with Schleiermacher's views of the original perfection of the world (as denoting not an original, now lost state, but the enduring structure of the world whereby the God-consciousness can always arise [§59]) and of the nature of the divine causality (as equivalent to the system of nature [§34, §46]) works to dissolve several intractable problems. Schleiermacher can deny a change in the world has occurred as a result of sin; that is, he denies the view that Adam, had he not fallen, would have been immortal, or that an unfallen humanity would not be subject to suffering or want.[20] The fear of death, we might say, and not death itself, is the result of sin (§75.1, §76.3). The mythological picture of a "fallen world" can be dispensed with (§59.2). So, too, the view that the individual's experiences of evils are the consequences of his or her particular sins is no longer to be maintained (§77). To be sure, the pious Christian will still regard evils as the punishment of sin; but this is a corporate reality, not an individual correlation (§76).[21] Finally, Schleiermacher's position leads

---

[20] See Kant's discussion of the natural, but mistaken, tendency of humans to relate the ills of life to transgressions: Greene and Hudson, 67-68 footnote; *Kants Werke* VI: 73-74, footnote.

[21] Exactly what Schleiermacher means in §§76-77 is somewhat elusive. Human beings are responsible for social evils: social evils are "dependant upon sin directly" (§76.2). Given a defective God-consciousness, "there emerges opposition between the individual beings, and what is furtherance to one will often for that reason become hindrance to another" (§75.1). Thus to experience social evil is to experience a *consequence* of sin. To the Christian consciousness, the consequence is experienced as punishment: this would seem to be the logic of "experiencing as." On the other hand, natural evils are not caused by human sinfulness. But given a defective God-consciousness, the consequences of finitude are *felt as* evils, and thus (as in the case

to a criticism of the preceding dogmatic tradition with its various attempts, based on the notion of "cooperation," to say that God is not the originator of evil, and yet evil somehow depends upon God (§48.3). God does not ordain evil in itself; rather, "God has ordained that the natural imperfections are regarded by us as evil in proportion as the God-consciousness is not yet dominant within us" (§82.2).

Given the abstractness of his *Glaubenslehre*, it is exceedingly difficult to grasp the practical import of Schleiermacher's claim that "man, were he without sin, would not feel what are merely hindrances of sensuous functions as evils" (§76.2). B. A. Gerrish has drawn our attention to a helpful passage from a sermon preached in 1800; although this text was written many years before even the first edition of the *Glaubenslehre*, it provides helpful clues to the practical import of Schleiermacher's statement:

> To be a religious man and to pray are really one and the same thing. *To join the thought of God with every thought of any importance that occurs to us*; in all our admiration of external nature, to regard it as the work of his wisdom; to take counsel with God about all our plans, that we may be able to carry them out in his name; and even in our most mirthful hours to remember his all-seeing eye; this is the prayer without ceasing to which we are called, and which is really the essence of true religion.[22]

This passage suggests what it means to be pious, that is, to have a higher self-consciousness that is dominant over the sensible self-consciousness. In Gerrish's paraphrase, "to be religious is to combine every thought of any consequence with thoughts of the omnipotent love that makes the world good."[23] Certainly, some of the thoughts of the greatest consequence are those we have in the face of the experience of finitude (experiences of suffering and death, poverty and oppression). To be pious, to have faith, means that such thoughts and experiences do not

---

of social evils) the logic of "experiencing as" comes into play. Thus evils, both natural and social, are experienced as the punishment of sin.

[22] SW II:1, p. 28. I am using Wilson's translation: *Selected Sermons of Schleiermacher*, translated by Mary F. Wilson, The Foreign Biblical Library, edited by W. Robertson Nicoll (NY: Funk & Wagnalls, n.d.), 38 (italics added). Gerrish draws attention to this passage in *Continuing the Reformation*, 162-64, as well as in B. A. Gerrish, *A Prince of the Church: Schleiermacher and the Beginnings of Modern Theology* (Philadelphia: Fortress, 1984), 65-66. For the dating of the sermon, see von Meding, 229. Obviously there is a methodological problem in utilizing a sermon nearly contemporary with the first edition of the *Speeches* as evidence for Schleiermacher's mature theological thought; I am assuming a basic continuity in his views that cannot be argued for here.

[23] *Continuing the Reformation*, 8.

finally undermine basic trust in the goodness of the world or in the divine wisdom and love in ordering the world. Schleiermacher does not deny the dark side of human experience; but he does maintain that the negative, destructive aspects — including death — need not undermine the Christian's trust in the Creator or in the goodness of Creation; they are not "evils," but inescapable consequences of finitude (or, in Schleiermacher's own language, "natural imperfections").

Later in the same sermon Schleiermacher comments on the real import of the Redeemer's prayer in the garden of Gethsemane as a model for Christian prayer:

> It should make us cease from our eager longing for the possession of some earthly good, or the averting of some dreaded evil (*Übel*); it should bring us courage to do without (*entbehren*), or to suffer (*dulden*), if God has so appointed it; it should lift us out of the helplessness into which we are brought by fear and passion (*Begierde*), and bring us to the consciousness and full use of our powers; that so we may be able in all circumstances to conduct ourselves as it becomes those who remember that they are living and acting under the eye and the protection of the Most High.[24]

Piety, then, does not change the world (bad things will continue to happen to good people); it changes how the world is experienced.

Further evidence that this is what Schleiermacher means can be found in the Christmas Eve dialogue. Ernestine portrays a Christmas eve long ago when she happened to glimpse Edward's oldest sister, Kornelia, along with her infant son and Edward himself at a Christmas eve service.[25] The characters in the dialogue of course know, and the reader is soon informed, that the unnamed infant will grow into manhood, only to fall as a soldier in the wars of liberation. The scene clearly evokes the image of the Madonna, and recalls a painful loss. How is evil understood here? Given the context of the dialogue as a whole, we might say that the pain of the death of Kornelia's son in war is taken up and overcome in the joy of the Christmas festival; or perhaps, better, the recollection of that event is incapable of diminishing the joy felt by the family at the birth of the Redeemer.

A second example might be drawn from Schleiermacher's own experience when his only son, Nathaniel, died at the age of nine. The grieving father took it upon himself to preach the sermon at Nathaniel's graveside.[26] Schleiermacher turns the sad moment into an occasion for

---

[24] SW II:1, 34; Wilson, 44 (translation slightly modified).
[25] Friedrich Schleiermacher, *Christmas Eve: Dialogue on the Incarnation*, trans. by Terrence N. Tice (Richmond: John Knox, 1967), 57-60.
[26] SW II:4, 836-840. Translated and discussed by Albert Blackwell, "Schleier-

admonition: "Therefore let us all truly love one another as persons who could — alas, how soon! — be snatched away."[27] In language reminiscent both of the *Speeches* and of Augustine, he admonishes himself and his listeners,

> Let us all more and more mature to that wisdom which, looking beyond the void, sees and loves only the eternal in all things earthly and perishable, and in all thy decrees finds thy peace as well, and eternal life, to which through faith we are delivered out of death.[28]

These words echo, in a different idiom, the viewpoint articulated in the *Glaubenslehre*: the attitude of pious submission (§78.2), of acquiescence "in all the evils of life as the expression of a divine decree passed upon us" (§82.2).

One final example comes from the sphere of Christian praxis. Schleiermacher draws from his understanding of evil the conclusion that, although the continuance of evil cannot be consistently willed,

> it is no less certain that the Christian consciousness could never give rise to a moment of activity specially directed toward the cessation of suffering as such — partly, of course, because such a moment would really be determined by the interests of the lower side of life, and partly because (since, in view of the aforesaid connection, suffering necessarily evokes the consciousness of sin) it is a disposition hostile to sin itself that needs to be aroused (§78.2).

The awareness of the dark side of human experience does not motivate, Schleiermacher is asserting, action to the alleviation of evil in itself. Thus when the Christian ethics commends hard work caring for the poor and the sick as part of restorative action, the point is not that the poor and sick need help; rather, such action is commended as a kind of calisthenics for those whose vocation is making them soft; it is a way of influencing the "flesh" of the one who acts (a way of restoring the proper balance of flesh and spirit) rather than as a way of reducing suffering in the world.[29]

---

macher's Sermon at Nathaniel's Grave," *The Journal of Religion* 57:1 (January, 1977): 64-75. Blackwell's translation has been reprinted in DeVries, 209-214.

[27] DeVries, 213.

[28] DeVries, 214; see Augustine's discussion of the death of his unnamed friend, *Confessions*, Book IV, chaps. 4-10.

[29] *Die Christliche Sitte, Beilage* B, 108; *Nachscrift*, 151-152, 154-157). The term paraphrased here as "calisthenics" is *Gymnastik*, a word that is used repeatedly in these pages. Schleiermacher is searching for a moral equivalent to the monasticism done away with by the Reformation; he alludes to *das eremitische Leben in der patristischen Zeit* as such a *Gymnastik*.

These passages serve, I hope, to illustrate the possibilities and suggest some of the limits of Schleiermacher's conceptuality with respect to the relation of sin and evil. The initial reaction, uninformed by a close inquiry into what Schleiermacher actually means, is only partially right. The experience of evil is, indeed, a matter of how you look at the world; but Schleiermacher is far from the insensitive optimism of a Pangloss.[30] What is at stake is one's confidence in the goodness of the world and in the omnipotent love of its Creator. What piety really means with respect to the dark side of experience is an attitude of acceptance of finitude and all that it entails. The shattering of confidence in the goodness of the world by misfortune, the experience of the limitations of finitude as "evils," is accordingly a matter of deficient (or perhaps misunderstood) piety.

Schleiermacher's revisionist understanding of sin and evil marks a clear gain in credibility. Four points should be recalled: (1) Schleiermacher's developmental account of the origin of sin (sinfulness is to be understood, not as the inherited consequence of a primordial fall but as the inevitable consequence of the evolution of natural creatures in a natural world);[31] (2) his replacement of the mythological picture of an original, lost, deathless state with the view that not physical death and suffering themselves, but the way they are experienced and interpreted, are the consequences of sin; (3) his corporate understanding of sin and evil that short-circuits any attempt to correlate an individual's misfortunes with his or her sins, thereby maintaining the constancy of the natural order; and (4) his dissolution of the conundrums surrounding God's "cooperation" with evil.

But if Schleiermacher's conceptuality allows him to make some clear gains in credibility, and offers some suggestive possibilities for interpreting the Christian experience of the darker side of life, it is not without its own unique limitations. Two are implicit in the preceding discussion.

First, the suspicion of a subjectivistic reduction of evil (*Übel*, misfortune) hovers around Schleiermacher's discussion. His conceptuality entails the assertion that evil (misfortune) is a matter of how you perceive it; given a sufficiently strong God-consciousness, that is, piety approaching the state of blessedness, the misfortunes of life will not be reckoned

---

[30] Voltaire (François Marie Arouet de Voltaire), *Candide, Zadig and Selected Stories,* trans. by Donald Frame (NY: Penguin, 1961). See Schleiermacher's rejection of the formula "best of all possible worlds," Chr. Gl. §59 Postscript.

[31] See the essay cited in note 7 for an extensive discussion of this issue and for my indebtedness to John Hick's "Irenaean type."

as evils. But while this characterizes the subjective consciousness of the believer, it does not take into account the objective consequences of misfortune. To take one example: Nathaniel's premature death at age nine cuts off all the potentialities he might have actualized given a longer life span. The objective consequence is a diminishment of the richness of life, not only of Nathaniel's experience and the experience of those around him, but ultimately of the divine life. The latter claim, of course, is inconsistent with Schleiermacher's insistence that God is in no respects dependant upon the world, and would lead to a discussion of the issues raised by process theology. But it is not necessary to pursue that thought further in order to make the point that the suspicion of a subjectivistic view of evil is not entirely unwarranted. The problem may be rooted as much in Schleiermacher's method (as theology of consciousness) as it is in his conceptuality, however. Schleiermacher would doubtlessly reply that it is not the task of Christian dogmatics to take into account such objective consequences of evil, but only to render an account of the Christian consciousness. Moreover, he would probably object that to raise the issue as I have is to have the mind set on the flesh. But that second suggestion points to a further limitation in the conceptuality.

Second, Schleiermacher's conceptuality has consequences for his view of Christian praxis that are troubling. Recall his view that care for the poor and suffering is a kind of calisthenics for the actor, not an attempt to change conditions. One need not embrace all that liberation theology has to say about "spiritualized" versions of Christianity to find troubling the view that only the higher self-consciousness finally matters, and that the motivations proceeding from the lower or sensible side of life are sub-Christian. The suspicion of a type of otherworldliness that I raised earlier, of a dualism of physical and spiritual existence, seems confirmed.[32]

---

[32] The "seems" in this sentence is deliberately chosen. The judgment must remain provisional, pending an investigation that is something more than a mere foray into *Die Christliche Sitte*. A more systematic inquiry into the nature of both restorative (purifying) action and disseminating activity is necessary. It might be objected that in so far as Christianity is a teleological type of religion in which "a predominating reference to the moral task constitutes the fundamental type of the religious affections" (Chr. Gl. §9.1), further inquiry into Schleiermacher's Christian ethics could only refute rather than sustain the suggestion of a dualism between spiritual and physical existence advanced here. But in so far as the moral action contemplated is "a practical contribution to the Kingdom of God" (Chr. Gl. §9.1) or "activity in the Kingdom of God" (Chr. Gl. §112.4), and in so far as the Kingdom of God itself is the "new corporate life" created by redemption (that is, a

The adequacy of the conceptuality employed in Schleiermacher's understanding of sin and evil is a crucial issue, for the technical distinction of the sensible and higher self-consciousness provides the conceptual backbone of his system. This distinction serves to structure not only his dogmatics, but his Christian ethics as well. When approaching the central categories of such a seminal figure as Schleiermacher, it is wise to tread with due humility and caution. If I cannot agree with Ogden's judgment that Schleiermacher has proceeded "uncritically" and "failed to respect the distinctive claims of the faith itself," nevertheless I do agree that there are limits to his conceptuality, and perhaps to his method as well.

---

spiritual reality), there are grounds for thinking that such a further inquiry would confirm rather than refute the criticism that is somewhat tentatively suggested here.

CHAPTER SEVEN

ETHICAL MONOTHEISM OR ETHICAL POLYTHEISM?: REFLECTIONS ON TROELTSCH, WEBER, AND JAMES

Mark A. Hadley

Ethical monotheism, in the words of Wendell Dietrich, "means a religious concentration and intensity that focuses singular attention on God in contrast to all creaturely reality." It entails the belief that the one God is the transcendent source and guarantor of moral value and "that monotheistic religion can structure and reinforce [human] moral consciousness."[1] God creates and enforces a moral order which provides guideposts for the construction of human culture and society. The key to this construction, as Jack Miles states it, is that "in one way or another, moral value shall have been placed above the other values that human beings properly recognize: power, wealth, pleasure, beauty, knowledge. . . ."[2] While such values may be recognized, they must be subordinated to moral ends; all moral ends are derivable from the one God.

The idea that there is one supremely powerful God concerned with human moral behavior is an ancient idea. It is found in Biblical texts such as Exodus and Leviticus which portray God as a lawgiver.[3] It is further found in prophetic texts such as Amos which gives voice to a God who cares more about human beings fulfilling ethical demands rather than performing religious rituals.

> Spare me the sound of your hymns,
> And let me not hear the music of your lutes.
> But let justice well up like water,
> Righteousness like an unfailing stream.[4]

Such texts, as Dietrich has shown so admirably with regard to Hermann Cohen and Ernst Troeltsch, provide the grounds for ethical

---

[1] Wendell Dietrich, *Cohen and Troeltsch: Ethical Monotheistic Religion and Theory of Culture* (Atlanta: Scholars Press, 1986), 1, 83.

[2] Jack Miles, *God: A Biography* (New York: Random House, 1996), 110.

[3] Miles notes the ambivalence of such a picture of God in Exodus who at times embodies "the seemingly anarchic behavior of God as warrior." Miles, 112.

[4] Amos 5:23-24. *Tanakh* (Philadelphia: Jewish Publication Society, 1985).

monotheism.[5] Yet these ethically oriented texts represent only one strand of the Bible. They do not represent an ancient or even medieval consensus about who God is and what is required of human beings. The judgement that the values represented by these texts entail the highest form of religious expression is of more recent origin. While the religious culture of ancient Israel and the subsequent religious traditions of Judaism and Christianity which derive from it may be the source of ethical monotheism in the West, ethical monotheism was not an immediately accomplished fact. It is an emergent entity.[6] Ethical monotheistic themes may have been present in the Biblical texts, but they do not attain central prominence in religious thought until the Enlightenment. It is Kant most prominently who provides the grounds for ethical monotheistic discourse in his *Religion within the Limits of Reason Alone.*

Dietrich's work has shown that to read the Biblical texts and traditions as warrants for a strictly ethical monotheistic religion is a *modern* interpretive choice.[7] As Dietrich notes, Cohen's reading of Judaism as ethical monotheism requires "a very selective and partial" reading of Rabbinic Judaism which gives "normative faith and significance to the prophetic faith," and an appropriation of Kant. Troeltsch's reading of Christianity as ethical monotheism warrants a similarly selective normative assessment of the prophetic ethos, and an appropriation of Hegel.[8] Cohen and Troeltsch stand in a tradition of modern religious thinkers going back at least to Kant who seek to reconfigure received religious ideas and traditions in the face of Enlightenment and post-Enlightenment criticisms. The general intellectual problem for such thinkers is how to reinterpret religious ideas and values which have lost their traditional meanings and influence and no longer serve as basic structures for individual and social life. The possibility of such reconstruction is, of course, an open question. There are plenty of intellectuals since the Enlightenment who have rejected the possibility of religious reconstruction. Ethical monotheism is but one response to the loss of traditional meanings and values.

---

[5] See Dietrich, 29-43. For example: for Cohen, "the prophetic writings are a decisively normative source from which the contemporary thinker derives a religion of reason out of the sources of Judaism. For Troeltsch the central Christian authoritative norm . . . must, for proper interpretation, be realigned with the prophetic faith and ethos of the Old Testament." 29.

[6] Miles, 111.

[7] Dietrich, 61.

[8] Dietrich, 84.

In the spirit of Dietrich's interpretation of Cohen and Troeltsch, I wish in this essay briefly to revisit Troeltsch's ethical monotheism and contrast it with two differing interpretive choices concerning religious ideas and values made by two contemporaries of Troeltsch who influenced his thinking, Max Weber and William James. The influence of Weber, who shared a house and many daily conversations with Troeltsch in Heidelberg, is well known.[9] Troeltsch's landmark work in the sociology of religion, *The Social Teachings of the Christian Churches*, owes much to Weber. Though less well known, James influenced Troeltsch's understanding of the psychology of religion.[10] If, as Dietrich has argued, Troeltsch recommends ethical monotheism as "a suitable base for modern culture,"[11] both Weber and James set forth, I would argue, versions of ethical polytheism. If ethical monotheism requires singular attention to God in contrast to creaturely reality, ethical polytheism, in the sense that I set it forth here, sees no need for such an exclusive focus upon the divine at the expense of creaturely, and specifically, human reality. Further, it requires the recognition of a plurality of legitimate values which cannot be solely or exclusively derivable from a singular divine source. Insofar as there is a divine reality, it is plural and not singular. Given Weber's cultural pessimism, polytheism is not so much an option as an inevitability due to the grinding forces of modern capitalistic and bureaucratic rationalism. In James's more optimistic mood, ethical polytheism is a living option which promises rich and exciting cultural possibilities in an increasingly diverse and democratic world. In setting forth the divergent perspectives of Troeltsch, Weber, and James, I do not intend to settle the argument between the ethical monotheists and the ethical polytheists, nor between the forms of ethical polytheism. My aim is essentially taxonomic and historical as I seek to explore the various meanings of ethical polytheism. However, after examining Troeltsch, Weber, and James in turn, and expanding upon the contrasts among them, I will conclude with a few questions regarding

---

[9] Troeltsch himself acknowledges this. See "Max Weber" in *Religion and History* (Minneapolis: Fortress, 1991), 362.

[10] The key texts here are *Psychologie und Erkenntnistheorie in der Religionswissenschaft* (Tübingen: J.C.B. Mohr, 1905) and "Empiricism and Platonism in the Philosophy of Religion: To the Memory of William James," *Harvard Theological Review* V (1912): 401-422. The latter is hereafter cited in the text as EP. For an overview of the connection between James and Troeltsch see Mark Hadley, "Religious Thinking in an Age of Disillusionment: William James and Ernst Troeltsch on the Possibilities of a Science of Religion" (Ph.D. diss., Brown University, 1995), esp. Chapter 3.

[11] Dietrich, 5.

the status of ethical monotheism in light of the challenges of Weber's and James's ethical polytheism.

1. Troeltsch's historical affirmation of Christian Absoluteness

Troeltsch's work must be seen as a response to a religious crisis. It is shaped by the context of the demise of the structures and prestige of European Christendom and the rise of a society dominated by the secular values of naturalism, relativism, and utilitarianism. In *The Absoluteness of Christianity and the History of Religions*, Troeltsch dramatically remarks upon "the religious chaos and religious devastation that threaten us from every side."[12] For Troeltsch, religion is an inescapable part of culture, so the question for European society is not whether there should be religious values and religious influences, but what form these take. A Christendom in demise leaves a vacuum in which all sorts of religious alternatives and substitutes thrive. These alternatives include other major religious traditions, a Goethean or Nietzschean inspired neo-paganism, and socialism; but none of these can possibly take hold in the way in which Christianity has.[13] Determining the future shape of European religious identity out of the demise of Christendom is Troeltsch's task.

Troeltsch's sense of religious loss and crisis is basic to shaping his intellectual agenda, and it is connected to his commitment to historical inquiry. In his early essay, "Historical and Dogmatic Method in Theology," Troeltsch witnesses to the eroding effects of the study of history.[14] The historical outlook represents the past and consequently the present in a new way. Cultural inheritances are not taken as absolute unquestioned norms and customs, but are reexamined in the context of their historical origin and development. Traditions become contingent

---

[12] Ernst Troeltsch, *Die Absoluteheit des Christentums und die Religionsgeschichte*, 2nd ed. (Tübingen: J.C.B. Mohr, 1912). English translation, *The Absoluteness of Christianity and the History of Religions*, trans. David Reid (Richmond: John Knox Press, 1971), 162. Hereafter cited in the text as AC.

[13] For this analysis of the religious crisis and religious alternatives, see especially "Logos and Mythos in Theologie und Religionsphilosophie" in *Gesammelte Schriften*, Vol. 2, 805-836. English translation, "Logos and Mythos in Theology and Philosophy of Religion," in *Religion and History*, trans. James Luther Adams and Walter F. Bense (Minneapolis: Fortress, 1991), 46-72.

[14] Ernst Troeltsch, "Historische and Dogmatische Method in Theologie," in *Gesammelte Schriften*, Vol. 2, 729-753. English translation, "Historical and Dogmatic Method in Theology," in *Religion and History*, trans. James Luther Adams and Walter F. Bense (Minneapolis: Fortress, 1991), 11-32.

entities which may be chosen or rejected depending upon their relevance to present and future needs. In theology the results are similar: "the historical method acts as a leaven, transforming everything and ultimately exploding the very form of earlier theological methods." The result is nothing less than "the disintegration of the Christian world of ideas" built by orthodox apologetics.[15] Historical thinking entails the possibility of relativism or skepticism because the Christian faith can no longer claim an absolute standpoint apart from history. There can be no appeal to a salvation history or to miraculous facts as these do not square with general historical inquiry.[16] Christianity stands or falls on the basis of such inquiry. If Christianity is so thoroughly shaped by contingent historical forces, on what basis can it make transcendent claims?

The threat of relativism posed by historical thinking is precisely this threat to Christianity's claim to ultimacy, perfection, and absoluteness. A full-fledged historical skepticism might conclude that Christianity is a merely relative and historical phenomenon which may have served the needs of earlier societies, but is no longer relevant to moderns. The religious truths which it sets forth would now be judged false. Troeltsch's dilemma is accepting historicism without affirming relativism. He wants to set forth a position which is able to assert the transcendent religious claims of Christianity without recourse to the strategy of dogmatic supernaturalism.

In *The Absoluteness of Christianity*, one of Troeltsch's more extensive discussions of the historicist dilemma for theology, he defines his own mediating solution to this dilemma. The essential problem, as Troeltsch sees it, is finding an Archimedean point amongst the competing claims of various religions: "How can we pass beyond the diversity with which history presents us to norms for our faith and for our judgements about life?" (AC, 61). The historical outlook has broadened knowledge of other religions and shown them to be analogous to Christianity. At the same time it has eroded confidence in the possibility of absolute values generally and of the absoluteness of Christianity in particular. If the traditional dogmatic supernaturalism is not an option, what are the possible solutions?

One apparent alternative that asserts the absoluteness of Christianity is a Hegelian or "idealistic-evolutionary" theory. It merits serious consideration as it rules out "every means of isolating Christianity from the rest of history on the basis of miracle," and presents "in a purely

---

15 "Historical and Dogmatic Method in Theology," 12.
16 "Historical and Dogmatic Method in Theology," 17, 20-23.

historical way the validity and significance of the Christian religion in statements as unequivocal as the doctrinal formulations of the early church" (AC, 60). Yet the idealistic-evolutionary idea of Christian absoluteness is also problematic because of its subordination of historical understanding to rational principles. While it avoids the appeal to a separate history of salvation and sets Christianity within the total context of the universal history of religion, it focuses too exclusively upon Christianity as a universal ideal rather than as a particular religious formation. According to this scheme, Christianity is the final culmination of the development of the religious idea. Other religions lead up to Christianity and are lesser manifestations of the religious idea. But in Christianity, religious history is complete; the universal principle coincides with its manifestation. As elegant as this solution is and as serious as it is about the total historical context, it ends up reintroducing a gulf between Christianity and other religions (AC, 82-83).

Ultimately, the idealistic-evolutionary theory is not historical enough. It reduces historical progress to the orderly march of reason and misses the idiosyncracies of history. It fails because modern historical understanding "knows no universal principle on the basis of which the content and sequence of events might be deduced. It knows only concrete, individual phenomena, always conditioned by their context and yet, at bottom, underivable and simply existent phenomena" (AC, 67). Christianity stands firmly in the midst of history and not, as the idealistic-evolutionary theory would have it, at the end of history.

Troeltsch believes that history is the domain of the individual. There are no unambiguous embodiments of absolute values, no pure universals working within the concrete particular. And religious values are no exception. A much greater historical knowledge of religions has undercut any claim that Christianity is the absolute religion. Indeed, there can be no religious formation which fully embodies absolute values. Christianity is one specific religious orientation among many and is subject, as all are, to diverse historical influences. These historical influences are integral to its shape and not simply vehicles for its timeless values. The values which it presents in large part reflect particular cultural situations. Christianity is thoroughly historical.

Nevertheless, through historical comparisons of the various religious formations, Troeltsch believes one can abstract each religion's values and on this basis make value judgements about each religious orientation. While no one religion can be the absolute religion, there are greater and lesser manifestations of religious value which might point the way toward absolute values.

The only course that remains, therefore, is the kind of scientific inquiry in which men strive as best they can to comprehend empirical, historical reality and to acquire norms from history by conscientious comparison and reflection. The study of history is not of itself the obtaining of such norms but the ground from which they arise. Historically delineated and actual norms are not necessarily norms we should acknowledge as valid for ourselves; they are disclosures of that principle from which we evolve valid norms (AC, 105).

It might be possible that historically oriented comparison and reflection leads to a rejection of all existing religious values. Yet even if no religion measures up, the course of comparison itself gives glimpses of absolute values from which a new orientation might be derived. If history is the locus of the individual it nevertheless discloses or points toward absolute values: "within the individual and nonrecurrent, there is something universally valid — or something connected with the universally valid — which makes itself known at the same time" (AC, 106).

Troeltsch is confident that such historical inquiry discloses that Christianity is the highest religious expression known to humankind. If it is not the absolute religion, if it cannot be fully shorn of its particular historical development among the peoples of the Mediterranean and of Europe, it is the fullest disclosure yet of the universally valid. In the spiritual evolution of humanity, it is "the purest and most forceful revelation of the higher world" and is thus normative for the present as well as for the foreseeable future. While Christianity may conceivably be surpassed by a higher revelation at some later point in history, this remote possibility should not overshadow its present sufficiency. If it is delusory to "possess the absolute in an absolute way at a particular point in history," it is no delusion to accept the absolute in a historical way (AC, 121, 122).

The historical acceptance of the absolute requires a careful study of Christian history attendant to the variety of social matrices in which Christianity has developed and thereby the recognition of the variety of Christianities. Such is the monumental task of *The Social Teachings*, which I will not rehearse here. Yet if in *The Social Teachings* Troeltsch will admit that "it becomes still less possible to find an unchangeable and absolute point in the Christian ethic," it is still possible to isolate certain elements of a Christian social ethos from the study of the various Christianities.[17] This ethos serves as the guideposts for a new "cultural synthesis" to respond to the crises of Western religion and culture.[18] A

---

[17] Ernst Troeltsch, *The Social Teaching of the Christian Churches*, trans. Olive Wyon (New York: Macmillan, 1931; reprint Chicago: University of Chicago, 1976), 1003, 1004.
[18] On the notion of cultural synthesis in Troeltsch, see Wendell Dietrich,

renewed Protestant Christianity, a monotheistic religion of personal redemption with a prophetic ethos, liberated from its ecclesiastical and dogmatic contexts becomes the ground for European culture and society.[19] While Troeltsch's historicist perspective requires ever renewed examination of the Christian ethos in response to contemporary cultural conditions, it does offer, Troeltsch thinks, a fitting response to the religious crisis facing Europe.[20] Christian monotheism can be reinvigorated to serve as the ground for cultural renewal. Troeltsch can confidently conclude that in its renewed form, "the Christian orientation contains today more than ever, a fountain of eternal youth that offers simplicity, health, and strength to a generation languishing under capitalism, determinism, relativism, and historicism."[21]

2. *Weber and the unceasing struggle of the gods*

Troeltsch's historicist reaffirmation of Christian values stands in stark contrast to Weber's rejection of the possibility of a cultural synthesis of the Christian ethos and modernity. Weber agrees with Troeltsch that the modern era in the West has been decisively shaped by the influence of Christianity, most notably by the inner-worldly asceticism of Calvinism. However, for Weber, the received religious values of the West are now fundamentally at odds with the values of modernity. The modern world is characterized by the presence of warring gods or conflicting value spheres (*Wertsphären*), each of which makes its claim upon modern persons, yet none of which can be rationally shown to take preeminence. The best that one can do is give the various gods their due insofar as one is called to do so by temperament and training. The decision to follow one over another is a necessary, yet rationally unjustifiable choice. Of all the gods to follow or value spheres to uphold, those who fully commit themselves to the religious ethos set themselves decisively against the modern world. In modernity, the "ethic of brotherliness" demanded by the most developed religions can only be

---

"Troeltsch's Treatment of the Thomist Synthesis in *The Social Teachings* as a Signal of his View of a New Cultural Synthesis," *The Thomist*, 57 (1993): 381-401.

[19] See Dietrich, chapters 2 and 4 for the outlines of this ethos and theory of culture.

[20] Dietrich provocatively raises the question whether or not Troeltsch's prophetic principle "opens the way to the conceivability of a religiously pluralist, secular society." Dietrich, 43.

[21] Ernst Troeltsch, "On the Question of the Religious A Priori," in *Religion and History*, 44.

carried out consistently in the intimate realm of personal relations, but not in the larger impersonal institutional realms decisive of modernity.

Weber's tour de force, "Science as a Vocation," somberly sketches the outlines of modernity: "The fate of our times is characterized by rationalization and intellectualization and, above all, by the 'disenchantment of the world.'"[22] The process of intellectualization has been going on for thousands of years and results from the desire of human beings to understand their world. Yet this process has accelerated rapidly with the experimental methods of modern science. Those various forces in life that once seemed irrational and beyond human control now become understandable and controllable. Science divides the world into an orderly and reliable series of causes and effects and thereby makes the world calculable. The idea of science is that "there are no mysterious incalculable forces that come into play, but rather that one can, in principle, master all things through calculation" (SV, 139).

However, the advance of science merely brings the advancement of technical rationality. It allows for the development of new technologies to manipulate and control the experienced world. It does not mean that human beings have a greater knowledge of how to live. The scientists of the Renaissance and the early modern period who were grounded in Christian ideas of providence naively thought that they were discovering the mind of God or the road to Him. The more recent utilitarian belief that science and its technical advancements might lead to greater human happiness is discredited as well. Today, according to Weber, no one believes that science "can teach us anything about the meaning of the world" (SV, 142). Science is, from this perspective, meaningless because it cannot teach us the most important question, which is how to live (SV, 143). What science can contribute beyond technical advancements is proper methods for thinking and clarity of thought (SV, 150-151). It can help the individual gain clarity about his or her ultimate values, but it cannot tell him or her which of these values is the best one to live by (SV, 151-153).

This is the modern situation of disenchantment in which there are no mysterious forces left, no theoretically unexplainable phenomena. God and the gods have vanished from the world. No magic is needed to manipulate the spirits beyond one's control, nor is any religious appeal to a personal deity necessary. "Technical means and calculations

---

[22] Max Weber, "Science as a Vocation," in *From Max Weber: Essays in Sociology*, ed. and trans. H. H. Gerth and C. Wright Mills (New York: Oxford, 1946), 155. Hereafter cited in the text as SV.

perform the service" (SV, 139). Science cannot take the place of religion nor can the scientist take the role of prophet or priest. All scientists who use the University lecture hall as a pulpit are worse than traditional religious preachers because the latter do not assume the mantle of intellectual integrity. Science is a vocation "organized in special disciplines in the service of self-clarification and knowledge of interrelated facts. It is not the gift of grace of seers and prophets dispensing sacred values and revelations, nor does it partake of the contemplation of sages and philosophers about the meaning of the universe" (SV, 152). It requires that one give up all such religiously based appeals.

Those who cannot accept the modern disenchantment of the world brought on by the scientific world-view should not look to the scientist as prophet but return to the earlier religious world-view. Yet they must do so at a price. They must make an "intellectual sacrifice" and retreat from this grim face of modernity. While Weber respects and understands such a choice, it is clearly not one he agrees with.

> To the person who cannot bear the fate of the times like a man, one must say: may he rather return silently, without the usual publicity build-up of renegades, but simply and plainly. The arms of the old churches are opened widely and compassionately for him. One way or another he has to bring his "intellectual sacrifice" — that is inevitable. If he can really do it we shall not rebuke him (SV, 155).

Such a choice is better than the choice of those who wait for new religious prophets and prophecies. It is better than the choice of those who evade the duty of intellectual integrity that science imposes and still seek for meaningful answers about how to live from it. But none of these alternatives face the modern situation squarely.

The Protestant Ethic and the Spirit of Capitalism adds a further dimension to Weber's understanding of modernity as it links the rise of scientific technical rationality with the economic rationality of capitalism.[23] The inner-worldly asceticism produced by Protestantism, especially the Calvinist varieties, led to an ethic of hard work and frugality among its members. While the accumulation and spending of wealth for its own sake was judged to be sinful by early Protestants, wealth earned by the fruits of one's hard labor was not. It was a blessing from God and a sign of grace to those who faithfully worked in their calling. Such wealth was not to be frivolously spent, but was to be saved and reinvested in work.

---

[23] Max Weber, The Protestant Ethic and the Spirit of Capitalism, trans. Anthony Giddens (London: Unwin Hyman, 1930). Hereafter cited in the text as PE.

When the limitation of consumption is combined with this release of acquisitive activity, the inevitable practical result is obvious: accumulation of capital through ascetic compulsion to save. The restraints which were imposed upon the consumption of wealth naturally served to increase it by making possible the productive investment of capital (PE, 172).

The capitalist economic ethic was born. As long as his "moral conduct was spotless and the use to which he put his wealth was not objectionable," the businessman "could follow his pecuniary interests as he would and feel that he was fulfilling a [religious] duty in doing so" (PE, 177). In turn, he could count on industrious workers who shared such ascetic attitudes. Economic inequalities were no longer morally and religiously objectionable, but were attributable to the hands of a Divine Providence.

For Weber, the religious underpinnings of the capitalist economic ethos are jettisoned by subsequent generations as capitalism matures and the increasing wealth it brings contributes a secularizing influence. The result is that the economic forces unleashed by ascetic Protestantism have shaped a world today in which material goods rather than religious values "have an inexorable power over the lives of men." The modern economic order of capitalism built by these early modern Protestants has become an "iron cage" from which there is no escape for moderns. It is "bound to the technical and economic conditions of machine production which today determines the lives of all the individuals who are born into this mechanism . . . with irresistible force" (PE, 181). Economic necessity forces most modern persons to conform to the dictates of the capitalist economy. Even the fortunate few free of such necessity are nevertheless tied to this mechanism as they pursue economic gain as an end in itself.

Like the scientific pursuit of knowledge, the economic pursuit of wealth has become its own distinct value sphere in the modern world at odds with religious values. In his essay "Religious Rejections of the World and Their Directions," Weber systematically outlines the various value spheres of modernity and their opposition to religion.[24] It is here that Weber's ethical polytheism comes into sharper focus.

In this essay, Weber assumes a general development of religion from naive, magical forms to prophetic and salvific forms. In the less

---

[24] Max Weber, "Religious Rejections of the World and Their Directions," in *From Max Weber: Essays in Sociology* (New York: Oxford, 1946), 323-359. Hereafter cited in the text as RR. For an extended discussion of this essay, see Robert Bellah, "Max Weber and World-Denying Love," *Journal of the American Academy of Religion*, 67/2 (1999): 277-304.

developed forms, there is a clear accommodation, if not integral connection, between religion and the various social dimensions of everyday life. In the more developed forms, there is a tension or even opposition between religion and the "world and its orders." The highest religions develop a world-denying ethos which rejects everyday values.

> The more the religions have been true religions of salvation, the greater has this tension been. This follows from the meaning of salvation and from the substance of the prophetic teaching as these develop into an ethic. . . . Indeed the further the rationalization and sublimation of the external and internal possession of — in the widest sense — "things worldly" has progressed, the stronger has the tension on the part of religion become. For the rationalization and the conscious sublimation of man's relations to the various spheres of values . . . have then pressed towards making conscious the *internal and lawful autonomy* of the individual spheres; thereby letting them drift into those tensions which remain hidden to the originally naive relation with the external world (RR, 328).

Weber conceives of the world-denying ethos as a "religion of brotherliness" or "objectless acosmism of love" in which the ethical demand requires a universal fraternity which goes beyond loyalty to the various worldly value spheres: kinship ties, economics, politics, aesthetics, erotic relations, and intellectual pursuits. "The religion of brotherliness has always clashed with the orders and values of the world, and the more consistently its demands have been carried through, the sharper the clash has been" (RR, 330). Interestingly, Weber's observations can encompass Troeltsch's prophetic ethical monotheism, for it is precisely when each of the value spheres *including the religious* is most highly rationalized that the tension is most acute. Rationalization is the process in which the mechanisms of each value sphere are increasingly harmonized or made consistent with the operative value. In large part, Troeltsch's project can clearly be interpreted as a process of rationalizing the Christian ethos. Further, for both Weber and Troeltsch, the prophetic impulses are key to the development of religion.

Weber gives extended attention to each of the value spheres and demonstrates how each one clashes with the religion of brotherliness. The particularity of kinship ties are devalued by the religious ethos. The dual layered ethic of kinship in which concern for the sibling, the parent, the neighbor takes precedence over concern for the stranger or enemy clashes with the religious demand for universal fraternity (RR, 328-30). While there have been affinities and alliances between religion and art throughout history, the aesthetic focus on form clashes with the religious emphasis on content. Both the iconoclasm of prophetic religion and the ecstatic transcendence of mystical religion are suspicious of the cultivation of form for its own sake that the aesthetic sphere promotes (RR, 341-43). The tension between the aesthetic and the religious spheres reaches its zenith in modernity. Art presents itself as an alternative form of religion, "a *salvation* from the routines of everyday life, and especially from the increasing pressures of theoretical and practical rationalism" (RR, 342). The same dynamic is at work between the religion of brotherliness and the erotic sphere. While sex and naive religion may have been intimately related in orgiastic rites, highly developed forms of religion aim to reject or control eroticism given its exclusivity, solipsism, and brutality (RR, 343, 348-49). Like art it presents itself as an alternative form of salvation from the rationalization of modern life (RR, 346-47).

Weber's conclusions about the economic sphere are consistent with his findings in *The Protestant Ethic and the Spirit of Capitalism.* Weber thinks that "no genuine religion of salvation has overcome the tension between its religiosity and a rational economy" (RR, 332). The religion of brotherliness and its emphasis upon charity and fraternity stands at odds with the most highly rational economic system, namely capitalism.

> A rational economy is a functional organization oriented to money-prices which originate in the interest-struggles of men in the market. Calculation is not possible without estimation in money prices and hence without market struggles. Money is the most abstract and "impersonal" element that exists in human life. . . . The more rational, and thus impersonal, capitalism becomes, the more is this the case. (RR, 331)

While the Puritan emphasis upon vocation escaped the tension between the economic and religious sphere, it did so at the price of renouncing "the universalism of love" that is key to the religion of brotherliness and thereby cannot be considered "a genuine 'religion of salvation'" (RR, 332, 333).

Like the economic sphere, the political sphere is based upon impersonal calculative mechanisms. As the rational economy focuses upon the logic of the market, rational politics resorts to the depersonalizing logic of bureaucracy (RR, 333-34). There is a further conflict between religion's renunciation of force and politics' foundation on the use of force. The political state "is an association that claims the monopoly of the *legitimate use of violence*, and cannot be defined in any other manner" (RR, 334). Politics allows for an ethic of justified means, where religion maintains an ethic of absolute ends.[25] Beyond this, the political sphere

---

[25] Weber makes these points more extensively in "Politics as a Vocation," in *From*

offers itself as an alternative form of salvation, like the aesthetic and the erotic, especially when it resorts to the use of force in the state of war. The patriotic fervor of warfare "makes for an unconditionally devoted and sacrificial community among the combatants" rivaling the highest forms of religious community (RR, 335).

The conflict between religion and the final sphere Weber considers in this essay, the intellectual, has already been anticipated in the discussion above of "Science as a Vocation." All that needs further emphasis here is that the pursuit of intellectual knowledge undoes the religious perspective of the world: "all religions have demanded as a specific presupposition that the course of the world be somehow *meaningful*, at least in so far as it touches upon the interests of men" (RR, 353). However, scientific investigation reveals otherwise. "The cosmos of natural causality and the postulated cosmos of ethical, compensatory causality have stood in irreconcilable opposition" (RR, 355). From the perspective of science, the world is irrational and has no meaning.

In the modern conflict between religion and the other value spheres, disenchantment reigns and religion loses out: "in the midst of a culture that is rationally organized for a vocational workaday life, there is hardly any room for the cultivation of acosmic brotherliness" (RR, 357). The rationalization and intellectualization of modern life return us, as Weber states it in "Science as a Vocation," to the situation of ancient polytheism, without the accompanying sense of enchantment. Christian monotheism had dethroned the ancient polytheism. Now, Christianity is itself dethroned.

> Today the routines of everyday life challenge religion. Many old gods ascend from their graves; they are disenchanted and hence take the form of impersonal forces. They strive to gain power over our lives and again they resume their eternal struggle with one another. What is hard for modern man . . . is to measure up to *workaday* existence (SV, 149).

While there is beauty and simplicity in the religious option of brotherliness, it is now unworkable in the spheres of everyday life.

The result is ethical polytheism. Weber requires us to choose among the various gods, the various forces, which have the modern person in their grip. This choice must be undertaken with the recognition that there can be no final reconciliation between the gods and no ultimately rational perspective for deciding among them.

Max Weber: Essays in Sociology, ed. and trans. H. H. Gerth and C. Wright Mills (New York: Oxford, 1946), 77-128.

This proposition, which I present here, always takes its point of departure from the one fundamental fact, that so long as life remains immanent and is interpreted in its own terms, it knows only of an unceasing struggle of these gods with one another. Or speaking directly, the ultimately possible attitudes toward life are irreconcilable, and hence their struggle can never be brought to a final conclusion. Thus it is necessary to make a decisive choice (SV, 152).

Neither science nor religious authority can decide for the individual. If one thinks science can lead the way, then one has a mistaken understanding of science. If one allows religious authority to make the choice, then one has already offered the necessary "intellectual sacrifice" required by an authentic and wholehearted religious commitment.

The modern situation of disenchanted polytheism reflects "a prophetless and godless time" (SV, 153). It entails a rejection of a wholehearted commitment to the religious ethos of brotherliness. Such brotherliness may still exist within the confines of personal life (SV, 155). Yet this religion of brotherliness can only live on if it is consistent with such polytheism by a partial commitment, as only one of the various values the modern person upholds.[26]

3. James and the democratic harmony of the multiverse

In his 1912 review essay, "Empiricism and Platonism in the Philosophy of Religion: To the Memory of William James," Ernst Troeltsch offers an appreciative, if critical, reading of James's empirical approach to religion. He initially notes the points of contact between them: their rejection of dogmatic presuppositions and authorities, the breadth of their data for study, and their open-ended pursuit of normative questions of meaning.

As with us the philosophy of religion is distinguished from the theology of the churches by setting out, not from a given theological norm of truth, but from the whole wide field of religious phenomena, so also with James. He, too, considers religion as a vast sphere of phenomena common to all mankind, within which no presumption lies in favor of minor individual circles. The goal, moreover, like the point of departure, is determined for him by no outside authority or dogma, but he compares and appraises the phenomena

---

[26] Weber's wife reports that Weber himself lived out this form of polytheism. "He never lost out his profound reverence for the gospel of brotherhood, and he accepted its demand relating to personal life." Nevertheless, Weber still had to make room for the "other 'gods,'" particularly the demands of the fatherland and of scientific truth." Marianne Weber, *Max Weber: A Biography*, trans. Harry Zohn (New York: Wiley, 1975 as quoted in Bellah, "Max Weber and World-Denying Love," *Journal of the American Academy of Religion*, 67/2 (1999): 299.

with entire freedom, according to a standard which the philosopher himself has to discover and justify (EP, 402).

While respecting traditional forms of religious life, both Troeltsch and James react against dogmatic theology and its ecclesiastical encumbrances. They move toward a consideration of personal piety. Both focus upon the psychology of the religious individual in his or her intercourse with the divine apart from sociological and historical considerations. Both see "an individualized and spiritualized form of Protestantism" as the highest form of religiosity (EP, 417-18). Troeltsch confesses that James's study of religion, "living, unprejudiced, saturated with reality grows on me." It is attractive because it displays the virtues of "marvelous freshness, freedom from prejudice, and sharpness of observation" which provide a model for further inquiry (EP, 420, 421).

Ultimately, however, Troeltsch rejects James's approach because of its grounding in a tradition of empiricism which can never rationally validate the truth of religious experience. Troeltsch appeals instead to a tradition of transcendental philosophy centered in the thought of Kant and Schleiermacher and stretching back to Platonic and Neoplatonic thought. This tradition validates the truth that all diverse forms of religious expression point toward God, the One which is the source of the Many. If James's empiricism leads him to take seriously the breadth and depth of religious data and makes him a master at understanding the psychology of religious expression, his thorough commitment to it leads to agnosticism, relativism, and skepticism regarding religion. James's anti-Platonic pragmatic empiricism "with its 'pluralistic universe,' its 'multiverse,' and its polytheism, does violence to the . . . basic sentiment of religion" (EP, 421). It must be decisively rejected.

Troeltsch's ambivalence toward James's work speaks to the affinities and differences among Troeltsch, James, and Weber and the modern religious possibilities they each perceive. All three begin from a point of religious loss or disenchantment. In an early letter to Oliver Wendell Holmes, James laments that, "if God is dead or at least irrelevant, then ditto everything pertaining to the 'Beyond.'"[27] Both Troeltsch and Weber could find some agreement with James's statement in the beginning of *A Pluralistic Universe*:

> The theological machinery that spoke so livingly to our ancestors, with its finite age of the world, its creation out of nothing, its juridical morality and eschatology, its relish for rewards and punishments, its treatment of God as

---

[27] As quoted in Ralph Barton Perry, *The Thought and Character of William James* (Boston: Little, Brown, and Co., 1935), 517.

an external contriver, an 'intelligent and moral governor,' sounds as odd to most of us as if it were some outlandish savage religion. . . . An external creator and his institutions may still be verbally confessed at church in formulas that linger by their own inertia, but the life is out of them, we avoid dwelling on them, the sincere heart of us is elsewhere.[28]

James is closer to Troeltsch than Weber, however, insofar as each sees the possibility of "reenchantment" or religious reinterpretation and renewal. Both would reject Weber's "cultural pessimism" and his picture of modernity as "an anarchic plurality of cultural values."[29] Hence, Troeltsch's sense of affinity with James. Yet James would reject Troeltsch's adherence to transcendental philosophy and Christianity as aspects of an outmoded form of monism which confers a sense of religious assurance, but does not do justice to the facts of human experience as lived.

Instead, James offers a "pluralistic hypothesis" in which there are multiple centers of value, no one of which is all inclusive. In such a hypothesis, "God" is only one center of value, one aspect of a wider spiritual reality in which human ideals are central. James argues for a humanistic and democratic moral and religious vision at odds with the autocratic heritage of Western monotheism. Like Weber, James's work may be interpreted as a form of ethical polytheism; but if Weber's ethical polytheism is centrifugal and anarchical, James's ethical polytheism is harmonizing. Where Weber sees an unceasing struggle of the gods, a chaotic competition among conflicting value spheres in a godless age, James perceives a creative transformation of human religious ideals in which old gods die and new ones are born, reflecting an evolution of human values. For Weber, the plurality of value spheres entails conflict and anarchy; for James, such plurality of values bespeaks healthy individual expression within a cooperative, democratic horizon.

In *The Varieties of Religious Experience*, James sets forth an intriguing conception of religious evolution.[30] "Nothing is more striking than the secular alteration that goes on in the moral and religious tone of men, as their insight into nature and their social arrangements progressively develop" (VRE, 263). Yet this process does not represent the end of religious values and purposes, but their transmutation. The death of the

---

[28] William James, *A Pluralistic Universe* (Cambridge: Harvard University Press, 1977), 18. Hereafter cited in the text as PU.

[29] These phrases are from Dietrich, 83.

[30] William James, *The Varieties of Religious Experience* (Cambridge: Harvard University Press, 1985). Cited in the text as VRE.

gods is a recurrent theme in human culture. Gods are to be judged according to their human fruits, and when their fruits are eventually deemed worthless, they are eventually discarded. "The gods we stand by are the gods we need and can use, the gods whose demands on us are reinforcements of our demands on ourselves and on one another" (VRE, 265). Religious and moral demands are tied together. Thus pagan versions of deity gave way to Christian ones, Catholic ones gave way to Protestant ones, and traditional Protestant ones gave way to liberal Protestant ones. In the same way, the religious conceptions of "all of us now living will be judged by our descendants" (VRE, 264). The judgement concerning particular religious values is based upon moral and intellectual grounds. "It is but the elimination of the humanly unfit, and the survival of the humanly fittest applied to religious beliefs" (VRE, 266). In James's judgement, religious evolution points in the moral direction of greater tolerance, diversity, and compassion. These values are supported by pluralistic religious conceptions.

In a survey on personal religious experience done by James Pratt in 1904, James gives a succinct statement of this pluralistic hypothesis. He responds that he has never personally experienced the presence of God, but that he has a dim sense of divine reality. He believes in God because of "the whole tradition of religious people, to which something in me makes admiring response" and because of "the social reasons." By social reasons, James means the possibility of sympathetic intercourse with higher powers. He identifies the most important element of religion as the "social appeal for corroboration, consolation, etc., when things are going wrong with my causes." To be religious is to know a wider world friendly and responsive to individual human desires and aims. God is not all in all in this wider world, but simply one among many spiritual agents having an effect upon human affairs: "'God,' to me, is not the only spiritual reality to believe in. Religion means primarily a universe of spiritual relations surrounding the earthly practical ones, not merely relations of 'value,' but agencies and their activities."[31] To believe in this plural wider reality is not to submit passively to it as an instrument of its ends, but to form an active partnership or social compact with it in the furtherance of shared goals.

It is true enough that in the conclusion to *The Varieties of Religious Experience*, James claims the Christian name for his own over-belief:

---

[31] William James, *The Letters of William James*, II, ed. Henry James (Boston: Atlantic Monthly Press, 1920), 212-15.

"God is the natural appellation, for us Christians at least, for the supreme reality, so I will call this higher part of the universe by the name of God" (VRE, 406). But this identification is a perfunctory nod to his mostly Protestant, Anglo-American audience and should not be read too literally. The main thing that James wishes to convey is the notion of an efficacious *more*, and not any deep connection to Christian doctrine or practice. As he explains in a footnote, "'God' is a causal agent as well as a medium of communion, and that is the aspect which I wish to emphasize" (VRE, 406 n. 32). The divine cannot simply be a passive ideal, but must be an active presence within the human world. And thus like the Christian God, James's "God" offers redemption from real evils such that "where God is, tragedy is only provisional and partial, and shipwreck and dissolution are not the absolutely final things" (VRE, 407).

Despite this similarity, James's over-beliefs cannot be so easily assimilated to Christianity. As he tells the psychologist James Leuba in a letter, he is certain that "the deeper voice" which he recognizes "is not old theistic habits and prejudices of infancy. Those are Christian; and I have grown so out of Christianity that entanglement therewith on the part of a mystical utterance has to be abstracted from and overcome, before I can listen."[32] The salvific possibilities which James's divinity offers are loosely defined and granted without any form of mediation. Further, James leaves the question open of the singularity and infinity of this divinity. In a postscript, James expands upon the last of his Gifford Lectures and discusses his "piecemeal supernaturalism." This "super-naturalism" is broadly construed and simply indicates the fact of effects of an ideal power of some sort within the natural world. But this position is consistent, James thinks, with the Buddhist doctrine of karma and of any "religion generally so far as it remains unweakened by transcend-entalist metaphysics" (VRE, 411). While this power may be called "God," it need not have the attributes often associated with this name.

> All that the facts require is that the power should be both other and larger than our conscious selves. Anything larger will do, if only it be large enough to trust for the next step. It need not be infinite, it need not be solitary. It might conceivably even be only a larger and more godlike self, of which the present self would then be but the mutilated expression, and the universe might conceivably be a collection of such selves, of different degrees of inclusiveness, with no absolute unity realized in it at all. Thus would a sort of polytheism return upon us . . . (VRE, 413).

---

[32] *The Letters of William James*, II, 211.

The monistic hypothesis requires an Absolute who guarantees the salvation of all, yet it may be that "there are different gods, each caring for his part" such that "some portion of some of us might not be covered with divine protection, and our religious consolation would thus fail to be complete" (VRE, 413). This pluralistic hypothesis holds out no religious guarantees, but only "the *chance* of salvation" (VRE, 414).

James reiterates these themes of pluralism and chance in the final chapter of *Pragmatism* entitled "Pragmatism and Religion."[33] James speaks of the great clash between "rationalistic and empiricist religion" in which "the great religious difference lies between the men who insist that the world *must and shall be*, and those who are contented with believing that the world *may be*, saved" (P, 135). James calls this latter pluralistic hypothesis meliorism: the belief that salvation is neither inevitable, as the optimism of the rationalistic religion would have it, nor impossible as some pessimists such as Schopenhauer might claim. Meliorism treats salvation "as a possibility, which becomes more and more of a probability the more numerous the actual conditions of salvation become." Salvation itself is an open-ended thing: "You may interpret the word 'salvation' in any way you like, and make it as diffuse and distributive, or as climacteric and integral a phenomenon as you please." But it deals in some manner with the realization of individual ideals as each "such ideal realized will be one moment in the world's salvation" (P, 137).

In pragmatically evaluating the empirical and the rationalist religion according to the total satisfaction which each gives, James favors the pluralistic hypothesis because of its emphasis upon human participation in the events of salvation. By requiring individuals to play an active role in bringing about the greater good of the universe, meliorism appeals to socially directed heroic energies. "It is a real adventure, with real danger, yet it may win through. It is a social scheme of co-operative work genuinely to be done" (P, 139). The monistic hypothesis leads, on the other hand, to a more comfortable passivity. This has some appeal for those requiring consolation and peace in the face of insecurity, but for James this is a minority opinion.

> Most of us, I say, would therefore welcome the proposition and add our *fiat* to the *fiat* of the creator. Yet perhaps some would not; for there are morbid minds in every human collection, and to them the prospect of a universe with only a fighting chance of safety would probably make no appeal (P, 140).

---

[33] William James, *Pragmatism: A New Name for Some Old Ways of Thinking* (Cambridge: Harvard University Press, 1975). Cited in the text as P.

While all have moments of discouragement and bewilderment in which the desire to escape from life becomes strong, most rise above these moments. Yet, James notes, some can never fully face up to the adventures of life and turn to the monistic or absolutistic scheme. It gives them the security of a God who is all in all and guarantees the salvation of all instead of the humanly dependent piecemeal salvation of pluralism.

In James's view, human effort is thus crucial to bring about the world's salvation. Yet meliorism or the pluralistic hypothesis is not mere moralistic striving, but is a genuine religious option. While it demands moral strenuousness — human toil to bring the world into a more ideal shape — this effort is religious as well. The meliorist believes that individual moral efforts are met by the cooperation of spiritual forces friendly to his or her larger goal. As a social scheme of work, each individual's religious efforts take place within human society and within a larger society encompassing the human and the divine: salvation is in the making by a plurality of powers. Hence, the friendly forces include both like-minded persons and superhuman forces. The meliorist may speak of God, but not as the optimistic rationalists do, as the Absolute power in the universe. Pluralism means viewing "God as but one helper, *primus inter pares*, in the midst of all the shapers of the great world's fate" (P, 143). While James's God may be first among the equal powers and principalities of the wider world, this God's effectiveness is bound up with human energies. James's judgement is that the source of moral value is not the one God, but a diverse wider world of spiritual agency.

Such a view is bolstered by *A Pluralistic Universe*, in which James describes the possibility of a superhuman consciousness which is not all-embracing, but must be finite "in power or knowledge, or in both at once" (PU, 141). The divine is an organism with a history of interaction with its environment.

> [B]ecause God is not the absolute, but is himself a part when the system is conceived pluralistically, his functions can be taken as not wholly dissimilar to those of the other smaller parts — as similar to our functions consequently.
>
> Having an environment, being in time, and working out a history just like ourselves, he escapes from the foreignness from all that is human, of the static timeless perfect absolute (PU, 143-44).

God's temporality means then that he is affected by his environment, most especially the human elements of that environment. His history is intertwined with human history. He evolves, too, according to the growth and decay of the parts. The wider world is thus "more like a federal republic than like an empire or a kingdom" (PU, 145). It is a "multiverse" of individual self-governing entities which loosely form a larger purposive entity. It is a democracy of the divine.

James would reject Troeltsch's notion of an Absolute even with the qualification that this Absolute can only be grasped relatively or historically. While there is a wider spiritual reality, a more, which impinges upon human affairs, it is not the all-in-all, the source and end of all creaturely reality and value. It is a diffuse and diverse divine reality intimate with and shaped by human concerns and desires rather than set apart from them. In an increasingly pluralistic and democratic modern world, the autocratic heritage of Western monotheism must give way to more evolved religious and moral conceptions which allow for human participation in divine activity and growth.

4. Whither Ethical Monotheism?

Although Weber might see James's democratic hopes and ideals as naive in the face of modernity's iron cage and James might see Weber's hardheaded analysis of modernity as one-sided and too pessimistic, taken together, James and Weber offer powerful criticisms of ethical monotheism.

Despite their clear divergences, both would agree that there is no single source of moral value. For Weber, there are multiple and competing value spheres derivable from the distinct activities which make up human social life. For James, the diversity of human interests and needs provides the substance of moral value.[34] Both, too, agree that monotheistic religion does not provide the best way to "structure and reinforce moral consciousness." For Weber, the monotheism of an ethic of brotherliness results in an intellectual sacrifice which unwittingly obviates tough moral thinking.[35] For James, monotheism limits rather than spurs human moral activity and supports outmoded forms of social organization and authority. Finally, both agree that ethical monotheism

---

[34] There is much more to be said in this regard which I do not have space for here, but I am especially thinking of James's comments in "The Moral Philosopher and the Moral Life": "there is no such thing as an ethical philosophy made up in advance. We all help to determine the content of ethical philosophy so far as we contribute to the race's moral life." William James, "The Moral Philosopher and the Moral Life," in The Will To Believe (New York: Dover, 1956), 184.

[35] See, especially in this regard, Weber's comments at the end of "Politics as a Vocation" about the contrast between an ethic of responsibility and an ethic of ultimate ends, 124-28.

is not the best ground for modern culture. Where Troeltsch sees ethical monotheism as the pinnacle of religious development and an invigorating resource for cultural renewal, Weber and James see it as belonging to an earlier, surpassed stage of human development. For Weber, the complexity of modern social organization limits the integrity of ethical monotheism to the private sphere. For James, monotheism is an exclusivist doctrine at odds with the modern values of pluralism, tolerance, and democracy.

As Dietrich's work has shown, Troeltsch's ethical monotheism is at least partly guilty of the last charge of exclusivism. In discussing Troeltsch's ethical monotheistic theory of culture and society, Dietrich notes Troeltsch's emphasis upon the unitary nature of culture despite his recognition of historical particularity and development. With the exception of his last writings, "one finds here no systematic conception of religious pluralism interior to a single state and culture."[36] There is an isomorphism between German culture and the Protestant Christian ethos. Insofar as Troeltsch's last writings reach beyond German religious and cultural traditions, they stay within the orbit of Christian Europe.[37] Troeltsch's recognition of an expansive religious pluralism is external to the European cultural sphere. While there may be other valid religious traditions, they cannot be integrated within European culture. This notion is underlined in the posthumously published, "The Place of Christianity Among the World Religions."[38] Reevaluating his earlier assumptions in *The Absoluteness of Christianity* about the supreme validity of Christianity among the world religions, Troeltsch here recognizes the equal validity of other major religious traditions, especially Hinduism and Buddhism. Nevertheless each religious tradition is bound up with "the historical, geographical, and social conditions of the countries in which it has taken shape."[39] Therefore, the only religion for the authentic development of European society and culture is Christianity.

This leads Troeltsch's ethical monotheism into a further dilemma. If Europe's fate is tied to Christianity, Christianity's fate is tied to Europe. The fate of other cultures are similarly tied to other religious traditions which are equally valid within their cultural sphere. Even with this

---

[36] Dietrich, 77.
[37] The cultural traditions so included are Anglo-American and French and the religious tradition is Catholicism. Dietrich, 79.
[38] Ernst Troeltsch, "The Place of Christianity among the World Religions," in *Christian Thought: Its History and Application*, trans. Baron F. von Hugel, et al. (London: University of London Press, 1923), 3-35.
[39] "The Place of Christianity among the World Religions," 22-23.

limited recognition of pluralism, Troeltsch's monotheism comes precipitously close to being transformed into an ethical henotheism, for Troeltsch explicitly states that the human experience of divinity is manifold. Troeltsch famously claims that Christianity is "final and unconditional for us," yet this does not mean that other cultures might "experience their contact with the Divine Life in quite a different way."[40] Despite the logical difficulties here, Troeltsch avoids a thoroughgoing henotheism with his assertion that it is still the one God who is yet manifest in differing forms. All religions have the same Source and End. He is ultimately confident that it is still possible "to apprehend the One in the Many."[41]

Weber might see Troeltsch's confidence as an exemplification of the intellectual sacrifice which ignores modern workaday existence. James would interpret it as a comforting, yet ultimately anti-moralistic and anti-democratic sentiment. For both, such a monotheism would hinder rather than further ethical thinking and practice. In an ever increasing climate of pluralism, Troeltsch's belief that it is still possible to seek "the One in the Many" in spite of social, historical, and cultural differences becomes today a question mark for contemporary constructions of ethical monotheism.

---

[40] "The Place of Christianity among the World Religions," 26.
[41] "The Place of Christianity among the World Religions," 35.

PART THREE

CHAPTER EIGHT

THREE IS NOT ENOUGH:
JEWISH REFLECTIONS ON TRINITARIAN THINKING

DAVID R. BLUMENTHAL

1. *Scriptural and Early Rabbinic God Language*

In earlier times, people did not ask questions about God language; they just used it. Talking to God, directly, brought people close to the Lord of creation and history. Addressing God, in a straightforward manner, drew them into relationship with the Lord of life. Imagine the intensity of relatedness between God and the person who said (Psalm 139:112):

> Lord, You have probed me and You know.
> You know when I sit and when I stand.
> You discern my yelling from afar.
> You sift through my life path and my sexual patterns.
> You have intimate knowledge of all my ways. . . .
> You encompass me, front and back. . . .
> Where can I run away from Your presence?
> Where can I flee from Your Face?
> If I go up to heaven, You are there.
> If I descend below, You are there too.
> If I fly with wings to the east, if I dwell on the western horizon, there, too,
> Your hand will guide me, Your right hand will grasp me.
> If I say, "Let darkness envelope me and night be light for me," even darkness
> cannot be dark for You, night will light up as the day, darkness and light
> are the same.

Or, imagine the intimate relationship with God of the person who said (Isaiah 66:13): "As a man is comforted by his mother, so shall I comfort you and you shall be comforted in Jerusalem." Or, imagine the imagination of the one who talked of God as follows (Psalm 78:59-66):

> God saw and got angry and He detested Israel greatly. He deserted His
> sanctuary in Shiloh, the tent He had set among humans. . . . He handed over
> His people to the sword and was angry with His inheritance. His young men
> were consumed by fire and His young women could not even wail. His priests
> fell by the sword and His widows could not even weep. But then the Lord
> woke up like one asleep, like a warrior intoxicated with wine.[1]

---

[1] Heb., *ke-gibbor mitronen mi-yayin*.

Even when trying to describe the ineffable nature of God, concrete language and real action were the rule (Isaiah 40:12-24):

> Who measured the waters in the hollow of his hand? or meted out the heavens with a span? or contained the dust of the earth in a measure? or weighed the mountains in a scale and the hills in a balance? . . . He spreads the heavens as a curtain, stretching them out as a tent to dwell in. He makes princes as nothing and human judges as if they had done naught. Scarcely are they planted, scarcely are they sown, scarcely have their stocks taken root in the earth, then He blows on them and they are dried up, the storm carries them away as straw.

The tendency to personalist language in describing and addressing God, especially in Scripture, is wellknown.[2] The question is, can it be improved upon? Prephilosophic rabbinic thought said, No. The language of the midrash, therefore, continued the earlier personalist understanding and expression. The following passage is typical midrashic language about God:[3]

> "God came down in a cloud and stood with him [Moses] there, and H/he called out in the name of God. God passed before him and H/he called, 'Lord, Lord, God, merciful, and kind, of great patience, and full of grace, and truth. Who stores up grace for thousands, Who forgives purposeful sins, rebellious sins, and inadvertent sins, and Who cleanses . . .'" (Exodus 34:57) — Rabbi Yohanan said, "Were it not written in Scripture, it would be impossible to say it: This teaches that the Holy One, blessed be He, wrapped Himself in a *tallit* like a *shliah tsibbur* [one who leads in prayer] and showed Moses the order of prayer. He said, 'As long as Israel sins, they should follow this order of prayer before Me and I will forgive them. . . .'"

Personalist language also remained the mode of understanding and expression for addressing God in rabbinic liturgy. "Our Father, our King, we have sinned before You. . . . Our Father, our King, inscribe us in the book of life." How else could one pray? Indeed, one might say that rabbinic Judaism intensified the personalist thrust of language about, and address to, God.

2. *The Philosophic Challenge*

Philosophic rabbinic Judaism, which begins in the ninth century, first raised the systematic question of God language. Which words, the philosophers asked, are to be taken literally — that is, which words have

---

[2]　On the term "personalist," see e.g., B. P. Bowne, *Personalism* (Boston: Houghton, Mifflin, 1908); and D. Blumenthal, *Facing the Abusing God: A Theology of Protest* (Louisville, KY: Westminster/John Knox, 1993) at the Index, "Personality."

[3]　*Talmud*, Rosh haShana 17b.

truth value as descriptors of, and modes of address to, God? And, which words are not to be taken literally — that is, which words are images and metaphors? Once raised, the question was, and still is, hotly debated. Some said that certain words are true while the rest are metaphors. These are the thinkers who taught the doctrine of "essential attributes." Saadia Gaon, tenth century Iraq, claimed there were five words/ideas that truly applied to God; the rest were images. Some claimed more; some claimed fewer. But the solution was the same: There is a legitimate but limited God language; theology and, to a certain extent, liturgy must conform to that language. Other philosophers said that no language at all is adequate to describe or address God. One can only advance in theological reflection by realizing how powerless human beings and the tradition are in describing and addressing God. These are the thinkers who taught the *via negativa*, the theology of negation, best represented by Maimonides in twelfth century Egypt. Many followed him, more or less systematically. But the solution was the same: One cannot describe, and therefore one cannot directly address, God. This theology, properly followed, leads to silence, to an acknowledgment of our inability to say anything coherent about, or to coherently address, God. Biblical and liturgical language is all metaphors and is to be used only with reservation.[4]

Each of these philosophical schools of thought led, in Judaism, Christianity, and Islam, to a configuration of serious problems. The school of negative theology, which denied especially the personalist language of Scripture and liturgy, ran into the wall of spiritual experience. Even the most radical of negative theologians had some form of spiritual experience, sometimes rooted in the intellection of God and sometimes rooted in the love of God. This led to the paradox of denying all language about God but affirming God as intellect or God as love. This paradoxical affirmation, in turn, was rooted in a form of religious experience that can properly be called "philosophic" or "intellectualist mysticism," which was a well recognized form of spirituality in the Middle Ages.[5]

---

[4] On these two schools of philosophic Judaism, see *Facing*, 6-31, 246-48 and D. Blumenthal, "Croyance et attributs essentiels dans la théologie juive médiévale et moderne," *Revue des études juives* 152 (1994): 415-23; also available on my website <http://www.emory.edu/UDR/BLUMENTHAL>.

[5] On "philosophic mysticism," see D. Blumenthal, "Maimonides: Prayer, Worship, and Mysticism," *Prière, Mystique et Judaisme*, ed. R. Goetschel (Paris: Presses Universitaires de France), 89-106; reprinted in *Approaches to Judaism in Medieval Times*, ed. D. Blumenthal (Atlanta: Scholars Press, 1988), 3: 1-16; also available on my website (see n. 4); and D. Blumenthal, *Understanding Jewish Mysticism*, vol. 2 (New York: Ktav Publishing, 1982), 386.

The school of essentialist theology, which asserted some but not all language of God, ran into the wall of the unity of God. Even the most elegant essentialist theologian had some form of pluralism in his conception of the divine. God, in God's essence, was limited, but always more than one. It is in the context of essential attributes that Jews understood the problem of the trinity: Granted that God could, in God's essential divinity, be three — or four, or five — how could God also be only one? A good question — for Jews, for Christians, and for Muslims.[6] Insofar, however, as the doctrine of the trinity claimed more than the identity of three dimensions within the essence of God, Jews did not, and do not, understand it. Jews simply denied, as a form of polytheism, that the persons of the trinity could be more than essential attributes of God. (The other problem Jews had with the trinity was its use as a tool for persecution, forced conversion, and religious murder. The trinity has not been experienced by Jews as the embodiment of God's inalienable and grace- filled love.)

Nonphilosophic Judaism took another tack on the matter of God language. Nonphilosophic — and postphilosophic[7] — Judaism followed in the footsteps of the biblical and early rabbinic tradition and simply did not get tangled up in the question of when a word is true and when it becomes only an image, of when a phrase is real and when it becomes only a metaphor. This stream of the tradition adopted the doctrine that some words/ideas were more important than others, but rejected the conception that other words and images are somehow not valid expressions of, and address to, the divine. I think this was due, in the first instance, to a loyalty to the earlier, traditional language of Scripture, midrash, and liturgy which is, everyone agrees, personalist. I think, too, that the nonphilosophic return to what Scholem called "mythic" language[8] was also due to a recognition of the limited affective range of philosophic Judaism. The rarified rational mysticism of the philosophic rabbis was not the favored cup of tea of everyone. Rather, these others found the expression for their own experience of God in the

---

[6] H. A. Wolfson, *The Philosophy of the Church Fathers*, 2nd ed. (Cambridge, MA: Harvard University Press, 1964), chaps. 7-15; idem, *Studies in the History of Religion and Philosophy*, 2 vols. (Cambridge: MA, Harvard University Press, 1973, 1977), at indexes.

[7] See for example, A. J. Heschel, *The Prophets*, 2 vols. (San Francisco: Harper and Row, 1962); and M. Kadushin, *The Rabbinic Mind* (New York: Jewish Theological Seminary, 1952), cited in *Facing*, 7, 12, 25-29.

[8] G. Scholem, "Kabbalah and Myth," *On the Kabbalah and Its Symbolism* (New York, Shocken Books, 1969), chap 3.

personalist language of the earlier tradition and built their theologies and liturgies in that language, rejecting the intellectualist, restrained speech of the philosophers.[9]

3. *The Zoharic Response*

Probably the most imaginative, and powerful, nonphilosophic response in the personalist tradition of thinking about and addressing God is to be found in the *Zohar* (end of the thirteenth century Spain) and in the tradition that developed from it.[10] This world view became known as "The Kabbala," which is a somewhat too restricted use of the term. It taught that God Godself is made up of ten dimensions, called *sefirot* (sing., *sefira*). These *sefirot* are not extradeical hypostases, like the intellects of the neo-Aristotelian philosopher theologians. Nor are they attributes of God, like the essential or accidental attributes of the other philosopher theologians. Rather, the *sefirot* of the *Zohar* are extramental — that is, they are real and not just mental constructs of the human mind — and they are intradeical dimensions of God's very being — that is, they are inside God, integral parts of God. Furthermore, the *sefirot* are not static; they interact with one another. Thus, God's *Hesed* (grace) interacts with God's *Gevura* (God's power to draw lines, set standards, and make judgments). Thus, too, God's *Tiferet* (compassion, mercy) draws on God's *Hesed* and God's *Gevura*. All three draw on God's *Hokhma* (knowability) and God's *Bina* (intuitive understanding), as well as upon God's *Keter* (ineffability). God's *Malkhut* (ruling ability) is God's Face to creation, God's Name by which God is known. *Malkhut* is the point of contact between God and the world; it is where the spiritual energy of humanity and of God meet and interact.

This interactive and dynamic system of the dimensions of God can be graphically portrayed as a tree, as a human being, as well as in

---

[9] Since I claim that the philosophers also had a form of mysticism, I cannot label the nonphilosophers "mystics." Further, the nonphilosophers also include liturgists and halakhists who were not mystics in its narrow sense or philosophers. For a typology of Jewish mysticism, see *Understanding Jewish Mysticism*, 2 vols. (New York: Ktav Publishing, 1978, 1982).

[10] To call the *Zohar* "nonphilosophic" is, technically, not quite correct. Part of the *Zohar* is rooted in Maimonidean philosophic concepts and terms (e.g., the use of "intellects"). Further, the doctrine of the *sefirot* is, in a way, a development of Saadia's essential attributes. The picture is, thus, not black and white. However, the basic intradeical and dynamic conception of God envisioned by the *Zohar*, and in particular its view of evil, is surely contrary to both schools of philosophic theology; hence, the use of "nonphilosophical."

various more abstract representations. These representations are widely available and form the core of "kabbalistic art." The clearest is given in Figure 1 (p. 194).[11] Further, the *Zohar*, unlike modern literature, is written in a style which regards multiple imagery as a fine art. Hence, each *sefira* is depicted with multiple metaphors and even with multiple meanings. An inkling of the complexity of this system is given in Figure 2 (p. 195).

4. *Texting*

The following text,[12] which uses the image of the common flame, best illustrates the dynamic and interactive quality of the *sefirot*:[13]

> Rabbi Simeon began by saying: There are two verses [that contradict one another]. It is written, "For the Lord your God is a devouring fire" (Deuteronomy 4:24) and it is also written, "And you who cleave to the Lord your God are alive, all of you, today" (Deuteronomy 4:4). We have reconciled these verses in several places, but the [mystical] companions have a [deeper] understanding of them. . . . Whoever wishes to understand the wisdom of the holy unification, let him look at the flame that rises from a glowing coal, or from a burning lamp, for the flame rises only when it takes hold of some coarse matter.
>
> Come and see. In the rising flame there are two lights: one is a radiant white light and one is a light that contains black or blue. The white light is above and it ascends in a direct line. Beneath it is the blue or black light and it is a throne for the white. The white light rests upon it and they are

---

[11] See *Understanding Jewish Mysticism*, 1: 116-18, for three diagrams. I proposed the third of those diagrams when I was first at Brown University with Wendell Dietrich, to whom this volume is dedicated. I have, however, much in Wendell's tradition, continued to ponder these matters and have rethought the translations I used then. I now propose those in Figure 1.

Students of these sefirotic trees will note that sometimes *Hesed* is on the right and sometimes on the left. The rule is quite simple. *Hesed* is always on the left; the issue is the point of view of the reader. If the reader considers the representation to be a roadmap, then right on the image corresponds to the reader's right and so with the left. If, however, the reader considers the representation to be a person, i.e., in face-to-face position, then left on the image corresponds to the reader's right and vice versa. The latter form of representation is a mirror; the former a diagram.

[12] I first used these texts in "Confronting the Character of God: Text and Praxis," *God in the Fray: Divine Ambivalence in the Hebrew Bible*, ed. T. Beal and T. Linafelt (forthcoming); also available on my website (see n. 4).

[13] *Zohar* 1: 50b-51b, modified from F. Lachower and I. Tishby, *The Wisdom of the Zohar*, trans. D. Goldstein (Oxford: The Littman Library and Oxford University Press, 1989) 1: 319-20. The *Zohar*, although it exists in translation, is not comprehensible without an explication. Tishby's three volumes do that. For a shorter presentation based on Tishby's method, see *Understanding Jewish Mysticism*, 1 (1978), 101-91. For syllabi on teaching the *Zohar*, see my website (see n. 4).

connected together, forming one whole. The black light, [that which has] blue color, is the throne of glory for the white. And this is the mystic significance of the blue.

This blueblack throne is joined to something else, below it, so that it can burn and this stimulates it to grasp the white light. . . . This [blueblack light] is connected on two sides. It is connected above to the white light and it is connected below to what is beneath it, to what has been prepared for it so that it might illuminate and grasp [that which is above it]. This [blueblack light] devours continuously and consumes whatever is placed beneath it; for the blue light consumes and devours whatever is attached to it below, whatever it rests upon, since it is its habit to consume and devour. Indeed, the destruction of all, the death of all, depends upon it and therefore it devours whatever is attached to it below. [But] the white light which rests upon it does not devour or consume at all, and its light does not change. Concerning this, Moses said, "For the Lord your God is a devouring fire," really devouring, devouring and consuming whatever rests beneath it. . . .

Above the white light rests a concealed light which encompasses it. Here is a supernal mystery and you will find all in the ascending flame. The wisdom of the upper realms is in it.

The *Zohar* begins this passage in classical midrashic style by showing a contradiction between two verses, one of which speaks of God as a consuming fire while the other advocates cleaving to God. It then goes on to draw an analogy to the common flame which is attached to a dark coal, which it must consume in order to burn. The flame itself is composed of two parts — a blueblack center, which is attached to the wick or coal, and a white periphery which encompasses and rises above the blueblack center.

In this passage, the *Zohar* depicts the central sefira — which is *Tiferet* — as the white part of the flame. It rests upon the *sefira*, which is the point of contact with creation, *Malkhut*, here depicted as the blueblack part of the flame. At the end of this passage, the *Zohar* calls attention to the invisible part of the flame — the zone of invisible heat which surrounds every fire — and interprets it as *Keter* (God's ultimate ineffability).

Finally, the *Zohar* notes that the blueblack part of the flame, *Malkhut* (God's ruling ability), consumes the coal or wick to which it is attached. The coal and wick are material; they depict creation, particularly humanity. Having decoded the symbolism of the passage, we can address the theology.[14] The *Zohar* teaches here that God's compassion (*Tiferet*, the white part of the flame) is interactive with God's providence (*Malkhut*, the blueblack part of the flame) or governance. Energy flows from compassion to governance and also from governance to compassion.

---

[14] For a good explication of the difference between symbol decoding and theological interpretation, see *Understanding Jewish Mysticism*.

God is in discussion with Godself, so to speak, on the issue of how best to act in creation — just as there can be no flame without both a blueblack and a white light and the interaction between them. The *Zohar* also teaches here that God's very energy depends on creation — just as, without the wick or coal, there can be no flame. This means that God's providence is fed by human action and, further, that that energy is passed on even unto God's inner being, God's compassion. To put it differently, spiritual energy generated in creation rises up into God's Self. This human-generated spiritual energy, according to the *Zohar*, actually sustains the dimensions of God's very being, God's providence, God's compassion, and God's ineffability — just as the wick or coal sustains the blueblack, the white, and even the invisible parts of the common flame.

Finally, the *Zohar* teaches that, for most of creation, this feeding of energy to the divine is consuming; that is, that it results in the death of created beings. This death-into-God is the purpose of most of creation. Death is not only a part of the natural action of God's governance; it adds energy to God.

The text continues:[15]

> Come and see. The only stimulus that causes the blue light to burn and to grasp the white light is that which comes from Israel, who cleave to it below. Come and see. Although it is the way of the blueblack flame to consume whatever is attached to it beneath, Israel, who cleave to it beneath, survive as they are. This is the meaning of "And you who cleave to the Lord your God are alive — " . . . to the blueblack light that devours and consumes whatever is attached to it beneath and yet you who cleave to it survive as is written, "alive, all of you, today."

Here, the *Zohar* takes another theological step and identifies the stimulus that sustains the flame as being the Jewish people.[16] They, in their proper zoharic observance of the commandments, feed spiritual energy first into *Malkhut* and then into *Tiferet*. Performing the *mitsvot* with the proper zoharic intent allows the Jewish worshiper consciously to direct energy into God. It allows the Jew to interact directly with God, not just in dialogue but in interaction, in a conscious directing of spiritual energy into God. This ability to feed spiritual energy back into God through the zoharic observance of God's commandments is the height of interactivity with God. It is the purpose of Jewish existence. It gives

---

[15] Ibid.

[16] The *Zohar* did not envision non-Jews (and Jewish women) as participating in this process.

life; hence, the verse from Deuteronomy 4:4, which contrasts with Deuteronomy 4:24, in which contact with the Godhead results in death.

The theology of the spiritual interaction of humanity and the dimensions of God's very being is repeated and extended in an important way in another passage:[17]

> Rabbi Judah said: When the righteous increase in the world, the Assembly of Israel exudes a sweet perfume, and she is blessed by the Holy King and her face shines. But, when the wicked increase in the world, the Assembly of Israel does not exude sweet perfumes, so to speak, but she tastes of the bitter "other side." Then is it written, "He has cast down earth from heaven" (Lamentations 2:1) and, then, her face is darkened.

To decode this passage, one must know that "Assembly of Israel" is not the Jewish people; rather, it is *Malkhut* (God's Face to creation). Similarly, the "Holy King" is not God but is *Tiferet* (God's compassion). To "exude sweet perfume" is to radiate positive spiritual energy. To have a "face shine" is to experience joy, bliss. Finally, "earth" is *Malkhut* and "heaven" is *Tiferet*.[18] The theology of this passage is deceptively clear. It teaches that the righteous, by their righteousness — that is, by their zoharic observance of the commandments, especially prayer — consciously return energy into God; that is, the righteous return positive energy into *Malkhut,* the outward dimension of God that governs creation. *Malkhut,* then, radiates that positive spiritual energy into *Tiferet,* the more inward compassionate dimension of God's being. With this positive unification of the outer and inner dimensions of God — that is, with the union of compassion and providence inside the Divine — God Godself experiences bliss! This understanding of the human-divine relationship in which humans help God unite Godself parallels that of the previous passage, with the addition that the *Zohar* teaches, here, that God Godself experiences bliss. The really new idea in this passage is that the wicked, by their wickedness — which includes, but is not limited to, their nonzoharic observance of the commandments — return negative energy into God. This, in turn, means that God (that is, *Malkhut*) does not radiate positive spiritual energy into *Tiferet,* and God Godself does not experience bliss. In fact, the passage teaches that when the wicked prosper, God is drawn toward the "other side," the dark side, of God's own being, and then God Godself experiences darkness, which

---

[17] *Zohar* 3: 74a; Tishby, 1: 364.

[18] Part of the great art of the Zohar is that most of its passages can be read on a simple midrashic level referring to God and the Jewish people. Texting by *double-entendre* is an art lost to contemporary theological writing.

is absence-of-bliss, but is also anger and dangerous power. When the wicked prosper, God Godself is fragmented — as the passage says, "earth" is separated from "heaven"; that is, *Malkhut* is severed from *Tiferet*. To put it succinctly: When the righteous prosper, God's governance and compassion act together, and God is in bliss. But, when the wicked are ascendant, God's ability to govern is severed from God's compassion, and God is subject to the dark side of God's nature, and is depressed and dangerous. This is a remarkable double theological statement: first, that God is influenced by the actions of humans, for better but also for worse; that the human capacity consciously to direct energy into God can have bad, as well as good, consequences — not just in this world but also inside God.[19] Second, and perhaps more revolutionary, the passage is clear — and it is typical of zoharic thinking — that God has a "dark side"; that, within God Godself, is the capacity to act in ways that are wrong, evil, sinful.[20] It is passages like these that led me in *Facing the Abusing God: A Theology of Protest* to dare to use the term "abusing" of God, as reviewers familiar with the *Zohar* have noted.

The *Zohar*, and the tradition that developed out of it, including Lurianic kabbalah, then, constitutes a reappropriation and a deepening of the personalist language of the biblical and earlier rabbinic tradition. It produces textual, spiritual, and theological insight into God in a very, very personalist mode. As Walter Brueggemann, in another context, has noted: "Thus, we need to consider not only mutations in the social processes, or mutations in the articulations of God which serve the social processes, but *mutations that are said to be going on in the very person of God.*"[21] Interestingly, Christian theologians seem to have sensed this. When, in 1553, the (otherwise good) Franciscan brothers ordained the burning of all Jewish books in the Campo dei Fiori in the center of Rome, they specifically ordered copies of the *Zohar* to be removed from the pyre.[22] In a more constructive vein, counterreformation Catholic scholars developed a whole theological enterprise called "Christian Kabbala" which translated and commented upon the *Zohar* and related

---

[19] This passage does not spell it out but other passages draw a further conclusion — that, when the wicked prosper, God actually radiates negative spiritual energy to creation, with disastrous consequences.

[20] See Tishby, vol. 2, part 2.

[21] W. Brueggemann, "A Shape for Old Testament Theology," *Catholic Biblical Quarterly* 47: 35, italics original.

[22] C. Roth, *History of the Jews of Italy* (Philadelphia: Jewish Publication Society, 1946) chap. 7; Tishby, 1: 278.

texts.[23] The reasons for this are quite direct: First, Christians easily found trinitarian allusions in the *Zohar* in the groupings *Keter, Hokhma, Bina*; or *Hesed, Gevura, Tiferet*; or *Netsah, Hod, Yesod*. Second, there were zoharic texts that lent themselves easily to a trinitarian interpretation. One well-known rabbinic saying teaches that the world was created by ten acts of creative speech, each act corresponding to one occurrence of the Hebrew *vayomer*, "And God said," in the first chapter of Genesis. However, if one counts the occurrences of that word, there are only nine. The *Zohar*, along with other sources, takes the other creative word to be the first word of the Bible, *bereshit*, "In the beginning." This yields the following rendering of the opening two words of Scripture, *Bereshit bara'*: 'The first-creative-speech-act created . . .' or, as Christians probably heard it, 'the Logos created. . . .' One zoharic text goes even further, understanding the second word of the Bible, *bara'*, "created," in its Aramaic sense, *bra*, "son," as follows:[24]

> *Bereshit bara'*: *Bereshit* — is a saying [that is, a creative speech act]. *Bara'* — is half a saying [that is, a second and partial creative speech act]. Father and Son (Heb., *'av uven*); concealed and revealed.

To the author of the *Zohar*, "Father and Son" are the *sefirot, Hokhma* and *Tiferet.* To the Christian reader, the allusion was clearly trinitarian.[25]

Finally, I suspect that part of the Christian interest in the *Zohar* stemmed from the distinctly feminine character of *Bina* and *Malkhut*, as opposed to the distinctly masculine character of *Hokhma, Tiferet*, and *Yesod.* This leads to a theology which is trinitarian; perhaps, Marian.

5. *Three is Not Enough*

The historical interlude of the Christian reception of the *Zohar* in counterreformation Italy aside, it seems to me that a more profound theological question has arisen: If God can, indeed, have personalist dimensions as part of God's own inner being, why should there be only three such dimensions? If God can, indeed, encompass different levels of being, all of which are equal within God's innerness, why should there not be as many such levels as necessary? To put it clearly: If God's being is plural, why only Father, Son, and Holy Spirit? Why not Ineffability, Knowability (Father), Intuition (Mother), Grace (male), Judgment

---

[23] See *Encyclopedia Judaica*, 10: 643ff; Tishby, 1: 278, 338.
[24] *Zohar*, 2: 178b, "Sifra DeTsniuta."
[25] Y. Liebes, *Studies in the Zohar* (Albany, NY: SUNY Press, 1993), chap. 3.

(female), Compassion (Husband), Eternity, Awe, Fecundity (male), and Providence (Bride, Mother) — all of which are equally integral to the divine whole? To put it in declarative form: The zoharic dialogue with the trinity leads to the statement: Three is not enough! God, in God's fullness, is more than three. God, in Whose Image humanity is created, has more than three dimensions. The awesome complexity of the human personality — in which Image humanity is created — suggests that there are many more than three basic dimensions to God's personhood. Indeed, if we, humans, are more than trinitarian, certainly God is more than three.

Jewish readers of the *Zohar* and its related literature knew all this. The nonphilosophers were struck by the very depth of its insight into God, and into humanity, and made the *Zohar* into a holy book, probably the third holiest in Judaism after the Bible and the Talmud.[26] Jewish rationalists of philosophic or halakhic bent were struck by the almost heretical pluralism within the divine and objected strenuously to teaching, publishing, and translating the *Zohar*. In fact, the charge of the *Zohar* being a book that aids and abets trinitarian thinking precisely because the *sefirot* are integral elements of God Godself, was first made by Jews,[27] and it is surely one of the reasons why the *Zohar* may not be taught to Jews who are too young or uneducated, or to Christians.

Jewish rationalist hesitations notwithstanding, the question remains: If God's being is plural, why only Father, Son, and Holy Spirit? Why not Ineffability, Knowability, Intuition, Grace, Judgment, Compassion, Eternity, Awe, Fecundity, and Providence — all of which are equally integral to the divine whole? If we, who are complex beyond three, are created in God's Image, God must be complex beyond three. I must admit that I am in sympathy with this question and with the theology it generates. There could, of course, be more than ten dimensions to divine, and hence to human, personhood. The choice of ten is an historical and exegetical artifact of the documents and culture which created this system, ten being an ideal number in late antique and medieval thinking. However, the personalist orientation of the system is, to my mind, right on the mark. It is biblical, midrashic, and liturgical, and it concords with our commonsensical experience and understanding of God. Furthermore, the subtlety of the understanding of personhood in this

---

[26] D. Bakan, *Sigmund Freud and the Jewish Mystical Tradition* (New York: Schocken Books, 1958, 1965) maintained that Freud had studied the *Zohar*. I find the suggestion intriguing but the evidence skimpy — the *Zohar* is almost impenetrable without direction, in addition to which Freud's copy thereof has never been found.
[27] Tishby, 1: 30, 358.

theology is remarkable. Each of us is many, and yet one. Each of us relates in many ways, and yet is somehow consistent in who she or he is. When we lose our oneness, we have multiple personality disorder and, when we lose our multipleness, we are too rigid to be fully in the world. God, too, according to the texts and according to our common-sense experience of the divine, is many and yet one. God, too, relates in many ways and is somehow consistent in who God is.[28] In a universe in which we are created in God's Image, it cannot be otherwise. In a creation in which the Creator is present in Personhood, the most powerful and insightful understanding of personhood is the best theology.[29]

---

[28] Indeed, our most imaginative texts tell us that there are moments when even God loses God's oneness or God's multipleness, and then God is lost. On the relationship between multidimension and unity, see *Facing*, chaps. 4-5.

[29] This theology which denies the perfection of God in favor of the multipleness of personhood has generated fierce resistance. For an analysis of this, see D. Blumenthal, "Theodicy: Dissonance in Theory and Praxis," *Concilium* 1 (1998): 95-106; also available on my website (see n. 4).

THE SEFIROTIC TREE

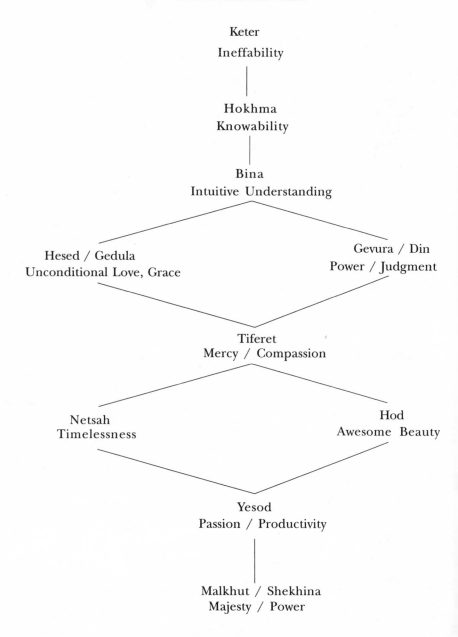

Keter
Ineffability

Hokhma
Knowability

Bina
Intuitive Understanding

Hesed / Gedula
Unconditional Love, Grace

Gevura / Din
Power / Judgment

Tiferet
Mercy / Compassion

Netsah
Timelessness

Hod
Awesome Beauty

Yesod
Passion / Productivity

Malkhut / Shekhina
Majesty / Power

Figure 1

CHART OF IMAGES

Keter
= ineffable, inexpressible, preverbal, unknowable in its being
Eheyeh, crown, hidden one, the ancient one, the encompassing one, will, place of
   the tefillin, Ein Sof

Hokhma
= verbal, conceptual, expressibility, knowledge, intellectual wisdom
Yod, father, Eden, hidden thought, brain

Bina
= emotional knowledge, understanding, intuition
sea, great river, repentance, upper temple, upper mother, Elohim; Hey; heart,
   inaudible sound; halo of the flame

Hesed / Gedula
= unmerited love, grace
Abraham, white, light, first day of creation, El, right arm, mountain of light

Gevura / Din
= power to set limits, physical as well as moral; demanding; source of "other side";
   judgment, mountain of darkness
Isaac, Pahad, red, second day of creation, Elohim, left arm

Tiferet / Rahamim
= compassion, mercy; loving judgment, just love
Jacob, Vav, YHVH, Written Torah, yellow / green, King, Tree of Life; male,
   father, son, lover; center, solar plexus, audible sound, heaven, sun

Netsah
= eternity, infinity, timelessness
one of the twins, Zevaot, Moses, right thigh

Hod
= awesome beauty
one of the twins, Zevaot, Aaron, left thigh

Yesod
= passion/desire, fundamentality, source of blessing and vitality, fecundity,
   productivity
male organ, river, Shaddai, extension of Tiferet, lower part of the Vav, Shabbat,
   Joseph

Malkhut / Shekhina
= face to the world, governance and providence, source of judgment; point of entry
   into the realm of the sefirot
sea, earth, Oral Torah, sound as speech; female, daughter, lover, consort; Assembly
   of Israel; David, Bathsheba, Rachel, Miriam, Esther; blue or black, changes to
   red; Face, mouth, feet; Adonai, Elohim; Hey; Tree of Knowledge of Good and
   Evil; gateway, receptacle; flower; the Depths; lower Eden; tabernacle, lower
   temple; lower mother; moon
when under the influence of the "other side": deserted wife, darkened light

Figure 2

CHAPTER NINE

THEOLOGICAL REALISM

KATHERINE SONDEREGGER[1]

Christian theology is a system of *realism:*[2] it seeks to lay hold of, to enter into and describe the real, or, more properly put, the Real. This is the proper work of Christian faith: to know, confess, and love the Real. And this is God's proper work of grace: to be known as the Real Presence among us, laying hold of us, and entering into our misery and need, to judge and love us to the end. The law of faith is the rule of the Real, a Divine and a human act, both Spiritual and material, corporate and individual, other-worldly and utterly mundane, entering deeply into the life and death of Christ.

Faith is the laying hold of and being laid hold of by the Real: so far most of Christian theology is in agreement. But it is no small matter to

---

[1] Those who have had the pleasure and privilege of working with Wendell Dietrich as a teacher and colleague will recognize how much this essay owes to him: the subject-matter, the theologians cited, the commitment to central questions of method and, more importantly, to central claims of the Christian faith. He is a consummate scholar; but a passionate theologian too. I hope to pay a small tribute to that theological side, and what he has taught me about its rigors and beauties, here.

[2] Much has been written on realism, both in epistemology and in metaphysics. My own understanding of realism, I hope, is evident in the text: that objects exist in their own right, have their own causal powers, and identity conditions. I have a similarly common sense view of realism in epistemology: that knowledge corresponds to the object it seeks to know. There are, of course, many complex versions of realism; "critical realism" appears the most popular among theologians. Such realism seeks to appropriate the critical idealism of Kantians, and the criticism of modernism into a conviction that some reality meets our thought of it. Sallie McFague is a realist of this kind; Gordon Kaufman may be. George Lindbeck in an influential book on theological method, *The Nature of Doctrine* (Philadelphia: Westminster Press, 1984) argues for a theological realism that works on the analogy of a useful and appropriate map: with its use we "know how to go on," as Wittgenstein said of rules. Lindbeck matches this realism with a kind of moral test: that the good practioner of the faith demonstrates the truth of the "first order" confession of faith. Many Narrative Theologians have been influenced by Lindbeck's "post-Liberal" understanding of doctrine and its modest realism. As I hope will become clear, I think there may be another way around these thickets of modern epistemology and method.

determine just what this realism means. For most theologians, even most anti-theologians, agree that Christianity intends to address something real. It does not set out to describe or send aloft a mist of illusion and self-deception; it seeks to know and to be known by the God some scholastics called the Most Real Being. Now, it is in formulations of just this kind that controversies over realism break out. I have laid out the Object of Christian faith in frankly realist terms, both metaphysical and epistemological. I have assumed that God exists, and exists as a sturdy, concrete, Spiritual Object: God is a metaphysical reality. And I have assumed that we know such a God, and that this God knows us: faith is an epistemological act — among others — of the knowledge of God. But it is easy assumptions of just this kind that have come under fire in our western modernism. Constructivism and subjectivism,[3] two competitors to the kind of realism I have assumed, sharpen the terms of debate; and we will find our way with their aid.

With their aid, and not without: For we will not understand rightly the debates in modern theology if we begin with the conviction that the competitors to robust realism are frank anti-realists. The modern and post-modern theologian as thorough-going anti-realist is a straw man, easily cast aside. We will not make progress along this line because it makes of theology a simple and straightforward contrast between the real and the imaginary, between true belief and false, between our side and theirs: and we know our cause is just! Such a position is as much a caricature of realism as skepticism and easy relativism is of contructivism and subjectivism. A robust realism in theology recognizes that it is no small matter to affirm, and affirm cheerfully, that we encounter objects external to ourselves and know them truly. It understands that much of modern western thought has been given over to careful, dogged, and profound questioning of just these commonsense claims. And it knows all too well the desire to write 'real,' 'objective,' and 'true,' as though the words themselves must be guarded by skepticism before

---

[3] I consider these schools of modest epistemological realism, for they do not disclaim a reality lying beyond the knowing subject, though our knowledge of it is an active feature of its reality. Gordon Kaufman is a constructivist in that he considers "reality" or "subject and object" imaginative constructions of our active thought; and a realist in that he advocates a "reflective consciousness" that recognizes the vital role played by reality in any experience we call human. Schleiermacher is a subjectivist in that he begins in the subject of knowledge and considers human consciousness a summation of the world of nature. He is a realist in that the world is given to consciousness and is the source of our knowledge of that which lies beyond thought.

used. A robust realism neither succumbs to the temptation to put quotation marks around the objects of thought and nature, nor minimizes the temptation. It makes common cause.

Common cause dictates that robust realism in theology finds its way with the aid of constructivists and subjectivists, and not without. Friedrich Schleiermacher, the subjectivist, teaches the robust realist the centrality of the believing subject. Note: Schleiermacher teaches robust realism about the believer, not about the dangers of non-objectivity, or the problems of experience, or the difficulties of foundationalism. To be sure, Schleiermacher has weaknesses as well as strengths, costs as well as generous legacies. But we must be careful, when writing about Schleiermacher, to find the right categories for his thought. The great architect of Liberal, academic theology in Germany in the 19th century, Schleiermacher defies the easy labels associated with his name.[4] We will not enter far into his thought, for example, if we assume that Schleiermacher had no place for objectivity in theology, or was a mystic in matters of faith, or was an anti-realist in metaphysics or ethics.[5] These tags do not identify Schleiermacher because they overlook the subtlety of his system and of his subjectivism. In *The Christian Faith*, the work of his maturity, Schleiermacher shows a marked commitment both to the Divine Source of theology and to its realism. What Schleiermacher demonstrates to theology is the richness, but also the cost of epistemology as a starting-point in theology. Karl Barth was fond of saying that we could not understand a theologian's work without seeing that thinker's place in the history of doctrine.[6] So too we cannot under-

---

[4] I capitalize liberalism when it refers to German academic theology dependent upon Schleiermacher.

[5] These were charges directed at Schleiermacher by the Dialectical Theologians of the interwar years, though more by Barth's allies in those years than by Barth himself. In a surprising irony, Schleiermacher is more often accused these days of a realist failing: foundationalism. See Lindbeck *The Nature of Doctrine*, (Louisville: Westminster/John Knox, 1984), chap. 6. IV, and in another vein, Mark Taylor *Erring: a Post/modern A/theology* (Chicago: University of Chicago Press, 1984), chap. 4. Though traditional foundationalism may be difficult to defend now, I certainly do not consider it a lost cause, or worse, an embarrassing one. A modern foundationalism of the kind Alvin Plantinga defends in "Reason and Belief in God" in *Faith and Rationality* (Notre Dame: University of Notre Dame Press, 1983), 16-93, seems most persuasive to me.

[6] See for example, Barth's analysis of German academic theology against the backdrop of the Enlightenment: *Protestant Theology in the 19th Century* (Valley Forge: Judson Press, 1972) [*Die protestantische Theologie im 19. Jahrhunderten* (Zürich: Evangelische Verlag, 1994)] and his comments on Calvin's place in the development of modern theology in "No!" in *Natural Theology*, P. Fraenkel, trans. (London: G. Bles, 1946).

stand Schleiermacher historically without a recognition of the terms governing debate at the beginning of the 19th century in Protestant Germany. More importantly, we cannot understand Schleiermacher *theologically* without a knowledge of just these things.

The beginning of modern philosophy in Europe — a period stemming from Descartes and Locke — may be recognized by its "turn to the subject" of knowledge. This movement in philosophy is decidedly epistemic in focus: how do we know the reality of other minds or of other objects beyond ourselves? Such preoccupation with a doctrine of knowledge should not surprise us. To turn to the human subject, to explore our reality or "inwardness," is to be struck by the encompassing nature of thought, stamped on all ideas and objects. The realm of human subjectivity — or consciousness, as a later generation would term it — seems to accompany every response to reality, from sensation to concept, from certainty to radical doubt, from an idea of extended object to my brute encounter with it. "The world is given to consciousness," Schleiermacher wrote;[7] to speak of reality was to speak of subjectivity; and to speak of subjectivity is to speak epistemologically. Epistemology must govern the entrance to all other philosophy; it is the royal road.

But it is also the narrow gate. What appears under other terms a magnificent and splendid realm may become an airless room. How can I know anything beyond myself? How can I encounter an object truly? How can I ever escape my own imagination, be correct, be corrected? Radical skepticism and radical idealism haunt epistemology. Little wonder that 19th-century modernism makes of these doubts the corrosives of historicism, ideology, and relativism.[8] And little wonder that Schleiermacher would seek a dogmatic system at once epistemic and subjective, overcoming the problem of knowledge within the living consciousness of faith.

---

7   *The Christian Faith*, trans. H. R. Mackintosh and J. S. Stewart (Philadelphia: Fortress Press, 1928), §4.2; *Die christliche Glaube*, M. Redeker, ed. (Berlin: De Gruyter, 1960), §4.2.

8   Well-known examples: Ernst Troeltsch, *The Absoluteness of Christianity and the History of Religions*, trans. D. Reid (Richmond: John Knox Press, 1971) [*Die absolutheit des Christentums und die Religionsgeschichte* (Tübingen: Mohr, 1902)]; Karl Marx, *The German Ideology*, in R. Tucker, ed., *The Marx-Engels Reader* (New York: Norton,1972); Friedrich Nietzsche, *On the Genealogy of Morals*, trans. C. Diethe (New York: Cambridge University Press, 1994) [*Zur Genealogie der Moral in Jenseits von Gut und Böse* (Frankfurt am Main: Insel, 1984)]; and in another vein, Wilhelm Herrmann's massive attempt to ward off these corrosives in *The Communion of the Christian with God*, R. T. Voelkel, ed. (Philadelphia: Fortress Press, 1971) [*Der Vehrkehr des Christen mit Gott* (Stuttgart: Cotta, 1903)].

In the *Christian Faith*, Schleiermacher first lays out the contours of a Christianity turned to the subject of belief. Not simply the Introduction, but the entire dogmatics itself is a comprehensive, elegant, and systematic presentation of theology as a form of human knowledge or faith. We would miss the entire force of this modern movement of thought if we complained that Schleiermacher's subjectivism lacked theological objectivity. For the whole program of modern epistemology is directed to the aim of showing objectivity *through* subjectivity. We know the world in so far as, and only as, it forms the content of our inwardness: our subjectivity embraces within it the objectivity that makes human life possible. Now, Schleiermacher follows this modern program faithfully.

The world, he writes, is given to consciousness, though the given does not depend upon consciousness, but rather on God's all-knowing causality. In our self-awareness, we experience freedom and dependence, a movement beyond and a movement toward ourselves. Our own selfhood is a "brute primitive": we do not deduce or argue for it, but discover it, always accompanying these encounters with the system of nature. We are the moment, the mediating point, between action and reception, a laying hold of the whole and a standing over it and apart. Never at rest, never static or alone, the human subject rises and recedes in this interplay of passion, knowledge, and will, each taking up the world and acting upon it in turn. Schleiermacher captures a fully dialectical self, open to introspection and in that introspection, open to the world.

Indeed, it is the very certainty of my inner experience — my conviction that I am a part of the system of nature — that answers skepticism about the objective world. Schleiermacher argues for a form of *ad hominem* defense against radical doubt: "a little introspection," he counsels in the Introduction, will show that the inner and outer world is given thus to the self. No one could live a skeptical life; no one could exhibit such a starved and solitary experience. The poles of inner and outer, subject and object, freedom and dependence, joy and sorrow, part and whole: these are the self, now summing up the whole, now surrendered to the remote and vital All. Such selves, Schleiermacher teaches, come to their full stature and maturity in utter dependence on God, the form of Christ's perfect fidelity. The human subjectivity Schleiermacher wishes to teach us about is a *faithful* subjectivity: we are most fully human in our lively awareness of utter and simple reliance upon God. All Christian doctrine is reflection upon this inner life of utter trust and need; it is "pious awareness uttered in speech." This movement from piety to doctrine, from inner awareness to abstract dogma, has been called the "method of experience," and is taken to be the hallmark of modern Protestantism.[9]

It was Barth, after all, who drew our attention to this leading characteristic of Schleiermacher; Barthians who made it anathema. To those who have studied Protestant controversy during the interwar years, the debate over the "method of experience" is familiar territory indeed. Nothing appears so clear from that period as the conviction that Schleiermacher gave us a false starting-point; and that a new method or starting-point must be found. It is customary, in fact, to see Barth as the proponent of a new method in theology: the analogy of faith. And that *analogia fidei* is widely taken to be metaphysical or objective: theology begins with the sovereign reality of God, and in God's grace comes to conform theology's words to His gracious truth. On this reading of modern Protestantism, Schleiermacher does not concern himself with knowledge, the subject-matter of epistemology; he rather develops a theology of experience and uses pious awareness as the method to shape doctrine. Barth, not Schleiermacher, returns to epistemology, it is argued, for only Barth can speak of a Divine Object that is *known* in faith. Schleiermacher does not know; he experiences or feels. Christian faith, Schleiermacher argued famously in his Introduction, was "neither a knowing, nor a willing, nor a doing"; faith was a feeling, a pious consciousness. It was to escape such pious vaporings that Barth launched his assault upon "religion," the religion of Schleiermacher. Barth rediscovered the Reformation theme: the gracious freedom of God. And in that freedom, faith comes to know God truly, and in that knowledge to find human freedom, the joyful obedience to a gracious Lord. Such is the well-worn path from Schleiermacher to Barth, a path smoother and better marked than the one outlined here; why should we not follow it?

The answer lies, I think, with Schleiermacher himself: his understanding of faith, and faith's role in the economy of modern Liberalism. We can catch better sight of this by clearing away that old war-horse of

---

[9] This method was not without adherents in Roman Catholicism: Johann Adam Möhler shows Schleiermacher's influence directly; Karl Rahner in *Spirit in the World*, trans. W. Dych (New York: Continuum Press, 1994) [*Geist in Welt* (Freiburg im Breisgau: Herder, 1996)], and *Foundations of Christian Faith*, trans. W. Dych (New York: Seabury, 1978) [*Grundkurs des Glaubens* (Freiburg im Breisgau: Herder, 1976)] replicates Schleiermacher's pattern though not, I think, intentionally, but rather because of common epistemological convictions. George Lindbeck in *The Nature of Doctrine* groups Schleiermacher and Rahner together explicitly as "experiential/ expressivists," though Rahner represents a "hybrid" position, encompassing more propositional content in doctrine.

Barthian polemic, that Schleiermacher desecrated the Reformation, handing the faith of the Reformers over to the natural theologians of Catholicism — and worse. As B. A. Gerrish has shown, in *Tradition in the Modern World* and *The Old Protestantism and the New*,[10] Schleiermacher did not abandon but continued the themes, hallmarks, and convictions of the Reformers, and the *Christian Faith* can be seen rightly as faithful successor to Calvin's *Institutes*, faithful even in its developments and departures from Calvin. We need not be convinced, I think, of every detail in Gerrish's re-appraisal to acknowledge the force of his position. Like Barth, Schleiermacher stands as a faithful son of the Reformation; as Calvin develops Luther for another generation, so these disciples continue Calvin's "true religion" for another time. Though Calvin appears a different man altogether in Barth's portrait than in Schleiermacher's, we should not be startled. "The knowledge of God and ourselves" that Calvin places at the head of the *Institutes* cuts a very different figure against the backdrop of Liberalism than against post-war modernism. This is not to say that Barth did not recover something Schleiermacher lost in the Reformers; quite the contrary. From the second volume of the *Church Dogmatics* forward, Barth recovers the *metaphysical realism* of the Reformers, and that is no small achievement. But Schleiermacher shows us, as little else can, what a starting-point in epistemology does to shape the legacy of the Reformation, even a full and well-guarded legacy. As Gerrish has put this point so well: "It can readily be seen that the concept of piety functions as a dogmatic limit rather differently in Schleiermacher than in Calvin. Schleiermacher's approach is rooted strictly in a theory of knowledge and is not, like Calvin's, simultaneously tied up with a doctrine of sin."[11] Calvin's religious piety becomes Schleiermacher's faithful subjectivity; and that is no small achievement, either.

Christian faith, even as a "modification of feeling," is a form of knowledge: that is the bearing for our discussion here. It is easy to imagine the opposite from Schleiermacher's treatment in the Introduction: that faith stands opposed to knowledge. His justly famous thesis, §3 of the *Christian Faith*, runs: "The piety which forms the basis of all ecclesiastical communions, is, considered purely in itself, neither a Knowing nor a Doing, but a modification of Feeling, or of immediate self-consciousness." He follows this general definition with a specification: "§4: The

---

[10] B. A. Gerrish, *Tradition in the Modern World* (University of Chicago Press, 1978); *The Old Protestantism and the New* (University of Chicago Press, 1982).
[11] Gerrish, *The Old Protestantism and the New*, 201.

self-identical essence of piety is this: the consciousness of being absolutely dependent or, which is the same thing, of being in relation to God." Schleiermacher here appears to be offering both a method and a denial. A method, because we are to find the foundation and form of doctrine in "immediate self-consciousness." A denial, because we are not to consider faith a matter of knowledge or act but of feeling, the immediate awareness of relation to God. Closer inspection — and perhaps a little introspection! — will lead us, however, to another conclusion. For Schleiermacher offers here an account of feeling that does not *deny* knowledge, but affirms it *under the province of piety.*

The Introduction lays out a parallel account to secular epistemology, a faithful response to Divine reality that, in joyful receptivity, knows its Lord. Such receptivity cannot be knowledge as his generation defined it, because to know meant clear and exhaustive possession of the object, against which we feel the freedom to control, compare, and counterinfluence the Other of thought. God cannot be Object to our thought in this way. Schleiermacher was too good a Calvinist to accept creaturely autonomy and control towards God in the act of faith. Schleiermacher rejects the wide-spread conviction of the older Protestant orthodox that faith is firm assent to dogmatic proposition: "In all other more typical fields of knowledge the only measure of conviction is the clearness and completeness of the thinking itself. Now if it is to be the same with *this* [religious] conviction, then we should simply be back at our old point, that he who thinks the religious propositions most clearly and completely, individually and in their connections, must likewise be the most pious man"(*Christian Faith* §3, 10) — a conclusion Schleiermacher rejects. Secular knowledge rested upon the *given*, the object present to thought and sensation. Like Kant, who held that "concepts without percepts are empty," Schleiermacher argued that knowledge was a form of mental action built upon objects given for our reception and response. Over against these givens, we experience the inner passivity, but also the inner freedom that knowledge demands.

In discussing his definition of "absolute dependence," Schleiermacher notes the pervasive and ever-widening scope of self-consciousness; against the world of nature, even as against the tyranny of autocrats, we sense a measure of freedom and control. "Towards all the forces of Nature — even, we may say, towards the heavenly bodies — we ourselves do, in the same sense in which they influence us, exercise a counter-influence, however minute" (§4, 15). From such premises Schleiermacher must clearly reject faith's Object as given and faith's task as [secular] knowledge: "Any possibility of God being in any way *given* is entirely excluded, because anything that is outwardly given must be given as an object exposed to our counter influence, however slight this may be" (§5, 18). The reciprocity of self-consciousness, the giving and taking up, the extending, ordering, and grasping, and being grasped in turn, the freedom and lively dependence on another: all these movements of the inner life belong to knowing and doing, the realm of the human alive to the system of nature.

Piety cannot belong to *this* realm, not "in itself," for it is an inwardness far deeper and richer than such worldliness permits; it is unreflected life in immediate relation to God. Schleiermacher builds his description of piety from the structure of immediate self-consciousness. Now feeling, as Schleiermacher understands it, is a house with two wings: the Self or Subject and the Other. They are "co-determinates," as these post-Kantians would put it, and fill the whole compass of the inner world. They are best expressed in the language of feeling, of course, however awkward: a "self-caused element and a non-self-caused element" or a "being and a having-by-some-means-come-to-be" (§4, 13). Not surprisingly, it is the last of these elements that interests Schleiermacher:

> This latter element presupposes for every self-consciousness another factor besides the Ego, a factor which is the source of the particular determination, and without which the self-consciousness would not be precisely what it is. But this Other is not objectively presented in the immediate self-consciousness with which alone we are here concerned. For though, of course, the double constitution of self-consciousness causes us always to look objectively for an Other to which we can trace the origin of our particular state, yet this search is a separate act with which we are not at present concerned. In self-consciousness there are only two elements: the one expresses the existence of the subject for itself, the other its coexistence with an Other (ibid).

Note here that Schleiermacher gives us a description not simply of self-consciousness, but of experience as a whole; even more, of the *Christian Faith* as a whole, under the terms of subjectivity. In these few lines we are really in the presence of Schleiermacher's system, compressed and distilled of the alloys of history and dogma. To be alive is to find oneself in the midst of Another. Like Aristotle's political animal, we need not introduce society into the individual; we need only uncover it, already there. But this Other does not appear under the guise of Object: it is not given "outwardly" or present in that sense. Rather, the Other *determines* my inner life. I discover my own reality as one given to me — "non-self-caused" or "having-by-some- means-come-to-be" — so that my own life is knit up in another's, and dependent on its power.

The Other, Schleiermacher insists, does not inhabit the Self concrete-ly or bodily; he is no mystic. Rather, the Other plays a transcendental role: it is the ground and source of my possible inner experience. I discover in myself a correlate, something that is not my own, an inheritance and a resting-point; I am not alone, nor have I made all that I am. I receive. And in that reception I have joy and sorrow; I find food for act and reflection. I am not submerged, or synthesized with the Other, nor is my inner life crushed by its determining power. Rather I discover my activity, my "self-caused" powers and spontaneous being in the reciprocity with the Other. The dialectics of self-consciousness uncover a self whose freedom *depends upon* the causality of the Other. But more important still, my sense of freedom — my integrity, purpose and self-direction — moves in a world I have received; and this whole, the "co-determinates" of my being, rests entirely, absolutely and utterly, on Another.

So we have come through the subjective to the Objective: faith is the experience of absolute dependence upon God. Now, faith for Schleier-macher is the essence of "co-positing": all that I am and have, I receive from Another. Faith does not have to generate gratitude; it *is* gratitude, a grateful reception. The more I sense my life in God's hands, alive to my utter need and debt, the more pious I am. Faith may give rise to doc-trines, to creeds, to ecclesiastical communions, to revolution and retreat; it can ground "objective consciousness." But it remains a higher feel-ing, a passion distilled of vacillation and fatigue. It is constant, in season and out; in it, all reality is enflamed with Divine quickening. Faith is the name Schleiermacher assigns to this steady relatedness to God. In straining to speak of the scope of this relation, Schleiermacher will even allow, for a moment, the language of the given: "It can indeed be said that God is given to us in feeling in an original way; and if we speak of an original revelation of God to man, or in man, the meaning will always be just this, that, along with absolute dependence that charac-terizes not only man but all temporal existence, there is given to man also the immediate self-consciousness of it, which becomes a conscious-ness of God" (§4, 7-18). Faith is original revelation, immediate to aware-ness, accompanied always by praise and act. Never static, never cheese-paring or small, faith is the ready embrace of all that is given that I may give back in turn. Faith, as Calvinists so finely say, is where God's acts are met with human praise.

So the stage is set: faith is knowledge according to its Object, piety in response to Divine revelation. When theology turns to the subject, Schleiermacher counsels, it must turn to a *believing* subject, not a neutral or skeptical inquirer. That, I believe, is the lesson Schleiermacher heard in Kant's critical philosophy, and not another, more generally expected and assumed. An earlier generation of Schleiermacher scholars were inclined to see in Schleiermacher the direct application of Kant's stricture against speculative metaphysics.[12] The rational science of God, Kant argued, could no longer be pursued, as knowledge demanded sense impression, a manifold not available from abstract, Divine ideas. Schleiermacher, it was thought, laid this lesson to heart; his *Christian Faith* at last offered a method free from Kantian prohibition. Not without cost, to be sure: Christians now speak of feeling and inwardness, not knowledge. But Schleiermacher allowed theology to begin again, sweeping together the shattered remains of orthodoxy, and displaying them now as the archeological distillates of feeling. We may have all that we had before, but we must submit it to Kantian critique; it will emerge, but changed. Feeling is a province of retreat, inward, private, untouchable: theology may have its dogma if it stay within its limits, protected, but isolated as well. So far, an older, Kantian, interpretation of Schleiermacher.

But we need not see Kant's influence, however strong, in such a direct and critical fashion. For Schleiermacher, though a careful student of Kant, borrowed and learned from a range of German intellectuals, from speculative idealists to Romantics in philosophy and letters. More important still is his Moravian upbringing and later life in the Church, a widely admired preacher and pastor. Such a profile is not to replace philosophical argument with biography; rather it aims to show the *place* of Kant in Schleiermacher's theological program. The *Christian Faith* does not seek to answer Kant directly, nor to remove theology from the realm of epistemology, as Kant may have wished. Schleiermacher would not consider such a straightforward philosophical task proper for theology; it had better things to do. Theology has its own theme: that phrase of Barth's could be Schleiermacher's, as well. The Introduction to the *Christian Faith* does not seek to answer or clear away philosophical

---

[12] See for example: John Dillenberger and Claude Welch, *Protestant Christianity* (New York: Scribners, 1954); Wilhelm Pauk, *The Heritage of the Reformation* (Glencoe: Free Press, 1961); Richard R Niebuhr, *Schleiermacher on Christ and Religion* (New York: Scribners, 1964) (though the Kantian influence is principally in ethics); and Martin Redeker, *Friedrich Schleiermacher*, trans. J. Wallhausser (Philadelphia: Fortress Press, 1973) (though Fichte is mentioned in Schleiermacher's ethics); this interpretation does not hold for Emmanuel Hirsch, who, in *Geschichte der neuern Evangelischen Theologie* (Götersloh: C. Bertelsmann, 1952) Bd. IV, K. 46, "Die Anfänge Schleiermachers," argues forcefully for the over-mastering influence of Fichte.

objections, nor does it try to escape them. Rather, the Introduction demonstrates what a theological system looks like under the conditions of German Liberalism. Schleiermacher was a fully modern Christian intellectual; his theology exhibits the Reformation as a modern intellectual achievement. Feeling, or immediate self-consciousness, is the modern, Liberal expression of the knowledge available to piety. Not private, not inward only nor isolated, this pious knowledge embraces the world, its history, cultures, and aims, now under its own terms. Schleiermacher aimed to *free* theology of philosophical constraint, not hem it in. Properly understood, faith authorizes theology to speak freely and boldly in the modern world. Its own knowledge, its own method, its own sources and norms: that is dogmatic theology under the province of piety.

Faith knows its Other as is fitting: as the ground and source of all that I am. To be sure, this is a Copernican revolution in theology: the believing subject, not the Divine Object, is the center around which doctrine turns. But no Protestant, Schleiermacher argues, should expect it otherwise. God cannot be known without faith: no one can say Jesus is Lord apart from the Holy Spirit. We do not approach God as a "subject of inquiry," nor as a reality to be compared, even at infinite distance, to other realities; indeed, we do not approach God at all. Rather, we know in faith the God who approaches us, has already claimed and caused us, and undergirds every moment of thought and will. As a form of self-consciousness, faith conforms to the pattern of knowledge. Like secular knowledge, faith does not possess the Object directly — it does not exist "inside our head," any more than trees or tables or train tables fit inside our minds. Like secular knowledge, faith responds to a given — though the given of revelation, the consciousness of absolute dependence upon God. Like a secular doctrine of knowledge, a doctrine of faith aims to justify commonly shared beliefs, and hopes to limit knowledge to what can be secured, warranted, or grounded in certainty. Like secular epistemology, religious epistemology guards the entrance to all other fields of thought.

We can, of course, speak of the Objects of dogma — they constitute the "second form" of dogmatic utterance — just as we can speak of the realities of transcendent metaphysics. But, Schleiermacher counsels, we must acknowledge what those statements *mean*. For a Kantian, transcendent metaphysics remains an Idea of Reason; we recognize its meaning when we are alive to its moral aim to shape thought and action. For a Schleiermacher-inspired Liberal, dogma remains the language of theology; we recognize its meaning when we see it as the objective translation of subjective faith. Faith gives us acquaintance with the Objects of its field: we are immediately aware of the Other of theology at the basal point of our existence. And this Other, central to the theologian's life, accompanies our acquaintance with the worldly other: our "temporal self-consciousness," as Schleiermacher termed our everyday experience, encompasses the world as the other of our daily, inner life. This unique religious knowledge, pious awareness, combines with the knowing and doing of everyday life. It grounds them, edifies and sanctifies them, and gives them the moral direction they seek. Faith gives to human life an inner compass and certainty. Like secular knowledge, but more deeply and thoroughly still, faith is self-evident certainty: it is immediate and absolute relation with the Other. Like the secular epistemologies Schleiermacher knew well, his religious epistemology changed everything it touched. The landscape of thought is ineradicably altered, and the old objects along familiar pathways are lit up by a foreign light.

But more than familiar pathways are made foreign to us: suddenly knowledge itself seems an odd state of affairs. For just what would it mean to call awareness of this kind "knowledge"? We might concur that Schleiermacher presents Christian faith under the *form* or pattern of epistemology; but do we really know anything at all in faith? Here, I think, we encounter the greatness, but also the great cost of Schleiermacher's turn to the subject in theology. We take the true measure here of what it means to insist upon the *believing subject* in the ordering of theology. Now, knowledge is true belief about the other.[13] How shall we gain this state about the Divine Other? Schleiermacher acknowledges the Pauline formula, much admired by Barth: we know in that we are known of God. We have a living Reality, not natural object, as aim to our knowledge. But this cannot be the type of knowledge gained by encounter with conscious beings like ourselves, nor even through their knowledge of us: for that is reciprocity, dialogue, *das Zwiegespräch*. We have no such power or status before God. Rather, the Word of God is near us, on our lips and in our hearts: we look *within*, not without, for knowledge of God. Now such inner knowledge is not propositional, nor mystical, but immediate and original. Feeling is the direct, independent certainty that I am the Lord's. Such knowledge *is* a lively joy; it

---

[13] I take this to be Schleiermacher's definition of knowledge, and one I endorse, though I do not mean to set this definition off against "knowledge by acquaintance," as much of what Schleiermacher counts as knowledge comes from direct experience of another in awareness.

could not count as knowledge of *this* truth if I had a cold indifference or wariness in its presence. All other knowledge stems from or accompanies this joyous certainty. Higher-order knowledge in theology — the work of dogmatics proper — arises from a translation of faith's original knowledge into categories of abstract or historical thought. Secular knowledge or action does not go out into the world alone, but is rather borne by an agent fully alive to the Divine work on us. No deed or act of thought, in this sense, can be wholly secular; Schleiermacher does not restrict religious knowledge to one intellectual or political domain. Rather, I know God's claim on me as I turn to thought or labor, as I know another in love or fear, as I rest when night comes or awake to tend the sick. I walk always ordered by God's governance. Now this is pious knowledge as Schleiermacher understands it: to be always conscious of the Lord of lords who dwells in unapproachable light, whom no one has ever seen or can see.

This is the great scope and richness of epistemology in theology; but there is also cost. Shall we pay the price? The answer rests on how we interpret our common cause with Schleiermacher. From his subjectivism, we learn the centrality of the believing subject; from his doctrine of faith, the knowledge of God as immediate and non-Objective: which shall we embrace? I have argued for the former; the cost of the latter, I believe, is too high. Schleiermacher's epistemology lays out a knowledge of God that demands human receptivity of a Lord never Objective to consciousness. To be sure, this epistemology gives us genuine knowledge; and knowledge that yields objective content when translated and re-cast. But only when re-cast. We cannot know God directly or fully as a Personal Lord, as Living Judge or Deliverer, or Divine Object of any kind; that is a *façon de parler*. God does not speak in revelation; does not address us in Word; does not encounter us at great remove, to judge and redeem; does not hear prayer. God does not suffer to appear in the swaddling clothes of scripture or sacrament, or bend down to be taken into our hands, sinners' hands. Rather, we are asked to *see through* these images to the scientific form they most truly bear: the joy and sorrow that are mine as I welcome or resist the Divine Other of the higher life.

But scripture does not bear witness to a Personal God who must be seen through to be grasped in knowledge. The faith of the Bible is the lively encounter with a Holy Judge and Redeemer, the End of sinners. Precious in this Lord's sight is the death of his saints; this is the One who kills and makes alive, covers all in disobedience to have grace upon all. Now Schleiermacher can make use of all these Biblical phrases; but only in Whiggish history. We see now what they meant, and we receive their testimony as tributes to the faith of an earlier age. We distill and preserve them under our own, scientific terms; they are kept at home, but under strict orders. The constraint that chafes many Evangelicals is particularly in evidence here. There are rules, complex and inviolate, that govern dogmatic work. Epistemology is a stern task-master. If pleased, everything is permitted; but the task-master must be pleased. We cannot rest easy with the objective or personal language of Scripture and tradition, nor can we address ourselves to interpreting dog- ma or the Bible without complex means of translation and justification. Just as Bultmann sought to translate the pre-modern world view into a scientific age, so Schleiermacher sought to express the language of preaching into an epistemological age.[14] Both hope that a kind of "folk-piety" can be rendered scientific, and in that way credible to an intel-lectual world come-of-age. These are worthy aims, and any systematic theologian must face the same task. But the epistemological strictures of Liberalism, from Schleiermacher to Bultmann, cannot allow the real work of theology to be done among the living world of Biblical Objects and acts. Always we must work off-stage, among a deeper, or higher, or more rarefied apparatus, and always it is more difficult on return to speak of the God and Father of our Lord Jesus Christ than it was before.

Many of these objections, I am sure, are familiar to readers of Karl Barth. And I would not wish to claim any originality for them! But we can see now that Barth attempted to answer these objections from within epistemology itself, a task not far from lifting oneself up by one's own hair. Little wonder that Barth had to throw his considerable weight against the most radical planks in epistemology, threatening to bring the house down around him. Barth's lectures in the years just before and after the First World War show a thinker striving to speak of theo-logy's Object through applying the force of dialectic. He remains within the categories of religious epistemology: revelation and faith, immedi-acy and the given. But they are now applied in opposition, in distance and asymmetry, a shattering of Schleiermacher's epistemology Barth would call the "vacuum of faith." Barth now would speak of the Divine Subject of theology; he would write approvingly of our encounter with a Lord who summons and commands. And, to be sure, he would use metaphysical or dogmatic language, as Bruce McCormack notes,

---

14 Examples of Bultmann's translation project: *New Testament and Mythology*, trans. and ed. S. Ogden (Philadelphia: Fortress Press, 1984); and *Theology of the New Testa-ment*, trans. K. Grobel (New York: Scribners, 1951-55) *[Theologie des Neuen Testaments* (Tübingen: Mohr, 1980)].

without flinching or elaborate apology.[15] But such ontology in those years served an epistemic end: he had to dissolve Schleiermacher's doctrine of faith before he could find credible means to affirm the believer's knowledge of the Personal God. It was for that reason that Barth could not entertain positive predication of God *in the believer's mouth*, nor a doctrine of revelation that yielded more than God's knowledge of us sinners. Only a return to a classical epistemology — an analogical predication based on God's gracious condescension to thought — allowed Barth to leave epistemology quietly behind. That, I believe, was Barth's path through the landscape of Liberalism, and theology, I think, should follow him; but on an easier path.

Christian theology should *begin* with metaphysics, not arrive there after much delay. Robust realism in theology holds that we order theology to its metaphysical Object: God's reality, God's mighty work, God's righteousness and mercy are the proper foundation and entrance to theology. The advantages to such an approach are not hard to find. Contemporary theology stands shoulder to shoulder with the past: with the Reformers, with many medieval doctors of the Church, with the Church of late antiquity, with the faithful of every age, all of whom spoke without hesitation about the frank and certain reality of God. More importantly, the Bible speaks in just this way: God is the Subject of the Bible, the living, holy and righteous Judge and Lord of creation, the Beginning and End, the Rock against whom many stumble and fall. The God of Israel reigns: that is the starting-point of the Bible. And Christian theology could do worse than beginning where the Bible takes its start.

Could do worse than? Surely such a transformation in starting point and method deserves more fanfare than that! Can a metaphysical starting-point simply "have advantages"? Can it say no more on its behalf than simply counting up eminent predecessors? There are complex problems in the history of modern thought that are being handled roughly here — or not handled at all. An easy conscience about metaphysics in theology, critics might say, shows a romantic longing for the past, or a retreat into "common-sense realism," or worse, "naive realism"; it ignores the thicket of problems moderns and post-moderns raise about ideology, about reification, about onto-theology, about discourse and power. It returns to a "second naivete," but without all the work. It drops back into "first order statements" without recognizing it is

---

[15] Bruce McCormack, *Karl Barth's Critically Realistic Dialectical Theology* (Oxford: Clarendon Press, 1995), chap 3.

theology not religious utterance. Divine metaphysics does not seem to understand that the old Science of God can no longer be done, that propositional realism and correspondence theories of truth are hardly victories won, and that knowledge of such realities is a vexed problem indeed. These are objections raised by the theory and method of academic modernism, and could be multiplied without effort.

And they are complex problems, to be sure. But they need not be *answered* by a robust realism before it gets underway. That is because these complex objections, theories, and methods exist within a shared frame or quiet assumption: that the *real* work in modern thought is done in epistemology, and the *real* problem in modern theology is encountered in the quest for justified belief in the Objects of scripture and dogma. Certainly Schleiermacher shared this assumption, as did Ritschl and Herrmann, Troeltsch, Tillich, and Barth; so too, Gordon Kaufman and Sallie McFague. All of them saw in epistemology the entrance or the barrier; all saw metaphysics as another country, now lost to sight, to be pursued or forgotten as the home of another age. But we need not see things this way. We do not need to dismantle this frame of thought, defeat its premises, break its hold from within. We may simply and quietly affirm that we see things in another way.

That is the nature of first principles, after all; they win us long before we win through to them. We may begin with them. Indeed if they are deep first principles, we must begin with them. We do not justify *them* but they justify all the rest: they are "properly basic."[16] In light of a fresh starting-point, we may find our common cause with those who begin elsewhere. We recognize their constraints and promise; we learn from their preoccupations and achievements; we lean upon them when we enter their field. But we need not accept the premise that metaphysics must be approached through epistemology, nor need we justify robust realism before the court of critical theory. We begin where we must; and we seek God's gentle leading.

Now that is not to say that robust realism does not recognize the demand for clear method and a doctrine of knowledge in theology. It would be a poor thing indeed for dogmatic theology to shear off the complex and sensitive achievement of modern academic theology as though it had no place. Such immiseration of theology could scarcely benefit dogmatics, and would demonstrate only that the real *force* of

---

[16] Alvin Plantinga developed this term in service of modern, post-classical foundationalism in religious epistemology in "Reason and Belief in God"; my interest, however, is metaphysical, not epistemological, and so copies his form, not his aim.

modern thought had been lost on us. Rather, a metaphysical starting point in theology should welcome modernism; but in another place. Epistemology and the problems of method swept in its wake belong to the doctrine of the person. It is the human person as creature of God who is called to know God, and to justify that knowledge before the Divine Truth. Our common cause with subjectivists and constructivists, with epistemic realists of all sorts, is in part a recognition that questions in the knowledge of God must be raised, and raised in earnest. To a robust realist, of course, these questions are in a sense already answered: the real Object they seek to know has been found; or rather this Divine Object has already found us. But in another sense, the questions of true knowledge of God remain open for the robust realist, too. Indeed, as Anselm taught us long ago, the Divine Answer provokes our questions, driving the believer to earnest searching, this time in unmatched seriousness as the task is done before the Holy God.[17] This pattern — from metaphysical claim to epistemological question — characterizes robust realism as a whole as it enters into the elaboration of doctrine. Indeed, we might call this pattern the *method* of robust realism in theology, should that term not seem freighted down by its path through the 19th century, and too grand a term for such a modest practice.[18] The relation of metaphysics to epistemology, or Object of theology to those

---

[17] Anselm of Canterbury, *Proslogion* in *Monologion and Proslogion*, trans. T. Williams (Indianapolis: Hackett, 1996); I take this position of humble openness before the God whom we seek to be the basic attitude of scripture and the basis of the doctrine of Scriptural authority in Protestant dogmatics.

[18] As a technical term, "method" has taken on greater and greater ballast during the modern period. When Schleiermacher used this term — he refers often in the *Christian Faith* to the constraints of his "method" — he usually meant his religious epistemology: we speak doctrinally of those elements present to us in piety. Schleiermacher's descendants developed highly technical forms of this epistemic method, some more value centered as in Albrecht Ritschl, some more historical as in Ernst Troeltsch or Wilhelm Herrmann (allowing Herrmann his idiosyncratic use of "history"). "Method" by the turn of the century came to mean "academic discipline" or means of justifying a field's special knowledge. In this sense, post-modernism is a "method" or perhaps, "anti-method." But method need not take on all this freight to remain useful to theology. Method can also refer to a more simple task of shaping doctrine: how should the multiple concerns or *loci* of the faith be organized? What form should they take? Method in this sense is instrumental: it generates doctrines in a particular form, following a particular pattern. Schleiermacher has a method in this sense too: the Supernatural becomes natural. All Christian doctrine conforms to this shape, including, wonderfully, his religious epistemology. Robust realism has a method in this sense too: the metaphysical Reality precedes and shapes the creaturely question. It is not "grand theory" but rather an informal guide or handy pattern; we see how to go on.

who know the Divine Reality, will form the natural province of robust realism. But such a relation exists among the modern and post-modern epistemologists as well. Epistemology has metaphysical correlates or implications, if it makes claim to know another truly. Schleiermacher's assumption of the Other into pious consciousness and his strain to turn Other into Object in his system shows the realist drive in this most modern of Christian thinkers. Indeed it is this very effort to arrive at the objective through the subjective that ties academic method in theology to modern philosophy on one hand and robust dogmatic realism on the other.

But the common cause robust realism makes with the history of academic theology is stronger than a shared pursuit of the Object of theology. More important still is the shared commitment to the believing subject of theology, the faithful Christian. Robust realism in theology will make no progress in service of its Lord if it turn its eyes away from the very creature the Lord God was pleased to make and in whose flesh the Lord was pleased to dwell. The weakness of Protestant rationalism was not its propositionalism; that was its strength. Protestant orthodoxy, like Catholic, medieval orthodoxy before it, recognized a metaphysical Object when it saw it. It could speak plainly and boldly about the metaphysical dogmas of the faith. But it did not take into account, from its first steps into dogmatics, the believing subject — that *we creatures* are the ones making these bold confessions; and that is its weakness. To be sure, propositional orthodoxy has always included a doctrine of the human creature, fallen, called to faith, covered in grace and restored to the sanctified life. But these are doctrines *about* the believing subject, third-person accounts, as it were, or species of the "objective consciousness," as Schleiermacher would put it. It is fitting, of course, for theology to encompass objective, metaphysical doctrines about humanity. Any robust realist would embrace theological anthropology as an essential metaphysical doctrine. But robust realism needs more. If alert to the tradition stemming from Schleiermacher, it will be alive to demands for a direct, first-person account of the believing subject in the reality of faith. I am the one who confesses that the Lord of Israel reigns; I the one who as sinner receives grace upon grace; I the one who as lost puts on death and in that dying is found by the Lord of life.

Such confession is more than a test of piety for the dogmatic theologian. To be sure, it is no small matter for theologians to believe what they write: like academics of many sorts, academic theologians, too, find authenticity an elusive prize. But more is at stake here than that, for piety of this kind, even the most authentic, is a depth *added* to a dogmatic system. It seals the presentation of doctrine with confession, a personal testament concluding the work. This is needed and welcome; but there is more. A metaphysical theology must find room for the believing subject *in the act of belief.* It must seize the rich legacy of Schleiermacher to theology: that the metaphysical doctrines themselves are uttered, even now, by those called and judged by Christ. It must have, that is, a *doctrine of faith.* This is no small matter; nor the main matter. But metaphysical realism written without faith, the faith that confesses the Reality of God, cannot claim the legacy of modern academic theology, nor the richness of the modern turn to the subject. It has not made common cause with the movement that shaped intellectual life within and beyond the Church, and shapes it still.

Note that once again, Christians start out in dogmatics armed with something far more modest than ringing endorsement or material entailment. Robust realism finds itself in a modern world; it works among its neighbors, heirs, sometimes grateful, sometimes restless, of the modern in philosophy and letters. We recognize in Schleiermacher, above all, but in his descendants, too, a greatness undiminished by its flaws: a generosity of spirit; a complexity and nuance; a self-inspection and inwardness; a coherence, rigor, and elegance of system; a conservation and enriching of the Reformation gospel that can only be welcomed in a dry time like our own. And in accompanying doctrine with faith, we pay tribute to that subjectivism that explored the self in service of the Church. It is to acknowledge the methodological landscape Hans Frei called "Relationalism:"[19] the joining together of Object and subject of theology in the knowing believer. Robust realism will transform this landscape, even as metaphysics transforms the dogmatic starting point. And to be sure, realism in theology need not take this step nor take Liberalism, in philosophy or theology, to heart; but it may. And I believe it should. To join metaphysics with the believing subject is the aim of a doctrine of faith, the aim of robust realism in theology.

---

[19] Hans Frei, "The Doctrine of Revelation in the Theology of Karl Barth" (Ph.D. diss.), Yale University, 1956, 27.

CHAPTER TEN

ETHICAL MONOTHEISM IN AN AGE OF PROBABILITY: WHAT IF GOD DOES PLAY DICE?

PETER J. HAAS

One of the first courses I took as a graduate student at Brown was Wendell Dietrich's course in nineteenth-century thought. It made me confront for the first time in a serious way how dependent modern moral thinking is on the intellectual legacy of the nineteenth century. On numerous occasions I have returned to the challenge represented by Wendell's courses. Below is yet another attempt to deal with the issue he so deeply cared about, the legacy of the nineteenth century and the collapse of its assumptions in the light of twentieth century developments.

Einstein's plaintive cry that "God would not play dice!" was his response to the implications of the new Quantum Mechanics that emerged in the 1920s. It was one theoretical physicist's reaction to the hypothesis of another. But it stands as well as the last cry of over two thousand years of moral thinking in the West. For as disorienting as the new physics would be to Einstein and his colleagues, the new cosmology it brought with it proved equally disorienting for religious and moral thinking. This cosmology threatened the very foundations of Western thinking about morality: the notion that a reasonable and knowable Good was built in to the cosmos. Einstein was perfectly correct in saying that if Quantum Mechanics was right, then the inherited vision of an understandable cosmos, a comprehensible God, and a universally available rational ethics would be lost. In the end, as it turned out, it seems that God indeed does play with dice, and religious thinkers and moral philosophers are still trying to figure out how to make sense in that new world of a post-Newtonian, dice-playing physics.

1. The Foundations of Western Moral Thinking

It is possible to divide the history of Western speculation on the nature of the right and the good into three broad categories: the classical view that has its foundation in Aristotle and lasted until the Renaissance; the modern, which took shape in the Renaissance and reached its classical articulation in the work of Isaac Newton; and the "post-modern," which was ushered in by the Quantum cosmology of the twentieth century. Each of the first two views of the underlying structure of reality had room for an ultimate good, an objective notion of the right, that was in principle open to human understanding, however that might occur. Whether such is possible in the third, "post-modern," world view is still up for grabs. In this essay I want to look briefly at where we have been in the Western intellectual tradition, and where we seem to be heading.

It was Plato who laid the foundation of all subsequent Western thought about the nature of the good. According to Plato, and his most famous student, Aristotle, everything we know in the cosmos consists of two metaphysical components: form and matter. The formal (or ideal) component gives an entity its character and definition; the material component gives the entity physical being in time and space. The forms reflect an ideal realm, one that was perfect, eternal and unchanging. Knowledge of this realm, obtained through reason and rational insight, was true knowledge. This was the realm of the True and the Right and the divine. The material substratum, on the other hand, was the abode of physical imperfection, impermanence, decay, and death. It was the source of all the change and unpredictability of the world of our perceptions. Knowledge of this was necessarily contingent and fleeing, and so in some sense not completely true.

An abiding problem growing out of this philosophy was to account for how these two realms relate to each other. Under Aristotle and his followers, the view took hold that the cosmos was actually a great spectrum, with earthly materiality at the one end and the divine empyrean at the other. In between these two extremes was the rest of cosmos, in which the materiality of the earth became progressively more rarified and purified as one moved out toward the empyrean. Thus one encountered pure earth at the center of the cosmos and then, in order, the spheres of water, air and fire. Beyond fire, one entered a sphere so rarified that it no longer acted according to the rules of material physics. This was the celestial realm, based on aether, in which the moon, sun, and planets were located. These could still interact with the physical world (we can see the planets) but they move in perfect and eternal circles. Finally, beyond even this, was the realm of the fixed stars, and then the domain of the divine, which is no longer physically visible, but apparent only to the mind's eye.

The central organizing principle of this version of classical cosmology was that of hierarchy, and this came to play a central role in religion and moral speculation as well. Scientists after Aristotle noted that hierarchies suffused the physical world. The flora and fauna on earth, for example, could be arranged in an hierarchical order: from greatest tree to meanest weed. Similarly, people comprise the highest order of life on earth with other plants and animals designed either to serve humans directly or to serve those that served humans directly. This principle of hierarchy could be found even in human society. Human communities each have their head and then a descending order of classes and castes, each meant to serve the one above and so contribute to the welfare of the whole.

It was on the basis of this hierarchy of beings that classical Western religious morality was built. The Good and Right was always represented by the highest element of the spectrum. In the cosmos as a whole, it was the divine that contained in itself the full potential of the perfection of all entities. Each individual being, mired in the materiality of the lower realms, was deemed to be good only insofar as it could actualize in its physical being the ideal type to which it "aspired." This was true of humans as well. Being good, in a moral sense, meant actualizing in the concrete reality of your day-to-day life your potential to reflect the ideal human type. The more you were able to overcome the seductions of the material realm and focus on your higher function, namely to serve those above you and the larger ideal of the just society, the better you were morally. There was at least in principle an objective standard of good moral conduct that could be recognized by all reasonable people.

This cosmology was taken up in pretty much its pure form by all the great Western religions: Christianity, Judaism, and Islam. Each stressed the need for transcendence, and each saw sin as residing in the pull of the material and self-centered over against that call of the more perfect ideal embedded in the divine. Despite all the arguments of the specifics of this ethic, everyone could agree on the basic outlines within which the discussion was to occur. Morality could be mapped out on the cosmology of the day.

This was the orderly, and thoroughly worked out, scheme that began to fall apart in the sixteenth century. Copernicus dealt the first blow by displacing the earth from the center of the solar system and placing it among the planets. Now to be sure Copernicus never claimed that the earth was actually a planet like all the others, only that this was a "bookkeeping" maneuver to make calculation simpler. Nonetheless, his new approach to astronomy opened the possibility of thinking of the earth not as the unique abode of matter different in degree and kind from the planets, but as something like the rest of the solar system. This process of decentering the earth was brought to its conclusion with the publication of Newton's universal law of gravity.[1] For Newton, not only was the Earth no longer in the center of the universe, but it is principle was no different from any other massive planet. All the planets, like the earth, were bodies of mass and all of them, like the earth, obeyed the same laws of physics, including gravity. In this universe there was no longer the essential distinction between heaven and earth, between the celestial realm and the terrestrial realm.

In short, the hierarchical model of the classical cosmos was replaced by the notion that the entire cosmos was a sort of great machine. But what remained was the conviction that the reality of the cosmos was in principle knowable. It is true that now the source of that knowledge was logic and mathematics rather than philosophy and religion. But thinkers still did not doubt for an instant that people could know the Truth and the Right. The laws of morality, like the laws of physics, were still attainable by the human mind. It was Simon de Laplace who gave articulation to the implications of this cosmology, noting that for the new physics everything was in principle knowable and so there was no longer any need for "the God hypothesis."

But Laplace was still something of a radical. Not all thinkers, Newton included, were convinced that "the God hypothesis" was completely superfluous. Many subsequent thinkers continued to feel a need to aver God's existence and concern, even while maintaining that the cosmos was a great and logically functioning mechanism. For the theological heirs of Newton, such as the Deists, God's presence was still felt not only in the operation of gravity, but in the intelligence manifest in the complexity of the cosmological machine. So even if God was not directly active at every moment, nonetheless we experience the activity of the divine benevolence by living in a world constructed in such a way as to be orderly and bountiful.

The nineteenth century added one important element to the mechanistic view of the cosmos, namely, the notion of history. One impetus was to account for why, if the universe was such a logical and orderly system, this had not been noted until recently. The answer lay in the development of human consciousness. Like an individual person, the human macrocosm has been engaged in a process of growing up, of reaching a kind of intellectual maturity. So in primitive times, people were only able to grasp so much. By classical times, human intellect

---

[1] Published in his *Principles of Natural Philosophy* in 1687.

had achieved a higher state of abstraction, and in the Renaissance, an even fuller appreciation of the nature of reality. And in each stage the applicability of human insight became wider and wider. We had now come to the point in which we were able for the first time to appreciate the real truth of the cosmic order and so produce a true and universal ethic. It was just out of this combination of trust in human logic and the innate sense of the divine creation that developed in the mid-to-late nineteenth century the theological claims labeled ethical monotheism.

2. *Ethical Monotheism*

The basic idea behind ethical monotheism was that monotheism represented the latest and so highest and most rational form of religion and alone among religious systems offered a solid foundation for a universally acceptable ethic. It took seriously the nineteenth century fascination with the historical process. We can take as a prime example of this way of thinking Solomon Formstecher, a German philosopher and rabbi who lived from 1808 to 1889. In 1841, Solomon Formstecher published *Die Religion des Geistes*. In this work, Formstecher drew on a number of trends that characterized nineteenth-century thought. He seems to have drawn, in particular, on the growing body of literature on the History of Religion, which claimed to be able to find the true meaning of religion by tracing it back to its origins. By the middle of the nineteenth century, the consensus had emerged that the development of religious thought had indeed undergone a history, a progressive development toward its fulfillment. At the beginning was animism, the conviction that all living things, and even non-living ones, were imbued with a certain spirit or power. Gradually, the human mind came to abstract these powers out of specific concrete physical entities and to place them as independent forces above nature. Thus was born polytheism. Over time polytheism became consolidated into fewer and fewer deities until final monotheism emerged. At this point the various forces in the world were no longer seen as independent, and in fact often in struggle with each other, but as manifestations of a single deity, therefore of a single logic and purpose. Now a truly universal religion and ethic were for the first time possible. From here the debate was as to whether the development of monotheistic religion was the end of the human intellectual journey, or whether humankind was now ready to grow on beyond religion to the even more mature state of science.

Formstecher, for his part, had no doubt that monotheism was the final ideal of religion, and he had no doubt that it offered the best hope for an ethic. For him there was no improvement beyond ethical monotheism, for this unified all. In his view, the monotheistic God of the West, and of Judaism in particular, was a real supreme being, not a philosophical construct. This real supreme being is a being of infinite goodness and benevolence, and has passed knowledge of this down through revelation. It is the apperception of this revelation that constitutes the religious insight of monotheists. The spirit of this religion is the consciousness within the minds of real men and women of the absolute moral values revealed by God. And because this moral vision comes from a single transcendent source, and not from the multiform complexity of nature as do philosophical ethics, it reflects an overarching unity of purpose. The morality of ethical monotheism is universally true because it comes from a single all-encompassing source.

Formstecher was neither the first nor the last to adopt this view of ethics. In fact, the notion of a kind of ethical monotheism is still invoked. Dennis Prager, a Jewish public intellectual, has made it part of his mission to popularize a version of ethical monotheism as a needed antidote for what he regards as the moral collapse of America.

> We need to revive the notion that there is a single mind and purpose behind creation, and so an objective source of what is really good or bad. The alternative is to fall into a situation in which any ethic is as good as any other, and so into a situation in which there is really no ethic at all.

This view was, of course, fully compatible with the received cosmology of the nineteenth century, because it averred the basic reasonableness of the cosmos and the innate ability of people to perceive the truth. God might be hard to understand, or even impossible to approach through the study of nature, but ultimately, God is real and his revelation transmits to us a unitary moral truth. So much even an Einstein could accept. But then where does one go when the universal laws of physics and human reason turn out to be contingent? This is the question, as we said, that quantum mechanics insistently raises.

3. *Twentieth Century Cosmology*

Einstein's Theories of Relativity seemed to contradict the optimism upon which Western science, and ethics, was based. In particular, Einstein's cosmology seemed to undercut the very possibility that there were given absolutes out there against which motion and position could be measured. His theories further implied that the validity of human rationality was by nature limited because of our inability to perceive more than three physical dimensions. So any conclusions on the character of the world or the values that were embedded in it had to qualified to the extent that all that we "see" is a distortion of a larger, more complex and complete reality.

Yet in a deeper way, even Einstein can be seen still to be an heir to this knowable cosmos. Despite the radical nature of his theories and despite limitations his theory seemed to place on human perception and understanding, Einstein remained at heart a nineteenth-century thinker. At the end of the day, he was still sure the universe made sense, albeit from a different perspective than that of everyday experience. It was still amenable to mathematization; its behavior on grand scale could still be intelligibly accounted for. The space-time continuum was a rigid grid within which cosmic events had a definite location.

So despite initial impressions, Einstein's theories could still provide the basis for a whole school of moral philosophy. What Relativity tells us is that whatever we say about a body can only be said in relation to something else. There is no absolute motion to the earth, for example. We cannot say that it absolutely and objectively revolves at a certain speed or orbits in a certain direction. But we can say that in relation to the sun, for example, it rotates at a certain rate or orbits in a certain direction. In other words, the character something has in the cosmos is a function of its relation to other bodies.

This epistemological insight can be transferred with relative ease to ethics. The idea would be that each moral agent is like a mass in the cosmos. Alone and without context, calling this or that act moral or immoral would be like measuring the movement of a mass that is alone in the cosmos. Actions can take on moral character only in relationship to some other. It is in fact the very existence of the other that makes the I of a moral agent meaningful to begin with. This is, of course, the major point of Buber's *I and Thou*. One knows that one is an "I" only when one becomes aware that there are other things, "non-I's" out there. These can then be treated as "its" or "thous," and the character of those relationships reflects back and creates the character of the original I, which is amorphous before relationships begin. So what we are as moral agents is relative to the "others" over against which we position ourselves. In this, the moral thinking of Buber takes its place as the epistemological parallel to Einstein's relativity. The cosmos is constructed out of relationships, as is human life. What makes the human microcosm different, and so moral, is that we can choose the character of the relationship.

But there is still a sort of nineteenth-century positivism lurking in the background of this scheme. It is that the other is really out there and has some existence independent of my relationship with it. How I relate to the other may be arbitrary, but the very existence of the other is a given.

4. *Quantum Mechanics*

It was just this surety, stretching over thousands of years, that quantum mechanics threatened to sweep away. For developers of this physics, looking at the atomic and subatomic level, the laws of physics as we thought we knew them simply do not apply. In particular, Quantum Mechanists started to tell us, there is no longer active anything like a direct link between "cause" and "effect," a relationship that constituted the very foundation of classical, Newtonian physics. Laplace, for example, could be so sure of the human ability to know fully the past and to predict the future, because every event is the result of some finite series of causes, and is itself the cause of a finite number of effects. This relationship was stable and predictable. What Einstein and all his predecessors assumed, the comfortable mechanical predictability of the cosmos God created, was being shown to be a nothing more than a play of probabilities at its most basic level. It was, indeed, as if God were playing dice.

The problem that Quantum Mechanics was designed to answer grew out of a series of questions about light that came to stand at the center of late nineteenth-century physics.[2] Einstein himself, it will be recalled, was concerned with light and related electromagnetic waves. Two problems stood out in particular. One had to do with the very nature of these phenomena. It had been assumed, and it was in fact theoretically necessary according to Newtonian physics, for these phenomena to be corpuscular in nature. That is, light was assumed to consist of a stream of particles — photons — just as electricity was assumed to be a stream of particles—electrons. But by the middle of the nineteenth century it had become clear that matters were in fact much more complex. Studies continued to show that light, electricity, magnetism and the like propagated like energy waves and not like streams of physical particles. So physicists had to come to the conclusion that there were two sets of laws that described the governance of the cosmos: laws of physical interaction and laws of energy waves. The problem with light was that sometimes it acted in accordance with the corpuscular laws and at other times in accordance with the energy wave laws. So the first question

---

[2] A summary of this history can be found in Nick Herbert, *Quantum Reality: Beyond the New Physics* (Garden City: Anchor Press/Doubleday, 1985), 31ff.

was how to account for the strange tendency of light to cross over this supposed boundary.

The second problem was the question of quanta. Light interacted with matter in a very puzzling way. If, for example, I were to shine light of a certain intensity on a metal, I could get the metal to release electrons at a certain energy level. The energy in the light simply bounced the electrons out like waves washing a boat ashore.[3] The strange part is that if I increase the intensity of the light, I increase the number of electrons released, but not the intensity with which they fly off. It would be like a small wave knocking only one boat in the harbor into the shore at 10 miles per hour while a heavy wave would knock five boats ashore at 10 miles per hour. So we could measure the strength of a wave not by how fast it propelled boats, for all boats are propelled equally, but how many boats were moved at all. Thus if one gradually increased the power of the wave, one would see its increase in discrete jumps: one boat, then two, then three and so one. These discrete steps of particle emission at the sub-atomic level were termed "quanta." The question was, why would energy always interact with matter in such bundles?

In 1925, a first step to a solution appeared in the form of a Sorbonne dissertation on light quanta published by Louis de Broglie. De Broglie made the counter-intuitive claim that formulas treating energy waves and formulas treating matter could be translated into each other, that is, that they were mathematically equivalent. In other words, not only did energy waves display certain corpuscular features (light could be treated as a stream of photons), but matter also always had certain wave features associated with it. So wave-ness and its particle-ness are inextricably bound together. While making a great amount of mathematical sense, however, the implications of this theory pushed physics through the looking glass into the strange Wonderland of quantum mechanics. The problem was that while physicists thought they understood the mechanics of matter and the mechanics of waves, they did not understand the mechanics of something that was both simultaneously.

It took a while for the full impact of de Broglie's radical claims to sink in. The first impulse of most physicists was still to deal with the familiar world in which matter is corpuscular and energy is wave-like. They took de Broglie's point either to be a convenient mathematical sleight-of-hand or, at most, the claim that particles and waves were closely associated. Only slowly did physicists appreciate the implications of de Broglie's work, namely, that the distinction between waves and particles

---

[3] The analogy is taken from Herbert, *Quantum Reality*, 37.

was entirely artificial and even arbitrary. That is, one had to be ready to say that at the subatomic level waves and particles were the exact same thing.[4] Einstein had already taught us that energy and mass were related (e=mc^2), but only in the wake of de Broglie did the implications of this equation really become apparent. To put it bluntly, matter, as matter, does not exist.

The question then arose as to how to relate these experimental results to the underlying reality. In 1925, Erwin Heisenberg proposed a theory, based on different matrices of measurement, that was to underlie his subsequent Uncertainty Principle. In his article, he addressed the difficulty experimenters were having in measuring both the position and the momentum of electrons. Heisenberg showed that one of the implications of de Broglie's work was that knowledge of both a subatomic particle's position and its momentum at any one time was *in principle* impossible. On an abstract level, this was because momentum and position were being measured on two different matrices. On the experimental level this manifested itself in the fact that in the very act of determining the position of an electron, one had to destroy its momentum, and vice versa. This was so because experimentally one had to treat the electron either as a particle (to measure its position), or as a wave (to measure its momentum), but one could not set up an experiment to treat electrons as both a particle and a wave at the same time.

Within the year, two alternative theories were proposed for explaining why quantum mechanics worked. Erwin Schrödinger proposed a wave theory, while Paul Dirac proposed a transformational theory. The details need not detain us. What is important is that physicists now had three different, yet equally valid, claims as to how experimental results relate to what was being measured. So the question was to account for the underlying reality, if there was one, that would account for this.

One of the earliest hypotheses is the so-called Copenhagen interpretation. This interpretation rests on the fact that light, for example, can be quite adequately measured as an energy wave or as a flow of corpuscles. That is, light can be made to act one way or the other depending on how

---

[4] To be more accurate, the idea is that subatomic particles have no "body" and so by nature have no fixed location in time or space. They do have certain probabilities of being at a certain place at a certain time, and these probabilities can be mapped out using wave equations, producing what we might call probability waves. A good summary of this is Boris Kuznetsov, "Quantum-Relativistic Retrospection and the History of Classical Physics: Classical Rationalism and the Nonclassical Science," in *Historical Studies in the Physical Sciences*, ed. Russell McCormmach (Philadelphia: University of Pennsylvania Press, 1971) vol. 3, 128-129.

the experimenter sets up the experiment. Or to put matters another way, an atomic "phenomenon" is neither wave-like nor corpuscular until an observer intervenes and, through observation, makes it one or the other.[5] Reality, in other words, does not exist out there already, but is the result of the interaction between object and subject. In terms that might be familiar to a nineteenth-century philologist, we could say that experimental reality is all an interpretation but that there is no underlying Urtext.

A rather famous example of how this works is through a mind experiment devised by Erwin Schrödinger. In the experiment, Schrödinger proposes placing a cat in a box along with a piece of radioactive material that has a 50% chance of giving off radiation over the time of the experiment. The box also contains a radiation detection device that would release a poisonous gas, thus killing the cat, if radiation was detected. Schrödinger's question was what state the cat would be in at the end of the experimental period but before anybody had looked into the box. His answer was that the cat would be 100% in both possible states (alive and dead) simultaneously, each state fully superimposed on the other. It is only when someone takes off the lid and looks that the cat finally becomes fully alive or fully dead. In other words, until the observer intervenes, there is no underlying reality.

But this is hardly the most radical of interpretations to grow out of Quantum Mechanics. For example, there is the so-called Everett interpretation. This interpretation begins with the question of what happens to Schrödinger's potentially dead cat when we open the box and find a living animal. The answer, in the Everett interpretation, is that it has popped into, or created, a parallel universe. In fact each atomic or subatomic event must be taken to produce its own reverse reflection in an alternative universe, of which there must be an infinite number. In this way, each probability is fully realized somewhere.

All these theories end up arriving at the same place, albeit from different directions. They all end up telling us that there is no single underlying reality that we can somehow objectively know, based on our experience. All we have is interpretation of what is in principle only a partial view. To be sure there have been attempts to interpret quantum mechanical results in such a way as to maintain a knowable and understandable reality. But these so far fail to deal with one of the theoretical implications of quantum physics, probability over long distance. The

---

[5] Cf. Arkady Plotnitsky, *Complementarity: Anti-Epistemology After Bohr and Derrida* (Durham: Duke University Press, 1994), 102f.

problem can be illustrated with the following mind experiment. Imagine we have two atoms of a radioactive substance that has a half life of one year. This means that we can say with full confidence that one of the particles will give off radiation within the next year and that the other will not. We cannot, of course say, which one will and which one will not. Now suppose we separate them and move them apart at the speed of light, so that there is no chance that the one can communicate with the other. We watch the one in our laboratory. At the end of the year it must be the case that one has "popped" and the other has not. There is of course no cause which will determine which will and which will not. But we can say that the fact that ours popped means that the other did not, or conversely that ours did not because the other one did. In other words, the "cause" for an observed phenomenon on the sub-atomic level may not be local. What we experience out there is not an a priori given, but is itself one probable outcome of unseen and even unknowable forces. It is not merely that we perceive reality in a distorted way, it is that the reality we do perceive is partial, contingent, and arbitrary.

5. *Conclusion*

So what does all this mean for ethics? One apparent implication is that the nature of reality is much more contingent than we thought. The modern physics of Newton, as the classical physics before him, assumed a world with a built-in and predictable logic. Right and wrong were matters of objective judgment. Even Einstein could aver that while we could not say anything about, say, the absolute motion of the earth, we could a) say something objective about its motion relative to the moon, and b) take the existence of the earth and the moon for granted. Even Buber, whose thinking bears remarkable parallels with Einstein, as I noted above, saw much more contingency in this relationship. For Buber, the relationship between the "I" and the "It" or the "Thou" was not an objective relationship between two given and already defined entities. The relationship also influenced the very definition of the entities, especially the "I." This is of course what gives the moral relationship its urgency. In the very process of forging relationships with "others" I define myself.

But quantum mechanics suggests that the contingency of moral self-definition goes even further than this. The "Other" is also always itself being defined by our relationship to it. So there is neither an "I" or an "it" in the beginning, but only the possibility of a relationship. The "I" and the "Other" both emerge in a dialectic relationship with the emergence of the relationship between them. I not only create a relationship with the Other, but I create the Other to begin with as I create myself. If this is so, then the moral character of the cosmos, or at least of that portion of the cosmos that affects us, rests on our perceptions and choices to an even larger extent than previous cosmologies had allowed.

This brings us back to the optimism of late nineteenth-century thinking, exemplified as we said in the notion of ethical monotheism. This notion rests on the claim there is a single unifying intelligence which not only gives unity to all of Creation, but imbues that Creation with moral value. But if anything like the Copenhagen, or even Everett, interpretation is correct, then the cosmos we experience is not a given, but itself more openly contingent than we had ever dreamed. This means that we can no longer complacently assume that we are growing in moral maturity. As the Nazi genocide makes strikingly clear, it is really in our hands to create Utopias or Holocausts, and there is no force out there to intervene. God does indeed seem to play dice and to depend deeply on the outcome of the roll. What Quantum Mechanics suggests is that we ourselves may in fact be the dice.

CHAPTER ELEVEN

THE DISAPPEARING GOD OF ETHICAL MONOTHEISM

ROBERT GIBBS

Tomorrow (and today) the possibility of ethical monotheism appears foreclosed. If we now raise its possibility again, then two questions will immediately strike us: 1) Does ethics need theology? and 2) Is the climax of theology a distinctively ethical moment? I phrase these two questions not primarily for a historical study about what some thinkers once thought, or even what Jews or Christians or Muslims once held. Instead, I wish to describe the possibility that even in an era where theology and ethics seem to have so little to say to each other, the topic is not only not concluded but is rather one where even the most basic landmarks may need re-locating. I offer here a brief contrast of two Jewish thinkers, Franz Rosenzweig and Emmanuel Levinas, a contrast that, insofar as it succeeds, will implicate us in a complex re-thinking of why we require ethics and theology thus to meet.[1]

My initial premise will be that Rosenzweig is engaged in a theological enterprise in *The Star of Redemption,* a performance in which God is present, commanding, and in relation with human beings.[2] I will leave aside the question of how 'ethical' his account of theological relations is but will instead contrast this relational divine presence with Levinas' discussion of God as not present, and indeed, as never having been present but as having always already passed by.[3] Levinas is clearly writing ethics, but his need for theology, for any discourse about God or even for any relation to God, is far from obvious. The shift from a theology of relations to an ethics with a divine absence is the focus of

---

[1] This essay hopes to honor both the man, Wendell Dietrich, and his scholarly work on Jewish philosophy. In ongoing conversation he has continuously encouraged and challenged me to pursue these questions with the greatest possible probity.

[2] Franz Rosenzweig, *Der Stern der Erlösung,* in *Franz Rosenzweig: Der Mensch und sein Werk: Gesammelte Schriften* (The Hague: Martinus Nijhoff); trans. William W. Hallo as *The Star of Redemption* (Boston: Beacon Press, 1971).

[3] Emmanuel Levinas, *De Dieu qui Vient a L'Idée* (Paris: Librairie Philosophique, J. Vrin, 1982); trans. Bettina Bergo as *Of God who Comes to Mind* (Stanford: Stanford University Press, 1998).

this paper: it is the disappearing God of my title. We have a few essays where Levinas reads Rosenzweig, and especially *The Star*, and so are justified raising the contrast as a shift. In addition, because a few of us have now explored their relation in detail[4] this paper raises questions in a less historical manner. Just what the personal and historical factors may have been for this shift I leave unexplored here. But the initial shift as a disappearing allows us to return to Rosenzweig and read *The Star* with specific questions about divine presence and how the relations of speaking are themselves an ethics. And that also raises the harder question for Levinas: to raise the question of the intimacy of the absence of God and the idea. At that point, we may see that even more than a theology of absence, the possibility of ethical monotheism requires a theology of disappearing but not a disappearance of theology.

If we begin at the center of the book *The Star of Redemption*, we find a relation between God and the ensouled human: revelation as love. In speaking the command "Love me," God reveals God's love to a human soul.[5] The soul is not only beloved but also confesses being loved. The soul is faithful. Revelation is the dialogue of love and faith. What love provides is the immediacy of the present moment, an urgent affirmation of the soul in the form of the command. The soul, through confession and ongoing dialogue, discovers its condition of being loved and makes the moment of revelation into a knowable state of being loved wherein God is recognized as both lover and creator. For Rosenzweig this dialogue is no play of ideas, nor in any sense susceptible to the doubts of self-deception. The very interchange, and the inequality of the partners, and indeed the lapse of time that this dialogue takes — these all characterize the *Erlebnis*, the lived experience, of revelation. To make the point more sharply: all lived experience is grounded in this most basic dialogue, in attending and responding to the divine command to love God. It is not an exceptional experience, but experience in its most exemplary form. The present moment of the command to love is the orienting moment of all human existence in time, the moment that makes us live in time and that shows us the meaning of life.

---

4 Wendell S. Dietrich "Is Rosenzweig an Ethical Monotheist? A Debate with the New Francophone Literature," in *Der Philosoph Franz Rosenzweig (1886-1929)*, ed. Wolfdietrich Schmied-Kowarzik, (München: Verlag Karl Alber, 1988), 891-900; Richard A. Cohen, *Elevations: The Height of the Good in Rosenzweig and Levinas* (Chicago: University of Chicago Press, 1994); Robert Gibbs, *Correlations in Rosenzweig and Levinas* (Princeton: Princeton University Press, 1992).

5 Rosenzweig, *Star* 197/177 (citations are to the original/translation).

But Rosenzweig is anxious about the epistemological significance of this elevation of *Erlebnis* and of God's revelation, which he calls the *Ereignis* (the event). *Erlebnis* and *Ereignis* are not *Erfahrung* — the traditional term for sense-experience. They are inherently linguistic, but *Erfahrung* seems to be non-linguistic. (One might pause here to think about the kind of sense-experience needed to listen or to read, but the point is that hearing a word spoken is not simply hearing sounds because the interpersonal dynamics exceed what could be catalogued in physiological records.) *Erlebnis's* excess, however, also opens into a realm where anything, any fanaticism or illusion, becomes possible.[6] The discipline that Rosenzweig requires, then, is language as the medium of lived experience, and grammar as the science (the organon) of language. The limits of grammar will be the limits of our knowledge about lived experience. The essence of revelation, then, is the grammar of language in which revelation occurs.

While many philosophers would presume that the primary function of language is to describe what is the case in the present tense and in the third person indicative, Rosenzweig discovered that the present moment occurs in an imperative, an imperative in the second person ('you'). Descriptions fix things in the past; imperatives reveal the urgent present; and exhortations, which Rosenzweig calls cohortatives, impel us into the future. The key moment is the imperative that reveals the speaker in speaking to the interlocutor: from I to you. God appears in *The Star* as a lover who commands love — becoming present in revealing love. The more demanding questions about whether God commands other commands, or indeed, whether in other people's commands God commands I leave aside. Rosenzweig does not confine God to the role of commanding lover, but our lived experience arises and is oriented from that role, from that moment of speech — to which the faithful soul responds, affirming that it is loved. From that command and its response, our language then goes on to perform other relations with God. We recognize God as the creator of the world when knowing and describing the world as filled with determined things. And we hope for God as redeemer of both humanity and the world in exhortation when we call others to join with us in praising God. In each of these three relations (Creation, Revelation, Redemption), our lived experience arises in the performance of speaking or singing. It is not in the first instance that God is the topic of our speaking, but rather that we talk about the world,

---

[6] Ibid., 123/111.

talk to each other, and indeed talk with each other — and in those relations God is experienced in relations with the world and with the human soul. From the perspective of the loving dialogue, God appears as the Creator that makes a world of nouns and verbs, a world in which things have been made. God also appears as the one who will redeem when we exhort each other to join together, thanks to God (appearing in the dative). Were the loving revelation missing, we would still speak about the world that was made and might still try to join together, but we would not experience God's love and role in our everyday speech.

This God who is experienced in speaking created the world, loves us, and will redeem us — of such a God there is much to say, and to whom there is much to say — is a God for theology but also for prayer, even for screaming to.[7] Such a theological vision might be classified as ethical because its access to these relations occurs in speaking with other human beings. It becomes a discourse theology, in the way that Habermas proposes a discourse ethics — but if it is then also a theological discourse ethics, it would be because the norms of grammar are then understood as norms for the relations between people and are obligating precisely in the way language is used. The latter claim, that it is not merely discourse theology but also ethics, is one I wish to keep in question.

Before shifting to Levinas, however, I must note that we have skewed our reading of Rosenzweig by ignoring the theological import of the two outer parts of *The Star*: Parts I and III. Part I has an intricate and rigorous construction of the hidden God, while Part III concludes with a remarkable discussion of how God is Truth.[8] The first part offers us a theology of impossible experience as pure conditions of linguistic experience. The third part offers a theory of verification that explores how the lived/ linguistic experience of Part II becomes actual in communal practices. The big picture, alas, is much bigger and the implications for theology yet more diverse and complicated. Indeed, the ethical side is less clear with the widening of the horizon, but the monotheism becomes much more emphatic through the various parts.

To shift to Levinas' work, however, is to focus on that aspect of speaking that cannot be experienced, the non-phenomenality of the otherness of the other person, to which I should respond. In my work, I have focused on the way that Levinas' exploration of responsibility examines the practices of listening and speaking (and eventually reading

---

[7] Ibid., 206/185.
[8] Ibid., 432/388.

and writing).[9] Thus, from Part II of Rosenzweig's *The Star* to Levinas there is a direct connection, focusing on the saying of language, on speaking language. Levinas' main concern is with my responsibility for the other person, on the exigency to which I must respond. His analysis depends on a certain exhaustion of epistemological interpretation, as the otherness of the other inverts the structures of intentionality: it is not that there is something I cannot intend or grasp about the other, but that the other person faces me, and bears intentions towards me. That breaking out from my horizon of meanings occurs in listening to the other, in drawing near to the other person, in becoming a sign for the sake of the other person. My interlocutor is not apparent to me, or is not merely apparent, but has the authority to break with her appearance, to refuse my meanings, to interpret her words to me. Levinas calls *the face* that breaking away from my image of her, away from appearance.[10] Not only is the face not some image of God, some presence of the other person in her skin, it is not something but is a performance, a breaking away from appearances. A breech in the totality of phenomena. In his later works, Levinas would hesitate to say that the face "is," because what it does is break with being, break towards what is beyond being, which is not some kind of being beyond, but is not a being at all.

Such an ethics produces an infinity as a responsibility that increases the more I do, because the other's reservoir of authority that arises when she faces me obliges me infinitely. The discussion of infinity and its place in Levinas' thought will occupy us below. Here we see something else, that God is introduced into this dialogue which is not a dialogue, into this asymmetrical assignment of responsibility to me. God is not present, but has been by, has passed by.[11] To clarify my point, we need to consider what God does not do in Levinas' account. If in Rosenzweig's theory of language God could appear in three modes: as interlocutor (You), as object of discourse (Creator: He), and as the one to whom we give thanks together (in the dative), then in Levinas' only that dative mode is left.

9 See my *Why Ethics?: Signs of Responsibilities* (Princeton: Princeton University Press, 2000).

10 Emmanuel Levinas, *Totalité et Infini*, 4th ed. (The Hague: Martinus Nijhoff, 1971); 1st ed. 1961; trans. Alphonso Lingis as *Totality and Infinity* (Pittsburgh: Duquesne University Press, 1969), 146/171.

11 Emmanuel Levinas, *Autrement qu'être ou au-delà de l'Essence* (Dordrecht: Martinus Nijhoff, 1974); trans. Alphonso Lingis as *Otherwise than Being or Beyond Essence* (The Hague: Martinus Nijhoff, 1981), 188/148.

Levinas distinguishes the saying from the said: the performance of speech (the pragmatics) and the content of what is said (the semantics). Ethics is not a matter of semantics, much less syntax (the relations between words), but rather arises in the saying, in the respons-ability, the way I should respond to the other person. What can be transcribed, the sense-experience, is the said. The concretization and taking on of form that occurs, transforming the saying into the said, is inescapable but also is a mode of betrayal. Philosophy is called to reduce this betrayal, to attend to the saying in the said.[12] God is not to be found in the said, precisely because God exceeds any said. Theologians have tried to coin a said adequate to God's transcendence, but fail — in part because they are not, according to Levinas, pursuing the task of philosophy, which is to reduce that betrayal. Levinas is not willing to continue the traditions of theology, but instead insists on breaking with any ontotheology.

But more decisive by far, is Levinas' resistance to speaking to God. The very immediacy of dialogue in Rosenzweig is denied. Despite the radical interpretation of the face-to-face in Levinas, or perhaps because of it, God is not the person to whom I speak nor the one whose voice I hear. Levinas goes so far as to interpret even Jewish prayer as a process of shifting away from the invocation of God. In his philosophical works, Levinas fashions a term for this non-interlocutor position: *illeity*.[13] It bears within it both the French *il* and means 'him-ness', but also the Latin *ille*, and so meaning 'that-oneness,' or even the 'over-thereness.' The third personness of this term is made to contrast with the I-you of Rosenzweig, Buber, and Marcel. God is not an it, not present in sense-experience, but is also more remote, more other than an interlocutor.

Indeed, for Levinas the key to thinking illeity is to think about a mode of absence, of something that was never present. God's transcendence is only evoked as never having been present. Theologically we might construe this as an inaccessible act of creation, or even of an internal self-relation in God prior to creation. Such a God is not 'real' — so why does Levinas need such a God in his thought? He often considers the phrase 'death of God', and even argues that atheism is a condition for ethics.[14] We do become aware of this absence by a trace of God in the saying, in relation to another person. What we 'have' is only a trace, an enigmatic absence. We 'see' the traces of withdrawal, like the

---

[12]   Ibid., 206/162.
[13]   Ibid., 188/148.
[14]   Levinas, *Totality*, 30/58.

swipe of the cloth where the handkerchief has wiped away fingerprints. Not a sign, not an intentional trace meant to lead us back to God, because there is no back-there to get to. God is not a transcendental condition for experience, but absolutely removed from experience. No sense-experience, no lived-experience, no dialogue.

Levinas' sole exception is the possibility of witnessing to God. An example would be the statement: "Thanks to God, Here I am for you."[15] I can speak to the other person, and in witnessing to my responsibility to her, I can invoke God, in the dative. Not speaking about God or to God, but due to God. This closely follows Rosenzweig's account of cohortation in his discussion of redemption, and it introduces some theological themes into Levinas' thought. It displaces the familiar statement: "I believe in God," (as well as the more pious "I believe God"). Again, God is not a proper theme for responsive discourse. But also, God is to be thanked, to be the indirect object of discourse. For Levinas, God's glorification occurs in human speaking. We are to glorify God by witnessing to our infinite responsibilities to each other. God is not the cause of our responsibilities, but is to be thanked and is the one thanks to whom we are assigned our ethical responsibilities. While Rosenzweig could anchor the word God in the love dialogue, depending on the faithful soul's utterance, and from that anchor recognize God as Creator and invoke God as Redeemer, Levinas is left only with that latter invocation, and with God as a term that requires continuous disruption.

At this point, we need to return to the more basic questions about ethical monotheism. Levinas' thought seems to have only a limited role for God. But that role is connected to a specific epistemological task, arising in the articulation of the ethics of responsibility. Levinas regularly refers to Descartes, and to the discussion of God in the *Meditations*. [16] For Levinas, God comes to mind as an idea in which I think more than I can think. The infinite is 'experienced' as an excess beyond experience. Exactly what is at stake in the rhetorical move to Descartes I leave aside here, but this presence of the infinite in the finite, this opening within my horizon of something that breaks with my horizon — this is a logic of God, a theo-logic. Levinas, unlike Descartes, does not claim that this arises in self-reflection, but rather is the breaking out of my consciousness of the other person — the way the face breaks with its forms or images. The infinition of responsibility occurs in this disruption of my consciousness by something that exceeds my powers of consciousness

---

[15] Levinas, *Of God . . .*, 122/75.
[16] Levinas, *Totality*, 187/211.

— which Levinas can conveniently then call my moral conscience (*conscience*, in French). For our purposes, moreover, this excess becomes the mark of the saying of a sign, and even more of a writing. For the word means more than the author means it to mean. It becomes an excess of meaning in the future which Levinas calls inspiration.[17] All saying/writing performs this theo-logic, this logic of the infinite in the finite — without ever making God present. The idea itself is not real, not present, not experienced, not certain, not spoken about or to. God comes to mind as what cannot appear in or for the mind. But we think, speak, and write about God precisely to accentuate and articulate the way that we are responsible for others beyond what we can re-present in an appearance.

This ethical logic of excess, this kind of ethical monotheism, is remarkably close to Hermann Cohen, for instance, and also to Maimonides and to many other Jewish philosophers. For much of the Jewish philosophical tradition, God has been understood as an idea, and indeed, as an idea with little 'personal' presence, and for whom both speaking about and speaking to is at best strained. Indeed, precisely because Levinas is struggling with ethics first and only introduces this specific theology in order to clarify the excess of responsibility, we see that ethics governs his claims about God (and perhaps that we should be calling this Monotheistic Ethics — except that in this case the adjective seems more central to the term than the noun).

But then we need to return to Rosenzweig, again. For his theological discourse ethics is in fact linked to both a social theory for its verification, and more interestingly here, to a theory of absence and withdrawal. Rosenzweig knew that the recourse to lived experience was dangerous. Grammar alone was not discipline enough, for the empiricism of rules (in contrast to the empiricism of sheer events) did not offer cognition of the contingency in revelation. That is, speaking speech could not show the freedom to speak without recourse to a thinking about unspoken language. God's revelation of God's love must be not merely an event, but must be set in a framework where God could have remained hidden. Existent love has a certain essential compulsion, but that love exists requires a contingent moment. That is, even God's entry into language must display God's freedom to abstain — but that will

---

[17] Emmanuel Levinas, *L'Au-delà du Verset* (Paris: Editions de Minuit, 1982); trans. Gary D. Mole as *Beyond the Verse* (Bloomington, Ind.: Indiana University Press, 1994), 204/171.

mean" for Rosenzweig that not only God, but human beings and the world itself have to be conceived of as withdrawn.

That world of withdrawal, where relations are not and so where lived experience cannot be our guide, that world is presented in Part I of *The Star*, as each of the three elements (God, Human, World) are constructed as inaccessible to language and to experience. Logic, in a particularly twisted way, obtains and the mathematics of the infinitesimal functions as parallel to grammar in the world of lived experience in language.[18] As for the temporality of this world without experience, why it is of course a past that was never present — the time of Levinas' illeity. But while Levinas announces the withdrawal of God, the 'experience' of the infinite, Rosenzweig constructs the God who hides from humanity (the Greek gods and also an interesting relation to Buddhism and Taoism). Such a hidden divinity (which is likely not a unique/monotheist God) is a condition for the self-revealing, loving God experienced in human language. The possibility for revelation is a rhythm between the hidden and the revealed, and only as such can *Erlebnis* produce the kind of meaning we seek.

Rosenzweig's infinitesimal constructions parallel Levinas' idea of the Infinite — each secures the withdrawal from experience of God, a withdrawal which marks not the passing away of Divine Presence, but rather, the impossibility of Divine Presence as a condition for the relations performed in speech. Such is monotheism, a theo-logic that offers little succor to those who seek a religious experience of a fully present God. (And lest we think that this philosophical scruple about Divine Presence is merely a polemic against Christian doctrines of incarnation, we should pause and ask ourselves whether the Passion, as well as the Ascension do not also point to an impossible presence? Not that Christian theology should deny the doctrine of two natures, but that Christian theology also examines whether either of the two natures are immediately present, or whether, like a Word, must not always suffer in anticipation of a future meaning. But the question of how monotheism and a theo-logic of withdrawal distributes over Jewish and Christian doctrine far exceeds this paper.) In Levinas' essay "God and Philosophy," he raises suspicions about the familiar division between the God of Abraham and the God of the Philosophers.[19] He suggests in many of his Jewish writings that the philosophical concepts of God (and here I recognize a theo-logic of a past God who was never present) are a true

---

18 Rosenzweig, *Star*, 23/20.
19 Levinas, *On God...*,96-7/57.

interpretation of the Jewish tradition, especially from the Sages of the Talmud on. Hermann Cohen is surely closely aligned with such a theo-logic.

But the Ethical in ethical monotheism depends on the relation of this theo-logic of withdrawal, of the idea of the Infinite, to the ethical responsibility for the other person. Rosenzweig shows in the very architecture of *The Star* that revealing oneself depends on a possibility of remaining concealed. The fact of love is free; even if the discourse of love is an imperative, and even if love is precisely this revealing of oneself in language. All we need do is see that the relations of love and faith are originary for ethics, and we can see that the possibility of a radical novelty even in love between human beings must depend on a contingency that is best termed divine. Rosenzweig's analysis of the relation between the withdrawn divinity and the revealed unique God is in the service of the contingency, rather the freedom, that is performed in human response, in human responsibility.

If we have drawn Levinas and Rosenzweig too closely together here, it was in order to think through the withdrawal of God as intrinsic to the freedom of responsibility in ethics. The idea of God, then, as idea that exceeds our ability to think, is not a simply transcendental condition for ethics, nor a postulate (although it resembles a postulate). It arises in a reflection in the service of the assignment of my responsibility, even as it censures any thought or image I have of God. But in the contrast between Rosenzweig and Levinas, we see a possibility for legitimated discourses about and to God to disappear. For Rosenzweig, it is hard to imagine the dative discourse ('thanks to God') without the speech from and to God. By accentuating the gap in the time of every word we might push Rosenzweig still closer to Levinas by arguing that the speech to and about God is not really a way of presenting God or a way of God appearing, but we would then lose the space that the thinkers open in disagreeing. The topic, for us, is richer and clearer if we maintain the disagreement and the distance between these two thinkers.

The topic itself is determined by its disappearing God, by a God whose possible presence is bound to a necessary withdrawal. Even a God that could be discussed and to whom we could pray would require an intimate connection with a withdrawn God, a God who is passed in a past that was never present. I now can return to the opening questions with a clearer interpretation.

1) Ethics does need a theology, but it is a theology of withdrawal, a theology where the hiddenness of God serves as the inverse of the freedom of human response. But such a theology gives us no knowledge of

God, and refuses to make the hidden God even a transcendental condition for ethics — because the withdrawal is also the withdrawal behind a transcendental horizon. Both the freedom and the obligation of responsibility requires an otherness that can break through my consciousness — without becoming simply available for me. With Rosenzweig, moreover, we might still raise the question of whether this orientation toward the other person is the only direct relation, and whether we cannot also have direct relations with both the world and with God.

2) The relation of theology to ethics, however, is more open. It raises the question of whether in Rosenzweig the center of his theology is the recognition that God loves me, or the recognition that God loves me freely. The contrast is between a theology of relations that makes the *Erlebnis* of those relations the center or a theology that understands the freedom and hence responsibility in those relations as the center. Rosenzweig is not resuscitating Schleiermacher and thus insists that theology have the discipline not only of grammar, but also of the rhythm of logic and language. What Rosenzweig asks us is whether the ethical moment, the moment of human responsibility, deserves to be the center, or whether, whatever the necessity for confining access to thelogical relations to a way through human language, still the drama exceeds the bounds of ethics. Indeed, the question doubles up with a concern that the ethics of responsibility itself should require the relations to the immediate dialogue and the discourse about God as Creator. The story of experience, told in human words to other humans, is a story of God's life from creation to revelation to redemption. And if we suspect that in such a story ethics is not central enough, then we might well find in Levinas' refusal to re-think the theological relations a privilege for ethics. Such concerns, however, define the ongoing concern with Ethical Monotheism — a permanent tension between the priority of ethics and the idea of God who disappears, even in coming to mind.

CHAPTER TWELVE

EMMANUEL LEVINAS AND ETHICAL MONOTHEISM

DAVID NOVAK

1. *Faith and Ethics: Ancient*

When speaking of "ethical monotheism," one raises the question of the normative character of the human and of the divine. For "ethics" covers those norms we see governing the realm of human interaction; "monotheism," the human affirmation of one unique God in faith, covers those norms we see governing the realm of divine-human interaction. "Ethical monotheism" itself is a modern term, but in order to appreciate how a recent contemporary Jewish thinker like Emmanuel Levinas (1906-1995) is connected to it, we must first see its ancient roots. Only then can we see how Levinas enters an ongoing conversation, making his own specifically modern contribution to it. And, of course, that contribution, as well as the whole enterprise of ethical monotheism, must be critically examined.[1]

In the classical rabbinic tradition, there are several ways by which the commandments of the Torah are distinguished. One of the most prominent of these ways is the division of the commandments into the categories of "what pertains between God and humans" (*bein adam lemaqom*) and "what pertains between humans themselves" (*bein adam lehavero*). One can see this specific categorization of the law as having several meanings.

First, in what is usually considered the *locus classicus* of this categorization, we read, "Rabbi Eleazar ben Azariah interpreted the scriptural verse, 'from all your sins before the Lord you shall be cleansed' (Leviticus 16:30), to mean: for transgressions between God and humans, the Day of Atonement atones; for transgressions between humans themselves, the Day of Atonement does not atone until one appeases the other

---

[1] Ethical Monotheism, which is a central issue in modern Jewish thought, has been a central issue in the teaching and scholarship of Wendell Dietrich. Over the years, I have learned much from conversations and written exchanges with Professor Dietrich about the meaning and historical background of Ethical Monotheism. Let this essay be a token of my gratitude to him.

person."[2] Here it seems as though the normative relationship with God is taken as two termed when the one offended is divine, but three termed when the one offended is human. That is, God must be directly appeased when God alone has been offended; God must be indirectly appeased when a human being *and* God have both been offended by another human being.[3] In other words, even though the interhuman relationship is included in the divine-human relationship (God is also offended when a human being is offended), its integrity must still be respected so that one may not use his or her claim on reconciliation with God as a means, a shortcut as it were, to ignore the need for interhuman reconciliation. As such, every transgression immediately against another human being is ultimately a transgression against God, while the converse is not the case. A three-termed relation necessarily includes two terms just as a two-termed relation necessarily excludes a third term.

This first meaning of the above categorization of the commandments concerns how one reacts to two kinds of transgressions, depending on who has been offended. Nevertheless, it suggests that there might be more to the distinction between the two kinds of relationships than just a question of reconciliation after a transgression. This distinction suggests a second meaning: initially one is to act differently towards another human being than one is to act towards God. Here one's intention before the act itself is to be different depending on the object of his or her act. The very quality of the respective acts themselves is to be essentially different.

One can see that the quality of these acts is different when the difference between the gravest transgression in each category is compared. The gravest transgression against God is idolatry; the gravest transgression against another human is killing.[4] Nevertheless, there are exceptions to the prohibition of killing another human being; thus, minimally, self-defense is not only not prohibited as murder, it is mandated as life-saving.[5] When it comes to idolatry, however, there are no exceptions. It is, truly, the only act for which there is no exception in Jewish law. Idolatry may never be practiced; under no circumstances is it valid.[6] When it comes to killing, though, the human other usually

---

[2] *Mishnah*: Yoma 8.9.
[3] See *Babylonian Talmud*: Yoma 87a re I Sam. 2:25.
[4] See Maimonides, *Mishneh Torah*: Rotseah, 4.9.
[5] See *Babylonian Talmud*: Sanhedrin 72a-b.
[6] See ibid.: 90a; also, Maimonides, *Guide of the Perplexed*, 2.33 re Exod. 20:2-3.

has the prior claim, but in self-defense I have the prior claim over that of another human.[7] Yet, as the absolute prohibition of idolatry indicates, the divine other always has the prior claim. Even God himself does not waive that claim. Thus when performing a commandment having a human object, there is always an element of contingency, which is not always the case when performing a commandment of which God is the direct object.

So far we have seen the distinction between interhuman norms and divine-human norms operating on two levels: one in the different results of the acts done in each realm; two, in the different ways the acts done in each realm are intended. But, does the distinction go even deeper? Can we distinguish between the way we know the two types of norms even before we are ready to do them or react to them as the third meaning of the distinction? That is, is there an essential difference between the specific *nature* of the interhuman commandments and the specific *nature* of the divine-human commandments? At this point we can see the fundamental divide between those in the Jewish tradition who could be called "fideists" and those who could be called "rationalists."

The fideists are those who would assert that the only reason to obey any commandment in the Torah is because God has commanded it.[8] Thus, there is no difference, for example, as to *why* one avoids eating pork and *why* one avoids committing murder. All commandments only have one general reason: God's will is to be obeyed. The two differences noted above between interhuman commandments and divine-human commandments are in their eyes differences of *how* not *why*; that is, God *happens* to be a party in interhuman reconciliation, and idolatry *happens* to be the one indispensable norm. In their view, it seems, the Torah could have just as easily not made God a party in interhuman reconciliation, and the Torah could have just as easily made idolatry a dispensable norm.

The rationalists, conversely, are those who assert that for at least some of the commandments of the Torah God has *reasons* for commanding them the way he does, and that some of these reasons are so evident their commandments are to be kept even before or apart from the actual promulgation of these commandments as commandments of the

---

[7] See, e.g., *Babylonian Talmud*: Baba Metsia 62a re Lev. 25:36; Maimonides, *Mishneh Torah*: Rotseah, 1.9 re *Babylonian Talmud*: Sanhedrin 72b and *Mishnah*: Ohalot 7.6.
[8] See David Novak, *Jewish Social Ethics* (New York, 1992), 25-29; *Natural Law in Judaism* (Cambridge, 1998), 64-72.

Mosaic Torah revealed to the Jewish people at Mount Sinai. These commandments, then, are not to be taken as arbitrary; in justice God could not have ruled otherwise. Thus, regarding the whole area of interhuman violence, for which the Torah sees the Flood in the time of Noah as God's just reaction, the thirteenth century Spanish Jewish theologian Nahmanides writes, "and the reason (*ta`am*) is because this is a rational commandment (*mitsvah muskelet*). There was no need for a prophet to so admonish them. Furthermore, it is something which is bad both for God and for human creatures (*la-beriyot*)."[9] Earlier, discussing the same theme, he writes: "it is a rational matter (*inyan muskal*) not needing the Torah."[10] Nahmanides, of course, is not in any way denigrating revelation. Instead, he is indicating that the prohibition of interhuman violence is something one brings to revelation to be elevated into the covenant intact; it is not something that revelation initially presents to practical human knowledge as a novelty.

If one were to designate the interhuman relationship by the modern use of the word "ethics," and if one were to designate the divine-human relationship by the modern use of the word "faith," then one could say that for this medieval Jewish rationalism, ethics leads into faith rather than being strictly derived from it. For the fideists, however, every valid norm must be directly derived from faith. Each side has the task of marshaling canonical texts needed to support its position. But, the rationalists have an easier task inasmuch as they only have to show the inherent rationality of *some* of the revealed norms, whereas the fideists have to show the inherent nonrationality of *all* of the norms. But that would require showing the uniqueness of every norm of the Torah, something clearly belied by the fact that many of the ethical norms of the Torah seem to be implied by pre-Sinaitic Torah narratives, and many of the ethical norms of the Torah have analogues in other systems of law.[11] That is why, I think, full blown fideism had to wait for modern times, functioning as a reaction against the attempts of specifically modern rationalism to reduce all revelation to reason, and to a type of reason in which God is by no means necessarily present. Thus, modern ethical monotheism can very well be seen as a form of modern rationalism, having ties, to be sure, to ancient Jewish rationalism. Levinas' Jewish thought is no exception.

---

9 *Commentary on the Torah*: Gen. 6:13.
10 Ibid.: Gen. 6:2.
11 See *Babylonian Talmud*: Yoma 67b re Lev. 18:4.

2. *Ethics and Faith: Modern*

In modern times, the relation between faith and ethics presented by ancient rationalists (and that includes medievals) has been fundamentally altered. The most radical and influential alteration of that relation was made by Immanuel Kant. And Kant had a special influence on Jewish thinkers because his emphasis of ethics seemed to have much resonance in the Jewish tradition. As the Mishnah stated about Jewish civil law, in which so much ethical discussion takes place, "one who wants to become wise should study Jewish civil law (*dinei mamonot*) since there is no aspect of the Torah greater than it; these laws are like a flowing source of water."[12]

Nevertheless, Kant presented the relation of faith and ethics in a very different way than it had been presented by the ancient (and medieval) thinkers, be they Jewish, Christian, or Muslim. These thinkers, it could be said, looked upon ethics as an anticipation of revelation. That is, through ethics one inferred what God seemed to have commanded in the most evident and immediately necessary area of human life: our interactions with other human beings. This inference, as it were, whetted one's appetite for the more direct receipt of what God has commanded in the more mysterious and remote areas of human life, which involve our more direct relationship with God himself, a relationship having cosmic significance. In this area we can anticipate next to nothing, for we only know about God what God himself tells us of himself in revelation.

Moreover, such inferences about what many called "natural law" (namely, law pertaining to human nature) most often presupposed what has been called "natural theology," which are conclusions about divine creation and governance of the universe derived from ordinary human sense experience of the natural order. But Kant began his critical philosophy with an assault on natural theology.[13] By means of carefully crafted and elaborate arguments, Kant seemed to have demolished natural theology, concluding that our immediately universalizable experience of the natural world tells us absolutely nothing about God, even as creator let alone as lawgiver.

For Kant, ethics is not derived from faith, even from the rationally constituted faith of natural theology, and ethics does not lead into faith inasmuch as he seems to have made no place at all for revelation.

---

[12] Baba Batra 10.8. See *Babylonian Talmud*: Baba Kama 30a (the view of R. Judah).
[13] Immanuel Kant, *Critique of Pure Reason*, B70-73, 659-670.

Revelation is not immediately universalizable since it is historically contingent: it only occurs in one event not all time; in one place not everywhere. Instead, ethics is derived from my own human autonomy, which requires that I universally legislate to and for myself and all other rational beings *as if* I myself were God creating a morally coherent universe in which, minimally, I too have to live.[14] Kant called this universe the "ethical commonwealth" or the "kingdom of ends."[15] It is clearly a human construct. But where does faith come in?

Despite the fact that some students of Kant's thought are convinced that Kant was either a crypto-atheist or that his thought leads to atheism even if he himself was unable or unwilling to take that step, he did explicitly make a place for faith. Now for him, faith becomes belief, that is, faith is not a response to a direct experience of the presence of God; instead, it is the intellectual acceptance of certain propositions human reason, in this case ethical reason, constructs about God. Such belief in this type of "good" God is required as a postulate of ethical reason. Without belief in an all-powerful and beneficent God, wouldn't our autonomous willing of our own happiness be an absurdity? For in the real world of impersonal causes, there seems to be no room at all for the efficacy of moral action. All we can do is properly will our acts in the beginning; we cannot make them succeed in the end. But willing only for the sake of willing can be easily dismissed as fanciful (and rationally dangerous) wishing. Therefore, the very exercise of our morality involves thinking about God.[16] Hence, ethics includes religious faith as "belief" within itself. Nevertheless, faith in the richer ancient sense is lost here. Accordingly, ethics is neither derived from faith above it nor does it lead to faith beyond it. Faith of this type has lost its fully transcendent intention.[17]

It is also clear that for Kant only a certain type of religious belief will serve ethics properly. It would seem that type of belief is one that has little if any connection to law. Faith as belief is a form of inwardness. Ultimately, it comprises a feeling of how the world ought to be and how it might actually come to be so. Law, conversely, suggests external authority, something that can only be a rival to true moral autonomy. Moreover, law suggests someone who arouses feelings of fear rather

---

[14] See Immanuel Kant, *Religion Within the Limits of Reason Alone*, trans. T. M. Greene and H. H. Hudson (New York, 1960), 157, note.
[15] Ibid., 87-91; *Groundwork of the Metaphysic of Morals*, trans. H. J. Paton (New York, 1964), 100-103.
[16] Immanuel Kant, *Critique of Practical Reason*, 1.2.2.5.
[17] Cf. Paul Tillich, *Dynamics of Faith* (New York, 1957), 4-16.

than the feelings of affection for a God who can be counted on to be beneficent to us. On both counts, though, Judaism fails the test of Kant's ethical theology. For Kant, Judaism is preeminently the religion of law, the religion concerned with a God demanding obedience to his purposes not ours, and a God who is primarily seen as a punishing enforcer of his law not ours.[18] Here Kant laid the groundwork for much of what came to be liberal Protestant theology in the nineteenth century, including its new, ethically formulated, anti-Judaism: Jewish "legalism" in contrast to Christian moral spontaneity; the "wrathful" God of the Old Testament in contrast to the "loving" God of the New Testament. So, how then could Jewish thinkers possibly rely on Kant for the formulation of their Jewish ethical monotheism?

3. Hermann Cohen's Neo-Kantianism

Although Hermann Cohen (1842-1918) was not the first Jewish thinker to turn to Kant for philosophical guidance, he was the Jewish thinker who did so with a philosophical power that set the tone for all subsequent modern Jewish philosophers, Levinas included. His critical appropriation required him to alter considerably Kant's views of God, law, and Judaism. Concerning all three views, he showed the error of Kant's conclusions, using principles that themselves could be justified in a Kantian way. And concerning all three views, he basically reinterpreted Kant from out of his reading of what for him are the classical sources of Judaism: Bible, Talmud, Midrash, and Maimonides.

Concerning Kant's view of God, Cohen rightly senses that such a God could hardly be considered the Absolute. Kant's God seems to be totally subsequent in importance to autonomous human moral subjects, doing their bidding as it were. Cohen is quite critical of Kant on this point, seeing this as an unacceptable return to the very "eudaimonism" Kant had otherwise rejected, namely, the Aristotelian view that the purpose of all ethics is the attainment of happiness.[19] Kant held that happiness is only the final result of ethics; the purpose of ethics, however, is to do what is right because it is right.[20] So, if God were only the guarantor of happiness, then God's ethical role could only be secondary. For Cohen, conversely, God's role is much more exalted, and it is the role for God

---

[18] Kant, *Religion Within the Limits of Reason Alone*, 116-118.
[19] Hermann Cohen, *Der Begriff der Religion im System der Philosophie* (Giessen, 1915), 51.
[20] Kant, *Groundwork of the Metaphysic of Morals*, 61-68.

Cohen sees as the central God-idea developed in the classical Jewish sources. In Cohen's view, God is not only the creator of all moral purposes; God is Being itself that enables all human becoming (that is, all human moral striving) to approximate its purpose and efficacy. Cohen sees this human striving to approximate God in the Jewish ideal of the Messianic Age.[21] Indeed, it is Jewish messianism that enables Jewish thinkers to appropriate Kant's idea of moral autonomy in a way that enhances their commitment to Judaism, especially their commitment to Jewish social ethics. Faith, then, is not just something ethics needs as a subsequent postulate; instead, faith in God as Being is the very foundation of ethics itself in its teleological striving, its purposeful attempt to be as much like the creator God any finite creature possibly can become. God, then, is much more than a postulate; rather, God is what Cohen called "origin" (*Ursprung*).[22]

Moreover, Cohen's very Jewish insistence of the social character of ethics leads him to emphasize a much more exalted role for law than Kant could have done. Cohen does not see a great chasm between the internality of ethics and the externality of law as does Kant. Instead, Cohen sees ethics functioning for law like logic (by which Cohen means what we now mean by "methodology") functions for natural science. Indeed, ethics grounds (that is, provides an intelligent foundation for) law similar to the way mathematics as scientific methodology provides an intelligent foundation for physics.[23] Interestingly, in his great work on ethics, Cohen is quite reticent, it seems, to provide any actual examples of how ethics grounds law. But in his great work on Judaism, his last work (published a year after his death), Cohen clearly saw Jewish law as the prime example of how a specific system of law is developed by universally valid ethical principles, which function as its ever-present ideals.[24]

When one sees how Cohen departs from Kant on the question of God and the question of law, he or she can better appreciate how Judaism becomes, perhaps not the only but certainly the most complete, ethical monotheism, which for Cohen is a religion of reason.[25] Nevertheless, although one must always see Cohen in the background of the ethical

---

[21] Hermann Cohen, *Religion of Reason Out of the Sources of Judaism*, trans. S. Kaplan (New York, 1972), 35-49, 236-268.
[22] Ibid., 63-70.
[23] Hermann Cohen, *Ethik des reinen Willens*, 5th ed. (Hildesheim and New York, 1981), 65.
[24] Cohen, *Religion of Reason*, 338-370.
[25] Cohen, *Religion of Reason*, 11-15.

monotheism of Levinas, between Cohen and Levinas stands the ethical monotheism of Martin Buber (1878-1965). There is a definite line of philosophical development from Kant to Cohen to Buber and then to Levinas. In order to situate Levinas properly in that line of development, none of its components should be short circuited.

4. *Martin Buber's Turn to the Human Other*

When ethics is seen as what Buber liked to call "philosophical anthropology," there is hardly any thinker who does not use the terms "I" and "thou." *I and Thou* is, of course, the title of Buber's central work, a work whose influence has continued unabated now for more than seventy-five years since its initial publication in 1923. Yet, despite his most famous use of these terms and their correlation, Buber was not the first Jewish thinker to use them. Hermann Cohen, in his idea of the "fellow human being as companion" (*der Mitmensch*) has used the terms quite explicitly.[26] Nevertheless, there is a great difference between Cohen's use of the terms and Buber's.

Cohen's view, despite its use of classical Jewish sources about neighbor-love, is still basically Kantian. In Kant's own view, the other person who is the object of my moral concern is only known *after* I have already known myself as a moral subject, a rational creator of moral law.[27] This other person, then, is essentially an analogue of my own fully conscious moral personhood. Thus our commonality, upon which we build a human society together, is the subsequent interaction of our mutual autonomies, and the source of each of them is independent of the other. They only come together in the end. Rational human association is based essentially on a common property, initially private and only subsequently public. It is the most morally inspiring version of the "social contract," precisely because it sees society as more than merely the means to individual, selfish, ends. Instead, society becomes an "ethical commonwealth." In Cohen's development of this social ethic, the richness of the traditional Jewish imagery of the Messianic Age gives a more solid, historically developed meaning and content to an idea that in Kant is still rather vague.

Even though Cohen does speak of the necessity of a moral object for the full development of the moral subject, his notion of human being-together is from here (I) to there (thou) and then towards the ideal that

---

[26] Ibid., 14-17, 128.
[27] See Kant, *Groundwork of the Metaphysic of Morals*, 95-96.

unites both of them. Neither the human other nor the messianic ideal can be said to be truly transcendent, that is, neither of them comes from there (beyond) to here (me). Instead, there is a line of steady moral progress from here to there, from becoming to Being. Like a subject creating its own object, so in Cohen's idealism does the idea of the moral subject create its own object as the means to its attainment, along with that object, of their common, as yet unrealized, ideal. In this ethics, God lies on the foreseeable horizon. Thus Cohen emphasizes in a number of places that there is no function for God outside morality.[28] There is no nonmoral or supermoral relationship with God.

In Martin Buber's understanding of the I-Thou relationship, conversely, there is no progressive trajectory from the moral subject to the moral object to the moral ideal. By the very utterance of "thou" (the inadequate English rendition of Buber's use of the German familiar second person pronoun *du*) the I is drawn into a relationship that he or she does not himself or herself create. Instead, the other person, whom one can only address in the second person, but never describe in the third person without losing his or her uniqueness, calls the heretofore self-encapsulated I into an uncharted and unpredictable new space between them.[29] In place of a moral trajectory from the particular persons to the universal moral ideal, Buber sees the very transcendence the individual person seeks as coming to him or her from the other person to whom he or she is truly capable of saying "thou." Any attempt to situate that other person in a world I have already laid out for myself is to reduce a thou to an "it," a thing.[30] By becoming an it, that person loses the very transcendence I so deeply desire. In the modern age, with its ever increasing mechanization of living persons, epitomized by the growth of technology, Buber's powerful presentation of both the possibility and the reality of a truly interpersonal relationship has proved to be steadily attractive to many. Nevertheless, this presentation of the realm of the interpersonal in and of itself does not yet provide an answer to the question of ethics or of faith or of the relation of one to the other. It is not too clear how it is an ethical monotheism.

On the level of faith, Buber designates God as "the eternal Thou."[31] So, whereas a human person can be turned into an it and still retain his or her personal identity (for example, a lover who is also a professional

---

28 See Cohen, *Der Begriff der Religion im System der Philosophie*, 32.
29 Martin Buber, *I and Thou*, trans. W. Kaufmann (New York, 1970), 62-67.
30 Ibid., 82-85.
31 Ibid., 123-124. Cf. Abraham Joshua Heschel, *Man Is Not Alone* (Philadelphia, 1951), 126-129.

colleague), to describe God in any way, which is to speak *of* God rather than *to* God, is already to turn God into what is not God, namely, an idol as it were. Thus Buber develops a theology, without which his understanding of the personal realm between humans themselves would become nothing more than a form of psychology. It would be about human emotions rather than a larger reality which (better, to whom) humans intend in the very acts of their own self-transcendence. This is the ontological dimension of Buber's philosophical anthropology, and it is indispensable. Yet, there are two ways one can see Buber's theology in relation to the realm of the interpersonal for humans.

On the one hand, one could see Buber's theology recognizing that there is a separate relationship with God over and above the direct relationships humans have with each other. The relationship with God is greater because God is only *Thou*, never *It.* Thus the relationship with God in faith is one that is all or nothing, unlike the relationship with another human person that inevitably descends into a relation of entities rather than remaining a relationship of full persons.[32] We do not, as in the words of Plato, "fly from the world and become like God."[33] The relationship with God is in this world and not in one beyond it. Accordingly, since we share this world with other human persons, our own personal relationship with God cannot simply displace it. Somehow or other we must connect our relationships with these lesser thous to the relationship with the Thou of all thous. Yet, the question here is that, unlike the rabbinic tradition which, as we have seen, constitutes a set of commanded acts (like the Sabbath and Festivals) as being "between humans and God," Buber does not do so. That silence leads one to think of another option for interpreting his theology, which might be more accurate.

Perhaps it is more plausible to see Buber's theology as not recognizing a separate relationship with God. For Buber might very well mean by his designation of God as the eternal Thou a kind of "thouness," that which makes all immediate thous what they are and not something else. In other words, the eternal Thou might well function like a Platonic form, into which all lesser replicas of it participate. Thus, for Plato, there is a form called "the Good," in which all acts we call "good" participate, even though the form of the Good is greater than any sum of the lesser goods that participate in it and draw their being from it.[34] In

---

32   Buber, *I and Thou,* 126-128.
33   Plato, *Theaetetus,* 176B.
34   See Plato, *Republic,* 505A-506B.

this way, the eternal Thou is the One who enables all lesser thous to be thous for however finite a period of time he or she encounters them. And that is surprisingly similar to the way Plato sees justice enabling all just acts to occur in the finite period of time in which those who do them are present to each other. Considering the fact that Buber has such an aversion to "ritual," which is the only area of human action one could consider having God as its direct object, it would seem that there is no relationship with God that is not mediated by a human thou.

Just as the connection between Buber's philosophical anthropology and Buber's theology is questionable, so is the connection between Buber's theology and Buber's ethics. For ethics deals with general principles and rules that extend over a endless period of time and which include a describable class of persons. This is what makes ethics subject to the logic of classes and not just function as spontaneous action. In ethics, it is the status of the person that determines what is to be done or what is not to be done in relation to him or her. But does not putting a person in such a preconceived category, by Buber's own criteria, make that potential thou into an it? What then is the relevance for ethics of Buber's understanding of the reality of interhuman relationships and what anyone else would call "ethics"? Yet, certainly, any thinker operating within Judaism needs to make a connection between theology: what can be said of or to God, and ethics: what can be done to or with other humans.

Buber's problem stems from his great aversion to law, especially Jewish law (*Halakhah*) as a system of generally and perpetually binding commandments. For Buber, law — any law — is the prime example of what is it-thinking.[35] Law is regarded as fundamentally depersonalizing. The most Buber can admit is the presence of particular commandments, that is, imperatives for a particular individual at a particular time only, stemming from the call of a thou to an I for an immediate response.[36] That, of course, excludes any imperative that can be generalized in either time (for persons in the past or future) or space (persons beyond those who are present here and now). The most one gets is a commandment that is a singular event in one place only. How one can possibly build a community with such an individualized ethics might very well be the greatest problem in Buber's thought, certainly his Jewish thought. And that would seem to affect the Jewish validity of his theology as well by so excluding God as lawgiver.

---

[35] Buber, *I and Thou*, 156-162.
[36] Ibid., 159.

5. Levinas' Ethical Monotheism

It seems that it has taken a very long time finally to get to Levinas, who, ostensibly anyway, is the subject of this essay. Nevertheless, that has been necessary in order to locate Levinas properly in the history of Jewish thought, indeed within the history of a certain kind of Jewish thought, one specifically modern (ethical monotheism, that is), with ancient roots to be sure. For the usual way of looking at Levinas is to see him as coming out of the philosophical tradition of Husserl and Heidegger. While that is undoubtedly true (and Husserl and Heidegger have influenced several important modern Jewish thinkers), Levinas must also be considered a Jewish thinker with a set of questions coming straight out of the Jewish tradition. On the question of ethical monotheism, where then does Levinas exactly enter into the conversation?

In a brief but highly suggestive essay on human rights, Levinas writes,

> These rights are, in a sense, *a priori*: independent of any power that would be the original share of each human being in the blind distribution of nature's energy and society's influence. . . . Prior to all entitlement: to all tradition, all jurisprudence, all granting of privileges. . . . Or is it perhaps the case that *it's a priori* may signify an ineluctable authority . . . the authority that is, perhaps — but before all theology — *in* the respect of the rights of man itself, God's original coming to the mind of man.[37]

And following up on this second possibility, Levinas writes shortly thereafter, "surely this is the trace of God in man, or more precisely, the point in reality at which the idea of God comes only to man."[38] What we need to ask is how "God's original coming to the mind of man" is "before all theology." Isn't any talk of God "theology" (which literally in Greek means "God-talk")? And wouldn't the traditional Jewish assertion that all law, whether directly or indirectly, is the commandment of God thereby imply that theology is prior to ethics, logically coming before it rather than after it?

These questions might be answered when we look at a more explicit statement of Levinas concerning ethics and theology.

> [T]he Other is not a *new edition of myself*; in its Otherness it is situated in a dimension of height, in the ideal, the Divine, and though my relation to the

---

[37] Emmanuel Levinas, *Outside the Subject*, trans. M. B. Smith (Stanford, Calif., 1994), 116-117.
[38] Ibid., 118.

Other, I am in touch with God. The moral relation reunites both self-consciousness and consciousness of God. Ethics is not the corollary of the vision of God, it is that very vision. Ethics is an optic, such that everything I know of God and everything I can hear of His word and reasonably say to Him must find an ethical expression.[39]

Here Levinas is moving quite close to the position of Hermann Cohen, namely, God is only known as the transhuman foundation needed by ethics. But Cohen is much clearer by what he means by God than is Levinas. God is Being, who functions as both the underlying cause and overlying end of ethics. God is the underlying cause of ethics inasmuch as God alone is able to make ethics efficacious, that is, make the ideal, towards which human ethical actions strives, ultimately effect the real. And God is the overlying end of ethics in that the very ideal of ethics is to become like God, what many have called the "imitation of God."[40] Thus Cohen gives us quite a coherent ethical monotheism.

The same cannot be said about Levinas. That seems to be the case because Levinas has an abhorrence for any kind of ontology, that is, any theory of being as a whole out of which ethics is then subsequently derived.[41] Instead, Levinas wants ethics to be wholly autonomous, that is, he wants us to see the ethical claim made by the human other upon myself as having an immediate authority requiring no external justification. This, it would seem, makes Levinas' theology in relation to his ethics different from the same relation in Cohen, however much he is similar to Cohen in refusing to see any role for theology other than an ethical one. For even though Cohen remains a Kantian in beginning with the moral autonomy of the morally challenged person, ultimately he sees God or Being as the source and end of all moral action. As we saw, that is a considerable departure from Kant.

In his description of the ethical reality, Levinas avoids the use of the term "autonomy," for that term as it has come down to us from Kant means the primacy of the "I" creating, as it were, its own objects and its own rules for them. For Levinas, an autonomous person is premoral.[42] In fact, Levinas is advocating "heteronomy," a concept Kant abhorred because it robs the self-sufficient moral self of the primacy of its own

---

[39] Emmanuel Levinas, *Difficult Freedom*, trans. S. Hand (Baltimore, 1990), 17. See Levinas, *Totality and Infinity*, trans. A. Lingis (Pittsburgh, 1969), 78-79.

[40] See *Religion of Reason*, 94-99.

[41] See Emmanuel Levinas, *Otherwise Than Being*, trans. A. Lingis (The Hague, 1981), 3-19.

[42] Levinas, *Totality and Infinity*, 119.

self-legislation.[43] (The Greek *heteros* is like the French *l'autre*). Thus ethics itself is autonomous, not being derived from any ontology, even the idealistic ontology of Hermann Cohen. Nevertheless, that autonomy is only in relation to anything outside ethics itself; within ethics itself we have the most extreme form of heteronomy possible. For it is the other who makes claims upon me that are, for Levinas, in no way to be reciprocated. The ethical relationship is essentially asymmetric. Indeed, that is a primary criticism of Levinas directed against Buber, namely, Buber has an ontology of cosmic relationships *into which* the ethical relationship between humans fits as a part of this larger whole.[44]

The relation of ethics and theology in Cohen and in Buber, in contrast to that relation in Levinas, seems to have a close affinity in general. The specific difference between them is, however, that Cohen sees law as the integral component of interhuman, ethical, relationships, whereas Buber has an abhorrence of law. The problem that Buber has along these lines, which is a problem neither for Cohen nor for Levinas, is that it is hard to see how any I-thou relationship could be possible unless the parties were already, minimally, committed to the moral norm: do not harm anybody else. For Levinas, conversely, that is no problem at all. Our moral obligation to respect the integrity of a different person from myself (the otherness of the other one; or as Levinas could have said in French: *l'autrui de l'autre*) is more primary than whether I have an intimate, reciprocal, relationship with that other person.[45] Indeed, morality is heightened more with strangers than it is with our friends, from whom we might very well expect reciprocity, something in return for our respectful efforts. Strangers make claims upon us for which we have no right to expect anything in return. Thus the very protection strangers require from us itself requires the otherness, the heteronomy, the anonymity of law.[46] Thus Levinas is critical of the essential role reciprocal mutuality plays in Buber's idea of I-thou relationships. And one could see him making the same criticism of Cohen's idea of ethics being rooted in the experience of the other (what Cohen called the *Nebenmensch*, the person next to me) as *fellow* person (what Cohen called the *Mitmensch*, the person along with me).[47]

---

[43] Kant, *Groundwork of the Metaphysic of Morals*, 92-93.
[44] Levinas, *Totality and Infinity*, 68-69, 101, 155.
[45] Actually, Levinas states, "L'absolument Autre, c'est Autrui" (*Totality and Infinity*, 39).
[46] Ibid., 39, 78.
[47] Cohen, *Religion of Reason*, 128.

The reason, it seems to me, that Levinas' theology is so difficult to specify is because theology can only be ontological, and Levinas is opposed to ontology altogether, including metaphysical theology.[48] The ontological concerns of both Cohen and Buber are concerns for transcendence. What is it beyond the immanent interhuman realm that truly grounds it? That has always been the prime concern of theology. Levinas, too, is concerned with transcendence, but for him ethics itself is transcendent. As such, it seems that the transcendence ontology seeks in God (either as Being or in Being even beyond God as in Heidegger), Levinas finds in the other person as the ethical object. Therefore, one must ask whether for Levinas the other person functions for the ethical subject like God. And, if so, how does Levinas avoid the quintessentially modern atheism best formulated early in the nineteenth century by Ludwig Feuerbach: not man in the image of God, but God in the image of man?[49] In other words, how is God to be taken as anything more than a human projection, something the ancient prophets of Israel would have surely called an idol?

Perhaps Levinas would have answered that his ethics is protected from such an accusation because his ethics is not at all projective. That is, it is not the subject who, as in certain forms of idealism, creates its own object. Instead, the object comes to the subject making its claims on the subject before he or she can do anything or even think anything. So, it might be said that any attempt to construct an anthropology, a theory of the human from which ethics is then inferred, is idolatry (what Levinas calls "totalizing").[50] In other words, any attempt to see the ethical object who comes to me only after I have in any way prepared myself for him or her or them is already to have compromised the true irreducibility of ethics. In that way, I ought to see the trace of God's face in the needy person before me, or the trace of God's voice in cry of such a person for my help. The French saying, *un Dieu defini c'est un Dieu fini,* for Levinas, might well mean that the mystery of God is what is present in the ethical object before me. It is what prevents me from reducing that object to what is immanently human, from what we already know

---

[48] Levinas, *Totality and Infinity,* 77-81. Generally, "metaphysics" refers to the type of ontology begun by Plato and, especially, Aristotle. So, there is more to ontology than metaphysics, although Levinas seems to use the two terms interchangeably, perhaps because he is also opposing the ontology of Martin Heidegger (1889-1976), which also departs from traditional metaphysics quite radically. See ibid., 45- 48.

[49] See Ludwig Feuerbach, *The Essence of Christianity,* trans. George Eliot (London, 1893), 33-34.

[50] Levinas, *Totality and Infinity,* preface.

about ourselves. Like any true revelation, the presence of the other before me is always a surprise. To use the title of a great work by Levinas, it is always "otherwise than being," and otherwise than ontology as the theory of being. Thus we might say that "otherness" (*l'autrui*) is what saves the other (*l'autre*) from becoming like me. Accordingly, "God" is *l'autrui*, the Most Other (what Levinas could call *le plus autre même*), the name we are to give transcendence, and that transcendence does not ground ethics from without but, rather, grounds ethics from within. Only within ethics can one experience what onto-theology means by transcendence. But, to derive ethics *from* any onto-theology is, for Levinas, already too late for ethics.

6. *Conclusion*

Although it had and still does have its lesser thinkers, modern Jewish ethical monotheism can be seen in the interchange of the thoughts of Cohen, Buber, and Levinas.[51] Nevertheless, modern (or some would say "postmodern") traditionalist Jewish theology has some significant problems with the ethical monotheism of all three of these thinkers. The problems are those that lie on the border of faith and morals, especially on the border of theology as the theory of faith and ethics as the theory of morals.

When it comes to ethics, the biggest problem comes from Buber. I do not think he ever overcame his own suspicion that the I of the I-thou relationship is only the "single one" of Kierkegaard. Jewish ethics must be seen in the primary context of the community; indeed, the I-thou itself, whether with God or with humans, is always part of the we-thou of the covenant.[52] The covenant is communal: a plurality extending through time. And, whereas God has an individual life outside the covenant, human individuality is totally contained within the covenant. As such, I do not see how one can have such a community, culminating in the messianic kingdom of God, without the institution of law. As

---

[51] Franz Rosenzweig (1886-1929) has been consciously excluded from this list since he is a theologian by the definition offered here. See his *Star of Redemption*, trans. W. W. Hallo (New York, 1970), 198-206, where God is the first speaker, hence all interhuman speech must finally be justified by what God has revealed to Israel. This is theology (albeit not of the usual kind). Surely that separates him from Cohen, Buber, or Levinas. Thus the affinities Levinas himself (*Totality and Infinity*, 28) and some of his disciples see between him and Rosenzweig seem to be exaggerated. Cf. Robert Gibbs, *Correlations in Rosenzweig and Levinas* (Princeton, 1992), 17-33.

[52] See Martin Buber, *Between Man and Man*, trans. R. G. Smith (Boston,1955), 40-82.

Franz Rosenzweig tried to convince his friend Buber, law is rooted in commandment; it is what gives it structure and duration. Without commandment, without hearing the commanding voice of God, law degenerates into political coercion. But that need not be the case. Thus the problem is not law, but improperly grounded law.[53] When it comes to law, Buber sounds more like Martin Luther or Karl Barth than he does like the whole normative Jewish tradition. His problem is very much like the problem of contemporary liberal Judaism, which cannot make up its mind about law in Judaism at all.

But even Cohen and Levinas, who do not have Buber's problem with law (especially Jewish law, of which Levinas, especially, was quite observant), do have his problem with the connection of law to theology. The problem is that for all three of them theology cannot be done except within ethics. In the case of Cohen and Buber, that theology still suffers from Kant's reduction of theology to ethics. It is very much like what Kant called a "metaphysic of morals," or what we might today call "metaethics." That is, something ethics, unlike natural science, still requires to be coherent. Thus distinguishing the realm between humans and God from the realm between humans themselves is still only formal but not substantive; it is a distinction without a difference in reality. And in Levinas' case, it is not even that. For Levinas will not permit us even to contemplate any realm wherefor ethics must wait, as it were. Yet, the normative Jewish tradition clearly requires us to serve God before man, even though there rarely has to be an explicit choice of God *in lieu* of man.[54] Thus the core problem with all three thinkers, and especially with Levinas, is that they have all overestimated the role of ethics in Judaism. To overestimate the role of ethics is just as erroneous as to underestimate it.

Perhaps the philosophical problem has been that Cohen, Buber, and Levinas, each in his own way, refused to become a Jewish theologian. Instead, each in his own way attempted to formulate a philosophy and then appropriate those aspects of the Jewish tradition that agreed with it. Thus, instead of affirming the whole Jewish tradition and its authority, which they could have done with every bit as much philosophical skill, each of them used Judaism to confirm some philosophical position or other. As the Jewish philosopher Leo Strauss (1899-1973) well under-

---

[53] See Franz Rosenzweig, *On Jewish Learning*, ed. N. N. Glatzer, trans. W. Wolf (New York, 1955), 72-92; also, David Novak, *Jewish-Christian Dialogue* (New York, 1989), 81-84.
[54] See *Babylonian Talmud*: Berakhot 19b.

stood, one must decide whether to be a philosopher using some theology or a theologian using some philosophy. Neither philosophy nor theology can totally appropriate the other.[55] Either option, philosophy or theology, can be done well and with great integrity. But Jews can only learn *from* Judaism *through* our own theologians, who are essentially responsible to speak the whole Torah as the fullest truth (*torat emet*) possible in this world, and by which everything is to be taken as true or false.[56] For that reason, I think "ethical monotheism" is not the way Jews should be speaking of Judaism, even Jewish ethics. To be sure, having learned much from the philosophers, we Jews have to continue to use such terms as "ethics" and "ontology." They are quite helpful. Nevertheless, in speaking of the relation of theology and ethics, we had better return to the ancient conceptuality of the realm "between humans and God" and the realm "between humans themselves" in order properly to speak and do what is required of us as Jews in the world. That is what we might call the vocational question addressed to all modern and postmodern Jewish thought.

---

[55] Leo Strauss, "The Mutual Influence of Theology and Philosophy," *Independent Journal of Philosophy* 3 (1979), 111-118.
[56] See *Babylonian Talmud*: Baba Kama 41b re Deut. 6:13 and R. Samuel Edels (Mahrasha), *Hiddushei Aggadot* thereon.

CHAPTER THIRTEEN

THE LAW OF NATURE AND THE NATURE OF THE LAW: DAVID NOVAK AND THE ROLE OF NATURAL LAW IN JUDAISM[1]

Louis E. Newman

Natural law theory has a long and complex history in western ethics and jurisprudence.[2] Though its origins extend back to the Stoic dictum "Follow nature," it received its classic articulation in Aquinas' moral theory, thereby securing a preeminent place in all subsequent Catholic moral theology.[3] During the Enlightenment, it found adherents in legal and moral thinkers such as Grotius, Hobbes, and Locke, and thereby had a profound influence on the doctrine of "natural rights" that lies at the heart of American legal and political theory. Among contemporary scholars, natural law theory informs the work of Josef Fuchs,[4] Germaine Grisez,[5] and John Finnes,[6] among others. Despite significant differences of opinion among natural law thinkers over the centuries (and notwithstanding a long history of critics), natural law thinking has plainly

---

[1] It gives me great pleasure to dedicate this article to Wendell S. Dietrich in appreciation for all that he has given me in the twenty years since I first became his student. I am forever indebted to him for the breadth of his learning, for his compassion and generosity of spirit, for his mentoring me in graduate school, and for his friendship ever since. It is my hope that this essay, insofar as it treats the nature of ethical monotheism, will be a fitting, if inadequate, tribute to his life and work.

[2] A general overview of natural law theories can be found in Richard Wollheim's excellent entry on "Natural Law" in *The Encyclopedia of Philosophy*, vol. 5 (New York: Macmillan and the Free Press, 1967), 450-54. For a good, brief introduction to the history of natural law thinking, see Arthur L. Harding, ed., *Origins of the Natural Law Tradition* (Port Washington, New York: Kennikat Press, 1954). A useful recent collection of essays on the subject can be found in Robert P. George, ed., *Natural Law Theory* (Oxford: Oxford University Press, 1992).

[3] Aquinas' views on natural law are expounded in his *Summa Theologica*, prima secunda, 1-2, 94.

[4] Josef Fuchs, *Natural Law* (New York: Sheed and Ward, 1965).

[5] Germaine Grisez, "The First Principle of Practical Reason," *Natural Law Forum 10* (1965): 168-201.

[6] Finnes, John, *Natural Law and Natural Rights* (Oxford: Clarendon Press, 1980).

played a pivotal role in the history of western ethics, theology, and jurisprudence.

Given the richness and persistence of the natural law tradition, it is hardly surprising that Jewish thinkers for centuries have explored the extent to which natural law plays a role in Judaism. Among contemporary Jewish philosophers and theologians, none has devoted more sustained attention to developing a theory of natural law than David Novak. Over the past decade Novak has devoted much of his prodigious scholarly efforts to constructing and defending a theory of natural law within Judaism, as well as tracing its theological implications for relations between Jews and non-Jews.[7] His most recent treatment of the issues, *Natural Law in Judaism*,[8] greatly expands upon his earlier reflections and represents by far the most extensive and sophisticated explication of natural law by any contemporary Jewish thinker. Before turning to the details of Novak's theory, however, it will be helpful to review briefly the characteristics of natural law in general. This will enable us to situate Novak's views within the natural law tradition, and to appreciate the ways in which he both appropriates and departs from the views of other natural law thinkers. In the concluding sections of this paper I will offer a critical analysis of Novak's views, as well as a more general assessment of the problem of natural law in Judaism.

1. *Natural Law: Issues of Definition*

The definition of natural law offered by Leo Strauss, one of Novak's teachers, provides a useful starting point. "By natural law is meant a law which determines what is right and wrong and which has power or is valid by nature, inherently, hence everywhere and always."[9] This definition highlights the first and most obvious criterion of natural law, that it must be "natural," something independent of human decision and prior to all human law-making or norm-setting. Natural law is discovered, not invented. It is "built in" to the fabric of the world and, in particular, to the very nature of human beings. Natural law, thus, stands

---

[7] See especially David Novak, *The Image of the Non-Jew in Judaism: An Historical and Constructive Study of the Noahide Laws* (New York and Toronto: Edwin Mellon, 1983); *Jewish-Christian Dialogue: A Jewish Justification* (New York: Oxford University Press, 1989); and *Jewish Social Ethics* (New York: Oxford University Press, 1992).

[8] David Novak, *Natural Law in Judaism* (New York: Cambridge University Press, 1998).

[9] Strauss, "On Natural Law," in *Studies in Platonic Political Philosophy* (Chicago: University of Chicago, 1983), 137.

in opposition to the entire tradition of western moral thought from Hume onward that insists upon a radical disjuncture between "is" and "ought," that from the way things are we can draw no conclusions about how they ought to be.[10] Natural law theorists, by contrast, believe that the "nature of things" does provide a source from which the basic principles of morality can be derived. Natural law, then, is believed to transcend the values and laws of particular cultures and countries, of all historical periods and places.[11]

A related but separate criterion of natural law is stated succinctly by Joseph Boyle. Natural law refers "to a set of universal prescriptions whose prescriptive force is a function of the rationality which all human beings share in virtue of their common humanity."[12] This definition focuses our attention on how natural law is discovered, i.e., through reason. It is through our rational faculty that we recognize order in the world. And because reason is the common possession of all humankind, it assures universal access to the natural law, at least in theory.

It should be apparent that these two criteria of natural law are closely related. Natural law is unchanging and universal, first because it is dictated by the natural order (which is understood as unchanging) and second because it is known through reason (which is understood as capable of grasping the necessary truths of nature). In a sense, the universality of natural law is twofold: it is both applicable to and (in principle) knowable by all people.[13]

Finally, natural law theorists have generally recognized that natural law, at best, provides a set of general moral principles, not a full-fledged

---

[10] Hume, *Treatise of Human Nature*, Book III, part 1, section 1 (New York: E.P. Dutton & Co., 1949).

[11] In Josef Fuchs's striking formulation, "Natural law is the superior court, so to speak, for all humanity and is independent of the changing legislation of today and tomorrow. It is the criteria of every law and of every juridical order" (Fuchs, *Natural Law*, 8). In this respect there are connections between international law and natural law with its closely related doctrine of intrinsic human rights. See, for example, the United Nations' Universal Declaration of Human Rights (1948).

[12] Joseph Boyle, "Natural Law and the Ethics of Traditions," in *Natural Law Theory*, ed., Robert P. George (Oxford: Clarendon Press, 1992), 4.

[13] It is important to note here that Strauss and Boyle's criteria represent related, but logically separate, dimensions of natural law. There is a substantive, in a sense metaphysical, aspect of natural law, embodied in the claim that there exists a set of moral norms the content of which is dictated by *nature*. And there is an epistemological aspect of natural law, embodied in the claim that human reason, which is universal, enables us to discern its principles.

system of moral rules.[14] Explications of natural law invariably include prohibitions against murder, appropriation or destruction of another's property and other norms necessary to a stable society. Even so, natural law theorists have generally acknowledged that the detailed rules necessary for governing social life are not dictated directly by natural law, but ought merely to be consistent with it. Natural law, then, is not a surrogate for "positive," humanly enacted law, but rather a set of a priori, universal moral principles that both ground and transcend all human moral and legal action.

Given this characterization of natural law, there is reason to suspect that it is foreign to the spirit of classical Judaic thought. It seems axiomatic that the ultimate source of moral and legal authority in rabbinic Judaism is located in God's commandments as conveyed in Scripture and interpreted by the rabbis. Torah, understood as encompassing both Scripture and the tradition of rabbinic interpretation, defines both the means by which God communicates the divine will to Israel and the parameters of classical Jewish moral and legal theory. And that theory would seem to require that Jewish moral and legal obligations flow, not from *nature*, but from the special, *supernatural* relationship between God and Israel. Moreover, these norms are understood by the community as authoritative, not because they are rational, but because they are revealed as divine commands. Thus, the defining characteristics of natural law — being dictated by nature and being authoritative because of its rationality — appear to be at odds with fundamental principles of Jewish theology.

Notwithstanding this apparent incongruity, a series of Jewish thinkers from Saadia Gaon in the ninth century[15] to Joseph Albo in the fifteenth[16] to David Novak in the twentieth have insisted that natural law does indeed play a role in Judaism. They have been motivated, at least in part, by the notion that the revelation that is Israel's alone cannot be the whole of God's moral message. There were, after all, moral violations (and so, by inference, moral rules) prior to the giving of the Torah

---

[14] See Thomas E. Davitt, "St. Thomas Aquinas and the Natural Law," in Arthur L. Harding, ed., *Origins of the Natural Law Tradition* (Port Washington, New York: Kennikat Press, 1954), 40-42.

[15] Saadia Gaon, *Book of Beliefs and Opinions*, trans. Samuel Rosenblatt (New Haven: Yale University Press, 1948).

[16] Joseph Albo, *Iqqarim* [Principles], 5 vols., ed. and trans. Isaac Husik (Philadelphia: Jewish Publication Society, 1929-30). See also Ralph Lerner, "Natural Law in Albo's Book of Roots," in Joseph Cropsey, ed., *Ancients and Moderns: Essays on the Tradition of Political Philosophy in Honor of Leo Strauss* (New York: Basic Books, 1964), 132-47.

at Mt. Sinai and, moreover, even after Sinai God's moral concern clearly extends to all humankind. What then are these pre-Sinaitic moral obligations that continue to be incumbent upon all people? How would we come to know them? Natural law appears to provide answers to both these questions.

The question of whether Judaism recognizes natural law, then, must be broken down into two separate (though related) questions:

A) Can we find within classical Jewish sources evidence of moral norms that exist independent of the covenant between God and Israel and, if so, are these understood as linked to a concept of the natural order, and/or

B) Can we find within classical Jewish sources evidence of moral norms that are "rational," that is, obligatory for all people because reason dictates that they be followed, independent of Israel's covenantal responsibilities?

The first possibility, it should be noted, directs our attention to norms that exist outside the covenant, and so are applicable to all human beings qua human beings. The second possibility could also include norms that are communicated to Israel through divine revelation, but which would be obligatory by virtue of their rationality alone or, as one source puts it, "even if the Torah had not been given."[17] Novak, as we shall see, affirms both possibilities.

2. *Novak on Natural Law*

David Novak's discussion of natural law draws upon the whole range of classical Jewish sources as well as the broad sweep of the western philosophical tradition. Because of his thorough knowledge of both sets of sources, he is able to offer an extremely nuanced reading of the biblical and rabbinic texts that bear on natural law, as well as to locate his own moral theory in relation to those of major philosophers from Aristotle and Kant to Rorty and Rawls. Given the subtlety and complexity of his discussion, it will be possible here to offer just a brief summary, one that captures only the essential elements of his position.

---

[17] Two rabbinic sources are regularly cited in the context of discussions of natural law. "If Torah had not been given, we could have learned modesty from the cat, aversion to robbery from the ant, chastity from the dove and sexual mores from the rooster" (B. Erubin 100b). [Commenting on Leviticus 18:5 — 'You shall keep my ordinances and my statutes']: "This (statutes) refers to those commands which had they not been written should properly have been written. These include the prohibition of idolatry, adultery, bloodshed, and blasphemy" (B. Yoma 67b).

In keeping with the passages from Strauss and Boyle cited above, Novak defines natural law as "those norms of human conduct that are universally valid and discernible by all rational persons."[18] He believes that a theory of natural law is essential for contemporary Jews given the most pressing issues of our day, those being 1) the need to define the relationship between Judaism and the modern secular, pluralistic society in which Jews find themselves, 2) the need to condemn the Holocaust on universal, rather than particularist, grounds, and 3) the need to create a Jewish, but democratic, society in the State of Israel. Each of these challenges, Novak believes, underscores the need for a moral theory that is both Jewish and universal, that has its roots in classical Jewish theology, yet whose scope extends to members of all communities. Natural law alone, he thinks, can meet these challenges.

Novak is quick to point out that his theory of natural law departs in significant ways from the views associated with Aristotle and Aquinas. Most importantly, Novak eschews a natural law theory grounded in teleological thinking, that is, in a notion of the telos or goal of all human beings. Recognizing that any such notion is extremely difficult to justify philosophically, Novak prefers to ground natural law in theology (rather than metaphysics). All societies and cultures, he argues, must ultimately confront and acknowledge the natural order that is the precondition for human society. In doing so, they will be led to acknowledge the limitations that nature imposes on human life and concomitantly to reflect on the moral norms indispensable to human flourishing in society. Within the Judaic tradition, such reflection takes the form of a theology of creation.

Novak insists that natural law, then, far from being a "foreign import improperly grafted onto" Judaism,[19] is intrinsic to it, for it flows directly from classical Jewish reflection on creation and the moral norms that existed prior to the revelation of the Torah at Sinai. Similarly, Novak is concerned to identify what reason knows of its own accord, independent of revelation, for this too will point toward a set of universal, moral norms, the hallmark of natural law. Accordingly, Novak finds evidence of natural law in Judaism in four separate places: A) within the narratives of Genesis, B) in the concept of "Noahide Law," C) in the rabbinic tradition of searching for the "reasons for the commandments," and D) in the philosophical presuppositions of the covenant between God and Israel. Each of these sets of sources bears on the

---

18 Novak, *Natural Law in Judaism*, 1.
19 Novak, *Natural Law in Judaism*, 62.

question of natural law in a somewhat different way and poses somewhat different problems.

A) *Biblical Narratives*

A number of narratives appear within the book of Genesis that presuppose moral norms, even though (in the biblical chronology) these events occurred prior to the revelation of the law to Israel. The first of these is the story of Cain, who is held accountable for the murder of his brother Abel despite the fact that Scripture records no explicit prohibition of murder at this time. Novak asks,

> So why is he guilty anyway? The only cogent answer is that it is already assumed that he knows murder is a crime. And how if not by his own reason? And what is that reason? Is it not the fact that he and Abel are brothers, that is, minimally, they are equal enough by virtue of ultimately common ancestry so that neither of them has the right to harm the other for his own individual advantage.[20]

So, Cain is held accountable for his act because it violated a basic principle of natural law, a moral principle that he knew (or should have known) simply by the exercise of his reason.

The idea that there is a source of moral knowledge outside of God's revelation is assumed by other biblical narratives as well. Novak points in particular to the encounter between Abraham and God over the destruction of Sodom and Gomorrah. Abraham challenges God with the rhetorical question, "Shall not the judge of all the earth do justly?" (Genesis 18:25). Abraham's question would make no sense, Novak argues, if he did not have access to moral standards independent of God's direct commands.[21] In his most recent treatment of this story, Novak contends that Abraham is here insisting that God serve as the model for human justice. "The justice of God must be the archetype for human justice, especially for his covenanted people. Without this cosmic justice, natural right cannot be maintained."[22]

The story of Abraham and Abimelech provides yet further evidence, if somewhat more indirectly, of a natural law implicit in the biblical narrative. Abraham, while travelling through the territory of Abimelech, a Philistine king, passes his wife Sarah off as his sister out of fear that otherwise Abimelech might kill him in order to acquire Sarah. When Abimelech discovers the ruse and challenges Abraham's deceit,

---

[20] Novak, *Natural Law in Judaism*, 34-5.
[21] Novak, *Jewish Social Ethics*, 31.
[22] Novak, *Natural Law in Judaism*, 41-2.

he defends himself by saying he had assumed, "surely there is no fear of God in this place" (Genesis 20:11). Novak interprets the phrase "fear of God" as indicative of a natural law perspective.

> 'Fear of God' means the elementary decency that requires human beings to restrain their desires out of fear/respect for the rights of other humans, in this case the right to inviolable marriage, because of the way God has created humans and their dignity. . . . To violate the 'fear of God' is to violate the order that God has enabled humans to know through their very nature.[23]

In these and other biblical passages, Novak discerns principles of natural law at work, for they give evidence of a pre-Sinaitic morality that, by definition, is universal.

B) *Noahide Law*

Possibly the most significant body of data that bears on the question of Jewish natural law concerns the so-called "Noahide laws." In his exhaustive and masterful study of this material, Novak has demonstrated that the concept of a universal law, applicable to all descendants of Noah, arose in Tannaitic times and continued to be a source of theological and legal interest throughout the centuries.[24] The classic articulation of the Noahide commandments is as follows:

> Seven commandments were the sons of Noah commanded: concerning adjudication, concerning idolatry, concerning blasphemy, concerning sexual immorality, concerning bloodshed, and concerning robbery and concerning a limb torn from a living animal.[25]

These seven commandments, which Novak understands as broad moral principles rather than specific enforceable laws, represent the universal moral order that God has established for all people and that all people can discern through rational reflection on human experience, quite apart from God's revelation.

As Novak demonstrates, those who reflected on Noahide law did so from two perspectives. On the one hand, they regarded these seven commandments as the universal law applicable to all people. In this sense, Noahide law embodied a Jewish theory of non-Jewish ethics. On the other hand, they viewed Noahide law as reflecting the norms obligatory for Jews prior to the Sinaitic revelation. As Novak writes,

---

23 Novak, *Natural Law in Judaism*, 48.
24 See Novak, *The Image of the Non-Jew in Judaism*.
25 Tosefta Abodah Zarah 8:2.

First, comparatively speaking, it [the Noahide] designates the non-Jew actually standing before Jews here and now. The Noahide is the 'other' with whom Jews desire to discover some significant commonality without, however, sacrificing the singularity which is theirs because of the covenant. . . . Second, ontologically speaking, the Noahide is the non-Jew, situated in the natural order of creation itself, who the Jews themselves had been before being chosen by God and given his Torah.[26]

Novak sees in the two dimensions of Noahide law an important insight into the character of natural law. It must be constituted, he thinks, both through comparative, empirical study of the commonalities among actual societies, as well as through reflection on the ontological status of humanity per se, which is the precondition for the emergence of that distinctive community called Israel. Indeed, at other points in his work, Novak criticizes theorists who ignore either the comparative/empirical or the ontological/theological dimension of natural law.

The specific content of Noahide law, as Novak understands it, accords well with a theory of natural law that emphasizes the basic rights of all human beings. These rights are grounded in a theory of the "minimal conditions that enable otherwise differing persons to at least live in peace together and to pursue their own respective visions of what the good is for them."[27] From this perspective, natural law (Noahide law) need not rely on any particular conception of "the good" for all human-kind, any telos of human life in general. Rather, it presupposes only that human beings are *by nature* creatures who can live together only when certain moral principles are accepted. That is, it presupposes that God has so created us that these moral principles are fundamental to any social reality. Noahide law, then, expresses this minimal, natural, divinely ordained moral order that all humans can recognize if they reflect rationally on their own nature.

C) *The Reasons for the Commandments*

Novak finds yet another source of Jewish natural law in the long history of rabbinic reflection on the "reasons for the commandments." Much of this reflection relates to the reasons for the ritual laws, such as the diet-ary restrictions and the rules concerning the mixing of diverse seeds or garments, which do not appear to have any rational basis. Leaving aside these rules governing obligations to God (alone), Novak focuses on the reasons for the commandments that govern the moral obligations of one

---

[26] Novak, *Natural Law in Judaism*, 158.
[27] Novak, *Natural Law in Judaism*, 155.

person to another. These rules are to be obeyed, he argues, not only because God commanded them (though that, of course, would be a sufficient reason). Rather, "the commandments are to be obeyed because to obey them is to attain what the wisely beneficent creator has intended as good for us."[28] That is, there are intrinsic benefits to the performance of our moral obligations that we can recognize through the use of our reason, quite apart from the revelation of God's law in Scripture.

By the same token, Novak notices that within Scripture itself some commandments are explained in relation to God's creation of the natural world. Thus, capital punishment for the crime of murder is justified by God's creation of humankind. "Whosoever sheds human blood by humans shall his own blood be shed, because in the image of God He made humans" (Genesis 9:6). Similarly, the requirement to observe a universal day of rest on the seventh day is explained by reference to God's creation of the world in six days and God's rest on the seventh (Exodus 10:10-11). The fact that the reasons given for these commandments are universal means that the Scriptural authors believed that these rules could be understood even by those outside the covenant. And this, of course, is one hallmark of natural law.

D) *Reason as the Basis of the Covenant*

But Jewish natural law could also express itself in the form of a moral principle at the foundation of the entire religious-legal system. Here Novak proceeds, not by exegesis of Scriptural or rabbinic texts, but by philosophical inference. He contends that the covenant between God and Israel presupposes natural law principles or, in a more theological vein, revelation presupposes creation. This is so, Novak thinks, in several distinct respects. First of all, Torah itself would not be intelligible were it not for the fact that human beings possess reason. Hence, reason is a necessary prerequisite for revelation or, as Novak puts it, "humankind must have its own intelligent speech in order for God's revealed speech to be intelligible to them. Thus intelligent human speech, which is human reason, is the presupposition of revelation itself."[29] Moreover, the covenant as a kind of contract "presupposes the norm that promises are to be kept. . . . Without this presupposition, a contract would have no duration and would be, therefore, meaningless. This natural law precondition seems to be an integral part of the convenantal [*sic*] theory in

---

[28] Novak, *Natural Law in Judaism*, 65.
[29] Novak, *Natural Law in Judaism*, 30.

Scripture."[30] Novak thinks that revelation (divine speech) and covenant (a form of contract) would be simply unintelligible were it not for the pre-existence of human reason and an appreciation of the meaning of mutual promises respectively.

But Novak believes that the actual content of the Torah (and not only the fact of revelation) presupposes certain natural law principles. He suggests, for example, that the Israelites' acceptance of the covenant must be understood as flowing from their recognition of the "goodness" of God's law. According to Novak, "In order for the people to know that God's commandments are right for them, they obviously have to possess some knowledge of what is right in general. This precondition is simply unavoidable."[31] Similarly, in his most recent treatment of natural law he argues that "natural law or its equivalent . . . had to be in place for Israel to be enough of a human community, with insight into the nature of human sociality, to be able to accept the Torah from God. Only then can their existing polity be elevated and become a holy people."[32] Novak's point, it seems, is that a certain basic level of moral discernment must already be in place before the Israelites can understand and make a rational decision to accept the Torah from God. That natural, pre-existing moral order is captured in natural law.

3. A Critical Assessment of Novak's View

There can be no question that Novak has offered us a brilliant argument for the existence of natural law in Judaism, one that simultaneously appropriates in critical fashion certain elements in the natural law tradition and reinterprets classical Jewish sources in light of that tradition. Accordingly, his construction of a natural law "out of the sources of Judaism" (to borrow a phrase from Hermann Cohen) makes important contributions to our understanding both of Judaism and of the natural law tradition in general. Certainly, Jewish natural law has never received a more cogent or comprehensive defense than Novak's. For just that reason, a close examination of Novak's theory enables us to discern

---

[30] Novak, *Jewish Social Ethics*, 34. This view is shared by Shubert Spero, *Morality, Halakha and the Jewish Tradition* (New York: Ktav, 1975), 81; and also by Daniel J. Elazar, *Covenant and Polity in Biblical Israel* (New Brunswick, N.J.: Transaction Publishers, 1995), 23: "In its theological form, covenant embodies the idea that relationships between God and humanity are based upon morally sustained compacts of mutual promise and obligation."
[31] Novak, *Jewish Social Ethics*, 34.
[32] Novak, *Natural Law in Judaism*, 146-7.

more clearly just what is at stake in the debate about natural law in Judaism.

It must be said at the outset that Novak's work as a whole is persuasive. In the face of the evidence he adduces it will henceforth be extremely difficult for anyone to argue that universal principles of morality, grounded in creation and/or reason, play no role whatsoever in Judaism. Yet, I want to suggest that not all the evidence here is equally persuasive. Indeed, the case for Jewish natural law may not be quite as strong, and the concept itself not quite as coherent, as Novak makes it out to be.

With respect to the biblical narratives that Novak cites, the interpretations he offers are not always the most plausible readings possible. To interpret "fear of God" in Genesis 20:11 as indicative of a rational standard of moral behavior, for example, is less plausible than to understand this phrase more literally, as referring to a place where Abraham believes people do not recognize and worship ("stand in awe of") God. The moral limits that this entails are probably those that God imposes, not those that people recognize through any rational faculty of their own.

Further evidence of forced interpretations emerges when we turn to Novak's account of Abraham's confrontation with God over the fate of Sodom and Gomorrah. Novak is at pains to explain how the famous line, "Shall the judge of all the earth not do justly," does not imply that God is subject to human moral standards, but nonetheless does imply that God must be a paradigm of moral behavior that is rationally understandable to humans. His "elaborate paraphrase" of Abraham's question is worth quoting at length.

> You are the free creator of the world and everything in it. Your creation is certainly without any necessity. You could have created another kind of world altogether . . . or no world at all. . . . But if you choose to be involved in the world with your human creatures, especially as their judge, then you must function as the archetype and model of justice. There is certainly more to that involvement than mere justice. . . . But there are prior conditions, first and foremost being that the covenant must include a morally intelligible form of polity, both in terms of the internal relationships of the members of the covenanted community one with the other, and their relationships with others outside their community. The minimum of that involvement in justice is that judicial decisions be made fairly (what we now call 'due process of law'). You are the archetype of justice in the world, and the model of justice for the people with whom you are making this covenant. Justice is a result of your divine freedom. This freedom, unlike human freedom, is unconditional and wholly original. With us humans, however, it is different; for us, justice is a natural necessity. . . .[33]

---

[33] Novak, *Natural Law in Judaism*, 46.

But why not take Abraham's statement at face value? He wants to hold God accountable for violating standards of justice that obtain within the human community. There is no implication whatsoever that Abraham has confronted, much less solved, the problem of the relationship between God's moral freedom and human moral freedom. The problem here is not that Abraham could not have thought about such things, but that there is no reason to assume that he would have. No reason, that is, unless one begins with the supposition that there is a universal, rational moral order and that evidence of it can be found in the narratives of Genesis.

In general, the degree of philosophical sophistication that Novak ascribes to the characters in Genesis (or to the authors of the narratives in which they appear) seems quite out of keeping with the overall lack of philosophical discourse in the biblical corpus. Indeed, the biblical books display remarkably little interest in philosophical questions,[34] and there is little reason to believe that the biblical authors had so clear or consistent a philosophical position as Novak attributes to them. It appears that he approaches these materials with an idea of what natural law is and a belief that it must be present in these stories of pre-Sinaitic life, and then finds what he must find to support his theory. In the process more straightforward (though, from a natural law perspective, less agreeable) readings of these stories are never considered.

When we turn to the Noahide Laws we face a different set of difficulties. Here it is quite apparent that these principles represent a rabbinic theory of universal morality. The issue is whether all the specific provisions of Noahide Law square with the claims that Novak makes on behalf of natural law. By way of example, consider the prohibitions against idolatry and against eating a limb taken from a living animal. Neither of these prohibitions appears to be required by the fundamental character of human sociality, which is the hallmark of natural law as Novak describes it. In the first instance, Novak attempts to circumvent this difficulty by insisting that the sin of idolatry is to "see oneself as God's equal," and that "idolatry breeds violence."[35] But when the rabbis included idolatry in the list of Noahide Laws they almost certainly had in mind the worship of idols, the reverence for that which is not divine, and this religious practice does not have any necessary connection to

---

[34] The obvious exception here is the wisdom literature, widely regarded as late in authorship and as influenced by a cross-cultural wisdom tradition in the ancient near east. Even here, philosophical modes of thought may not have been indigenous to ancient Israelite culture.

[35] Novak, *Natural Law in Judaism*, 35.

violence. (Consider Buddhists, who would certainly qualify as idolaters by rabbinic standards, but who practice radical non-violence.) The prohibition against eating a limb from a living animal is even less obviously related to natural law, either as understood by western philosophers from Aquinas on or as reconstructed by Novak himself.

The "comparative approach" to natural law as Novak describes it also encounters difficulties. It is Novak's contention that natural law is constituted in part "from the bottom up," that is, by comparing the minimal moral standards operative within human societies and so constructing a concept of the morality requisite to human social life in general. But adopting this empirical, lowest common denominator approach, Novak must contend with those societies that have failed to embrace even these minimal moral principles. From the biblical and rabbinic perspectives, some societies apparently were assumed not to affirm these minimal moral standards (and, in point of historical fact, we know of societies today that do not).[36] But why is it that these societies do not disintegrate, contrary to the assumptions of this comparative approach to natural law? It seems that Novak can only discount such societies as "fundamentally flawed" and "unworthy of the human persons to whom they are addressed."[37] But this is to undermine the point of natural law, which was, like the *ius gentium* in Roman law, to be an articulation of universal law, that is, law practiced universally by all nations.

When Novak insists that some form of natural law constitutes the logical preconditions of the covenant other questions arise. Novak reads the creation of the covenant at Sinai as a story of Israel's response to God's benevolence and of Israel's recognition of the intrinsic moral benefits of observing God's law. On Novak's account, Israel's choice to accept this covenant is deliberate and rational. But it is equally possible to interpret their decision to covenant with God as based, not on moral or rational considerations, but on fear of God's awesome power, which is surely the dominant motif of the Exodus narratives. In fairness, it must be conceded that the biblical authors did not fully articulate a concept of what lay behind Israel's decision to accept God's offer of the covenant. Accordingly, Novak's conclusions in this regard remain in the realm of philosophical/exegetical speculation. Novak's claim that "natural law or its equivalent . . . had to be in place for Israel to be enough of a human

---

[36] See the now classic study of the Yanomamo Indians who regularly practice brutal revenge in intra-tribal conflicts; Napoleon A. Shagnon, *Yanomamo: The Fierce People*, 5th ed., (Fort Worth: Harcourt Brace College Publishers, 1997).
[37] Novak, *Natural Law in Judaism*, 162.

community, with insight into the nature of human sociality, to be able to accept the Torah from God," is subject to similar questions. It is not apparent that the Israelites accepted the Torah because it confirmed or conformed to some prior insight that they had into human sociality, rather than, say, because it was offered by God. Certainly, the biblical text offers no suggestion that they first evaluated the content of Torah by the criteria of natural law or its equivalent and only afterward accepted it. Again, Novak can read the biblical account in a way that accords with his natural law theory, but only by making some questionable assumptions.

In reviewing the full scope of Novak's theory, one cannot help but conclude that, despite its minimalness in some respects, it is extraordinarily bold and far-reaching in others. That is, Novak is very careful to avoid the pitfalls of earlier natural law theorists who were inclined to claim too much, that human nature was fixed in a particular way, that a certain set of "goods" were universally to be desired, etc. Thus, he acknowledges that there is no "Olympian perspective" from which we can view human life, as it were, sub specie aeternitatis.[38]

Yet, despite this caution, Novak makes extraordinary claims on behalf of natural law — that Scriptural exegesis, philosophical analysis, comparative moral and cultural analysis and a theology of creation all confirm the truth of natural law. Novak insists at various points that natural law is intrinsic to Judaism, that it is the necessary corollary of the doctrine of creation, the necessary presupposition of Torah and the necessary precondition for all human sociality. Despite Novak's valiant efforts to make all these philosophical and theological lines converge on natural law, the reader is left wondering whether he risks violating the very rabbinic principle that he himself adduces, "one who grasps too much, grasps nothing." It is not clear whether natural law can be made to serve all these masters at once. To demonstrate that it can, Novak would have to say more about the actual *content* of natural law, the specific moral principles that it comprises, rather than focusing exclusively on the theoretical construction and justification of it. Only then can he make good on his claim that natural law provides answers, or even essential resources, for the central problems that Jews face in the modern world.

In the end, the strongest evidence that Novak offers on behalf of Jewish natural law may be the "reasons for the commandments." Here, after all, the rabbis explicitly offer rational reasons for divinely revealed

---

[38]   Novak, *Natural Law in Judaism*, 137.

commandments. It is in this context that Novak directly addresses what appears to be at the heart of the natural law controversy — the relationship between reason and Torah, in other words, between creation and revelation.

4. Reflections on Nature, Law, and Natural Law in Judaism

As a form of ethical monotheism, Judaism affirms the existence of a single God who is the creator of all life and the author of human history, who establishes both the natural order and the moral order of the universe, and who calls humankind to account for its moral failings. The natural and universal implications of this view are tempered for Jewish thinkers by one further basic theological assertion — that this God also entered into a unique covenant with a single human community, Israel, by revealing Torah to them and choosing them to exemplify God's will to the nations of the world. In one sense, then, God's creation of the world (and of humankind in particular) means that we are creatures endowed by God with moral discernment and that we therefore stand in an irreducibly moral relationship with a God who both created us for moral purposes and judges our moral conduct. But in another sense, the moral order for Jews is established through God's special revelation to them in Torah, which contains the perfect and comprehensive expression of God's will and constitutes the source of all religious and moral norms.

Creation and revelation, then, represent two aspects of God's relationship with the world or, viewed from human perspective, two means by which God's power in the world is experienced. Both of these dimensions of God's involvement with the world have normative implications. The question at hand is how the normative order established by creation is related to the normative order established through revelation. Or, more specifically, how is the moral order that God has created naturally and for all of humanity related to the moral order that God has established "supernaturally" for Israel alone? Novak openly acknowledges that this is the central theological issue underlying the natural law debate when he writes, "If natural law is an apt designation of the universal ethics one finds in the Jewish tradition, it is now appropriate to see how the tradition constitutes that universal, natural law, ethics within the covenant itself. That will require an understanding of how the tradition connects creation and its nature with revelation."[39]

---

[39] Novak, Natural Law in Judaism, 91.

Novak's answer to this question is clear enough, though surprisingly it receives less attention in his book on natural law than it may deserve.

> [T]he normative content of the Sinai covenant need not be regarded as originally instituted at the event of the Sinai revelation. Even much of that content which is cultic, historical research has been showing to have analogues and precedents in other cultures. And that commonality is even more evident in the ethical teaching of Scripture, which, being more universal in essence, will have more easily discovered cognates elsewhere. Instead, the uniqueness of the covenant lies in its overall Gestalt, which constitutes a full and abiding relationship between God and a people on earth.[40]

In short, Novak understands creation and revelation as separate, but related, modes through which God's will is made known to the world. The point of revelation and of Torah is not that they introduce moral principles that we could not have discovered on our own through human reason. Rather, Torah reaffirms the moral truths accessible to us independently and places these moral requirements in the context of a covenantal relationship between God and Israel. As Novak puts it, "much of the law governing interhuman relationships found in the Torah is law that has been elevated into the covenant, not introduced by it. Much of that law can only be discovered by human reason, of which philosophy is the epitome."[41]

On Novak's view, creation and revelation are *complementary* and *correlative*. Creation establishes a normative world that retains its own integrity even after the Torah is given. Indeed, Torah adds little moral substance to that which follows from creation and which is embedded in the natural order. It follows that Israel's uniqueness is not that it has access to fundamental moral principles from which others are barred.

But, as I have written elsewhere,[42] within the history of Judaism the relationship between creation and revelation has more often been viewed as *sequential* and *progressive*. From this perspective, creation is only a prelude to revelation in the history of God's relationship to the world. God's will is only partially revealed to humanity at large, but is fully revealed to Israel at Sinai. It follows that the normative order

---

[40] Novak, *Natural Law in Judaism*, 60-61.

[41] Novak, *Natural Law in Judaism*, 177. With the words, "much of the law . . ." Novak appears to be introducing a qualification here, leaving open the possibility that the Torah does include moral truths that are not universally accessible to reason, but have been vouchsafed to Israel alone. He does not go on to specify what these are, however.

[42] See Louis E. Newman, *Past Imperatives: Studies in the History and Theory of Jewish Ethics* (Albany, New York: SUNY Press, 1998), esp. chapter 6.

established through covenant and Torah takes precedence over that established through creation. Any universal moral law, then, is but a precursor to Torah and is necessarily subordinated to it.

Novak, like many Jewish philosophers before him, has opted for one way of relating creation and revelation, according to which the implications of creation are not overshadowed by the event of revelation. This allows for the emergence of natural law both within and alongside of Torah. "Within," for Torah encompasses and affirms universal moral norms, and "alongside," for the values derived from the created order remain operative for non-Jews who are not recipients of God's revelation. From this perspective, the natural order constitutes a source of moral instruction, a "natural torah," as it were, more limited in scope than the Torah revealed at Sinai but significant nonetheless. And reason functions as a vehicle for discovering these universal moral norms, insofar as God has created us with the capacity to understand human nature and the order of existence. Accordingly, there are two parallel sources of moral truth, one universal, determined by nature and discovered by reason, and the other particular, determined by revelation and discovered in the words of Torah.

But plainly this more exalted view of creation and, concomitantly, of natural law comes at the expense, so to speak, of a more expansive doctrine of revelation. To the extent that the law of nature is emphasized, the law of Torah is correspondingly de-emphasized. To the extent that creation and its universal implications are central, revelation and its particularist implications are less so. While this view is surely theologically defensible (and, again, Novak has offered a most sophisticated defense), it raises a number of questions: What moral truths, if any, are revealed through Torah that are not accessible through reason alone? What are we to make of the many moral rules in Scripture concerning the care of the poor and the disenfranchised in society? These principles do not appear in most constructions of natural law, certainly not in the Noahide Law, and they are not evidently essential to human sociality. Can we be sure that there are no genuinely new moral truths conveyed in Torah that would not be evident from nature or reason? And what do we make of the fact that Scripture permits indentured servitude, a law almost certainly at odds with natural law principles?

In the final analysis, Novak's theory of natural law rests on his theological construction of Judaism. His view of Judaism is necessarily selective, for it rests on certain ways of construing the tradition, including biblical narratives, rabbinic concepts and theological categories. I have noted that these constructions are questionable at a number of points. But Novak will surely respond that his reading of the tradition is defensible, for it develops, albeit in a more philosophical vein, the moral implications of the doctrine of creation, views that have been present within the tradition from the beginning. There is a universal moral order within Judaism, for all human beings stand in a moral relationship to God, all have the capacity to discern God's will through the exercise of reason and through the observation of natural processes. And so the meaning and authority of Torah must be affirmed in a way that allows for an independent source of moral truth, one that operates outside of Torah for non-Jews and alongside Torah for Jews. Novak's is but the latest and most sophisticated attempt by a Jewish philosopher to synthesize the universal implications of creation with the particularist implications of revelation.

In conclusion, then, Novak can construct a Judaism that is hospitable to natural law only by limiting the moral significance of revelation in relation to creation. The extent to which his position is persuasive depends finally on whether we accept his way of construing the relationship between Torah as the embodiment of God's moral instruction to Israel and nature as the vehicle for God's moral instruction to humanity, inclusive of Israel. In the end, perhaps the debate over natural law in Judaism to which Novak has contributed so extensively will be resolved not on philosophical or theological grounds, but on practical ones. If, indeed, natural law thinking of the sort Novak advocates does contribute to the resolution of major issues facing the Jewish people, then to just that extent it will be embraced, together with the theological underpinnings that Novak articulates. If it is to survive, any theological reconstruction of Judaism must serve the needs of the people defined by that religion. Whether natural law will do so in the century ahead is a question that remains to be answered.

CHAPTER FOURTEEN

PLURALISM: A WESTERN COMMODITY OR JUSTICE FOR THE OTHER?

Francis Schüssler Fiorenza

Wendell S. Dietrich's contribution to scholarship is in many ways unique. He brings such a broad range of expertise in modern religious thought that enables him to offer penetrating comparative studies, such as his work comparing the liberal Protestant Ernst Troeltsch with the Jewish Hermann Cohen.[1] In addition, he has not only compared Roman Catholic theology with Protestant liberal theology,[2] but has also examined and commented on official Roman Catholic church documents.[3] Within this comparative work, Dietrich is also concerned with the relation of modern religious thought to social ethics and to theories of culture and society.[4] He has analyzed the relation between Ernst Troeltsch's interest in historical consciousness and relativism and his theory of culture and society and he has explored the different social consequences of ethical monotheism.

Dietrich's work has developed around comparative and social differences and deals with the social implications of theological differences. I have selected the topic of this essay to honor him in a way that expresses a certain continuity as well as discontinuity with the authors and issues to which Dietrich has dedicated his life work. As is well known,

---

[1] Wendell S. Dietrich, *Cohen and Troeltsch: Ethical Monotheistic Religion and Theory of Culture*, Brown Judaic Studies 120 (Atlanta: Scholars Press, 1986).

[2] See Wendell S. Dietrich, "Loisy and Liberal Protestants," *Studies in Religion/Sciences religieuses* 141 (1985): 303-311 and "Troeltsch's Treatment of the Thomist Synthesis in *The Social Teaching* as a Signal of his View of a New Cultural Synthesis," *The Thomist* 57 (1993): 381-402.

[3] See "Gaudium et Spes and Haering's Personalism" *Oecumenica* (1968): 274-283; and "Nostra Aetate: A typology of Theological Tendencies," in *Unanswered Questions: Theological Views of Catholic Relations* (Notre Dame: University of Notre Dame Press, 1988), 70-81.

[4] See his "Calvin's Scriptural Ethical Monotheism: Interpretation, Moral Conscience and Religious System," in John T. Caroll, et al., eds., *Faith and History: Essays in Honor of Paul W. Meyer* (Atlanta, Georgia: Scholars Press, 1991), 360-377.

Troeltsch revised the views expressed in his earlier treatment of the absoluteness of Christianity to a much more pluralistic view of religions. Previous generations have viewed Troeltsch's final essay as too relativistic. Today, however, when postcolonial and postmodernist currents abound, many view some of Troeltsch's opinions as excessively Eurocentric and modernist. The ethical monotheism of Hermann Cohen was combined with a strong advocacy of social ethics and socialism. The relationship among ethical monotheism, relativism, and social ethics was central to Wendell Dietrich's analysis of their work.[5] His lectures, travels, and projects have dealt not only with modernism, but also with colonialism, not only with social ethics but also with the Marxist-Christian dialogue and with Black Theology.[6] For this reason, in this *Festschrift* honoring Wendell S. Dietrich, I take up the issue of pluralism and relativism and treat them in connection with the criticisms raised by post-colonialism that modern Western advocacy of pluralism can be viewed as an expression of a Eurocentric market economy in which ideas, including religious ideas, are reduced to commodities.

In *The View from Nowhere*,[7] Thomas Nagel begins with the philosophical problem of moving from the perspective of a particular individual within the world to an objective view of the world. Even though Nagel does acknowledge the limits of objectivity and the merits of combining both perspectives, his ultimate goal is to achieve a view that is less subjective and more objective — a view from nowhere. Such a view should go beyond a view of the world based upon a particular subjective experience to a more objective viewpoint. Although I concur that it is indeed valuable for us to transcend the limitation of our particular perspectives, I question whether we can ever arrive at a perspective that would fully justify the title as *the* view from nowhere.

I speak and write from somewhere. It is the somewhere of a white, middle-class, male, Roman Catholic theologian, living in the United States, and teaching in a North American Protestant divinity school. That "somewhere" is one that is often criticized by African Americans as racist, by Third World citizens as colonialist or imperialist, by

---

[5] See also his "The Function of the Idea of Messianic Mankind in Hermann Cohen's Later Thought," *Journal of the American Academy of Religion* XLVII (1980): 246-258.

[6] In addition to his various lectures in South Africa, see also "Openings for Marxist-Christian Dialogue," *Theology Today* XXVI (1969): 208-211.

[7] See Thomas Nagel, *The View from Nowhere* (New York: Oxford University Press, 1986). See also his earlier and much more popular *What Does It All Mean?* (New York: Oxford University Press, 1984).

feminists as patriarchal or kyriarchial, and by liberation theologians as exploitive of other groups within the Americas, both North and South. What I find deeply troubling is that many speaking from similar perspectives fail to heed these criticisms. They sometimes allege that they are not speaking from a somewhere. Instead, they maintain that they represent a universal viewpoint or an objective viewpoint — a God's-eye view.

To address the topic of pluralism from somewhere requires that one take into account the particularities of where one stands. To do so involves several conditions. First, it requires that we take seriously the criticisms addressed to our particular viewpoint. Although we cannot stand independently of where we stand, we should at least attempt to understand and address those criticisms that are brought against our standpoints. Second and equally important, it requires that we examine what drives a standpoint to deny its very particularity and to claim universality, or a view from nowhere, residing in the space of truth. This contradiction between occupying a particular standpoint and thinking and writing as if one did not occupy it is a crucial and critical problem. To overlook this contradiction amounts to a "substitutional universalism," in which the particular is advanced as a universal and the subjective is passed off as the objective. Its presupposition is that it is presuppositionless. Often those occupying positions of dominance (if not domination) and influence (if not controlling power) are precisely those who allege that their particular standpoint is universal and their specific viewpoint is neutral. Consequently, it is precisely in such situations that they fail to acknowledge that their viewpoint is that of a particular race (white), a specific gender (male), a certain status group (intellectual), a definite nation (colonial), and a specific economic system (capitalist).

In addressing the problem of pluralism, therefore, as a white male academic of the United States I have to begin by asking: to what extent is the North American view of pluralism a very particular viewpoint and to what extent am I in danger of passing off this particular view of pluralism as universal or as pluralism itself? In other words: to what extent is pluralism really a view from a particular standpoint that needs to be analyzed and critically examined for both its particularity and for its claims to universalism?

My paper will begin with a description of various types of pluralism as a backdrop to the issue of religious pluralism. It will, however, seek to situate pluralistic discourse in the context of differences between the technological, economic, and communications substructure, on the one hand, and the formulations of cultural pluralism within the contemporary superstructure, on the other hand. Second, it will describe pluralism as a phenomenon of academic historical studies and of academic religious studies in order to ask whether such pluralism makes room for a genuine openness and justice to the culturally and religiously "other," or whether it entails a commodification of otherness that actually undercuts, if not denies, such pluralism. The third section will highlight ambiguities of the relation between religion and justice within the context of pluralism, especially as their ambiguities relate to two appeals: the appeal to justice as a criterion and the appeal to conversation as a means of convergence. The concluding section will argue that appeals to justice and to dialogue have ambiguities that are often overlooked. My own proposal seeks to deal with these issues by elaborating and combining three elements: the particularity of identity within concrete overlapping traditions and horizons, the responsibility for the suffering of others and the materiality of life, and the conditions of discourse and dialogue.

1. *Situating Pluralistic Discourse*

Pluralism is defined quite differently in distinct disciplines: legal theory, political theory, social theory, philosophy, and religious studies. Moreover, pluralism is a contested concept. Not only is there little agreement about the definition of pluralism, but also the way it is defined often determines its valuation. Definitions of pluralism include within them valuations of pluralism. Some definitions equate pluralism with relativism, skepticism, indifferentism and a host of other "vices."[8] Others view pluralism as the foundation of democracy, the acknowledgment of diversity and the openness to otherness. That pluralism is a contested concept[9] is obvious in the different significance and meaning attributed to pluralism in postmodern theory in comparison with modern philosophical and political theories. In this discussion of the types of pluralism, I am especially interested in situating pluralism in relation to the distinction between the superstructure and substructure of modern societies and in asking whether there exists apparent conflict or a hidden isomorphism that needs to be made explicit.

---

[8] For a taxonomy of these different "isms" from the perspective of a defender of pluralism, see Nicholas Rescher, *Pluralism: Against the Demand for Consensus* (New York: Oxford University Press, 1993).
[9] Gregor McLennan, *Pluralism* (Minneapolis: University of Minnesota Press, 1995).

A. *Types of Pluralism*

Pluralism has different meanings in different discourses. In *philoso-phical discourse*, one distinguishes an epistemological pluralism from an ontological pluralism. Epistemological pluralism underscores the limit-ed and perspectival nature of all knowledge. Such pluralism maintains that many different perspectives and viewpoints can exist in relation to one reality. Ontological pluralism, however, refers to the existence of a plurality of realities. This epistemological and ontological pluralism finds its correspondence in religious discourse also. Religious pluralism of the epistemological type argues that there is one ineffable reality or one ultimate reality, but that the many religions represent different per-spectives of that reality.[10] Ontological pluralism emerges in the recent advocacy of a new polytheism.[11]

A second type of pluralism is a *social-cultural* pluralism. The emphasis here is on the intertwinement between ideas and practices, institutions and selves. Religious pluralism based upon a social-cultural pluralism criticizes the Western narrative of history as linear and progressive. It underscores the diversity of religious beliefs as embedded in varied life-practices and cultures. Such a social-cultural religious pluralism is often advocated in postmodern, postcritical, and communitarian thought.

A third type is *political pluralism* where the emphasis is on the relation between interests and groups and power. Difference and diversity are related to issues of interest and power, which is left out of the first two types of pluralism. Whereas an epistemological pluralism elaborates the limits of our knowledge of reality and social-cultural pluralism expli-cates the intertwinement of religious beliefs and life practices, the politi-cal pluralism emphasizes that individuals and groups have different values, interests, and power. It is concerned about the use of power by dominant groups to suppress the values and interests of minority groups and individuals.

---

[10] John Hick, *An Interpretation of Religion: Human Responses to the Transcendent* (New Haven: Yale University Press, 1989); *Problems of Religious Pluralism* (New York: St. Martin's Press, 1985); *The Rainbow of Faiths: Critical Dialogues on Religious Pluralism* (London: SCM Press, 1995). For a perceptive sketch of the development of Hick's thought and its nuances, see Sumner B. Twiss, "The Philosophy of Religious Plural-ism: A Critical Appraisal of Hick and His Critics," *The Journal of Religion* 70 (1990): 533-568, reprinted in Philip L. Quinn and Kevin Meeker, eds., *The Philosophical Challenge of Religious Diversity* (New York: Oxford University Press, 2000), 67-98.
[11] David LeRoy Miller, *The New Polytheism: Rebirth of the Gods and Goddesses* (New York: Harper & Row, 1974).

Religious pluralism has often been defined in terms of epistemological pluralism, social-cultural pluralism, or political pluralism. Traditionally the issue of religious pluralism has been raised in terms of soteriology or salvation with three distinctive viewpoints.[12] An exclusive viewpoint maintains that truth and salvation are limited to a religious community. An inclusive view affirms the universality of the offer of God's grace to everyone so that individuals of other religions implicitly accept that offer of grace through their fundamental orientation to what they perceive as ultimate and absolute. Pluralists reject not only the exclusivist but also the inclusivist positions as an imperialistic imposition of a Christian view upon other religions. The inclusivist fails to acknowledge the other in its otherness. Appealing to an epistemological perspectivalism, pluralists argue that all religions, including Christianity, have a limited perspective of the ineffable divine or ultimate reality. Where they have sought some evaluative criterion, they have often appealed to human flourishing or social liberation.

The pluralist positions, however, waver between the poles of universalism and particularism. Hence, while they seek to acknowledge the validity of pluralism and diversity, they often introduce abstract or universal categories, such as an ultimate reality as a noumenon or ontological referent point for the diverse religions, or they look for an underlying unity beneath this diversity, or they appeal to human flourishing as universal criterion. Critics of _religious_ pluralism often draw on a _cultural_ postmodern pluralism in order to criticize the pluralist position as incoherent.[13] They appeal to the diversity and plurality of conceptions of justice in order to argue that justice cannot serve as a criterion to adjudicate religious views. The different types of pluralism and the debate between a religious pluralism based upon epistemic pluralism and one based upon cultural postmodern sensibilities provides the context for the following discussion of pluralism.

B. _Conflict between Superstructure and Substructure_

In my perspective, a certain dichotomy exists between the superstructure, using that term loosely to refer to culture and ideas, and the substructure of the economy and technology. On the economic and

---

[12] Francis Schüssler Fiorenza, "Christian Redemption between Colonialism and Pluralism," in Rebecca Chopp and Mark Taylor, eds., _Reconstructing Christian Theology_ (Minneapolis: Fortress, 1994), 269-302.
[13] S. Mark Heim, _Salvations: Truth and Difference in Religion_, Faith Meets Faith (Maryknoll, N.Y.: Orbis Books, 1995).

technological level, the world is becoming increasingly unified and interconnected. Modern technologies make communication almost instantaneous between all parts of the world linked up through the communication media of television, radio, newspapers, and the Internet. The market economy is increasingly a unified world economy so that a drastic drop in the stock market in Hong Kong almost immediately reverberates in Europe and then the United States. Increases in the rate of interest instantly attract capital that flees from one nation and flocks to another. A worker in one country wanting to strike for better wages has to fear not only that his union might not win the particular struggle for better wages and working conditions, but also that the company might very well move the factory outside the nation or outside the continent. The worker stands in a global market in which workers and jobs are treated as commodities just as money and products are. If capital moves to find the highest rates of return, jobs are transferred to where they cost the least. Finally, the ecological crisis underscores that we all live on one earth. Pollution generated by one country becomes acid rain in other countries. The extensive use of fossil fuel and other energy resources, especially in the industrialized countries of the Northern Hemisphere, my own in particular, contributes to global warming and may lead to devastating flooding in other nations in other parts of the globe.

If the substructure points to a technical, economic, and ecological world that is becoming increasingly unified, elements of the superstructure point in the opposite direction. On the level of the superstructure, one sees the celebration of heterogeneity, diversity, difference, and pluralism. The celebration of difference is often considered the transition point from modernism and modernity to postmodernism and postmodernity. What does this cultural pluralism and postmodernism entail? This is indeed a difficult question, for there are different postmodernisms.[14]

Amidst this diversity, postmodern theories have several characteristics that accentuate pluralism. One characteristic is their emphasis on the contingency of knowledge, the perspectivity of values, and the ambiguity of meaning in contrast to a traditional reliance on knowledge grounded on clear and certain evidence.[15] Another characteristic is the heterogeneity of rationality itself that emphasizes a pluralistic

---

[14] Wolfgang Welsch, *Ästhetisches Denken* (Stuttgart: Reclam, 1993).

[15] An example is the work of Richard Rorty. See his *Contingency, Irony, and Solidarity* (New York: Cambridge University Press, 1989).

understanding of reasoning over against a logocentric understanding of rationality as uniform, centered, and hierarchical.[16] A third characteristic is the variegated character of the imagination that emphasizes the imaginative creativity, multiformity, and openness instead of the primacy of the perceptual and visual. Instead of conceiving of the imagination in terms of representational objectivity or representational creativity, the imagination seeks to intimate the ineffable.[17] A further characteristic is the argument that the philosophical recourse to a transcendental self amidst cultural diversity overlooks the multidimensionality and opacity of the self. It posits the universality and transparency of the self, whereas in practice, the self exists as opaque, contextual, and ineffable. Moreover, the affirmation of the transcendental self and existentialist concern with the self might be less a universal than a middle-class occupation with the self. Or it might be an example of an anthropocentrism that overlooks the location of humans as one species among a multiplicity of variegated species, situated within the earth as one world of nature within a cosmos. Finally, among the characteristics of postmodern theories, there is a shift from an understanding of rationality as centrist and hierarchical to sensitivity for an aesthetic form of rationality.[18]

These characteristics feature a complex set of interpretations that increasingly challenge modern rationality on several fronts. They entail a critique of the universalism, representationalism, and anthropocentrism implied in certain conceptions of rationality of the modern west. And they also entail a critique of the differentiation and rationalization of modern culture. Whereas modern rationality sees the separation of the objective world of nature from the moral world and aesthetic world as advances in rational thinking, postmodern interpretations judge such distinctions and differentiations not as advances but as retreats. In their view, such distinctions bifurcate the human person, for they hierarchically order certain types of reason, values, and feelings in a way that denies genuine plurality and pluralism. They fail to recognize the otherness of the other in their variegated religions, reasons, values, and feelings.

---

[16] See Jacques Derrida, *Writing and Difference* (Chicago: University of Chicago Press, 1978).

[17] For a survey and critical confrontation, see Richard Kearney, *The Wake of Imagination: Toward a Postmodern Culture* (Minneapolis: University of Minnesota Press, 1988).

[18] For a critique of postmodern rationality, see Jürgen Habermas, *The Philosophical Discourse of Modernity: Twelve Lectures* (Cambridge: MIT Press, 1987).

C. Relation between Superstructure and Substructure

It would be misleading just to look at the difference between super-structure and substructure, for indeed a certain isomorphism or parallel-ism exists between the cultural affirmation of pluralism and the exten-sion of the substructure of the market economy. This parallelism, moreover, can be interpreted in two ways. On the one hand, it seems that the unification of the world through communications and tech-nology makes it possible for one to encounter pluralism. Hence it is precisely the unification of the world through the market economy and technological advances in travel and communications that makes the experience of pluralism possible. In addition, the increase in migration and movement in society in comparison to more insulated societies means that today one no longer encounters only persons with similar religious, ethical, and political values, as one might have previously. Many metropolitan centers and areas have become increasingly multi-cultural and offer the opportunity for a genuine pluralism. (Although such multiculturalism may be the exception, since these metropolitan centers often exemplify not so much pluralism, but rather microcosms of segregation and strife.)

On the other hand, one can question whether or not pluralism is compatible with the market economy so that pluralism really represents an extension of the market to cultural, ethical, and religious values. Is religious and ethical pluralism itself a commodification of culture with-in a capitalist system? This question refers not only to the marketing of American culture, as is evident through the spread of American movies, television programming, and cultural stereotypes, that exemplify how a central economic power influences and controls the cultural market of the periphery. It refers also to pluralism, religious pluralism, and even cultural otherness. Have these also become the commodified objects of consumption? One travels to other cities, museums, and cultural institu-tions as consumers seeking to taste and marvel at the cultural objects of others as objects of one's own curiosity and appetite. The strangeness and diversity of other cultures is reduced to a plurality of cultural objects that can be enjoyed. As such, cultural others stand at an objectified distance and become objects to be tasted and enjoyed rather than as otherness that challenges us in our very values and presuppositions.

D. Questions

In short, the above description of the tensions and parallelisms raises two basic questions that pull in different directions. *First,* and this is the question just raised: To what extent is pluralism itself an example of the commodification of the culture and the parallelism between culture and its economic and technological base? Or, as the question is posed in the light of postcolonial criticisms and accusations: Is pluralism itself just one of the many coercive and closed ideologies of the modern west? *Second*, to the extent that there is a disparity between the economic substructure and the post-modern culture, then the question emerges: How does postmodern advocacy of a heterogeneous pluralism function in a world that is becoming increasingly united ecologically, economically, and politically, where agreements and interchanges become practically necessary?

2. *Pluralism: Historical and Religious*

The first question is occasioned by elements of historical and religious pluralism within the North American academic situation. The issue is whether a certain commodification of culture takes place that results from the increased presence of scientific rationality in academic studies and from the increased dominance of the market economy across many areas of modern life. In addition, one can ask if the commodification of culture leads to a commodification of pluralism or whether there are instants of openness, if not resistance, that press beyond that such a commodified pluralism. Such openness may disclose the need for a pluralism that respects difference and at the same makes possible cooperation, so that there is both justice for all as well as for each.

A. *Historical Consciousness — A Commodification of the Past?*

Pluralism can be seen as a result of historical consciousness that studies and contextualizes the historical past so that the historical past becomes an object of difference. The historical-critical study of the past is a product of the modern European Enlightenment. Its approach differs radically from classical approaches to the past, even if some precedents do exist. The development of historical-critical consciousness has led to an enormous growth in our understanding of the past. Nevertheless, a historical-critical interpretation has several distinctive features. It seeks, not only through philological analyses, but also through historical analyses of the social, cultural, and political context, to produce a specific and determinate meaning of a specific text or event. The result of historical-critical analysis has been to objectify the past and the study of the past into a multiplicity of cultures and diversity of values.

Two differences are significant between the features of modern historical-critical studies and classic Christian interpretations. One concerns the singularity or plurality of meaning. Traditionally, interpretation sought a plurality of meanings as exemplified in the fourfold senses of scripture.[19] Not only scriptural texts have a multiplicity of meaning, but even past events, for example, an event described in the Hebrew Scriptures, could be viewed has having a typological meaning. The intent, however, of a modern philological and historical analysis is to arrive at a singular interpretation. It achieves this singular interpretation through an historical and contextual analysis that locates the text in the past — a past that is diverse from the present.

A second difference is the emphasis upon the method of interpretation as a kind of instrumental rationality. If a classical interpretation, such as Augustine's *De doctrina christiana*, advocated the necessity of personal asceticism and charity in addition to linguistic competency for the proper understanding of the Scriptures, the Enlightenment espoused an objective method that emphasizes linguistic and historical expertise to the exclusion of personal asceticism and charity. The interpretation of the texts seeks to exclude the prejudices of the interpretation. The historical-critical mode of interpretation remains a dominant practice despite criticisms: hermeneutical theorists point to the unavoidability of the hermeneutical circle and postmodern theorists point to the plurality and ambiguity of meaning.

The result is that the scriptures, as well as other cultural artifacts such as architecture, art, and texts, enjoy an independence from both their authors and recipients. They become objects of the past which we face and study. The past is then not that to which we belong but rather that which we can objectify, analyze, and interpret independent of our belonging to that past as normative. In addition, historicism views the past much more with the category of individuality rather than example. The past provides less normative examples that we can emulate than it provides world views that in their individual configuration stand in contrast to ours. The dominance of this historicism in our approach to the past remains despite all criticisms from a hermeneutical perspective, such as Gadamer's critique of historicism, and from liberation theologians indebted to this criticism.[20]

---

[19] Henri de Lubac, *Exègese medievale: les quatres sens de l' écriture*, Théologie, vols. 41-42 and 59 (Paris: Aubier, 1959).

[20] See Hans-Georg Gadamer, *Truth and Method*, 2d rev. ed. (New York: Continuum, 1994).

Historical studies objectify past cultures and this objectification leads to the pluralism of past cultures. These cultures become other in the sense of objects and as objects they are plural. Yet this objectification and distancing of the past and this separation of interpretation from spiritual exegesis has another side besides the commodification of the past. The objectification of the past acknowledges the otherness of the past. For example, the Hebrew Scriptures are then read in their Otherness and difference from the Christian Scriptures. The Hebrew interpretation of the Scriptures is acknowledged to have a legitimacy that it does not have in the Christian patristic reading where their reading is an interpretation of the Hebrew scriptures "according to flesh" in distinction to a Christian reading "according to the Spirit."

In summary, the commodification of the past that takes place through an instrumental study of the past has an ambiguous function. It can produce knowledge and information about the distant past and we understand the past as other to the present. That gain may also entail a loss. It can eliminate the claim the past has upon us and it can relate to the historical past as an aesthetic object instead of as a genuine otherness that challenges us.[21]

B. *Acknowledging Religious Pluralism or Religious Otherness?*

The understanding of religious diversity and the interpretation of religious pluralism has undergone a long development within modernity, which cannot be traced in this paper. Instead, I select a few salient features of this development along with some ambiguities. In the wake of the religious wars, one sees the beginning of the European Enlightenment underscoring the notion of natural religion. The particularities of individual Christian denominations were denigrated in favor of a natural and rational religion. At the same time, from another impetus, there was a search for a natural religion as an interpretive key to understanding the religions of the new worlds and the rights of the inhabitants of those worlds.

In the beginning of the nineteenth century, F. D. E. Schleiermacher's notion of individuality and G. W. F. Hegel's logical and developmental scheme can be seen as attempts to deal with pluralism.[22] Within the

---

[21] For an interpretation of Otherness in regard to Gadamer's hermeneutics, see James Risser, *Hermeneutics and the Voice of the Other: Re-reading Gadamer's Philosophical Hermeneutics* (Albany: State University of New York Press, 1997).

[22] For a description of Franz Rosenzweig's critique of Hegel's view of history in relation of Judaism, see Wendell S. Dietrich, "The Character and Status of the

Hegelian developmental framework, Protestant Christianity in its Berlin incarnation became conceptualized as the logical apex of the historical development of human religiosity, with Catholicism, Judaism and other religions lower down on the developmental scale. Though Schleiermacher's understanding of religion in terms of the self's relation to the whence of human existence avoids the developmentalism of Hegel, his interpretation of the self, focusing on the dialectic of freedom and dependency in relation to the transcendental ground of Being, becomes the differentiating point of interpretation of religions. In this schema Catholicism and Judaism are relegated to a lower stage. These attempts thereby acknowledge the plurality of religions, but only to the extent that they are placed within stages that are hierarchically structured. In our century, Troeltsch has criticized the idealism of Hegel's developmental approach and sought to take relativism increasingly seriously as his thought progressed. Nevertheless, his own articulation of an "essence" of religion beneath the diversity betrays the very same legacy of Idealism. Likewise, his assessment of the individuality of the modern spirit correlates with his conviction that the progressiveness of Protestant thought comes to maturation in the modern European spirit.

The development of the "scientific" and the comparative study of religion sought to apply a scientific rationality to the study of religions. It sought, through scientific objectivity and neutrality, to avoid both the dogmatic doctrinal approach to religion of classic orthodoxy as well as to avoid the developmental Eurocentric version of Christianity. What becomes of religious pluralism within the framework of this scientific rationality of religious studies?[23] In a way parallel to the course of the development of historical studies, the emancipation of religious studies from dogmatic theology has led to a proliferation of knowledge about diverse religions, just as the emancipation of historical studies from ecclesiastical did. Through knowledge of historical and social context, individual religions are interpreted in their diversity and plurality. However, such studies, with their search for objectivity and neutrality, often amount to an instrumental rationality that excludes from consideration precisely the central religious claims of the religions themselves.

Concept of History in Three Twentieth Century Systems of Judaic Thought: Cohen, Rosenzweig, Lévinas," in *From Ancient Israel to Modern Judaism*, Vol. 3, *The Modern Age: Philosophy*, eds. Jacob Neusner, Ernest S. Frerichs and Nahum M. Sarna (Atlanta, George: Scholars Press, 1989): 197-211.
[23] See Francis Schüssler Fiorenza, "Theology in the University," *Bulletin of the Council of Societies for the Study of Religion* 22 (April 1993): 34-39.

A curious academic situation emerged: whereas one studied literature or philosophy for their critical significance, one studied religions with a objective detachment and without asking for their critical relevance. Although the academic study of religion has sought to acknowledge religious pluralism, it has often interpreted religions in a way that denies pluralism insofar as the interpretation of the other religions has often taken place in terms of specific Western viewpoints. Here it is not just a question of a more narrow doctrinal interpretation of other reli-' gions from the perspective of Western monotheism or Christian soteriology or Augustinian views of the sinfulness of human nature. It is also a question whether such categories as "religion," "ritual, "myth," and "institution," are embedded in Western viewpoints of religion.[24] It is also an issue of the specific viewpoints implicitly present in a scholar's views of the sources.[25]

Moreover, a view of religion that defines religion with very specific criteria and characteristics, in applying its defined criteria of religion, may judge that sets of practices and beliefs not fitting its definition are not religious. Quite often the use of the category of world religions leaves many native and indigenous religions out of the spectrum. Consequently, other religions are seen not so much in their radical otherness as they are interpreted from the perspective of Christianity or the West or even systematically interpreted as an implicit Christianity (Schleiermacher) or anonymous Christianity (Karl Rahner).

In addition, there are the issues that Edward Said has raised in *Orientalism* that argue that the Western academic study of the orient utilized categories that constructed the orient as an inferior other.[26] From a different perspective, Philip Almond has shown how the scholarly interpretation of Buddhism was colored by specific British perspectives, to the degree that the Western view of Buddhism amounts to an invention of Buddhism.[27] More systematic is Benson Saler's challenge

---

[24] Wilfred Cantwell Smith, *The Meaning and End of Religion* (New York: Mentor, 1972).

[25] For example, Friedrich Max Müller introduced Schleiermacher's categories of religion into his study of ancient Indian Vedic sources. Edward Burnett Tylor used the notion of "soul" to interpret natural event and described religions as a kind of natural philosophy. Cf. Hans G. Kippenberg, "Rationality in Studying Historical Religions," in Jeppe S. Jensen and Luther H. Martin, eds., *Rationality and the Study of Religion* (Aarhus: Aarhus University Press, 1997), 164.

[26] Edward Said, *Orientalism* (New York: Pantheon, 1978).

[27] Philip C. Almond, *The British Discovery of Buddhism* (Cambridge: New York: Cambridge University Press, 1988).

in *Conceptualizing Religion* (1993) to the enthnocentricism of many essentialist constructs in the study of religion.[28]

These brief considerations lead to a result that is similar to the conclusion reached through the analysis of historical studies. The modern study of other religions often enters into the hazardous situation of failing to acknowledge the otherness of other religions insofar as it subsumes these under Western categories and conceptions of religion. Even modern attempts to avoid the use of traditional Christian categories or to avoid the application of monotheistic notions to understand these religions often do not suffice to prevent their subsumption under modern or Western categories. The rigorous extension of the historical method and its explanatory modes of analysis has had the advantage that religious studies have become increasingly self-corrective. It has increasingly become critical of the adequacy of analogies drawn from the West for the task of understanding other religions. Nevertheless, it too can fail to grasp the otherness of other religions to the extent that these very explanatory modes objectify and commodify these religions, removing from consideration the very claims these religions make.

3. *Religious Pluralism as Evading or Engaging Justice*

The issue of the commodification of religious pluralism and the interpretation of other religions from the perspective of particular categories raises issues of the relation between religious pluralism and justice. How are issues of religious pluralism and issues of justice related?

A. *Religious Pluralism as Consumer Choice*

Involved in affirmations of religious pluralism are epistemological positions that reduce religious pluralism to the cognitive and social content of religion. All religious beliefs and practices are only approximations to an ineffable and unknown truth.[29] Viewed only as approximation to an ineffable and unknown truth, religious beliefs and their ensuant practices then become separated from cognitive content or from moral norms about which genuine disagreement becomes possible. Instead,

---

[28] Benson Saler, *Conceptualizing Religion: Immanent Anthropologists, Transcendent Natives, and Unbounded Categories* (Leiden: Brill, 1993).

[29] Hick writes that his pluralist hypothesis has as its center the assumption of "a divine reality which is itself limitless, exceeding the scope of human conceptuality and language, but which is humanly thought and experienced in various conditioned and limited ways." *Problems of Religious Pluralism*, 104.

religion becomes a matter of consumer choice and individual preference. Even when these beliefs intersect with social arrangements and
political life, they remain as such objects of consumer choice. But if
religious choices are commodified, then, like watching a myriad of
television programs, choice is reduced to identity rather than difference.
The catchword concerning television programming remains valid:
"five hundred times nothing still equals nothing" is applicable to
religious pluralism. Pluralism is a genuine pluralism when the choice
entails challenge or difference and not simply a replication of the same.
If the Modern West advocates religious pluralism just as it distributes
hamburgers, then one has a multiplicity of the same commodity, but
not a genuine religious pluralism.[30]

Thomas Luckman's analysis of religion in the United States and in
Germany points to an invisible religion that exists along side of and
independent of the mainline churches and denominations in North
America.[31] His point is that to understand religion it is important not
simply to analyze institutional churches, their structures, and their
explicit beliefs, but it is important to look at the attitudes, values, and
practices that exist outside of and alongside of the institutional churches.
Here one finds the values, virtues, judgments, and beliefs of an
"invisible religion" that permeate a culture. Individual autonomy and
personal choice are two examples of the characteristics of this invisible
North American religiosity. The sense of choice, closely linked to a
pervasive consumer orientation, is articulated for what is religious,
sacred, and ultimate. An individual may be socialized within a particular religious world view but he or she may later, as a private consumer
does, choose from the assorted smorgasbord of ultimate meanings. In
light of this analysis, religious pluralism may be a feature of modernity.
With its emphasis on choice it is not simply a neutral pluralism
allowing religious choice, but is itself a specific religious configuration.
We have to be careful that we are not exporting an American invisible
religion under the guise of pluralism.

---

[30] Kenneth Surin, "A 'Politics of Speech': Religious Pluralism in the Age of
McDonald's Hamburger," in Gavin D'Costa, ed., *Christian Uniqueness Reconsidered*
(Maryknoll, NY: Orbis, 1990) 192-212; Lesslie Newbigin, *The Gospel in a Pluralist
Society* (Grand Rapids: Zondervan, 1989); Tom F. Driver, "The Case for Pluralism,"
in John Hick and Paul F. Knitter, eds., *The Myth of Christian Uniqueness* (Maryknoll,
NY: Orbis, 1987).

[31] Thomas Luckmann, *The Invisible Religion: The Problem of Religion in Modern Society*
(New York: Macmillan, 1967).

B. *Religious Pluralism as Engaging in Issues of Justice*

The claim to an objective and neutral scientific rational approach to the study of religion sometimes fails to consider the degree to which the religious traditions to be interpreted make truth and normative claims.[32] An instrumental rationality that studies religions as objects or that commodifies religion and leaves it to individual choice and preference undercuts the claims that religions make for social and political life. If one fails to consider religious claims or the intersection between religious claims and social and political life, one fails to consider what is at the heart of many religions. By not considering these aspects of religion as open to adjudication and debate, one relegates them to the realm of private experience and preferential choice.

Religion is integrally involved with questions of meaning, total or fragmentary, and with practices of life as they imply or relate to normative values. Consequently, the relation between religion and justice is integral to religious belief as well as to religious practice. Our ideas of God, ultimacy, and nirvana, or our ideals of practice as embedded in paradigmatic examples, such as Moses, Jesus, Buddha, and Mohammed, affect not only how we live individually, socially, and politically, but also the meaning and practice of social and political life. When many criticize the role and importance of justice in some pluralist conceptions of religion in liberation theologians, they overlook the degree to which these are integral to religious beliefs and practice. To allege that when one gets involved with justice one is secularizing religion is to overlook the degree to which religion and ethical practice, and religion and the social-political order have been integral to religious belief and religious practice from the very beginning — and this is true not just of Christianity, but of many religions. Consequently, to raise the question of justice is to raise a question that goes to the heart of where religious life crisscrosses with ethical and social life. To acknowledge religious diversity means to take seriously the religion of others not only in their religious claims, but in the integral intersection between religious claims and social-political life. If we are to take pluralism seriously, then the question becomes: How can we learn from the other in regard to both

---

[32] This point has been consistently argued by Wolfhart Pannenberg, *Theology and the Philosophy of Science* (Philadephia: Westminster, 1976) and equally rejected by Donald Wiebe, "The Failure or Nerve in the Academic Study of Religion," *Studies in Religion* 13 (1984); and "Why the Academic Study of Religion? Motive and Method in the Study of Religion," *Religious Studies* 24 (1998): 403- 413.

religion and justice? How can one both challenge others and be challenged by them?

C. *Religious Pluralism in Relation to Discourse and Justice*

How does one deal with pluralism? Two answers are especially important: One explores the interrelation between justice and religion; the other emphasizes the role of dialogue and conversation. Both solutions are open to criticism, as we shall show, first by examining the proposal based on the interrelation between justice and religion, and secondly by examining the appeals to dialogue and conversation. The problem with the first solution rests on the diversity of the criterion that one appeals to as a criterion for resolving issues of religious pluralism. There are different understandings of justice just as there are different conceptions of the good. There are contrasting cultural ideals of the good just as there are contrasting ideals of human flourishing. To appeal to justice or to the good or to human flourishing as a criterion to deal with religious diversity overlooks the ambiguities inherent in these notions.

1. *The Ambiguities of Justice.* One very strong and important approach to religious pluralism is to stress that the option for justice becomes a criterion by which the plurality of world views and the good is decided. Within Western liberal democracies, this position is advocated by many who maintain that a priority of the right exists over the good. Many religious pluralists will argue that justice is the criterion in which religious plurality can converge or be adjudicated. There is one basic and fundamental problem with such a solution. The question becomes whose justice or whose criterion? Classical utilitarians argued that the freedom and plurality of life-styles should be increased because it increases the pleasure and decreases the pain of the greatest number of its citizens. Utilitarians had a criterion of justice and that criterion was maximization, but such a calculus of the maximum overlooks the dilemma if this maximization is achieved on the backs of the minority within a country or outside the country. The happiness of the greatest number in one country is often gained at the expense of those in other countries, thereby satisfying the maximum at the expense of the rights of others. Classical utilitarian theories of morality had, in my opinion, no adequate answer to this question, and even though rule utilitarianism attempts to provide one and thereby overcome the weakness of utilitarianism, it remains a question of whether it can in fact sufficiently protect the rights of minorities.

Another example concerns contrasting views of justice. Two diametrically opposed views of justice exist side by side or, more properly, in conflict, within our culture. Varieties of these two contrasting views dominate our political debates and cultural rhetoric. One view understands justice primarily as an entitlement. This entitlement view of justice emphasizes primarily that an individual is entitled to what he or she has achieved; individuals should retain and enjoy the benefits of what they have earned through their efforts.[33] The other view interprets justice as egalitarian. Faced with physical, social, and economic inequalities, such a view of justice seeks to make it possible that the disadvantaged and disprivileged within society have opportunities equal to others. For example, the Rawlsian difference principle proposes that one should distribute to the disadvantaged so that they can have equal opportunity for freedom.[34]

These different conceptions of justice have their correlates in conceptions of religion. One can appeal within the history of Christianity to religious stances that appear to justify an entitlement view of justice just as one can appeal to the tradition of the option for the poor as an exemplification of the difference principle. Appeals to human flourishing as a means by which religious pluralism can find a meeting point need to take into account that contrasting visions of justice, the good life, and human flourishing abound.

2. *The Ambiguities of Conversation.* Another proposal is to appeal to conversation and dialogue as a means of dealing with pluralism. This proposal also has its problems. Conversation can be understood as simply replicating in the realm of ideas the market exchange. Ideas are exchanged in the realm of the market economy. How does the other become recognized precisely in their need so that they make claims on our understanding of justice? How does the other become recognized within the conversation so that a genuine encounter with pluralism and otherness takes place?

Today in the United States both minority groups and feminists point to the inadequacy of the notion of conversation as a basis for dealing with conflicts of interests and values as well as with ethical and religious conflicts.[35] They see conversation and discourse as the privileging of a certain mode of communication that is rationalist, hegemonic, and

---

[33] Robert Nozick, *Anarchy, State, and Utopia* (New York: Basic Books, 1974).

[34] John Rawls, *A Theory of Justice* (Cambridge: Harvard University Press, 1971).

[35] See especially Iris Marion Young, "Communication and the Other: Beyond Deliberative Democracy," in Seyla Benhabib, ed. *Democracy and Difference: Contesting the Boundaries of the Political* (Princeton: Princeton University Press, 1996), 120-235.

elitist. The historian Joan Landes argues that the rational sphere of reason is not merely accidentally, but essentially masculinist.[36] To emphasize conversation is to privilege logical argumentation, the force of better reasons, and rhetorical persuasion. It thereby re-enforces, as some complain, the logocentrism of the Modern West. The abstract proposal of conversation invites others to the banquet table but it sets certain requirements for participation that de facto excludes "the other."

Consequently, the problem with the proposal of conversation as the solution is that it replicates the very problem that it is supposed to overcome. Dialogue and conversation as a model may be setting the criterion of the participation in a way that excludes what it seeks to include. Recently Russell McCutcheon argued against the study of religion as a vehicle for cultural dialogue,

> [b]ecause it overlooks the many ways in which imperial powers are the ones most often interested in doing the understanding, and, more important, in doing the conceptual and material appropriating that seems to come along with such efforts to understand. The appropriation and subsequent domestication of their means (in this case, intellectual categories) for our ends (in this case, increased cross-cultural understanding) bears disturbing resemblances to earlier instances of economic colonialism, where the colonies' natural resources became the colonizer's finished products, profits, and eventually meanings.[37]

This view of religious dialogue as domestication and colonialization is similar to the criticisms of justice the diverse strands of postmodernism, postpluralism, and postcolonialism bring against modern western conceptions of rationality and justice.

4. Responsible Pluralism: Identity, Suffering, and Intersubjectivity

How does one take such criticisms into account? How does one reckon with the ambiguities of justice? One simple solution is to accept the critique as such as well as to accept the postmodern critique of universal language and international conceptions of justice. George Lindbeck exemplifies the acceptance of the critique when he writes: "As current East Asian challenges to the discourse of international human rights

---

[36] Joan B. Landes, *Women and the Public Sphere in the Age of the French Revolution* (Ithaca: Cornell University Press, 1988). For a different view, see Keith Baker, "Defining the Public Sphere in Eighteenth-Century France: Variations on a Theme by Habermas," in Craig Calhoun, ed., *Habermas and the Public Sphere* (Cambridge: MIT, 1992), 181-212.

[37] Russell T. McCutcheon, *Manufacturing Religion: The Discourse on Sui Generis Religion and the Politics of Nostalgia* (New York: Oxford University Press, 1997), 151.

illustrate, the universal languages (or 'Esperantos' as some have called them) in which Enlightenment modernity seeks to deal with the common problems of the global village are not likely long to survive the Western cultural hegemony under which they developed."[38]

Such an affirmation as its stands remains an unmediated claim unless Lindbeck further explores or examines the possible consequences of his critique of international human rights discourse as an example of Western cultural hegemony. Is the Enlightenment's affirmation unrelated to the tradition of Christian testimony and witness and not simply a *Deus ex machina* of universal language and reason?[39] In a world seeking international cooperation and exchange, what is to become of the United Nations and its International Declaration of Human Rights? Are we to say that when Amnesty International criticizes police brutality in New York City and Los Angeles, or the treatment of Palestinians in Israeli Courts, or the treatments of prisoners in democratic as well as totalitarian regimes, it is doing nothing more than expressing Western cultural hegemony?

A. *Identity within Overlapping Traditions and Horizons*

The alternatives are not between a view from somewhere and a stand from nowhere or between an abstract universalism and a concrete particularism or even simply between universalism and relativism. While it is correct to say that one does not speak or write from nowhere, but only speaks or writes from somewhere, it is incorrect to identify that somewhere as if it were an isolated island. In articulating the particularity of one's own standpoint one has to acknowledge that individuals, communities and nations have their identities by standing in a multiplicity of crisscrossing traditions. Consequently, persons do not have a single one-dimensional identity, but an identity constituted out of overlapping traditions and multiple horizons. We are not members of one community, but of crisscrossing communities, with overlapping traditions so that when we speak from somewhere, it is a somewhere with multiple horizons and traditions. This overlapping of traditions and horizons is neglected by a view of Christianity that isolates Christian traditions from modern traditions, as if they were polar opposites, or that regards

---

[38] George Lindbeck, "The Gospel's Uniqueness: Election and Untranslatability," *Modern Theology* 134 (1997): 423-450, quote from page 427.

[39] For a defense of rights with reference to Christian traditions, see Arthur J. Dyck, *Rethinking Rights and Responsibilities: The Moral Bonds of Community* (Cleveland, Ohio: Pilgrim Press, 1994).

Christian traditions in isolation from other religious traditions, as is sometimes done in the writings of George Lindbeck,[40] John Milbank,[41] and Stanley Hauerwas.[42] Many today have their horizons formed in and through their membership in diverse and intersecting communities — though I am aware that membership in overlapping communities may be more a characteristic of metropolitan than of rural settings.

As a Christian theologian, I have been formed through the tradition of prophetic concern for the orphan, widow, and stranger and I have been educated by the proclamation of Matthew's Parable of the Last Judgment where love for the least of the brethren is equated with love for Jesus and the criterion of salvation. My horizon includes Thomas Aquinas where the goods of the earth belong properly to God and hence one needs to give out of one's abundance to those in need. It also includes John Calvin who argued that since the human person is an icon of God, an injury against a human being is an injury against God. These traditions come to the fore and crisscross with the traditions of Latin American liberation theology which has developed the option for the poor that has become part and parcel of Roman Catholic Christian consciousness and integral to Catholic social teachings. I can justify this reading of the tradition, though I am aware that others give different readings of the tradition.[43]

However, I also stand in another tradition, namely, that of human rights. Some point to this tradition as a product of the Enlightenment's abstract rationality and as an example of Western hegemony. Yet this tradition has a long history. Its roots can be found not only in classic and Stoic philosophy, but also in medieval canon law.[44] The ethical universalism of the Enlightenment in regard to human rights stands in relation to prophetic traditions, even if the lines are not as direct as some

---

[40] See George Lindbeck, *The Nature of Doctrine: Religion and Theology in a Postliberal Age* (Philadelphia: Westminster Press, 1984).

[41] John Milbank, *Theology and Social Theory: Beyond Secular Reason* (Oxford: Blackwell, 1990).

[42] Stanley Hauerwas, *In Good Company: The Church as Polis* (Notre Dame: University of Notre Dame Press, 1995). For a critical analysis, see Max L. Stackhouse, "In the Company of Hauerwas," *Journal for Christian Theological Research* 21 (1997).

[43] Francis Schussler Fiorenza, "The Works of Mercy: Theological Perspective," in Francis Eigo, ed., *The Works of Mercy* (Villanova: Villanova University Press, 1991).

[44] See R. Tuck, *Natural Rights Theories: Their Origins and Development* (New York: Cambridge University Press, 1979); Brian Tierney, *Religion, Law, and the Growth of Constitutional Thought* (New York: Cambridge University Press, 1982); and James A Brundage, *Medieval Canon Law: The Medieval World* (London; New York: Longman, 1995).

nineteenth-century exegetes maintained with their emphasis on the ethical monotheism of the prophets, or if theologians draw different social consequences from it.[45] Consequently, any historical consideration of what is often labeled a product of the Enlightenment or modernity shows that this tradition itself overlaps and crisscrosses other traditions.

B. Suffering of Others and the Corporeality of Life

Suffering and pain are experiences that are on the seam of interpretation and experience. The metaphor of "seam" is selected because while experience does not exist without interpretation, pain and suffering involve an experiential dimension that permeates the interpretative.[46] Suffering is such that when another claims that he or she is suffering or he or she is in pain, I cannot on the basis of some preconceived assumptions deny that their expressions of suffering are true or are invalid. If I am to take the voices of others seriously, then when faced with their expressions of pain and suffering, I have to take responsibility. Responsibility comes not as an abstract universal, but comes as a response to the suffering of others.

The anthropologist James Clifford has argued that "the privilege of standing above cultural particularism, of aspiring to the universalist power that speaks for humanity, for the universal experience of love, work, death, and so on is a privilege invented by a totalizing Western liberalism."[47] Yet it is possible to conceive of responsibility for the other not through a universal experience of love, but through concrete experiences of Others in suffering. Such a responsibility does not stand above cultural particularism, but is rooted in specific and particular religious

---

[45] Although many refer to ethical monotheism, as if it were a unified interpretation of the prophets, it is one of Wendell S. Dietrich's significant contributions to clearly differentiate diverse proposals for ethical monotheism in Hermann Cohen and Ernst Troeltsch. See chapter 2 "The Prophetic Ethos in Dispute," in *Cohen and Troeltsh*, 29-43. Whereas Hermann Cohen saw the prophetic ethos of ethical monotheism as the basis of the principles of a just society, Troeltsch sought to appropriate the relativist critique of claims to universality and was much more reserved than Cohen about the applicability of these principles to a social democracy.

[46] This is not to deny that different cultures and religions interpret suffering differently. Martha C. Nussbaum makes this point strongly in the chapter "The Study of Non-Western Cultures," in idem, *Cultivating Humanity* (Cambridge: Harvard, 1997), 113-147.

[47] James Clifford, *The Predicament of Culture: Twentieth-Century Ethnography, Literature, and Art* (Cambridge: Harvard University Press, 1989), 263.

traditions that have anchored the responsibility for the stranger and for the Other in their religious beliefs.

Suffering and pain often relate to the corporeality of human life and to the material existence of the other. The corporeality of human life should not be understood individualistically or even anthropocentrically, but should include other species and the earth itself. We are embedded within Gaia.[48] Consequently, both immediacy and universalism adhere to the corporeality of life. An individual's experience of hunger, violence, illness, torture, and death are experiences with an immediacy to his or her corporeal existence. At the same time hunger, illness, death, and pain are universal experiences, though differently interpreted in different cultures. Nevertheless, their corporeal root has an immediacy in our hungering, facing death, and experiencing violence. We can conceive of ourselves in substitution for the other so that their pain and suffering is not incommensurable with ours, but crisscrosses with our own experiences and interpretations. Immediacy and universality are not separate but are interlinked.

Within academic debates about pluralism sometimes examples are used that often test the limits of our attitudes toward suffering. What if the person involved does not see it as an experience of pain and suffering but sees it as an opportunity? For example, some might suggest that colonial prejudices were at work when General Charles Napier in 1843 prohibited *sati*, which prevented a woman from being revered as a goddess in her village.[49] Is it an example of a pious religious practice enabling the widow to be revered or is it an example of institutionalized cultural misogyny? Without condoning the practice, Gayatri Spivak notes that it can be constructed as "'white men saving brown women from brown men.'"[50]

Another counterexample is the Christian Scientist's attitude to modern medicine. If one forces modern medicine upon a Christian Scientist is one not then imperialistically imposing a Western form of healing in

---

[48] Cf. Sallie McFague, *The Body of God: An Ecological Theology* (Minneapolis: Fortress Press, 1993).

[49] Peter Berger, *A Far Glory: The Quest for Faith in an Age of Credulity* (New York: Free Press, 1992) and Lourens P. Van den Bosch, "A Burning Question: Asti and Sati Temples as the Focus of Political Interest," *Numen* 37 (1990): 174-94. Van den Bosch notes that whether suttee or sati is religious depends upon your definition of religion; see 193, n. 76.

[50] Gayatri Chakravorty Spivak, "Can the Subaltern Speak?" in Patrick Williams and Laura Christman, eds., *Colonial Discourse and Post-Colonial Theory: A Reader* (New York: Columbia University Press, 1994), 66-111. Quotation from 93.

contrast to other forms of healing? Such examples, when a person's cultural and religious background might embrace what others outside of that culture would condemn, provide difficult limit situations. They are often appealed to as examples expressing a Western cultural, religious, and ethical hegemony toward other cultures. These counterexamples should not be made into a general rule, for the overwhelming number of cases are where suffering and pain are inflicted upon unwilling and unconsenting victims.[51] The examples need to be dealt with not on the basis of an a priori rationality but through a practical rationality that realizes that there is no neutral agency or rationality that can adjudicate different beliefs. Instead one struggles case by case to negotiate norms and values. Such a rationality is not so much transcendental as it is "piecemeal" and "prudential." As such it is a practical rationality that develops only as a result of discourse with those who are affected. In the case of medicine, one can distinguish — though it is contested — areas where Western medicine succeeds, where it fails, and where alternative approaches might be wiser. An a priori justification of one over the other fails to be a prudential rationality. Likewise, the difficulty of negotiating between misfortune and injustice provides complexities that cannot be easily resolved.[52]

Although sati or modern Western medicine are often discussed as examples of divergent rationality, there is, perhaps, a greater urgency to those political cases involving the imposition of violence against the will of individuals and peoples and deprivation of human rights. Two examples are recent statements by Israel's Supreme Court and by the President of China. At first, the Supreme Court of Israel refused to prohibit the use of torture against the Palestinians for the sake of the survival of the nation. Amnesty International and editorials in both *The New York Times* and the *Washington Post* sharply criticized the Court for a lack of respect for human rights in that decision. In turn, they were of course criticized for not understanding the imperatives of the local situation and the necessity of a nation to survive in a hostile environment. When the Supreme Court finally ruled to exclude the torture of prisoners, it was criticized by others for failing to grasp the priorities of the security of a nation.[53] In a similar manner, the President of China

---

[51] For perceptive comments on the rhetoric of torture, see Elaine Scarry, *The Body in Pain. The Making and Unmaking of the World* (New York: Oxford University Press, 1985).
[52] Judith N. Shklar, *The Faces of Injustice* (New Haven: Yale University Press, 1990).
[53] See the recent article "Israeli Court Bars Routine Use of Force in Interrogations," in *The New York Times* (September 7, 1999).

argued during his visit to the United States that the Western emphasis on rights is a cultural prejudice that does not take into account the necessity of social-political order in order to survive and to provide enough food for the nation. These two examples are significant because they involve not only the de facto use of violence, but the theoretical and moral justification of that violence. Moreover, the President of China explicitly rejects rights language as culturally determined.[54]

What makes these situations different is that the individual, namely, the one tortured or imprisoned, is not consenting to their suffering. It is their voices that call forth responsibility. We articulate this responsibility in terms of our religious tradition as it overlaps with modern traditions of rights in order to meet our responsibility to the other. The suffering and pain of others call out to us for our responsibility toward that suffering. Such a responsibility is concrete responsibility to the suffering and pain of others rather than a formal universalism. The rights language, negative as well as positive, attempts to deal with aspects of human life that are universal and crisscross with particular experience. It is not so much the imposition of a hegemonic universal on the other, but attention to the possibilities of suffering and violence that are concretely experienced and underlie religious, ethical, and rational attempts to formulate safeguards, be these in terms of Christian language about God's creation or an Enlightenment language about rights. This point is correctly made by Emmanuel Levinas when he underscores the priority of responsibility before freedom and when he emphasizes that this responsibility is a concrete responsibility to the suffering of another.[55]

C. Conversation and Democracy

The question is: can one structure conversation and dialogue so that it becomes a genuine acknowledging of the other? The issue is not simply that dialogue and conversation involve the acknowledgment of the other. But rather how can dialogue be open for and give due justice to the other in terms of their specific religious beliefs and claims? In other words, how can it take seriously their exclusivity claims and their truth claims in a way that enables them to enter into religious dialogue on

---

[54] For a discussion of the cultural critique of rights, see Jürgen Habermas, *Die Postnationale Konstellation* (Frankfurt: Suhrkamp, 1998).
[55] See Emmanuel Levinas, *Outside the Subject*, trans. Michael B. Smith (Stanford: Stanford University Press, 1993), 166-125.

their terms and not just in the terms of a Western understanding of religious belief and their practices?

The theological reception of the model of dialogue and conversation has been developed within the horizon of Gadamer's hermeneutics.[56] That model was developed within the humanistic ideal of education that had a specifically normative tradition with exemplary classics. The legitimacy of the transfer of this model to issues of religious and ethical pluralism of diverse traditions and nations has been challenged through several factors. The transfer of this model to the issue of pluralism does not take into account that it is often through power that classics become classics and are maintained as classics.[57] In addition such a model fails to take into account the diversity of traditions in which the very character of the tradition and its classics differ and fails to consider how cultural hegemony may affect the valuation of traditions themselves.

The proposed solution of conversation and pluralism requires the deliberate conception of democracy in which conversation and dialogue could take place. In *Social Contract*, Jean-Jacques Rousseau suggests that only a society in which no one was poor enough to have to sell themselves and no one rich enough to buy them could be democratic.[58] The importance of Rousseau's point underlies some important conversations going in the United States (which I cannot survey here) in regard to deliberative democracy and the institutionalization of deliberative democracy.[59]

A part of this conversation is to suggest the importance of a diversity of heterogeneous publics and networks within the public in a way that leads to the abandonment of a unitary model of the public sphere.[60]

---

[56] Hans-George Gadamer, *Truth and Method*, 2d rev. ed. (New York: Continuum, 1994).

[57] Jürgen Habermas has argued this point in his critique of Gadamer. See Jürgen Habermas's "Zu Gadamer's 'Wahrheit und Method,'" and "Der Universalitäts-anspruch der Hermeneutik," in *Hermeneutik und Ideologiekritik*, ed. by Jürgen Habermas et al. (Frankfurt: Suhrkamp, 1971), 45-56 and 120-159 respectively.

[58] Jean Jacques Rousseau, *On the Social Contract* (1762; Indianapolis: Hackett, 1987): chap. 11.

[59] See Seyla Benhabib, ed., *Democracy and Difference: Contesting the Boundaries of the Political* (Princeton: Princeton University Press, 1996); Amy Gutmann and Dennis Thompson, *Democracy and Disagreement* (Cambridge: Harvard University Press, 1996); J. Donald Moon, *Constructing Community: Moral Pluralism and Tragic Conflicts* (Princeton: Princeton University Press, 1993); John S. Dryzek, *Discursive Democracy* (New York: Cambridge University Press, 1990).

[60] See Nancy Fraser, "Rethinking the Public Sphere: A Contribution to the Critique of Actually Existing Democracy," in Calhoun, ed., *Habermas and the Public Sphere*.

Another element concerns the diverse strategies for overcoming or balancing inequalities of power and thereby ensuring a greater participation. Conversation and discourse models as resolutions to issues of pluralism and justice point to the mutual respect or egalitarian reciprocity enabling individuals and groups. Nevertheless, this remains an abstract ideal unless it becomes possible to institutionalize the conditions that make reciprocity possible or at least until one seeks it as a goal.[61]

5. A Responsible Pluralism

My paper began seeking to locate a typology of pluralism in relation to the contrast between current postmodern cultural pluralism and the structural unity of the world resulting from the increased interconnectedness of the market economy and from the technology of communications. The question was whether a contrast or implicit isomorphism existed between pluralist cultures and a unified substructure. I suggested that instead of genuine pluralism, we could be ending up with a commodified pluralism of the Modern West, in which pluralism is a product of Western cultural and economic hegemony. The growth of an instrumental academic rationality in its approach to diverse religions and their values can, instead of underscoring the otherness of other cultures, past and present, commodify their cultural, religious, and ethical values. It can reduce these religious beliefs and ethical values to objects of aesthetic choice and consumer preference. Political and social implications of religious beliefs for issues of justice are evaded by being commodified as objects of private choice and personal preference. The question then became: How does one deal with religious and ethical pluralism in a way that is much more than the commodification of religion and that takes seriously both the intertwinement of the world and the particularity of the other precisely in their claims? Furthermore, I suggested that the attempt to achieve a resolution through appeals to justice and to dialogue is inadequate unless such attempts take into account the ambiguities of these appeals, namely, the ambiguities of justice and the ambiguities of conversation. In attending to these ambiguities, my own proposal sought to combine diverse elements: a particular identity within overlapping traditions and horizons; suffering and the corporeality of life; conversation and democracy for a responsible

---

[61] Francis Schüssler Fiorenza, "Politische Theologie und liberale Gerechtigkeits-Konzeption," in Edward Schillebeeckx, ed., *Mystik und Politik. Johann Baptist Metz zu Ehren* (Mainz: Matthias Grünewald, 1988), 105-117.

pluralism. Through these three sets of arguments, I seek to avoid dealing with pluralism from within the stark alternatives of universalism or relativism.

I have suggested first that we have particular identities, cultural as well as religious. Our particular identities are constituted by standing in a plurality of overlapping traditions and with a plurality of crisscrossing horizons. Consequently, the abstract contrast between Enlightenment rationality and Christian tradition, between modern society and Christian community, is reductionistic in that it overlooks the plurality of communities, discourses, and traditions in which we stand.

In addition to this overlapping of traditions and crisscrossing of horizons, I pointed to the materiality of life and corporeality of human existence that humans share, even though they share it through different cultural traditions and different ethical and religious beliefs. This materiality of life provides one basis for the possibility of a communicative rationality. Discussions of difference often take place against the background of some shared knowledge that requires nuance in claims of differences rather than the simple affirmation of total incommensurability.[62] It is not only out of different traditions but also out of concerns about the integrity of human life that language about positive and negative rights emerges. From such a perspective, the listening to the voices of others and the responsibility to the face and speech of the other, as Levinas has so insistently reminded us, is a concrete phenomenological feature of human life rather than an abstract universal.[63] In addition, I have suggested that where conflicts emerge between different traditions, they need to be resolved through piecemeal and concrete reflections.

Finally, the crisscrossing of traditions and horizons, the facing of human suffering, and experience of the corporeality of life point to the need for conversation about how different religious traditions interpret life and justice. On this point I have suggested, but not fully developed, the relevance of recent reflections on deliberative democracy and the relation between power and conversation, and the relation between modes of communication and discourse. Appeals to discourse or to a mere procedural solution do not solve the problem of commodification. Instead a responsible pluralism should reflect on the conditions of conversation and on the intersection between religion and justice.

---

[62] Donald Davidson's point in "On the Very Idea of a Conceptual Scheme," in *Inquiries into Truth and Interpretation* (Oxford: Clarendon Press, 1984), 183-198.
[63] Emmanuel Levinas, *Otherwise than Being: or, Beyond Essence* (Pittsburgh: Duquesne University Press, 1998).

CHAPTER FIFTEEN

WALZER ON EXODUS AND PROPHECY

Jeffrey Stout

1. *Introduction*

Norms are implicit in the stories we tell, the complaints we voice, the questions we raise, and the arguments we exchange when criticizing society. To make our norms explicit is an act of interpretation, which enables us to make sense of their roles in the traditions they inhabit and to relate them self-critically to the society we wish to criticize. Social critics who think they are standing outside tradition altogether or that interpretation is inessential to their critical task are deceiving themselves.

That, in brief, is Michael Walzer's theory of social criticism. In what traditions, then, does Walzer stand and how does he interpret them? He describes himself as a social democrat, dedicated to gradual yet radical political change, but also as a Jew. As someone committed to practicing what his theory of social criticism preaches, he would seem to have at least two reasons for subjecting biblical texts in particular to interpretation. The first reason is that some biblical texts have played a formative role in the now somewhat secularized political culture of social democracy. To understand that role, one must interpret the relevant texts. The second reason is that his Jewishness gives him a stake in clarifying his relation to the normative sources of Jewish tradition. To argue Jewishly with one's Jewish friends and foes, one must interpret the relevant texts, many of which are biblical ones.

In *Exodus and Revolution*, Walzer reads the Exodus story from a "social democratic" point of view and finds it a "liberating vision" of "deliverance from suffering and oppression," a paradigm of gradualist but radical transformation.[1] In *Interpretation and Social Criticism*, he reads the Hebrew prophets from the same angle and declares Amos a

---

[1] Michael Walzer, *Exodus and Revolution* (New York: Basic Books, 1985), 54, xi, ix; hereafter cited as "ER."

paradigmatic social critic.[2] In this essay, I will be examining what Walzer does with these biblical texts and why, inquiring into the rationale and adequacy of his interpretive practice, but I will also be raising related questions about details of his theory, questions that pertain to his prophetic model of "connected criticism." In the concluding section I will ask what Walzer's relation to the hermeneutical principles of ethical monotheism might be.

2. Is the Exodus Story Liberating?

Walzer's interpretation of the Exodus story does not merely tell us some ways in which the text has been used. It would be possible, Walzer tells us, "to trace a continuous history from the Exodus to the radical politics of our own time" (ER, 25). But he immediately adds that he "won't try to do that." So what is Walzer's interpretation supposed to do? If we can figure out the answer to that question, we can go on to ask whether he succeeds in doing what he sets out to do and whether trying to do such a thing is worthwhile.

Walzer says that he is not making claims about what the original authors and editors of the story intended by it. Nor is he making claims about the relation between that story and the historical events that the story purportedly describes. It would not matter, from Walzer's point of view, whether those events happened or not. What matters is that the story of the Exodus has given rise over the centuries to certain meanings over which the original authors and editors exercise no control. The text, he implies, does not have one meaning but several (or perhaps many). Of these, Walzer is interested in only one, which he labels, "Exodus as revolution." His interpretation, it seems, is meant to give us this meaning. But what does it mean to give this meaning? How would you go about finding this meaning? How would you know you had it right?

Walzer does not answer these questions explicitly. He says that he is "following a well-marked trail, moving backward from citation and commentary to primary text, from enactments to acts or, at least, to stories of acts" (ER, 134). The point, I take it, is at least partly that this trail is itself an important feature of Walzer's own political culture, his tradition, not just as a Jew but as a democrat and as a kind of radical living in a modern, Western society. Walzer himself and many others before

2 Michael Walzer, *Interpretation and Social Criticism* (Cambridge: Harvard University Press, 1987); hereafter cited as "ISC."

him have traversed that trail. They have read the story as a model of revolutionary activity, and their reading of it has influenced their understanding of themselves. They might have behaved differently had they not read this story or had they not seen it as relevant to radical politics in their own day or had they not construed its relevance in the way they did. So to understand important aspects of his own political culture, Walzer needs to understand a particular story read in a certain way. His interpretation is to be judged, in part, by its ability to illumine those aspects of modern Western political culture.

So far, so good. But there is more, for Walzer does not merely seek to describe how certain important writers and political agents have interpreted the story. He proposes to stand among them. That means to stand with them in claiming that their way of reading the story is, on the whole, a valid one. It also means to take a stand on issues that divide those who read the story in this way into separate camps. In claiming that "Exodus as revolution" is a valid reading of the story, he seems to be saying that the well-marked trail really does lead back to the primary text, that it is not merely projected onto the text by its politically motivated readers. As he puts it, this reading "has a firm foundation in the actual words of Exodus and Numbers" (ER, 8).

Those words have undoubtedly fueled certain projects of political revolution. As Walzer demonstrated in his first book, *Revolution of the Saints*, the first modern revolutionaries were Calvinists who took Exodus as their inspiration and their model,[3] and they have obviously had many successors in using the story in this way. Walzer is right about this and right in holding that important aspects of political culture in the West are intimately connected with readings of Exodus as a revolutionary tract. But there is something odd about all such readings that Walzer neglects to mention. Revolutions are major political transformations that come about when oppressed people stay where they are and fight it out with their oppressors, hoping to replace one political order with another one. The story of Exodus, however, is nothing of the kind. It is rather a story about an oppressed group leaving the scene of oppression and going somewhere else.[4] Moreover, their ability to leave is secured not by their own struggle against the oppressors but by a god who sends plagues and kills countless first-born children. After wandering for forty years in the wilderness, they arrive in a land promised to them by

---

[3] Michael Walzer, *Revolution of the Saints* (New York: Atheneum, 1976).
[4] I first heard this point from Daniel Overmeyer, who was responding to the Gauss Seminars in which Walzer first laid out the arguments of ER.

their god but which is already occupied by other peoples. The Lord, through the prophetic voice of Moses, orders that these other peoples be utterly destroyed. The people follow these orders, and the promised land is theirs.

In short, the actual words of Exodus and Numbers tell a story of mass migration, conquest, and ethnic cleansing, not a story about revolution, and it is hard to imagine a story less in keeping with social-democratic sympathies. Walzer says surprisingly little to counter this objection. He would not deny that the objection is grounded in the story of Exodus as we have it. He knows that Exodus has an "Exodus as exodus" reading as well as an "Exodus as revolution" reading. But he implies that his book is about the latter, not the former. By delimiting his topic in this way, he allows himself to mention only in passing the modern uses to which "Exodus as exodus" has been put — when various groups of oppressed Europeans left Europe and traveled to the Americas, to southern Africa, and to Palestine itself, fleeing the scene of their oppression, sometimes construing their enterprise as divinely mandated, and subduing native populations in the promised land. There are other noteworthy uses about which Walzer tells us little or nothing — for example, by African Americans during the Civil War, or during the great migration north in the middle decades of the 20th century, or when articulating the desire to leave North American bondage for some other place.

"Exodus as revolution" is not about leaving, wandering, conquest, and genocide. Or rather, these activities, to which the "actual words of Exodus and Numbers" refer, become at most tropes or figures for something involved in revolutionary struggle. Leaving Egypt becomes a trope for rebellion against unfreedom — against both the literal condition of bondage and the spiritual vices, the metaphorical bondage, it engenders. Wandering in the desert becomes a trope for the long delay between the first moment of rebellion and the achievement of a free and just society. What, then, about conquering and genocide? Being a social democrat, Walzer doesn't like those parts of the story, so he holds them off as long as he can and then plays them down as thoroughly as he can. Yet they appear to have "a firm foundation in the actual words of Exodus and Numbers." They also have a long history as a source of inspiration for murderous behavior. They have inspired the unrestrained violence of Exodus-thumping revolutionaries no less than that of Exodus-thumping conquerors. Why not conclude, then, that Walzer's version of the story is significantly less faithful to the text than either the "Exodus as exodus" version or the militantly Calvinist variant of the "Exodus as revolution" version?

Walzer is most faithful to the text when discussing the theme of wandering. The length of the time in the wilderness is indeed essential to the story, and it does provide fodder for his gradualist radicalism. The story does imply both that radical change is necessary and that it does not happen over night. The story also vividly illustrates a truth underlying these by showing how a legacy of unfreedom can linger on in the behavior of victims even after the external chains of oppression have been broken. Walzer interprets the story's account of Israel in the wilderness, in effect, as a fable with morals. That is to say, he uses the story to exemplify general truths that can be stated and known independently of it. Taking the story in this way is plausible as far as it goes, because the general truths Walzer sees at work in the text do seem to make the right kind of connection with details of the story.

The trouble, of course, is that these are not the only details of the story. The story, when interpreted as an example illustrating general truths that are in keeping with social democratic sympathies, overflows with details that suggest other morals less in keeping with those sympathies. John Lyons, in his study of the rhetoric of example in Renaissance literature, calls this the problem of excess. "Example is excessive," Lyons writes, "because any [narrative] adduced to support a generalization will have characteristics that exceed what can be covered by the generalization." In a complex narrative, "the number of other concepts that can be illustrated by the narrative begins to threaten the control of the generality."[5]

Walzer is aware that there is a 20th-century version of the "Exodus as revolution" story which is morally and politically at odds with his own. This is the version he calls Leninist, which emphasizes the passages in which Moses purges his opponents and introduces a hierarchical organization founded on the Levites. Walzer acknowledges not only that this version exists but also that it emphasizes actual features of the story. He insists only that the story can be read differently, that his social democratic reading is valid too. Interpreters, he implies, are free to choose their own emphases. Walzer chooses to emphasize the role of Moses as educator of his people and his role as their defender before God, to de-emphasize his blood-curdling purge, his antidemocratic creation of the vanguard of Levites, and, curiously enough (for a champion of prophetic social criticism), his role as Yahweh's prophet.

---

[5] John D. Lyons, *Exemplum: The Rhetoric of Example in Early Modern France and Italy* (Princeton: Princeton University Press, 1989), 34.

In what sense, exactly, can the resulting interpretation claim to be a good one? In this sense, surely: that it expresses a more wholesome moral vision and implies a more defensible politics. As a fellow social democrat and gradualist radical, I can agree to that. But can Walzer's social democratic reading of Exodus reasonably claim to give the deeper, more thorough interpretation of the story as we have it? His opponents will argue that his engagement with the parts of the story he doesn't like is merely to wish they were not there. Even fellow social democrats will suspect that he has failed to test the prejudice that the story is an essentially liberating one. If we are going to test that prejudice rigorously, we will have to confront all the troublesome details that might adversely affect our overall appraisal of the story: the details played up by the Leninist reading, the details played up by migrating conquerors mindful of their former status as victims of oppression, and the details played up by people who read the story as an essentially religious one about God's character and deeds.

A democrat who is told that the story including all these details is liberating will want to ask, liberating for whom? No doubt, those who identify intuitively with the God-fearing Israelites and construe the story from their point of view will find it liberating. The Israelites are victims of oppression at the outset of the story, and their liberation from slavery puts them on a wandering path to the promised land. But not all the Israelites find their way to the promised land, and many people besides Israelites become victims before the story ends. It is ethically instructive to read the story from the vantage point of the characters who are victimized by practices other than slavery.[6] Walzer says that when he first grappled with the golden calf episode (Exodus 30:11-34:35) in his *bar mitzvah* portion his heart went out to the victims of Moses' divinely authorized command to kill the idol worshipers (ER, xi). He also draws attention to a long list of other victims of similar commands. In

---

[6] As Edward W. Said argued with such vehemence in "Michael Walzer's 'Exodus and Revolution': A Canaanite Reading," *Grand Street* 5 (1985-86): 86-106. For Walzer's response and Said's subsequent rejoinder, see "An Exchange: 'Exodus and Revolution,'" *Grand Street* 5 (1985-86): 246-59. I agree with Said on the importance of reading Exodus from a Canaanite point of view, but much of what he says about the details of Walzer's work in philosophy and social criticism strikes me as severely unfair. Part of my motivation in writing this essay is to return to the scene of their impassioned exchange now that the dust has settled. I want to see what can be made of the interpretive and philosophical issues Said and Walzer were debating if we disentangle them from the emotions surrounding Israeli treatment of the Palestinians.

Deuteronomy 20 the Hittites, Amorites, Canaanites, Perizzites, Hivites, and Jebusites "are explicitly excluded from the world of moral concern" envisioned by the story — which is a euphemistic way to say that God commands their "systematic extermination" (ER, 142). When read from the perspective of all such victims, the text hardly seems liberating at all.

Reading a story with its various victims in mind is often assisted by consideration of questions about the religious, moral, and political purposes informing its authors, editors, and early users. Walzer avoids these questions about the Exodus story because he wants to take the words of the story "straightforwardly, as they occur" (ER, 8). "The effort of modern critics to disentangle authorial traditions, to identify earlier and later fragments within the narrative, has not in my view produced a better understanding of the Exodus story, certainly not of the story as it has been read and reread, cited and elaborated." Walzer is surely right if all he means is that someone who wants to understand what Cromwell or Ahad Ha-Am thought Exodus meant will need to look at the whole story in its received, canonical form. The strands of the biblical text that modern scholars have distinguished and the intentions of the redactor who brought those strands together are simply irrelevant to that question.

If, however, you want also to affirm the actual story — and not merely some expurgated version of it — as liberating, you had better ask whether you are fully prepared to endorse the story's valuations and devaluations of the individuals and groups who are its characters. Investigation of sources and of the process by which they were brought together has the merit of reminding us to think of the devaluated characters and groups as real people who might have had their own stories to tell. Aside from satisfying our antiquarian curiosity, the value of asking how the devaluations were put in place once upon a time is a concrete reminder that we, too, as celebrators or users of the text, may become complicit in devaluations of our own. They may not be the same ones as those at work in the heart of an ancient author or editor, but they will probably have some parallel to those.

Some scholars hold that the earliest biblical form of the Exodus story — the one contained in the so-called "J" source — was part of a commissioned justification or nostalgic celebration of the house of David and its heroic founder, that the story's evaluations and devaluations performed a number of ideological tasks for supporters of the Davidic house. According to this view, the story explained how it could be that a usurper like David could actually possess divinely grounded legitimacy and favor. It united the diverse groups under David's rule by construing them as a single people, and it systematically devalued David's great enemies: Egypt, the neighboring groups not allied with David, and the residents of cities.[7] Jan Assmann has recently placed heavy stress on the Israel-Egypt polarity around which the story is organized.[8] According to Assmann, ancient Israel's monotheism was a "counter-religion." It asserted itself self-consciously over against a form of religious practice that already existed, and established its identity primarily by drawing heavily loaded normative distinctions between the old ways and the new. In this sense, it was revolutionary, and, like most revolutionary movements, it relied on a rhetoric of absolute polarities.

Whatever one makes of the more controversial assertions that Assmann and others have made about Exodus, the claim that the story revolves around a dualistic division of the moral universe is hard to deny. The ethical question for a social democratic reader is therefore how to avoid being tempted to endorse some modern analogue of the story's invidious distinctions between, on the one side, the evil empire of Egypt and the evil city-dwellers of Canaan, and on the other side, the benefits of Mosaic authority and purity. These distinctions are hard to de-emphasize without depriving the story of its main characters, God and Moses, and their most characteristic modes of action. As long as such distinctions remain in the text, there is a danger that it will remain a culture in which extreme forms of nationalist hatred, unbridled political violence, and religious authoritarianism can grow. The dualism implicit in the story seems so integral to it at the level of detail that a social democratic reader who wishes to de-emphasize it necessarily risks rendering both the plot structure and the main characters of the story unrecognizable.

Walzer acknowledges that the text includes such elements, but he stresses that generations of commentators have taken pains to guarantee that the commandment, "Thou shalt utterly destroy them," "could have no practical effect" outside its original context (ER, 143). Judaism and Exodus politics, he says, are "not found in the text so much as in the interpretations of the text" (ER, 144). This claim, which appears five

---

[7] See Robert B. Coote and David Robert Ord, *The Bible's First History* (Philadelphia: Fortress Press, 1989), which places the author of the J source in the Davidic court, and interprets J's version of the Exodus story as intended primarily for the Bedouin on whom David's rule depended.

[8] Jan Assmann, *Moses the Egyptian: The Memory of Egypt in Western Monotheism* (Cambridge, Mass.: Harvard University Press, 1997), esp. chaps. 1 and 2.

pages from the end of *Exodus and Revolution*, might frustrate readers who feel that on page 8 Walzer had led them to expect that his interpretation was to be judged in terms of its capacity to account for the "actual words of Exodus and Numbers." To such readers it might well seem that when the text does not cooperate with the meaning he ascribes to it, he shifts ground, and begins talking about something other than the text — namely, the broader traditions that the text inhabits. But when I go back to the book's early pages with this move in mind, it becomes clear that Walzer, though not entirely clear about the nature of his interpretive project, was not playing a game of "bait and switch" either. He proposes "to read the text in the light of its interpretations, to discover its meaning in what it has meant" (ER, 7). Just before he emphasizes the importance of having "a firm foundation in the actual words of Exodus and Numbers," he claims that his version of the story "has had a consistent place in the interpretive literature over many centuries" (ER, 8). He appears to be saying that it is not the text, by itself, that is normative for him, but rather the traditions within which the text has been read, argued over, and used. It would seem, then, that what makes one reading of the story better than another, according to Walzer, is its dialectical relation to the various voices and elements of the tradition, taken as a whole, not simply its capacity to account for details in the text itself.

What, then, is Walzer's view of Jewish tradition, taken as a whole? He does not state his view explicitly, so I will have to infer an answer from his interpretive practice. I suggest that his interpretations are usefully compared to those of the early 20th-century thinkers who saw Judaism as a form of ethical monotheism. Judaism, thus understood, is a tradition in which monotheism emerges from polytheistic beginnings and gradually becomes ethicized. "Ethical monotheism is commonly named as ancient Israel's signal contribution to Western civilization," writes Jack Miles.

> [The] elevation of morality over other goods in human life has been honored, wherever it has been achieved, as a tempering of the otherwise unquenchable human appetites for power, wealth, pleasure, and the rest. Morality has been, in that way, the price of peace and the basis of civilization, and the form of morality dominant in the West has been decisively affected by the emergence of ethical monotheism in Israel. *Emergence* is the term of choice, for historians of religion do not believe that ethical monotheism was achieved at a stroke in ancient Israel. Though decisive moments and pivotal individuals may be named, its development was gradual.[9]

---

[9] Jack Miles, *God: A Biography* (New York: Random House, 1996), 110, 111.

Ethical monotheists interpret the tradition as heading in a direction suggested by the emergence of belief in a single god who is essentially ethical, as well as supremely powerful, a god who deserves to be worshiped for moral reasons and shows interest in the ethical behavior and moral transgressions of human beings. They view the Bible as a collection of historical materials in which one can trace this emergence. That the Bible also contains expressions of earlier stages of human religiosity is only to be expected.

For ethical monotheism the Exodus story is an especially important text to focus on precisely because of the incomplete process of ethicization one can discern there. As Miles argues, ethical topics occasionally arise in the Book of Genesis, but God shows little interest in them. In the Bible as we have it, it is not until the Book of Exodus that God's interest in ethical topics picks up. In Exodus, however, the text's characterization of God alternates between what Miles calls "the ferocious, terrifying, and often seemingly anarchic behavior of God as warrior" and the "careful, severe but measured, and sometimes relatively benign language of God as lawgiver."[10] Ethical monotheism tends to read the Exodus story backwards, from the vantage point of the later, more fully ethicized form of religiosity expressed in the major prophets. It deals with the more disturbing aspects of the text by labeling them as archaic and thus distancing itself from them. The text appears liberating rather than morally odious because the very features that would seem ethically inspiring to an ethical monotheist are taken to be *emergent* — and thus, the salient, important ones. The story's reassuring meaning is largely determined by its having been placed in a teleological context that consigns everything at odds with the ethical impulse of ethical monotheism to the role of background. The more disturbing aspects of the text are regressive in the sense that the tradition was already in the process of leaving them behind. The Egypt-Israel polarity around which the text is organized need not be repressed to bring the story's values and those of ethical monotheism into harmony, it need only be ethicized. Ethical monotheism retains early monotheism's sharp distinction between true and false religion. It can appropriate the Exodus story, the grand narrative of Israel's ancient counter-religion, by placing it in a still grander narrative of ethical progress. Once placed in this teleological context, the disturbing elements of the story diminish in significance because they are assimilated, against the grain of the surface details of the story,

---

[10]   Ibid., 111, 112.

to the Egyptian side of the Israel-Egypt polarity. The ferocious, warrior God who commands and authorizes ethnic cleansing thus becomes identified with the (Egyptian, polytheistic) past from which monotheism was still in the process of emerging.

While Walzer's reading of Exodus appears to be indebted, wittingly or not, to the interpretive habits of early 20th-century ethical monotheists, he obviously lacks what Wendell Dietrich describes as their tendency to focus "singular attention on God in contrast to all creaturely reality."[11] This comes out most clearly at the end of Walzer's discussion of Exodus, when he condenses his interpretation into three points about what the story

> first taught, or what it has commonly been taken to teach, about the meaning and possibility of politics and about its proper form:
> – first, that wherever you live, it is probably Egypt;
> – second, that there is a better place, a world more attractive, a promised land;
> – and third, that 'the way to the land is through the wilderness.' There is no way to get from here to there except by joining together and marching (ER, 149).

None of these three points essentially involves reference to God. Walzer's summary version of Exodus is one in which Israel, not God, is the story's chief protagonist. Exodus, for him, is part of a longer story about the people of Israel and what they do in response to the various situations in which they find themselves.

As a fellow social democrat, I applaud the ethical and political sentiments expressed in Walzer's three-point summary. In particular, I hold that wherever we live, it is probably Egypt — if we take this to mean simply that every human community is disfigured by injustices to which we should be attentive and by which we ourselves are apt to be corrupted. But I also want to acknowledge openly that the biblical story seems to be saying something quite different. As I read it, the story says that if you belong to Israel and succeed in maintaining the purity of a collective identity purged of Egyptian vices, you will attain divinely authorized proprietary rights to the promised land, which is not Egypt at all. To make the story say something other than this, Walzer's summary in effect refashions the story. It does so primarily in two ways. First, it diminishes God's role in the story. God, far from being what the biblical text clearly makes him out to be (that is, the agent responsible for initiating most of the story's action), becomes a feature of the scene to

---

[11] Dietrich, *Cohen and Troeltsch: Ethical Monotheistic Religion and Theory of Culture* (Atlanta: Scholars Press, 1986), 1.

which human agents respond. Second, Walzer's summary collapses the beginning and ending of the story into its middle. The story's actual structure moves from an Egyptian starting point to a middle of wandering in the desert and concludes with arrival in the promised land, the place that is not Egypt at all. Walzer's summary version of story is all middle. Its message is that we are always wandering, always somewhat corrupted by injustice, always obliged to fight against the injustice in our midst, and never likely to arrive in the place that is not Egypt.

By collapsing the beginning and ending of the Exodus story into its middle, Walzer's summary transforms it from an epic into a romance, and the values conveyed by the story in this altered form are significantly different. It is romance, and not epic, in which the protagonists are essentially wandering from one episodic adventure to another. Epic narrative needs to impose more structure than romance because it tells a story the significance of which is determined by its ending and is typically foreshadowed at the start. In the case of the Exodus, the ending is arrival in the (non-Egyptian) promised land, which is foreshadowed in early stages of the story by mass migration from Egypt. The triumphant ending, which in the story is achieved by divinely authorized conquest and ethnic cleansing, determines the significance of the whole. What David Quint says of epic endings in the Virgilian tradition could apply as well to the Exodus: "With this goal, epic linearity — the sequential linking of events — becomes a teleology: all events are led, or dictated, by an end that is their cause." "The narrative shape of this history-as-triumph," Quint adds, "bears an affinity with . . . the plot that presents a whole with its linked beginning, middle, and end. . . ."[12]

For this reason, according to Quint, epic narrative tends to be freighted with the values of an ideology of victorious nation- or empire-builders. The recipe for producing a romance, which tends to be associated with the perspective of victims or losers, is precisely to weaken the differentiations of beginning, middle, and ending in such a way that the teleological shape of the narrative, its epic linearity, dissipates. If wherever we live, even in Israel, is probably Egypt, then we are still wandering and always have been, and the episodes that make up our story will inevitably be linked together only loosely, in the manner of romance.

It is no accident, then, that Walzer is at his best as an Exodus interpreter when discussing the wandering in the desert, because his way of

---

[12] David Quint, *Epic and Empire: Politics and Generic Form from Virgil to Milton* (Princeton, N.J.: Princeton University Press, 1993), 33.

reconfiguring the story, his collapsing of the beginning and ending into the middle, implies that episodic wandering is all we've had and all we're going to get. The promised land is transformed from an actual place into a utopia in the literal sense of that term. By undermining the progressive phases of the story as it moves through time and space, Walzer's summary gives us an Exodus that never leaves Egypt and yet is always in the desert. The people never arrive in the promised land, which is now "no place" at all, and hence they never stop wandering. By such means, a triumphalist epic is transformed into a social democrat's romance of reformist struggle against persisting, ubiquitous injustice.

Collapsing the beginning and end of any nation-building epic into its middle will tend to move it in the direction of a romance of adventurous wandering and diminish its potential for justifying nationalist ambition and the associated forms of violence. A similar effect could be achieved with respect to the *Aeneid* by emphasizing the Trojans' voyage from Troy to Italy while depriving the story of both its *telos* in the founding of a future empire and the foreshadowing of that *telos* in Book 1's prophecy that Aeneas will one day

> wage tremendous war in Italy
> and crush ferocious nations and establish
> a way of life and walls for his own people.[13]

In the case of the Exodus, however, something more is achieved, because the highlighted middle contains what David Damrosch has called the "anti-epic" elements of the Exodus epic.[14] These are the elements of the story that a latter-day advocate of the prophetic ethos would want to emphasize, given that they are, in Damrosch's terms, "reoriented to monitory rather than (or as well as) celebratory emphases" (NC, 50). What the people are doing as they wander in the desert is not presented as exemplary. To the contrary, "the guidance is to be negative: the people must learn to refuse to imitate the deeds of their ancestors, and only by knowing the disasters visited upon the people in the past can the people hope to avoid repeating them in the future" (NC, 49). So in its content, the middle of this particular epic story is just what a prophetic critic would want to emphasize and make use of in his social

---

13 *The Aeneid of Virgil*, trans. Allen Mandelbaum (New York: Bantam Classic, 1981), 1.367-9.
14 David Damrosch, *The Narrative Covenant* (Ithaca, N.Y.: Cornell University Press, 1987), 47- 50; hereafter cited as "NC."

criticism. A specialist in the rhetoric of admonition will have a stake in exploiting the text's monitory resources.

No doubt, the story is going to get higher marks from social democrats once it has been reconstructed it in this way. But Walzer seems conscious, when introducing his concluding three-point summary, that he will have trouble defending the account as a claim about what the actual words of the relevant biblical books say, because he deftly shifts from the phrase "what the Exodus first taught" to the phrase "what it has commonly been taken to teach." If the Exodus did not first teach what Walzer and I want to hear, are there precedents, at least, for treating the text in the way he treats it?

Walzer is very vague on what those precedents might be, but there are certainly precedents in the modern tradition of ethical monotheism. And I think Damrosch is right to suggest that ample evidence of resistance to "the norms of epic" in interpretations of the Exodus story can be found even in Deuteronomic times. He shows that the psalmist's stated reason for retelling parts of the story in Psalm 78:5-8 is connected to the admonition that the people "should not be like their fathers, a stubborn and rebellious generation, a generation whose spirit was not faithful to God." As Damrosch explains,

> Within the psalm, this perspective has interesting narrative consequences. The poet is so unconcerned to construct a normal narrative progression that he tells events out of order, first describing the people's most insistent murmurings against God, in the wilderness (vv. 13-41), then going back to describe the plagues in Egypt (vv. 42-55), and then moving ahead to the history of the loss and recovery of the Ark in the time of Saul, concluding with the anointing of David (vv. 56-72). God's saving activity is, of course, presented in glowing contrast to the rebellious infidelity of his people, but even God's actions in history are mysterious, only barely comprehensible, and his anger against the Egyptians is hardly distinguishable from his fury at his apostate people (NC, 49).

So if Damrosch is right, the anti-epic, monitory use of the epic story has been around for a long time. Notice that even the psalmist found himself, when using the story in this way, needing to collapse the teleological structure that gives the Exodus story its "epic linearity." The psalmist, like Walzer, does give an interpretation of the story, but in the sense that a jazz artist gives an interpretation of an old standard. In "performative" interpretation of this kind, some thematic and narrative elements from the original are retained, whereas others are dropped, and the overall narrative structure of the original is abandoned completely.[15]

---

[15] For an account of several varieties of interpretation, including the performative,

The only way to vindicate such a procedure as an interpretation, however, is to relinquish the claim, implicit in most varieties of interpretation, of fidelity or adequacy to what the original text says or means. One might as well admit that, like the jazz artist, one is really trying to produce something that is superior, at least for certain purposes, to the original. A "strong," performative interpretation of Exodus can be liberating even if the original story is not.[16]

3. Prophecy as Connected Criticism

In the prophetic rhetoric and violent acts of the Calvinists who marched behind Cromwell we can find much to admire. It is a courageous and noble thing to set oneself against rulers and nations, speaking and fighting on behalf of the weak and the oppressed. There is much to admire in the prophetic critic's concern for the rights of the least he and she — much that a modern democrat owes to the Calvinist radicals of the English Revolution. But there is also much to fear in the preaching and deeds of these men. The prophetic call, as Calvin put it, "to reduce the world to order" is often couched in a language of divine violence and vengeance. It typically claims for itself the power of what Calvin called celestial truth, and brooks no opposition.

At the very end of the Exodus story (Deuteronomy 34:10-12), it is written,

> And there has not arisen a prophet since in Israel like Moses, whom Yahweh knew face to face, none like him for all the signs and the wonders which Yahweh sent him to do in the land of Egypt, to Pharaoh and to all his servants and to all his land, and for the mighty power and all the great and terrible deeds which Moses wrought in the sight of all Israel.

---

improvisational kind, see Jeffrey Stout, "The Relativity of Interpretation" *The Monist* 69/1 (1986), 103-18, esp. 113: "We can recognize jazz saxophonist Coleman Hawkins's 1939 improvisational interpretation of 'Body and Soul' as the best yet recorded without being bothered by measures in the second chorus (e.g., 9-12) that have nothing in common with the original theme save harmonic foundation. In fact, the extent of variation is closely related to its greatness, and the interpretation is clearly superior to the original." Obviously, the values involved in Hawkins's case are aesthetic. Walzer's variations on themes from Exodus are governed by ethical and political values more than aesthetic ones. It might well be that there are aesthetic reasons for preferring the canonical version or the version given in the J source (as Harold Bloom has argued).

[16] I want to thank my colleague Shaun Marmon for reading a draft of this paper and especially for her comments on this section, which have helped me improve my argument significantly.

Moses may be the greatest of the prophets, but he has in common with the later prophets that he was raised up by Yahweh to speak in Yahweh's name. In Deuteronomy 18:18, Moses quotes God as saying, "I will raise up for them a prophet like you from among their brethren; and I will put my words in his mouth, and he shall speak to them all that I command him." In thus quoting God, Moses purports to speak for him, in his name and on his authority. As Nicholas Wolterstorff has put it:

> The prophet is one who speaks *in the name of* God. As a consequence, those who hear the prophet speaking, when he is speaking in his prophetic capacity, are confronted with that which counts as God speaking; the utterance of God is not something that a person just undertakes to do; God will "raise up" the prophet, as God raised up Moses. To be a prophet requires being deputized to speak in God's name. In addition, God will tell the prophet what he is to say, putting words in his mouth; the prophet does not devise the words by himself. The prophet is commissioned to communicate a message from God, and God will give that message to the prophet.[17]

Thinkers like Hermann Cohen and Ernst Troeltsch saw Hebrew prophecy as the first full flowering of ethical monotheism in the ancient world. In their eyes, it was a pivot on which the moral and religious history of the West turns, as well as a model for their own efforts in social criticism. Because they were committed to belief in the God of the prophets, they were bound to take prophecy at face value as a divinely authorized vocation. This did not keep Cohen from using prophetic motifs as building blocks for a religion of reason; nor did it keep Troeltsch from subjecting the prophets to an aggressively sociological analysis.[18]

In Walzer's treatment of prophecy, however, the theological component of ethical monotheism is missing. So for the prophets to continue playing their role as model social critics, he finds it necessary to deemphasize their claim to speak in the name of God. "Criticism is an adversarial proceeding," Walzer says, "and the relevant comparison is between the critic and his adversary, not between critics from one culture and critics from another. And Amos's adversaries also spoke in God's name, while the adversaries of contemporary social critics usually make no such claim" (ISC, 82 n.15). All would-be prophets in ancient Israel had the same resources at their disposal, the same "authoritative texts, memories, values, practices, conventions," whether they were attacking or defending the status quo. Among their shared conventions was the claim, "Thus saith the Lord!" On Walzer's reading, this claim

---

17   Nicholas Wolterstorff, *Divine Discourse* (Cambridge: Cambridge University Press, 1995), 48, italics in original.
18   As shown in great detail in Dietrich, *Cohen and Troeltsch.*

was no more significant in its ancient context than a modern critic's claim, "It is true!"

It is important to keep in mind, however, that the Bible sets prophetic discourse within a narrative context designed to settle conflicting claims to prophetic authority, a context that can cause more trouble for modern readers than Walzer lets on. Miriam, the singer, timbrel player, and sister of Moses, was also evidently a prophetess. She may have had some access to the various critical resources Walzer enumerates. But when she asks a crucial question about Moses and his appeal to divine voices, "Has the Lord spoken only through Moses and not through the likes of Aaron and Miriam?" the Lord's response to this question is twofold: first, to assert that he is not an equal opportunity delegator of the authority to speak on his behalf; and second, to turn Miriam white as snow, to make her instantaneously leprous. He does not do the same to Aaron, who joined her in asking the question. After Moses pleads their case, Miriam's sentence is bargained down to a seven-day exile from the camp. The Bible leaves no doubt, in the end, that it does not imagine the resources of genuinely prophetic speech to be available to everyone.

One kind of religious feminism insists on the necessity of choosing between the Bible's devaluation of Miriam and democracy, and then affirms Miriam as heroine and fellow victim — doing so self-consciously against the grain of the text. A feminist reading of the Bible insists on the importance of the question, "To whom does the text belong?" If the text is the work of a redactor who is himself doing the dirty work of patriarchal consolidation by incorporating into scripture a passage in which an admittedly great prophetess and female spiritual leader is delegitimated relative to Moses, then a democrat committed to feminism will have a hard time seeing the text produced by that redactor as the expression of a liberating vision.

When a new Moses or Miriam rises up from the people, and then looks down upon us, addressing us in God's name, the democrat's habit is to say, "Get down off your pedestal and speak for yourself." Walzer seems to underestimate the frequency with which the claim, "Thus saith the Lord," is still uttered in the public square, but he is surely right in holding that it poses a threat to the democratic assumption of equal standing. What, then, can prophetic social criticism mean in a democratic culture, if not that God authorizes some but not others to speak? Walzer would like to reclaim from the prophetic heritage a style of social criticism that is compatible with democratic sympathies. When he holds up the prophet as a model social critic, he is not, therefore, endorsing the kind of privilege as a divine spokesperson that Moses is said to have enjoyed. Nor, on the other hand, is he merely praising the ethical content of what Jeremiah, Amos, and other prophets said on behalf of widows, orphans, resident aliens, and the poor. He is also making a point about the need for what he calls *connected* social critics, critics who do not aspire for critical distance of the wrong kind or go about their critical business in the wrong way. The prophet Amos is a model social critic for Walzer precisely because he is connected to the society he is criticizing. He is not radically detached. He does not stand at a great distance from Israel. He interprets a world of shared meanings. His critical conclusions are rooted in that world.

Walzer asks "how much distance critical distance is" (ISC, 36). His most memorable answer is that "critical distance is measured in inches" (ISC, 61). What are we to make of this metaphor? I will argue that Walzer is actually talking about a number of different questions, that his metaphor of distance tends to conflate these questions, and that the best way of approaching them is to distinguish them clearly and address them separately. The first question is whether it is possible (or even desirable) to escape the limitations of our particular historical and cultural perspective and view society in the light of reason itself. The second question is whether social criticism should rely heavily on highly general ideals or abstract principles. The third question is whether the social critic can or should attempt to criticize only his or her own society. The fourth is whether the social critic needs to identify with, as opposed to feeling alienated from, the society he or she is criticizing.

Each of these questions is about a distinct kind of critical distance. A careful reading shows that Walzer is at least somewhat suspicious of each kind: of critics who attempt to escape history, of critics who rely heavily on abstract principles, of critics who speak across cultural boundaries, and of critics who pride themselves in alienation or disaffiliation from their own groups. His failure to distinguish these issues tends to create the impression that Walzer's arguments are cumulative — that there is a single opponent, the champion of critical distance, against whom all the arguments gradually mount up, and a single alternative model, the connected critic, whose various traits come together in the person of the prophet. I grant that there are some critics who champion critical distance in each of the senses I have distinguished. But it is surely possible to be more selective in appraising distance than Walzer proposes to be.

Let's begin with the first question, whether it is possible to escape from history and view our society "objectively" from the perspective of eternity or universal reason. According to Walzer, most social critics these days want to view us from afar. They fear that standing too close would blind them to the realities they propose to criticize. So when Walzer said, in *Spheres of Justice*, that he doesn't claim to have achieved any great distance from the social world in which he lives, it may have struck many readers as a revealing, and especially damaging, admission. But Walzer wasn't expressing shame or even modesty; he was simply indicating where he thought he had to stand in carrying out the task he had undertaken. Anyone,who wants, as Walzer does, "to interpret to one's fellow citizens the world of meanings that we share," cannot afford too much distance from that world. Stand too far back, and that world "loses its particular contours and takes on a general shape."[19] Interpretive social criticism is an inside job, an act of intimacy, a lover's quarrel. It needs a connected critic, not a radically detached one.

Walzer turns away from the paths of discovery and invention, which lead away from the moral world we already inhabit up to the heavens, a God's-eye view, the perspective of eternity. Only far above the city, we are commonly told, is critical perspective possible: that is where to discover or invent the principles of our criticism. Walzer, in contrast, prefers the path of interpretation. He stays in the city, walking its streets and squares with his fellow citizens, rising no higher than the top of a soap box. His social criticism is a kind of reflexive ethnography. It begins and ends at home, with its feet on the ground, making do with tools it finds at hand. Its method is participant-observation, its principal aim the critical understanding of familiar goings-on. It takes its stand within a particular cultural tradition, and it relies throughout on the critical practices of the tradition itself.

The interpretive social critic, to vary the metaphor, is in the same boat with the rest of us. As Walzer puts it in his discussion of Camus, the critic is "one of the crew, who can't leave before the passengers."[20] The boat, of course, is Neurath's — the one made famous by Quine. The vessel of critical thought can never be brought into dry-dock for complete overhaul but must be repaired, plank by plank, while remaining at sea. Plank repair is carried out on board, over deep waters. If you rip out too many planks at once, the boat sinks.

---

[19] Michael Walzer, *Spheres of Justice: A Defense of Pluralism and Equality* (New York: Basic Books, 1983), xiv.
[20] Michael Walzer, "Commitment and Social Criticism: Camus's Algerian War," *Dissent* 31 (1984): 431.

But this image makes some of us feel the need for critical distance all the more. Isn't Neurath's boat in fact a floating prison, a prison-house of language, a ship of fools? Isn't the social critic who remains on board condemned to preserve its fundamentals? What if the hull is rotten, eaten away by the acids of human desire and self-deception, as we have every reason to expect? What can interpretive social criticism do besides rearranging the deck chairs or repainting the captain's quarters?

Walzer's response is that we are all in Neurath's boat, whether or not we yearn for solid footing, and that we had better acknowledge it. Stand as far back as you please from any set of parochial commitments — as far back as your favorite radical critic has actually managed to stand — and you will still be in a particular culture at a specific point in its voyage through time. And that is not necessarily a bad place to be. Neurath's boat can become a prison, but it needn't be one. We lose nothing by admitting our place in it except the illusion of complete transcendence — a bad model of critical distance. The only alternative is to jump ship, which is madness, the death of critical thought.

This line of response is what makes Cornel West identify Walzer (and me, for that matter) with the pragmatic strand in American philosophical and social thought.[21] All three of us stress that the social critic speaks from within some culture at a particular point in its history and that the critic's task is to make the most of the critical tools available in that location, not to criticize society from a perfectly universal point of view above the fray. Why not? First, because there is no such point of view. Second, because when critics believe that they have achieved a perfectly universal point of view, not only are they guilty of hubris and self-deception, they are also sorely tempted to relax the habits of self-criticism. Third, because when critics rigorously avoid relying on critical tools obviously indebted to their own cultural-historical location, they are foolishly depriving themselves of concepts, arguments, and images that might well improve the subtlety, incisiveness, and appeal of their social criticism.

All of this seems right to me as a pragmatic critique of the philosopher's desire for complete transcendence of the society he or she would like to criticize. But I wonder whether it can be fully squared with holding up the prophets as model social critics. Walzer is right to emphasize that Amos, his chief exemplar, was in fact making use of ancient Judaic cultural tools in formulating his criticisms of ancient Israel. Amos was

---

[21] Cornel West, *The American Evasion of Philosophy* (Madison: University of Wisconsin Press, 1989), 3.

no philosopher worshiping at the shrine of universal reason. He was, however, claiming to speak from a point of view not that of a finite human being in a particular time and place. What point of view? Yahweh's, which is to say a God's-eye point of view. Walzer mentions this fact about Amos only in passing. This move not only plays down the religious dimension of the biblical materials, it leaves unaddressed the crucial issue of how a prophet like Amos acquired his authority as a social critic. One could easily get the impression, if one relied entirely on Walzer, that Amos wasn't a charismatic leader of ecstatics, but that is exactly what he was.

So far, we have touched only on the first kind of critical distance. Now let's turn to the second. Knowing that it is impossible to escape history completely doesn't tell us where in our cultural tradition to stand when practicing social criticism. The advocates of radical detachment and highly general principles could still be standing in the right place — the crow's nest, perhaps — even if they shouldn't have called it the perspective of eternity, even if the view from nowhere turned out to be somewhere after all.

Walzer argues against criticism from the crow's nest, but less conclusively than he argues against the hope for dry-dock. He thinks that the crow's nest's allure is its illusion of complete transcendence. If the illusion is dispelled, we need to be told why its vantage point is better than that of critics who stay down below, striving for thick descriptions rather than abstract principles. We should judge critics not by the alleged privilege of their standpoints but by the quality of the criticism they produce. Interpretive critics learn more, he thinks, by standing closer. Their thick descriptions engage with the ordinary motivations of fellow citizens and illumine the details of ordinary lives. Criticism from the crow's nest does not. It needs to be imposed from above, often coercively, through "an unattractive politics" (64). It has trouble telling us, without resort to "manipulation and compulsion," why we down on the deck should be moved by considerations that seem salient only from a distant and abstract point of view.

Walzer's opponents will have a different story to tell about the effects of critical distance. Any form of criticism can lead to an unattractive, coercive politics. The detached viewpoint of the philosopher is meant to expose harmful prejudice and constrain violent emotion. If some champions of detachment have behaved poorly in politics, this does not show, by itself, that detachment is itself responsible. It could show rather that some champions of detachment aren't as detached as they claim or that they're detached in the wrong way. Furthermore, the doubt lingers that connected critics are bound to be insufficiently radical, that despite their protestations to the contrary, their criticism tends to be merely cosmetic.

The history of social criticism, according to Walzer, proves otherwise. Nearly all social criticism, from Amos and Jeremiah to Camus and King, has come from connected critics, and much of it has been very radical indeed. This reply can be answered if Walzer's long line of connected critics turns out to be relying, implicitly or explicitly, on the principles of detachment. My guess is that they won't, that Walzer is right about the history of social criticism. My worry, however, is that his way of contrasting interpretation with discovery and invention sometimes suggests less scope for critical innovation than he actually wants to maintain.

As I put the point in another context: "Neurath's boat can travel the open seas, trade with foreign places, and send parties ashore in search of virgin timber. Its crew can take unimagined treasures on board, plunder shipwrecks for usable gear, and invent an engine to pull weight once pulled by oar."[22] That is why it needn't be a prison. Criticism benefits from thick description of its immediate surroundings, but also from dredging up old documents, from long visits to strange places, from flights of artistic imagination — from all the ways in which new moral possibilities can be brought into view. It does not simply rearrange cargo already on board.

The most interesting social critics, the Hebrew prophets not least among them, interpret shared meanings, but they also make something new out of the linguistic materials they find around them.[23] They remove, replace, retrieve, reorder, and reassemble parts of a cultural inheritance. The resulting invention can be a new vocabulary of criticism. A new vocabulary makes new claims and counter-claims possible, allowing us, if we are lucky, to discover things undreamt of by our ancestors. By making something new out of something found, the critic can find out new things — moral truths, for example, about the evil of slavery, the rights of women, or the value of separating church and state.

---

[22] Jeffrey Stout, *Ethics after Babel*, expanded edition (Princeton: Princeton University Press, 2001), 58f.

[23] Walzer is surely aware of this, but he calls attention to the creative dimension of interpretive criticism only rarely. He does so most explicitly in the following comments on the prophets: "[T]he coherence of Israelite religion is more a consequence than a precondition of the work of the prophets. . . . In fact, the prophets pick and choose among the available materials. . . . They are parasitic upon the past, but they also give shape to the past upon which they are parasitic" (ISC, 82-3).

Walzer says: "The claim of interpretation is simply this: that neither discovery nor invention is necessary because we already possess what they pretend to provide" (ISC, 19). I want to say: Criticism begins with interpretation, but it progresses to invention and discovery. I share Walzer's suspicions about the *paths* of discovery and invention, his doubts about the standard philosophical accounts of social criticism, but I am dubious of his apparent dismissal of discovery and invention.[24] Social criticism can be connected — eschewing both dry-dock and crow's nest — without being merely interpretive. It need not exclude discovery and invention.

When Walzer inveighs against too much critical distance, he isn't saying that James Baldwin should have stayed home in Harlem instead of criticizing American racism from abroad. The distance in question is metaphorical, but, as we have already seen, the metaphor isn't univocal. So far, we have distinguished two kinds of distance avoided by connected critics. One is the mythical distance of escape from history to a God's-eye point of view. The other is the philosophical detachment of abstract principles. Walzer's complaint about the first is that it is impossible. His complaint about the second is that it makes for bad criticism. Different arguments support each complaint. The former are more conclusive than the latter. But that is not the end of the matter, for there are at least two more kinds of distance to consider. One of these I shall call cultural distance, the other alienation.

By cultural distance, I mean the kind of difference in habit and attitude that separates us from members of some culture or historical epoch to which we do not belong. Can Walzerian social criticism move across cultural boundaries? Can those of us in one boat perform social criticism of another? Walzer does not deny that this is possible. His claim is that such criticism can be truly good (and social in the fullest sense) only if it approximates what the connected critic does from within. "The outsider can become a *social* critic," Walzer writes, "only if he manages to get himself inside, enters imaginatively into local practices and arrangements" (ISC, 39, his italics).

---

[24] Walzer's low regard for discovery seems related to the form of relativism asserted in the final chapter of *Spheres of Justice*, but I do not have space to pursue the matter here. Walzer claims, "A given society is just if its substantive life is lived in a certain way — that is, in a way faithful to the shared understandings of the members" (313). Even if the shared understandings of the members depend essentially on falsehoods? For an extended discussion of relativism and an account of moral philosophy that leaves room for interpretation, discovery, and invention, see *Ethics after Babel*, part 1.

What does this mean? Walzer does not say. But it surely doesn't mean adopting the other culture's attitudes or endorsing its practices and arrangements. Critical outsiders, like Tocqueville or Tutu in their visits to America, may need to approximate the insider's intimate knowledge of detail if they want their criticism to acquire depth and resonance. They don't, however, need to commit themselves to our practices, believe what we do, or become one of us.

Walzer says at one point that "[a]n enemy is not recognizable as a social critic; he lacks standing" (ISC, 59). This comment is true enough, if it means only that human beings often refuse to give standing to their enemies, more or less automatically discounting what they say. But sometimes even enemies can get through with social criticism we have to take seriously. Even if they don't, their criticism can still serve its purpose. Social criticism directed against one group can be addressed to another. The liberation theologian may declare herself an enemy of the colonial oppressors, hurling justified criticism at them, as the oppressors turn a deaf ear. The primary audience, however, may well be her fellow victims of oppression, whom she hopes to conscript into the anti-colonial struggle. She may lack standing with the enemy she criticizes, but not with the audience she means to address.

It is worth noting that Walzer's book, *Just and Unjust Wars*, assumes the possibility of social criticism across cultural boundaries. To know whether we have just cause in going to war, we must be able to say, from whatever cultural distance, that another nation has behaved unjustly toward us. And, as Walzer says, we may be obliged to intervene in affairs of another sovereign state — when, for example, "the violation of human rights within a set of boundaries is so terrible that it makes talk of community or self-determination or 'arduous struggle' seem cynical and irrelevant."[25] It is hard to see how we can know such obligations without practicing social criticism against actual and potential enemies.

In fact, Walzer excels at social criticism of his enemies. He was a persistent and effective critic of Soviet tyranny, and some of his most interesting criticism in the 1980s was directed against so-called authoritarian regimes.[26] In these cases he judged other governments and societies from a cultural distance, but we, Walzer's fellow citizens, were the intended audience. We need social criticism of this kind if we want

---

[25] Michael Walzer, *Just and Unjust Wars* (New York: Basic Books, 1977), 90.
[26] Michael Walzer, "Totalitarianism vs. Authoritarianism: The Theory of Tyranny, the Tyranny of Theory," *Dissent* 28 (1981): 400-3; "On Failed Totalitarianism," *Dissent* 30 (1983): 297-306.

to conduct ourselves justly in forming and breaking alliances with other states. The rejoinder that such criticism is not *social* reduces the dispute to a verbal quibble.

Walzer grants that Amos "prophesies against nations other than Israel," but when he does so, Walzer thinks, he is appealing in a necessarily thin way to a minimal code that governs "our contacts with all humanity." The importance of the prophetic model lies elsewhere, in Walzer's view. "It is a mistake," he says,

> to praise the prophets for their universalist message. For what is most admirable about them is their particularist quarrel, which is also, they tell us, God's quarrel, with the children of Israel. Here they invested their anger and their poetic genius" (ISC, 91-93).

Amos is a great prophet, Walzer thinks, because of the marvelously detailed way in which he draws upon a rich reservoir of shared meanings when speaking to his own people about their own transgressions. The God he imagines poetically is a connected social critic in the same sense that Amos himself is, for they are both parties to a covenant that involves the children of Israel, and they both draw on the shared meanings and common history that constitute Israel as a people.

> The line that Amos attributes to God, 'You only have I known of all the families of the earth,' could have come from his own heart. He knows one nation, one history, and it is that knowledge which makes his criticism so rich, so radical, so concrete (ISC, 93f.).

Walzer's interpretation of Jonah is meant to illustrate the vacuity of criticism directed across cultural boundaries. Jonah is a poor model for social criticism, according to Walzer, precisely because his mission is not to Israel but to Nineveh. I am happy to grant that Jonah is not a model social critic, but I think Walzer misses the main point of the Book of Jonah. I read the book, following Joseph Blenkinsopp, as a highly sophisticated, artful, and ironic critique of prophecy in the name of Yahweh's freedom, his sovereignty, and his compassion for people outside Israel.[27] It is an antinationalist critique of prophets. Why does the author of the book choose Jonah as a foil for this critique? Probably because a man of that name had acquired a reputation as an optimistic nationalist who predicted the fall of Nineveh. The author deliberately picks Jonah because his prediction did not come true. Nineveh did not fall until a century and a half later. So here the predictive aspect of

---

[27] Joseph Blenkinsopp, *A History of Prophecy in Israel: From the Settlement in the Land to the Hellenistic Period* (Philadelphia: Westminster Press, 1983), 268-73.

prophecy — another dimension largely ignored by Walzer and played down in ethical monotheism — is placed in question. In earlier parts of the story, Jonah's nationalism is satirized by juxtaposing him with pagan sailors whose behavior is presented as superior to his. Jonah is subsequently portrayed as someone resentful of Yahweh's freedom to change his mind. He has reluctantly heeded Yahweh's call and predicted the downfall of Nineveh. Walzer is right to point out that the author implicitly draws our attention to the Genesis story of Abraham and Sodom. But the point of doing so seems to have been that Abraham intercedes on Sodom's behalf, recognizing the possibility, rooted in divine freedom and compassion, that Yahweh will repent. Jonah does not intercede. To his surprise and consternation, the people of Nineveh respond positively, repent of their sins, and convert. Yahweh, seeing this, changes his mind compassionately and withdraws the harsh fate he has planned for Nineveh.

As Blenkinsopp has put it,

> [t]he most important implication of the story is that the freedom of God is not constrained even by the prophetic word. . . . More specifically and unexpectedly, he is free to respond graciously to true repentance and prayer on the part of Gentiles, even of traditional and archetypal enemies of Israel like the Assyrians. The irony is that *they* understand this but the prophet does not.[28]

Walzer's reading of Jonah is intended to show that Jonah is not a model social critic because he stands at too great a cultural distance from Nineveh. What Walzer ignores is the book's powerful critique of prophets who are blind to the virtues of neighboring peoples, narrowly nationalist in their moral outlook, and overconfident in their ability to predict the future even on the basis of Yahweh's word.

Let me now turn to the fourth and last kind of critical distance, the kind involving alienation or disaffiliation from one's own people. "The connected social critic can still say no to his own people, even when survival is at stake," Walzer writes, "it's just that he can't give up his principled interest in survival."[29] Walzer admires the prophets as critics who do not place the cause of justice over love of their own people. Principled interest in the survival of one's community comes first. Without it, Walzer thinks, commitment to justice makes no sense or becomes a dangerous abstraction. But one needn't believe this to be a connected

---

28   Blenkinsopp, *A History of Prophecy in Israel,* 271.
29   This comment comes from Walzer's response to David Bromwich in *Dissent* 32 (1985): 256-7.

critic in other senses of the term, and maybe we shouldn't believe it. The virtue of justice may be needed, not least of all, in determining the limits of love for one's community and when one ought to leave it or perhaps even let it die. Some connected critics express love for their community's way of life partly by refusing to act unjustly under any circumstances. It may be that their unwillingness to act unjustly contributes more to the survival of that way of life than acting unjustly in a situation of supreme emergency ever will.

Connected critics dissent. They question or denounce specific convictions and commitments held by their fellows. In that sense, they move away from us, become alienated, perhaps severely so. They can even suffer exile, literally or figuratively, as a result. But they do not, according to Walzer, quit the community. They do not cease thinking of themselves as one of us.

It would indeed be foolish for somebody to seek complete alienation from the community as an end in itself or in order to achieve the distance essential to social criticism. Walzer is right to suspect Sartre: his disaffiliation was phony, his disregard for the French Algerians heartlessly abstract, his silence on FLN terrorism hypocritical. I am reminded of Richard Rorty's telling remark that Sartre hated the bourgeoisie more than he loved anything else. I agree with Walzer, against Edward Said and others, when he says that Camus's loyalty to a particular community served social criticism better, even when it reduced him to silence. But Sartre and Camus aren't our only possible models, any more than the prophets are.

If extreme alienation turns the critic into an outsider, of sorts, what value is there in that? Perhaps more than Walzer lets on. If Tocqueville and Tutu, speaking as outsiders, can make us listen, why not the local critic who cannot in good conscience any longer identify with us? Extreme alienation need not be sought as an end in itself or as a means to critical distance, and it need not mean completely curtailing one's love or becoming a public enemy. It may simply be the unwanted outcome of commitment to justice at a moment when complicity in the people's injustice would itself be unjust. There may be circumstances in which love of justice moves me to renounce membership in my community. If that happens, and I state my reasons to my former compatriots, do I cease being a social critic? Will I fail to get through to them? Not necessarily. If they respect my judgment, and my renunciation rings true, it may speak eloquently to them. For all its possible inauthenticity, Simone de Beauvoir's insistence in 1958 that she was no longer a member of the French people still touched a nerve in France.

Gandhi, to take a better exemplar, enacted more than one symbolic disaffiliation. Each seems, from my historical and cultural distance, to have been authentic. Each had powerful effect as a moral statement. Together they make social identity seem more ambiguous, more open to realignment and moral scrutiny, than Walzer's examples would suggest. In one case, Gandhi marched to the sea and made salt, thereby breaking British law. He was saying to his British masters, on behalf of his fellows Indians: No, I will not be one of you, an empire's subject. Reidentifying himself as an independent Indian, not subject to British law, helped create the independent India of which he wanted to be a part.

In another case, toward the end of his life, he fasted while Muslims and Hindus tore newly independent India to shreds. He was saying: If this be India, I cannot take part. Few instances of social criticism have been felt more deeply by more people in any age. Gandhi loved India. In standing back from it, he wished it well, hoped for its survival. His loyalty to the community expressed itself in commitment to the virtues of that community at its best. Those virtues, in turn, excluded some means absolutely and set limits on his willingness to be a member in good standing.

In most of this section I have been considering the question of "how much distance critical distance is" and Walzer's answer that "critical distance is measured in inches." It should now be clear that the question conflates many distinct issues and that the answer is apt to make some kinds of distance seem less worthy than they are. I have tried to sort out the various kinds and to show that they require separate treatment, but it is equally important to see that once we give up the hope for a God's-eye point of view, whether it be the kind sought by philosophers or the kind claimed by prophets, there is little point to the general question of where to stand. I will elaborate on this conclusion in a moment.[30]

4. *Concluding Reflections*

The upshot of Walzer's biblically oriented work, I have suggested, is a prophetic conception of social criticism strongly reminiscent of the left-leaning ethical monotheism that German thinkers like Hermann Cohen and Ernst Troelstch worked out in the early decades of the 20th

---

[30] I presented the main arguments from this section of the paper at a plenary session of the Society of Christian Ethics a number of years ago. I wish to thank Michael Walzer for his generous response on that occasion.

century. One need only read Wendell S. Dietrich's elegant comparative study of Cohen and Troeltsch with Walzer in mind to be struck by the uncanny way in which their favored themes and questions — Troeltsch's especially — re-emerge in Walzer's work.[31] It would be inaccurate to characterize Walzer either as committed to ethical mono-theism or as self-consciously influenced by its principal exponents, but his relation to this tradition does shed light, I think, on the approach he takes as an interpreter of the Bible.

While it seems unlikely that he has looked closely at predecessors like Cohen and Troeltsch, and while he is always careful to avoid rely-ing on theological commitments like theirs, his interpretive practice is hard to make sense of without ascribing some of their assumptions to him — in particular, assumptions about the normative significance of the prophetic ethos in a reconstruction of the Jewish tradition, about the importance of the monitory middle of the Exodus story from the vantage point of that ethos, about the progressive ethicization of religion over the

---

[31] Walzer, like Cohen, is a Jewish philosopher, but his methodological commit-ments and his emphasis on cultural particularity more nearly resemble those of Troeltsch, a Christian theologian. Cohen belonged to the Marburg school of neo-Kantianism, whereas Troeltsch belonged to the Heidelberg Southwest Baden school. According to the latter, Kantian ideas, though important, need to be cor-rected by Hegel's insistence on viewing "religious beliefs and social ethical views as conditioned by and expressions of a social situation" (Dietrich, *Cohen and Troeltsch*, 2). As Dietrich argues in chap. 3, the Baden school accused Marburg neo-Kantian-ism of "being excessively formalistic, abstract and empty" (50) and of failing to do justice to the historical and cultural contexts in which normative ideas arise. Cohen, in a manner more like Ronald Green's or Thomas Nagel's than like Walzer's, stressed the importance of transcending one's own historical situation when engaging in normative thinking. Troeltsch was an interpretive thinker, struggling against Kantian formalism, in much the way Walzer now does. There is also an interesting parallel between Troeltsch's normative social theory and Walzer's important work on "complex equality" and "spheres of justice." "In Troeltsch's judgment, each differentiated sphere of culture is to be permitted to stand in relative independence without the attempt being made to demonstrate that sphere's evident or implicit religious significance. That is what taking seriously the secularization of modern culture means" (Dietrich, 27). Cf. Michael Walzer, *Spheres of Justice* (New York: Basic Books, 1983), esp. chap. 10. Also consider Walzer's *Thick and Thin: Moral Argument at Home and Abroad* (Notre Dame, Ind.: University of Notre Dame Press, 1994) in light of the following passage from Troeltsch's *Christian Thought: Its History and Application*, trans. Baron R. von Hügel (Westport, Conn.: Hyperion Press, 1979), 23f.: "What was really common to mankind, and universally valid for it, seemed, in spite of a general kinship and capacity for mutual understanding, to be at bottom exceedingly little, and to belong more to the province of material goods than to the ideal values of civilisation."

course of many centuries of human development, and about the value of reading the Bible primarily as a vehicle and reflection of such ethicization. Walzer does not explicitly endorse those assumptions, and he might be inclined to reject them once they are made explicit, but he would then need to offer some other way of justifying his interpretations of the Bible. I, for one, do not see how it can be done.

Walzer resembles the ethical monotheists, first, in selecting the Exodus story and prophets like Amos and Isaiah as his main points of biblical reference. He resembles them, second, in extracting from the selected biblical texts an essentially uplifting ethical impulse that is compatible with — and, indeed, meant to inspire — commitment to social democracy. He does this, as we have seen, by highlighting many of the same features of the texts that the ethical monotheists did while playing down features that appear to conflict with the kind of ethical message he and they would like to derive. One question that arises from this essay is how to vindicate the selectivity of his interpretations without resorting to his predecessors' assumptions about progressive ethicization. Another is how to retain the ethical emphases of ethical monotheism's readings of biblical texts to the extent that Walzer does while eliminating the theological dimension of his predecessors' position.

The thing that allowed his predecessors to play down aspects of biblical texts they deemed ethically retrograde was their claim to be interpreting the text from the cutting edge of advancing ethicization, for this is what justified highlighting the ethically "emergent" aspects of those texts at the expense of aspects that offend modern democratic sensibilities. If the contemporary significance of a biblical text consists in the contribution it has made to the process of ethicization, then aspects of the text that appear retrograde, from the vantage point of advancing ethicization, can safely be played down as inessential to its significance for us. But we have seen that Walzer plays down the theological aspects of the texts in much the same way that he and the ethical monotheists play down episodes that strike them as ethically retrograde in comparison with "the prophetic ethos" at its best. If he intends to justify his interpretive practice without relying on hermeneutical assumptions like those of his predecessors, Walzer owes us an explanation of how he proposes to do so.

The most straightforward way for Walzer to exploit the hermeneutical assumptions of his predecessors while maintaining distance from their theological preoccupations would be to say that while the idea of one God who cares about the ethical traits and deeds of his people may once have represented an ethical advance over previous forms of religious discourse, it can now safely be pushed away as a ladder for which we no longer have an essential use. Whether this is what he wants to say, I do not know. What seems clear, in any event, is that the themes and interpretive habits of the ethical monotheists continue to exert influence, however indirectly or unwittingly, on intellectuals who care about what the Bible says.

As for the question of critical distance, it is clear that all social critics stand somewhere, and that they are all bound to select and interpret the critical resources they draw upon. On these two points I agree entirely with Walzer. But I would argue that there is no particular distance from the object of criticism that makes the product of a social critic's labor good or bad. Good social criticism does not first find the right distance from its object and then fire away while holding its ground. It begins wherever it happens to be, struggles with whatever temptations present themselves under the circumstances, and travels whatever intellectual, emotional, and social distance from its object that the struggle demands.

The real interest of critical distance as a metaphor and of prophecy as a model for secular social criticism resides in those temptations: where to expect them, how to identify them, how to overcome them. The received view of critical distance that Walzer wants to displace has the virtue of drawing attention to the dangers of proximity and attachment: narrow-mindedness, bias, complacency, sloth, wishful thinking about the prospects of melioration, the unconscious desire to mask our complicity in injustice, an inability to empathize with those outside our circle, and so on. Walzer's secularized prophetic model, with its image of the critic as a party to a lover's quarrel, draws needed attention to the dangers of distance: the self-deception of perfect objectivity, the costs of abstraction and enmity, the false postures of romantic solitude, the unattractive politics of manipulation and compulsion, and so on.

But no vantage point is free from danger. Wherever social critics stand — whether with Moses or Miriam, Amos or Jonah, Sartre or Camus, Baldwin or Gandhi — temptations will abound. The perils of critical thought are insidious not only because they are so often shrouded in unconscious desire but also because each masquerades as an innocent means for avoiding the rest. As we step away from one trap, we risk falling backwards into another. We do well to remind ourselves of this as we draw our morals from Walzer's praise of connected criticism. For the dangers of close connection remain real, even if detached philosophers and Sartrian traitors have described them in the wrong terms and recommended the wrong remedies.

Where, then, do the best social critics stand? Neither here nor there. The best social critics are virtue in motion. We know them by the character of their movement from here to there. They need enough wisdom to recognize the temptations of each critical posture they assume and the ability to change position, courageously but temperately, as justice requires.[32]

---

[32] I wish to thank the editors for helpful comments on an earlier draft of this paper and especially for the opportunity to honor Wendell Dietrich's career as a teacher and scholar. My first exposure to Wendell came in the spring semester of 1970, when my radical friends and I all decided to enroll in his course on 19th-century Christian thought. Somehow we all ended up in the same discussion section, debating Hegel, Marx, Nietzsche, and the rest under Wendell's direction. None of us found it disturbing that Wendell's lectures were densely packed with information or that he had apparently never been schooled in the rhetorical techniques of eye-contact, informality, and animated inflection. We cared about the material, and knew that this man, in his own way and for his own reasons, cared about it too. He was evidently prepared to put every bit of his considerable intellectual powers into explaining it to us. I soaked up every word he uttered — until the semester ended somewhat prematurely when the student body went on "strike," with the faculty's official blessing, in response to Nixon's invasion of Cambodia. One unintended consequence of the strike was that we had the whole summer to work on our papers for Wendell's course. Mine was on Hegel. The extra time and the heightened sense of relevance combined to make that paper my first genuinely scholarly performance. After that I took every course in Wendell's sequence on the history of Christian thought, except for the course on early Christian thought, which I first audited from Wendell and took for credit when Giles Milhaven offered it a year later. This, by the way, was in the days before Jewish materials had made their way into Wendell's curricular offerings. It is to Wendell, more than to anyone else, that I owe my knowledge of Christian thought and my historically oriented scholarly conscience. Indeed, it was while reading Troeltsch and others with Wendell, not while conversing with Michael Walzer and Richard Rorty at Princeton some years later, that I first acquired both my interest in the issues treated in this essay and my preference for historical and praxis-oriented approaches to ethical and religious thought. I suspect that Wendell was quite taken aback when I asked him to read a passage from the Bible at my wedding, but it seemed only fitting to have him there along with many of my friends who had taken his course together in the spring of 1970. I look back with fondness and gratitude on what Wendell contributed to my life almost 30 years ago, and am pleased to count him among my friends today.

CURRICULUM VITAE

Wendell Sanford Dietrich

Professor of Religious Studies and Professor of Judaic Studies
Brown University, Providence, RI

Education

1951	A.B., *summa cum laude*, Princeton University
1954	B.D. *magna cum laude*, Yale University Divinity School
1961	Ph.D., Yale University, Religion

Dissertation Topic: Christ and the Church according to Barth and His Roman Catholic Critics

Academic Appointments

1958-60　Instructor, Department of Religious Studies, Brown University

1960-65　Assistant Professor, Department of Religious Studies, Brown University

1965-71　Associate Professor, Department of Religious Studies, Brown University

1971-2000 Professor of Religious Studies, Brown University

1981　Visiting Professor of Religion, Dartmouth College, Winter and Spring Semesters

1984-2000 Professor of Judaic Studies, Program in Judaic Studies, Brown University

1987　Visiting Professor of Religion, Princeton University, Spring Semester

1995,1998 Visiting Professor, Kaplan Centre for Jewish Studies, University of Capetown, South Africa

2000-　Professor Emeritus of Religious Studies, Professor Emeritus of Judaic Studies, Brown University

Books

Cohen and Troeltsch: Ethical Monotheistic Religion and Theory of Culture
Brown Judaic Studies, Scholars Press, 1986.

Chapters

"Calvin's Scriptural Ethical Monotheism: Interpretation, Moral Conscience and Religious System," *Faith and History: Essays in Honor of Paul W. Meyer* (John T. Carroll, Charles H. Cosgrove, E. Elizabeth Johnson, eds.) Scholars Press, (1991). 360-377.

"The Character and Status of the Concept of History in Three Twentieth Century Systems of Judaic Thought: Cohen, Rosenzweig, Levinas," *From Ancient Israel to Modern Judaism: Intellect in Quest of Understanding: Essays in Honor of Marvin Fox* (Jacob Neusner, Ernest Frerichs, Nahum H. Sarna, eds.) III, 199-211, Scholars Press. 1989.

"Is Rosenzweig an Ethical Monotheist: A Debate with the New Francophone Literature," *Der Philosoph Franz Rosenzweig (1886-1929) Internationaler Kongress Kassel 1986* (Wolfdietrich Schmied-Kowarzik, ed.) Freiburg: Karl-Alber-Verlag, 1988. 891-902.

"*Nostra Aetate*: A Typology of Theological Tendencies," *Unanswered Questions: Theological Views of Jewish-Catholic Relations*, University of Notre Dame Press, 1988, 2nd printing, 1995, 70-81.

"*Gaudium et Spes* and Haering's Personalism," *Oecumenica: Jahrbuch fuer oekumenische Forschung* (1968), Friedrich W. Kantzenbach and Vilmos Vajta, eds., Gutersloher Verslagshaus Gerd Mohn, 1968, 274-83.

"Yves Congar: The Church as Structured Communion," *The New Day: Catholic Theologians of the Renewal* (William Jerry Boney and Lawrence E. Molumby, eds.). Richmond, VA., John Knox Press, 1968, 21-33.

Refereed Journal Articles

"Troeltsch's Treatment of the Thomist Synthesis in *The Social Teaching* as a Signal of His View of a New Cultural Synthesis," *The Thomist*, 57 (1993): 381-402

"Shear-Yashuv's *Steinheim*," *Jewish Quarterly Review*, LXXXII (1992): 519-524

"Franz Rosenzweig: Recent Works in French," *Religious Studies Review* 13:2 (April, 1987): 97-103.

"Loisy and the Liberal Protestants," *Studies in Religion/Sciences Religieuses: Revue Canadienne/A Canadian Journal* 141 (1985): 303-311

"The Function of the Idea of Messianic Mankind in Hermann Cohen's Later Thought," *Journal of the Academy of Religion* XLVII (1980): 246-58.

Review article: Heinrich Ott, *Reality and Faith: The Theological Legacy of Dietrich Bonhoeffer, Theology Today* XXIX (1973): 449-53.
Review article: *Openings for Marxist-Christian Dialogue* (Thomas W. Ogletree, ed.), *Theology Today* XXVI (1969): 208-11.

Non-Refereed Journal Articles

"Jewish Perspectives on Christianity: Review Essay on Fritz Rothschild's *Jewish Perspectives on Christianity: Leo Baeck, Martin Buber, Franz Rosenzweig, Will Herberg, and Abraham Heschel, Midstream XXXXIV*: 1 (1998): 38-41.
"The Contextualization of Roman Catholic Modernism," in *Revisionist Modernism: Working Papers of the Roman Catholic Modernism Seminar* (1994): 87-90
"Rupp's *Culture Protestantism: German Liberal Theology at the Turn of the Twentieth Century,*" *Culture Protestantism and Catholic Modernism: Papers for the 1977 Annual Meeting of the AAR, Nineteenth Century Working Group*, 1977: 17-25.

Invited Lectures

"Three Early Twentieth Century Jewish Appraisals of Christianity: Rosenzweig, Buber, and Baeck," [revised version], Robert P. and Theresa Goldman Memorial Lecture, Hebrew Union College - Jewish Institute of Religion, Cincinnati, March 24, 1999.
"Three Early Twentieth Century Jewish Appraisals of Christianity: Rosenzweig, Buber, and Baeck," Kaplan Centre for Jewish Studies, University of Capetown, South Africa, August 12, 1998.
"The University of Capetown as an Instrument of Change in South Africa: The Role of Religious Studies," Africa Group, Watson Institute for International Studies, Brown University, February 12, 1998.
"An Assessment of Contemporary South African Jewish Studies," University of Durban-Westville, Durban, South Africa, August 22, 1995.
"Mordecai Kaplan and Contemporary American Judaic Religious Thought," Department of Religious Studies, University of the Western Cape, Bellville, South Africa, August 10, 1995.
"Reading Mordecai Kaplan in South Africa," Kaplan Centre for Jewish Studies, University of Capetown, South Africa, August 8, 1995.
"The Character and Status of the Concept of History in Three Twentieth Century Systems of Judaic Thought: Cohen, Rosenzweig, Levinas,"

Colloquium of the Jewish Studies Program, University of Washington, Seattle. October, 1988.

"The Concept of History in Some Twentieth Century Systems of Judaic Thought: Cohen, Rosenzweig, Fackenheim," University of Pennsylvania, Department of Religious Studies seminar on "History, Historiography and Religion," Semester II, 1986-87, March 27, 1987.

"Is Rosenzweig an Ethical Monotheist?" Princeton University, March 26, 1987.

"Is Rosenzweig an Ethical Monotheist? A Debate with the New Francophone Literature," Internationale Franz Rosenzweig- Konferenz Gesamthochschule Kassel Universitat, Kassel, West Germany, December, 1986.

"*Nostra Aetate*: A Typology of Theological Tendencies." "*Nostra Aetate*: A Symposium on Catholic-Jewish Religions in Celebration of the 20th Anniversary of the Vatican II Declaration *Nostra Aetate*," University of Notre Dame, South Bend, Indiana, October 28, 1985.

"Preface: Classic Options in Interpreting Cohen's Influence on Rosenzweig," Jewish Philosophy Section, AAR Meeting, Dallas, December 1983.

"Hermann Cohen's Objections to Ernest Troeltsch's Interpretations of the Prophetic Ethos," Jewish Philosophy Section, AAR meeting, New York, December 1982.

"The Function of the Idea of Messianic Mankind in Hermann Cohen's Later Thought," Faculty-Graduate Colloquium on the Modernization of Judaic and Christian Religion with Special Reference to the Philosophy of Religion, Concordia University, Montreal, February 15, 1979.

Papers Read

"Kohler's *Jewish Theology, Systematically and Historically Considered* and the Overcoming of Mendelssohn's Enlightenment Version of Judaism," Nineteenth Century Theology Working Group, AAR Meeting, Boston, 1999.

"The Contextualization of Roman Catholic Modernism," Roman Catholic Modernism Seminar, AAR meeting, Chicago, November 20, 1994.

"Christianity, Colonialism, and Black Nationalism in South Africa: A Comment," South African Research Program Workshop, Yale University, October 23, 1993.

"Black Theology and Black Consciousness: A Comment," Conference on "People, Power, and Culture: The History of Christianity in South Africa, 1792-1992," University of the Western Cape,Bellville, South Africa, August 15, 1992.

"Troeltsch's Treatment of the Thomist Synthesis in *The Social Teaching* as a Signal of His View of a New Cultural Synthesis," Nineteenth Century Theology Working Group, AAR Meeting, Kansas City, 1991.

"Herman Schell's Roman Catholic Modernism: A Critique," History of Roman Catholic Modernism Working Group, AAR Meeting, Anaheim, CA, 1989.

"*Imitatio Dei* and Martyrdom in Judaic Tradition: The Maccabean Literature and Theologies of 'Spiritual Resistance': A Reply to Lawrence Frissell," Biblical Theologians, March 11, 1989.

"The New Francophone Literature on Rosenzweig: An Appraisal," Biblical Theologians, November 1986.

"Critique of Gabriel Daly's Proposal for 'Defining Modernism,'" History of Roman Catholic Modernism Working Group, AAR Meeting, Chicago, 1984.

"The Current State of Roman Catholic Modernist Studies: Daly's *Transcendence and Immanence: A Study in Catholic Modernism and Integralism,*" History of Roman Catholic Modernism Working Group, AAR meeting, Dallas, December 1983.

"The Function of the Idea of Messianic Mankind in Hermann Cohen's Later Thought," presented in the section on Modern Jewish Religious Philosophy, AAR meeting, New York, November 1979. (revised version of a paper originally presented at Concordia University, Montreal, February 1979)

"Loisy and the Liberal Protestants," Roman Catholic Modernism Consultation, AAR Meeting, 1977.

"Papal Primacy as a Theological Issue: Methodological Observations on the Joint Statement on Papal Primacy by the Lutheran-Catholic Dialogue Group for the United States [1974]," Biblical Theologians, November 16, 1974.

"Moltmann's Dialectical-Critical Theory of Society and Culture: As Respondent to Moltmann's presentation 'Hope, Play, and Fantasy,'" American Academy of Religion, New York City, October 24, 1970.

"Rahner's Essays in Controversy with Marxism," Biblical Theologians, New York City, October 25, 1968.

Academic Awards

1950	Phi Beta Kappa
1951-52	Woodrow Wilson Fellowship
1954-55	Fulbright Fellowship for study in contemporary theology, St. Andrews University, Scotland
1957-58	University Scholar, Yale University
1966-67	Cross disciplinary Grant, Society for Religion in Higher Education, for study of theological and philosophical theories of man (project: Marxism as a humanism: a test-case for theological anthropology) at the Universite de Strasbourg, France
1967	Elected Post-doctoral Fellow, Society for Religion in Higher Education
1992	Travel Grant from Thomas J. Watson Jr. Institute for International Studies, Brown University and Curricular Development Grant, Salomon Fund, Brown University, for month-long study trip to South Africa to investigate "Religion, Apartheid, and Nation-Building" (August 1992).
1992	Elected member of The Center of Theological Inquiry, Princeton, New Jersey, for January-June 1993 (topic of project: "Divine Providence and Moral Action: Jonathan Edwards, Kant, Schleiermarcher, Barth's III 3, 4") (withdrew for health reasons.)
1999	Elected member of American Theological Society

September 2000

CONTRIBUTORS

David R. Blumenthal is the Jay and Leslie Cohen Professor of Judaic Studies at Emory University. He is author of several books in medieval Jewish thought, as well as works in contemporary Jewish theology. Among the latter are: *God at the Center* (1994), *Facing the Abusing God: A Theology of Protest* (1993), and *The Banality of Evil: A Social Psychological and Ethical Reflection* (1999).

Walter H. Conser, Jr. is professor of Religion and of History at the University of North Carolina at Wilmington. His publications include *Church and Confession: Conservative Theologians in Germany, England, and America, 1815-1866* (1984), *God and the Natural World: Religion and Science in Antebellum America* (1993), and the co-edited volume, *Religious Diversity and American Religious History* (1998).

Richard Crouter is the John M. and Elizabeth W. Musser Professor of Religious Studies and Chair of the Department of Religion at Carleton College. He co-edits *Zeitschrift für Neuere Theologiegeschichte/ Journal for the History of Modern Theology*, is editor and translator of Friedrich Schleiermacher, *On Religion: Speeches to its Cultured Despisers* (1799[1996]), and author of *Friedrich Schleiermacher: Between Enlightenment and Romanticism* (forthcoming).

Francis Schüssler Fiorenza is Charles Chauncey Stillman Professor of Roman Catholic Theological Studies at the Divinity School, Harvard University. He is author of *Foundational Theology: Jesus and the Church* (1984), *Beyond Hermeneutics: Theology as Discourse* (2002), co-author with James Livingston of *Modern Christian Thought*, vol. 2, *The Twentieth Century*, and co-editor of *Systematic Theology: Roman Catholic Perspectives* and *Habermas, Modernity, and Public Theology* (1991).

Robert Gibbs is a professor of Philosophy at the University of Toronto. He is author of *Correlations in Rosenzweig and Levinas* (1992), *Why Ethics?: Signs of Responsibilities* (2000), and co-author of *Reasoning After Revelation: Dialogues in Postmodern Jewish Philosophy* (1998).

Peter J. Haas is the Abba Hillel Silver Professor of Jewish Studies and Director of the Samuel Rosenthal Center for Judaic Studies at Case

Western Reserve University. He is author of *Morality After Auschwitz: The Radical Challenge of the Nazi Ethic* (1988), *Recovering the Role of Women: Power and Authority in Rabbinic Jewish Society* (1992), and *Responsa: Literary History of a Rabbinic Genre* (1996).

Mark A. Hadley is Assistant Professor of Religious Studies at Western Maryland College. He has taught at Syracuse University and Wheaton College.

Susannah Heschel holds the Eli Black chair in Jewish Studies in the Department of Religion at Dartmouth College. She is the author of numerous studies in modern Jewish thought, including *Abraham Geiger and the Jewish Jesus* (1998), and *Insider/Outsider: American Jews and Multiculturalism* (1998, co-edited with David Biale and Micahel Galchinsky).

Peter C. Hodgson is Charles G. Finney Professor of Theology at the Divinity School, Vanderbilt University. His most recent books are *Winds of the Spirit: A Constructive Christian Theology* (1994), *G. W. F. Hegel: Theologian of the Spirit* (1997), and *God's Wisdom: Toward a Theology of Education* (1999).

Louis E. Newman is Professor of Religion and Director of the Program in Judaic Studies at Carleton College. He is author of *Past Imperatives: Studies in the History and Theory of Jewish Ethics* (1998), and co-editor with Elliot N. Dorff of *Contemporary Jewish Theology: A Reader* (1999), and *Contemporary Jewish Ethics and Morality: A Reader* (1995).

David Novak holds the J. Richard and Dorothy Shiff Chair of Jewish Studies at the University of Toronto. He is author of *The Image of the Non-Jew in Judaism: An Historical and Constructive Study of the Noahide Laws* (1983), *Jewish-Christian Dialogue: A Jewish Justification* (1992), *Jewish Social Ethics* (1992), *Law and Theology in Judaism* (1974), *Halakhah in a Theological Dimension* (1985), *Covenantal Rights: A Study in Jewish Political Theory* (2000), *The Election of Israel: The Idea of the Chosen People* (1995), *The Theology of Nahmanides Systematically Presented* (1992), *Natural Law in Judaism* (1998) and *Covenantal Rights* (2000).

Peter Ochs is the Edgar Bronfman Professor of Modern Judaic Studies at the University of Virginia. His books include *Peirce, Pragmatism and the Logic of Scripture* (1998), *Reviewing the Covenant: Eugene Borowitz and the Postmodern Renewal of Theology* (2000), *Reasoning after Revelation: Dialogues in Postmodern Jewish Philosophy* (1998, with Robert Gibbs and Steven Kepnes), and the edited collections *The Return to Scripture in Judaism and Christianity* (1993) and *Understanding the Rabbinic Mind* (1990).

Katherine Sonderegger is Professor of Religion at Middlebury College. She is author of *That Jesus Was Born a Jew: Karl Barth's 'Doctrine of Israel'* (1992).

Jeffrey Stout is Professor of Religion at Princeton University. He is author of *The Flight from Authority* (1981), and *Ethics after Babel* (1988).

Theodore M. Vial is Assistant Professor of Religious Studies at Virginia Wesleyan College. His articles include "Opposites Attract: The Body and Cognition in a Debate over Baptism," *Numen* (1999), "Friedrich Schleiermacher on the Central Place of Worship in Theology," *Harvard Theological Review* (1998), and "A. E. Biedermann's Filial Christology in Its Political Context," *Zeitschrift für neuere Theologiegeschichte/Journal for the History of Modern Theology* (1996).

Walter E. Wyman, Jr. is Weyerhaeuser Professor of Biblical Literatures and Professor of Religion at Whitman College. His recent publications include *Revisioning the Past: Prospects in Historical Theology* (1992, co-edited with Mary Potter Engel) and "Rethinking the Christian Doctrine of Sin: Friedrich Schleiermacher and Hick's 'Irenaean Type," and "Revelation and the Doctrine of Faith: Historical Revelation within the Limits of Historical Consciousness (1994 and 1998, both in the *Journal of Religion*).

Titles Available from Brown Judaic Studies

Brown Studies on Jews and Their Societies

Brown Studies in Religion